GLOBAL INFORMATION TECHNOLOGIES

ETHICS AND THE LAW

THOMAS H. KOENIG
PROFESSOR OF SOCIOLOGY
NORTHEASTERN UNIVERSITY

MICHAEL L. RUSTAD
THOMAS F. LAMBERT PROFESSOR OF LAW AND CO-DIRECTOR
INTELLECTUAL PROPERTY LAW CONCENTRATION
SUFFOLK UNIVERSITY LAW SCHOOL

444 Cedar Street, Suite 700
St. Paul, MN 55101
1-877-888-1330

Printed in the United States of America

ISBN: 978-1-68328-573-1

Summary of Contents

Table of Contents

Table of Cases

GLOBAL INFORMATION TECHNOLOGIES

ETHICS AND THE LAW

Preface

The authors of this book frequently receive messages, usually in the form of telephone calls or emails from individuals and businesses, seeking practical advice: "My daughter has a learning disability and is being bullied at school. What can I do about it?" "I am receiving threats of a lawsuit for tens of thousands of dollars for illegal downloading. I think my grandson may have done something with my computer when he visited last month. What should I do?" "Our business computer system has been locked by people who are demanding payment in Bitcoin to unencrypt it. Should I call the police? If I decide to pay the ransom, where do I buy Bitcoins?"

"I was in the final stages of being considered for a great job when the hiring manager demanded that I turn over my Facebook password so that she could review all my postings, pictures and messages to see if I fit into the company's culture. Do I have legal recourse if I refuse her request and subsequently I am not hired?" "A humiliating picture of me has been posted on a website. They will not remove it. Can I force them?" "An ex-boyfriend is posting menacing rap lyrics to describe our relationship. I am scared. What can I do about it?" "Is my company liable for misappropriation of a customer's trade secrets if our computer system's inadequate security enabled the theft?" Both legal and ethical considerations are necessary to address these all-too-common, deeply troubling scenarios.

Ethical and legal issues often arise out of Internet use and misuse in the workplace. "I work in IT and my boss demands that I install software that monitors Internet and email communications so he can read everyone's messages. Can I refuse to agree to this request, which secretly invades the workers' privacy? If my employer disciplines me for refusing to comply with his demand, do I have recourse?" "Some of the workers are forwarding offensive jokes through our email system. Can they be fired for distributing these emails?" "My company wants to release software that does not have adequate security, which can potentially imperil customers' health information and third-party customer data.

How secure does a computer program need to be and what are my responsibilities if our security falls short of federally mandated standards for health care providers?"

We often receive questions about the uses and misuses of contract law terms in the workplace. "My company just added language to the terms of service agreement of their website that gives them the right to sue employees or customers who post anything negative about the company. Is this enforceable?" Increasingly, we are asked about how to protect or assert intellectual property rights. "I have invented a new software application that I believe can be very profitable. I am an independent contractor who freelances. Can I patent this software or does it belong to the company that retained me while I was developing the application? Does it matter that I created this code during my spare time and not during work hours?" "Can I review an applicant's public postings as part of our company's due diligence before hiring him?" This book will deal with both the legal and ethical aspects of these, and many other, common queries. Too often people ask these questions after their actions have already enmeshed them in a legal or ethical quagmire.

The twenty-first century computer professional works in an untidy world of uncertainty and rapid change. After studying this book, you will be able to apply leading ethical theories and basic legal principles to resolve emergent issues arising from the use of computer technologies. For example, a prominent political website contended that Donald Trump's presidential campaign made it nearly impossible to cancel recurring monthly campaign contributions. Similarly, some companies sign up customers for auto-renew payments without giving them notice. Is this tactic merely an ingenious way to ensure repeat campaign contributions and subscription renewals ("growth hacking"), or is this an unfair, unethical and illegal practice? If so, what legal remedies, if any, potentially address this controversial practice?

Courses with diverse titles such as "Computer Ethics," "Computers, Ethics, Society, and Human Values," "Ethical Issues in Computing," "Emerging Issues in Information Technology" and "Social Issues in Business" are taught in almost every institution of higher learning to help graduates cope with the ethical quandaries raised by technological advances. Computer science accreditors require that computer science program help students gain "an understanding of professional, ethical, legal, security and social issues and responsibilities."[1]

This book presents materials that will satisfy this requirement by using real-life illustrations of globalized dilemmas faced by computer professionals and discussing the laws that govern their possible responses. Both authors have taught, published and consulted in this field for decades, which provides them with in-depth knowledge of both the theoretical and practical aspects of the rapidly evolving field of computer law and ethics.

Thomas Koenig used a beta version of this book in his course entitled, "Computers and Society" in the fall of 2017. His class fulfills the requirement that all computer science majors at Northeastern University take a course examining the ethical, social and/or legal aspects of information technology. Michael Rustad uses this book as a required text in Suffolk University Law School courses entitled "Global Internet Law" and "Emerging Issues in Law, Information Technology and Transnational Business," which is for JD students, visiting legal scholars and post-graduates in Suffolk's LL.M. and SJD programs.

In the summer of 2017, he used the text in Suffolk's National University of Ireland–Galway summer program in "Current Issues in EU Business Law and Policy." This text is also appropriate for legal studies classes in business and the social sciences, as well as courses such as "Introduction to U.S. Law" for international students.

Why the Study of Computer Ethics & the Law Is Important

In this digital age, novel technologies are reshaping nearly every branch of the law. Connected devices are also directly affecting culture, economy, politics, communications and even personal relationships. Daily headlines describe conflicts over disruptive information technologies that often are resolved through judicial verdicts, regulatory decisions or new statutes. Each chapter of this book considers emerging quandaries of the information age, such as whether individuals should have the right to erase demeaning postings, whether copyright law should protect tweets, and how much cybersecurity should be required for cloud computing.

Ethicists, attorneys, legislators and other policymakers need the expertise of computer professionals to ensure that legal rules and regulations properly address the technology-driven issues that continually arise in diverse social settings. Workplace rights, cybercrimes, Internet security, civil lawsuits, intellectual property rights, Internet-enabled devices and robotics, online privacy and social media terms of use are among the rapidly evolving issues addressed in our book.

Computer professionals, lawyers, judges, corporate executives and government officials regularly confront perplexing choices that must be decided in a policy vacuum, without clear legal or moral precedent. Everyone, particularly students who are entering fields impacted by rapidly evolving technological changes, will benefit from reading an up-to-date account of how to resolve unsettled (and unsettling) dilemmas. Computer law and morality are presented in an applied format in this book, using concrete legal issues, regulatory actions and court decisions to illustrate the global consequences of unethical computing. Each chapter considers how other countries, particularly the twenty-eight nations of the European Union, evaluate and resolve these issues.

Forewarned is forearmed, and students who have thought about how to approach these problems will be better prepared when they later assume their professional roles. Whether they become employed in established technology companies, join a startup, work for a government agency, advocate for social change or litigate these issues as attorneys, this book's applied legal lessons will be of significant value. In an increasingly interconnected world, understanding how other cultures and legal systems deal with cross-national predicaments such as pursuing offshore cybercriminals, ensuring data protection or addressing online blasphemy in countries that have no tradition of free religious expression is critical.

Rapidly evolving technologies require computer professionals—and their attorneys—to be highly imaginative and extremely flexible. Practitioners who are not reflective and who take the approach that they should only "do what they are told" will not be upwardly mobile. They may expose themselves and their employers to civil or even criminal liability for their failure to comply with ethics and the law:

> In fact, unethical behavior of an employee can be very serious for a company and can be cause for dismissal. In order to understand professional and ethical behavior, it is necessary to go beyond an understanding of personal morality. You need to understand the kinds of situations that can and frequently do occur in the conduct of business that can have a serious negative impact on companies and their employees if these situations are not handled correctly.[2]

Prior to the development of the Internet and the World Wide Web, computer science departments did not devote much attention to ethics. Today, however, in addition to an understanding of software architecture, coding and design, computer professionals must play a central role in avoiding legal liabilities and ethical lapses. This is the first text to explore in depth how law and ethics interrelate. While many computer ethics books describe computer laws, this book demonstrates, in every chapter, how ethical perspectives culminate in legal developments.

Students who view computer science as an exclusively technical field are missing the big picture. Today, many of the purely mechanical roles in the information-based economy are outsourced to Third World countries where low-wage workers toil long hours in obscurity. "Developers are often natural problem solvers who possess strong analytical skills and the ability to think outside the box,"[3] but more is required to reach the top ranks of the profession. The Accreditation Board of Engineering and Technology, which accredits Engineering, Computer Science, and Information Systems programs, specifies six essential skills that are often imperative to career success. These non-technical qualifications include:

(1) The ability to communicate effectively

(2) The ability to understand professional, ethical responsibility

(3) The ability to function on multi-disciplinary teams

(4) Broad education necessary to understand the impact of engineering solutions in a global and societal context

(5) Recognition of the need for, and an ability to engage in, life-long learning

(6) Knowledge of contemporary issues[4]

Consider just a few representative career advertisements taken from a randomly chosen, recent computer science employment bulletin:

> *Lockheed Martin*: Seeking person with experience with computer vulnerability scanning and patch deployment with the highest standards of business ethics.
>
> *Lubrizol Corporation*: Bachelor's degree in computer science or a closely related field. Visionary Team Leader Required.
>
> *Ricoh*: Four-year degree in Computer Science, Systems Engineering or related field. Previous experience working in law firms with legal applications and end user IT support with ability to work with a broad variety of legal technologies.

A Computer Systems Architect for a top technology company cannot just be a skilled programmer. She is also expected to understand how humans from multiple cultures interact with information technology and must tailor computer systems to comply with cross-border legal, ethical and regulatory standards. An app developer marketing her product in Europe must comply with privacy regulations such as the General Data Protection Regulation and the EU/USA

Privacy Shield that governs data transfers outside the European Union. The European Commission has filed actions against Facebook, Google, Microsoft, Twitter and many other U.S. companies who did not revise their contracting practices for the European consumer market. Companies doing business in China need to modify their licensing agreements to comply with mandatory consumer law that prohibits licensors from eliminating warranties or limiting remedies in the event of software or hardware failures.

Computer forensics provides another example of a high-demand, fast-growing field that requires a cross-disciplinary approach.[5] These professionals need a basic knowledge of criminal statutes, cybercrime fighting techniques and a familiarity with hacker culture as well as high-level programming skills. Digital forensics experts uncover "smoking gun" evidence of wrongdoings such as trade secret theft, computer system intrusions and insider hackings. These experts also unmask insider and outsider cybercriminals threatening U.S. companies.

Information technology is upending a wide array of long-established business and personal practices. Firms on the cutting edge of technology, for example, are devising new methods of bypassing traditional recruiting channels to locate employees who are skilled, imaginative and self-motivated. Google experimented with using brainteasers that required applicants to show that they were imaginative and resourceful, but this method of testing applicants is on the decline. More recently, a Georgia Tech graduate reports that he was recruited through a Google search that he initiated:

> One morning, while working on a project, I Googled "python lambda function list comprehension." The familiar blue links appeared, and I started to look for the most relevant one. But then something unusual happened. The search results split and folded back to reveal a box that said "You're speaking our language. Up for a challenge?" I stared at the screen. What? After a moment, I decided yes, I was most definitely up for a challenge. I clicked through and landed on a page that called itself "foo.bar." The page resembled a UNIX interface, so I typed the command to see the list of files. There was a single one called "start_here.txt". I opened it and saw two sentences:
>
> *"Type request to request a challenge. Type help for a list of commands."*
>
> I typed "request" and half expected to see "Follow the white rabbit, Max." Instead, the screen displayed a paragraph outlining a programming challenge and gave instructions on how to submit my solution. I had 48 hours to solve it, and the timer was ticking.[6]

The recent graduate was intrigued by the task and solved the problem for fun:

> I set to work and solved the first problem in a couple hours. Each time I submitted a solution, foo.bar tested my code against five hidden test cases. Once my solution passed all of those tests, I could submit it and request a new challenge. Over the next two weeks, I solved five more problems. After I solved the sixth problem, foo.bar gave me the option to submit my contact information. I typed in my phone number and email address, fully expecting that to be the end of things. Much to my surprise, a recruiter emailed me a couple days later asking for a copy of my resume. I emailed it to him, and we set up a phone call. . . . Overall, I enjoyed the puzzles that they gave me to solve, and I'm excited for my first day as a Googler.[7]

Similarly, Apple is attempting to bypass traditional hiring channels through innovative tactics such as placing covert job advertisements where skilled and imaginative programmers will stumble across them.[8] Energy, talent and a driving curiosity are prized above paper credentials by firms battling to stay at the forefront of the IT revolution.

The state-of-the-art information technology companies are aware that narrow technical specialists quickly become obsolete in the rapidly evolving environment of information technologies. Innovative computer professionals who can learn from diverse fields, including the liberal arts, and who are intrigued by other cultures, will be better suited for the twenty-first century leadership. An information technology company doing business in Sweden, Brazil, Malaysia or South Africa must tailor their products to conform to cross-national cultural, ethical and legal norms.

Even small, highly specialized technology start-ups need to implement funding, employment and hiring practices that comply with the law. A recent episode of the television show, *Silicon Valley*, centered on the ethical dilemmas involved in faking the amount of website traffic as a ruse to obtain financing from venture capitalists. The head of the start-up confessed to the deception at the last minute and the investor withdrew the proffered seed money, leaving the viewer to decide whether the developer's honesty was admirable or a foolish mistake.

The ability to apply legal and regulatory principles in an ethical way is integral for success in the information-based economy. Computer professionals need to know how to protect their company's legal rights and how to avoid infringing on the rights of others. Cybertort liability may result from enmeshing your organization too closely with third party content creators that defames, invades the privacy, or steals trade secrets belonging to others. Even if a corporate counsel is on retainer, it is important for information experts to know when to alert attorneys to potential legal hazards before the risk turns into a full-blown crisis.

Many of the costly lawsuits discussed in this book could have been avoided through better preventative measures. Intellectual property, such as trademarks, copyrights, patents and trade secrets need to be carefully secured. Computer engineers need to know when they must consult with legal counsel to prevent problems dealing with specialized topics such as tort law, software licensing, data protection, tax law, securities regulation, products liability, environmental law, financial services, patent infringement, discrimination complaints and workplace regulations.

Computer professionals need to design solutions for the increasingly complex dilemmas that arise out of swiftly evolving information technologies. Privacy issues, for example, will become more pervasive as the Internet of Things products gather an unparalleled amount of personal information. Electronic payment systems will compile extensive data about your financial behavior. Self-driving vehicles will assemble comprehensive digital records of your driving behavior, including whether you complied with traffic laws and where you have been. Your smart refrigerator will be able to monitor whether you are complying with your doctor's dietary instructions and to communicate that information to your health insurer, employer, spouse or other interested parties. Who will have access to the information about your secret trips to the refrigerator for late night snacks or alcoholic beverages that will be recorded in a digital format?

With the expansion of the Internet of Things, new forms of targeted advertising will evolve. In a recent example, software began emailing a woman with advertisements for pregnancy products before she even realized that she was expecting a child. Are we entering an era in which, as in the words of Sun Microsystems's president, "You have zero privacy anyway? Get over it"?

Will law enforcement be permitted to view private information to document money laundering or terrorism? Can your probation officer use big data to monitor your behavior? Should policyholders be able to waive their privacy rights in return for an insurer being able to collect data about their activities? What security systems will be necessary to prevent paparazzi from spying on celebrities and other prominent people through Internet connected devices? Should electronic agents using blockchain technology be able to form legally enforceable "smart contracts"?

Globalized Internet communications lead to increased international understanding and harmonization, but also engender new forms of crime, oppression and social friction. Many observers call for international limitations of some cyberspace freedoms to undermine cybercriminals, state-sponsored espionage and terrorism, while others argue that online free expression is an inalienable human right. Will obscure hate groups be allowed to stir up religious discord through postings of the mass burnings of copies of the Qur'an; an action protected under the First Amendment of the U.S Constitution, but that also is likely to cause significant harm to American interests throughout the Middle East?

Social media websites, such as Twitter, have implemented "report buttons," allowing users to alert monitors to objectionable postings. Some users have objected to this, contending that it violates freedom of expression and robust discussion.[9] Facebook replaced its trending news topics curators with "objective" algorithms because of complaints that conservative media was being screened out.[10] However, eliminating human judgment led to an explosion of fake news stories, which now is being countered by linking these stories to fact-checking organizations. This book is designed to provide conceptual tools and insights to help future leaders approach such inevitable quandaries in a systematic and principled way.

How This Book Teaches About Code, Law, & Ethics

Every chapter of this book demonstrates the centrality of ethical and legal concerns. This method contrasts with other approaches where the text introduces abstract, ethical principles in the first chapter, and never applying these perspectives again in any subsequent chapter. The moral and legal frameworks that shape lawsuits, regulatory actions, criminal prosecutions, industry practices and cross-national treaties are explained in concise non-technical language.

Information technology professionals can no longer afford to be U.S. centric in their approach to website design, competition law, privacy and many other cross-national concerns. Both European Union and Chinese law, for example, provide consumers with mandatory rights that are not available to U.S. website users. European regulators recently struck down twenty-two clauses in America Online's terms of use agreement, whose anti-consumer clauses had previously been upheld by U.S. courts. The privacy practices of Facebook and other U.S. computer firms are under intense scrutiny by the European Commission for violating the fundamental rights of European consumers. Google faces large fines in Europe for giving its services priority over rival corporations in presenting search results.

At the end of each chapter, there are challenging (and we hope stimulating) problems relating to evaluating various legal and ethical issues such as the protection of personal data, preventing cybercrime, avoiding cybertort liability, implementing reasonable security, adapting electronic contracting and protecting intellectual property rights. These exercises center around case studies of complex moral and legal problems that will help the student learn to identify, conceptualize and resolve ethical problems. As most of these examples describe real world legal struggles, rather than abstract hypotheticals, students can look online for the most recent developments in similar disputes. Our overall goal is for students to learn to apply the principles of moral and legal reasoning to concrete problems arising from digital technologies.

Contents of this Book

Chapter 1: Basic Concepts in Computer Ethics & the Law

Computer scientists are the architects of the Internet, designing new applications and implementing operations on a global basis. Chapter One illustrates how information technology affects our daily lives in multi-faceted ways. Technological advances have created unique social conflicts in every historical epoch, but never has the speed of change been greater than in the modern era.

Every computer professional needs to anticipate and help resolve legal dilemmas resulting from new market conditions.[11] At the upper branches of the information technology field, computer scientists are working with legislators and regulators in testifying about the new ethical and legal issues raised by the ubiquitous applications of novel information technologies. Computer professionals often take the initiative in advocating for new legal rules on topics such as database protection and enhanced intellectual property protection.

This chapter concludes with a brief description of the social organization of the traditional professions of medicine and law, discussing whether computer science should follow a similar path. Professional associations such as the Association for Computing Machinery are updating their ethical codes to address the vast number of dilemmas created by advances in information technology. However, unlike medicine and law, there is no mechanism in the United States for such organizations to bar ethical violators from working in the information technology field.

Chapter 2: Applying Ethical Theories and the Law to Computers

Laws, both in the U.S. and globally, draw heavily from moral underpinnings. Chapter 2 provides a summary of the five principal ethical perspectives used to analyze and resolve the many moral dilemmas raised by emerging information and communications technologies. These five perspectives are: (1) Consequentialism; (2) Virtue and Duty Ethics; (3) Conflict Perspectives; (4) Social Contract Theory; and (5) Libertarianism. We focus on identifying the greatest strengths of each philosophical approach and how these perspectives are embodied in both technology law and personal moral codes.

Resolving ethical dilemmas often requires an understanding of public policy rationales. The Ryan Haight Online Pharmacy Consumer Protection Act of 2008, for example, prohibits Internet medical consultations to prescribe controlled prescription drugs. The U.S. Attorney for Florida successfully prosecuted the leader of an online pharmacy that illegally distributed hundreds of thousands of narcotic and other prescription pills. In January 2017, the organizer of the online pharmacy was sentenced to eight years in prison for creating this massive online pill dispensing operation. The great benefit of online pharmacies is their convenience and lower costs for consumers, which must be balanced against potential dangers to the public's health. Each subsequent chapter applies the five ethical perspectives introduced in this chapter to such substantive dilemmas.

Chapter 3: Cybertorts for the Information Age

Chapter Three emphasizes the role of private litigation in supplementing criminal law. Many cybertorts parallel civil actions in the brick and mortar world, but often contain a twist. A company or individual, for example, may be held liable for defamation after publishing or repeating false accusations in a blog, a tweet or a website posting. However, newspapers are held to a higher standard than websites in some situations because, under the Communications Decency Act, websites are immunized from any legal responsibility for third party postings.

Because of gaps in the criminal law and inadequate enforcement mechanisms, cyberspace injuries resulting from revenge pornography, online stalking, dark-side hackings and other socially harmful behavior would go unpunished if it was not for the tort system. Punitive damages are an example of a cybertort remedy that punishes and deters these types of malicious misconduct on the Internet.

Chapter 4: Cybercrimes: Ethics and the Law

Chapter Four provides a review of the existing laws used against cybercriminals, such as the Computer Fraud and Abuse Act (computer trespass statute), the Electronic Communications Privacy Act (federal wiretap act) and the Economic Espionage Act. Computer professionals need to be able to recognize if a crime has been committed and know which law enforcement authorities to contact, especially when dealing with cross-border criminals. Preventing insider crimes requires monitoring of employee access to sensitive information.

This chapter, like all the others, discusses global developments, which include attempts to coordinate international enforcement through the Cybercrime Convention. New statutes and criminal justice techniques are emerging to deter and punish international cybercriminals and state-sponsored spies. Whether to enforce online enablement of "crimes without victims," such as carrying transparently coded advertisements for prostitution is controversial because of sharp divergences between the major ethical perspectives about morality laws. The proper ethical and legal rules for punishing those who release confidential information for idealistic reasons are also hotly contested.

Chapter 5: Information Privacy

What does the right to be left alone mean in a world when we are connected to the Internet 24/7? Teens and young adults are increasingly "living their lives as if in a fishbowl." This chapter contrasts the U.S. piecemeal privacy approach to the European Union's treatment of privacy as a fundamental right. This chapter covers questions such as whether the U.S. should adopt Europe's "right to be forgotten" or maintain its current marketplace approach to online privacy. In February 2016, the EU and the U.S. agreed to a temporary Privacy Shield, which requires U.S. companies to self-certify that data entrusted to them is secure.

Web security, anonymity, censorship, human-computer interactions and many other Internet topics raise troublesome privacy-related issues. Should the FBI be able to order Apple to create a means to decrypt iPhone messages? When can stingrays be used to capture personal communications? When can cell phones of criminal suspects be searched without a warrant?

Chapter 6: Computer Contracts

Chapter Six contrasts U.S. and European consumer contract rules. The enforceability of sales, leases and licenses used in the information-based economy differ dramatically between these two legal systems. U.S. consumers are frequently surprised to discover that when they clicked "yes" to a hyperlink that they have often waived their right to a jury trial, to join a class action and can be forced to arbitrate disputes in distant venues. European consumer law prohibits anti-class action waivers, predispute forced arbitration, disclaimers of warranties and caps on damages.

The chapter examines the major contracting forms used in the information-based economy: sales, leases, and licenses. The First Sale Rule gives purchasers control over any product that they buy. For this reason, software is licensed rather than sold to enable computer companies to control the use of their applications after delivery to their customers. Licenses protect intellectual property by using contract law to prevent unauthorized distribution and copying.

Chapter 7: Patents, Copyrights & Computers

Chapter Seven applies legal and ethical perspectives to disputes over the best balance between the rights of intellectual property owners and the larger public interest. This chapter focuses on the two purely federal branches of intellectual property law: patents and copyrights. The U.S. patent system has been significantly revised by the passage of the America Invents Act of 2011. Similarly, federal copyright law has been significantly updated for the digital age.

Topics such as the patenting and copyrighting of software, the rights of employers to control code written by consultants and other employees and the operation of the free software movement are examined. European statutory and case law developments covering topics such as moral rights, database protection and secondary infringement are compared to recent U.S. legal developments.

Chapter 8: Trademarks, Trade Secrets & Computers

Chapter Eight examines the ethical and legal issues underlying trademark and trade secret protection. Software publishers seek trademark protection for their logos, trade names, products and even their websites. The trademarks of Apple, IBM, Google and Microsoft need to be aggressively defended in order to prevent them from losing their legal protection by becoming everyday words as happened to former trademarks such as "zipper" or "thermos."

Software companies use trade secrets to protect their source code, customer lists and other intangible assets that have an economic value if kept secret. High tech companies generally require their employees, joint venture partners, consultants and others to sign nondisclosure agreements to protect their secrets. Increasingly, the U.S. is including trade secret protection in international trade treaties such as TRIPS and NAFTA. In late 2016, Congress enacted the Defend Trade Secrets Act that gives trade secret owners a private remedy under the federal Economic Espionage Act.

About Us: Why We Wrote This Book

Both authors of this book have had a deep interest in ethical computing issues for more than forty years. When we first started working with computers in the early 1970s, keypunch cards were physically fed into a card reader. Mainframe computers were so heavy that they had to be kept in basements so that they would not crash through the floor. Tom Koenig was an undergraduate student at the University of California–Santa Cruz, which was just beginning to be impacted by the emergence of what would later be labeled Silicon Valley.

Computer access was so expensive that every program needed to specify a maximum amount of run time for fear that a mistake would result in an "infinite loop" that would burn up the employers' annual budget. Software came pre-installed as part of the computer system, which was leased from a few large suppliers such as IBM and Hewlett-Packard. System crashes were generally attributed to hardware failures, such as a burned-out component, rather than defective software. We were college sophomores in December 1968 when IBM made the monumental decision to unbundle software from hardware, which led to the emergence of an independent software industry.

Tom Koenig did his Ph.D. work at the University of California–Santa Barbara, where he studied under the guidance of the former head of the University of Michigan's Institute for Social Research's computer center. The late Professor John Sonquist, his mentor and dissertation chair, was a Quaker pacifist who was deeply distressed by the irony that the software code he had created was being deployed to guide intercontinental nuclear missiles. One of Professor Sonquist's major priorities was to make the DARPANET, the predecessor to the Internet, a mechanism to democratize information rather than to increase the centralized power of the military-industrial complex.

In 1969, UCLA's Network Measurement Center, Stanford's Research Institute (SRI) and the Universities of Utah and California at Santa Barbara established the first nodes for what would later be called the Internet.[12] While at Santa Barbara, Tom was one of the first sociologists to access and work on the DARAPANET, which was "slow, sluggish, and unreliable."[13] Remote connections were made through telephone modems, which would erase unsaved work whenever there was a glitch in the telephone line. During this era, there were no online "browsers." The term was applied to impoverished students who might browse books in bookstores to save money.

Tom's dissertation modified a networking program to examine how interlocking directorships among the 500 largest U.S. corporations correlated with their financial and political policies. His teaching career took him to Brown University in the mid-1970s and then to Boston's Northeastern University. Tom studied computer law as a Fellow at Harvard University Law School and later taught computer policy as a Fulbright Scholar at the University of Belgrade Law School in Serbia. Tom has placed many of his Northeastern University students in software and other technology firms. Today, he teaches large classes in "Computers and Society" and works with graduate students in Northeastern

University's Information Assurance, Law and Public Policy, and Sociology Ph.D. programs.

Michael Rustad's first position after completing his Master's Degree in Sociology was in the Computer Information and Systems Division of the National Institute of Education (NIE) in 1973. Like the University of California, NIE used mainframe computers weighing many tons and containing thousands of vacuum tubes. When Michael moved to Massachusetts in 1978 to begin his Ph.D. program, his first job was with Sheldon Laube at a startup called Optimum Computers in Auburndale, Massachusetts.

During his time at Optimum Computers, there were no sophisticated software applications or personal computers. Michael wrote some of the first user manuals for computer-based statistics with Sheldon Laube, who later became the first CIO of Innovation at PricewaterhouseCooper. He was ranked as one of the twenty-five most influential pioneers of Silicon Valley after founding "USWeb which was the world's largest Internet consulting firm during the Internet boom. That company grew from five people to 2,500 in more than 23 countries in fewer than 25 months."[14]

Michael completed his Ph.D. thesis and first book, *Women in Khaki: A Study of the American Enlisted Woman*, on an IBM Selectric typewriter. This IBM model was then state of the art, although it had no spell-check or word processing capabilities. You used "white-out," a small bottle of white paint, to cover up your typing errors. He did not use a personal computer until 1985 when Charles Nesson, his LL.M. advisor at Harvard Law School, suggested that he invest in one. Professor Rustad taught one of the first computer law courses at an East Coast law school, beginning in 1993.

Our goal in writing this book is to produce the first text that focuses on the intersection between computer ethics and the law in a globalized setting. The book provides compelling case studies from the European Union, China, the former Russian Republics and other countries. Computer professionals need to become familiar with radically different legal systems, as well as to gain a better understanding of how U.S. law constrains their activities.

Class Activities: Note for Instructors

The courses we teach at Northeastern University and Suffolk University Law School require students to give oral presentations and use classroom group exercises. We have designed interesting and provocative end-of-chapter exercises that can be used for class discussion, take-home assignments, or in-class presentations. Professor Rustad finds that these exercises work well when they are pre-assigned to students who are on-call to be experts on particular questions. Professor Koenig often divides his classes into research groups who are each responsible for presenting reports that explain specialized issues. We both find these exercises raise the level of class discussion and that students enjoy debating these hot button topics. Students who use these materials become more enthusiastic about understanding computer law, both to chart an ethical path and to avoid being drawn into legal quagmires when they become industry professionals.

This book presents a snapshot of a complex and rapidly changing field. We have tried to be as accurate and as up-to-date as possible and would greatly appreciate your feedback. Professors adopting this book can email either of us for access to a website where we update cases, discuss technological and legal developments, and do our best to keep the information in this book exciting and contemporary. Our website also contains ideas for examination questions, tips for teaching, PowerPoints, as well as links to interesting articles and legal developments. Whether you are a new instructor or an experienced professor, we would like to work with you to make adopting this book a great experience.

Acknowledgments

We would like to acknowledge the steadfast support of Suffolk University Law School Associate Dean, Pat Shin, who is a philosopher, as well as a lawyer, with a sincere interest in this project. Professor Koenig's Computers and Society students have provided numerous examples, edits and other improvements to earlier drafts of this book. Anton Ogandzhanyan provided consistently excellent editing advice that greatly improved the readability and coherence of the entire book. Alp Elci's astute comments and edits for each chapter, particularly for Chapter Two's review of the ethical perspectives, were of immense value. Micah Storkersen provided a number of useful editorial suggestions on multiple chapters.

Samantha Cannon has been a stellar research assistant for multiple semesters. James Contrino compiled exhaustive research on software-as-a-service or cloud computing as well as the latest case law on wrap contracts for Chapter 7. Nicole Anzuoni, Maureen DeSimone, Elizabeth Mollie Heintzelman, Samantha LeBrun, Noé Leiva, Robert Marin and Priscilla Santos provided us with expert assistance. Bob Bevill, a lawyer and computer professional with decades of experience, provided expertise and stellar research assistance.

Amanda Frederick proofread and contributed research to each chapter. Carly A. Herosian, Gabriele Ferrigno and Elizabeth Ejiofor edited and researched several chapters. Dr. Cambria Alpha-Cobb provided useful editorial suggestions in Chapter 8 on patents and copyright law. Elif Kavusturan, a Suffolk University Law School SJD candidate and a global IT attorney, provided insightful comments on cloud computing, software licensing and other computer contracts. Harel Talasazan, a Massachusetts IT attorney provided useful examples and editorial suggestions. Rebecca Huertas contributed research, edited each chapter, and co-authored the conclusion. Dr. Sarah Cortes' critical reading of the entire manuscript has been particularly valuable. Professor Rustad would also like to thank his wife, Chryss J. Knowles, for her editorial work and good cheer.

Thomas H. Koenig
Michael L. Rustad

November 1, 2017

---

1 Accreditation Board of Engineering and Technology (ABET), *Criteria for Accrediting Computing Programs*, 2016–2017.

2 University of Maryland–Baltimore, *What Do Graduates of Engineering, Computer Science, and Information Systems Programs Need to Know Beyond Their Technical Courses?* (2016).

3 U.S. News & World Report, *Software Developer Overview: #2 in Best Technology Job* (2016).

4 University of Maryland–Baltimore, *What Do Graduates of Engineering, Computer Science, and Information Systems Programs Need to Know Beyond Their Technical Courses?* (2016).

5 Computer Science Degree Hub, *Can I Get a Job in Forensics with a Computer Science Degree?* (2016), http://thehustle.co/the-secret-google-interview-that-landed-me-a-job.

6 Max Rosett, *Google Has a Secret Interview Process. . . And It Landed Me a Job* (August 24, 2015).

7 *Id.*

8 Kif Leswing, *Apple Hid a Job Listing on Its Website That You Need Serious Computer Skills to Find*, Business Insider (August 19, 2017).

9 *Twitter Adds In-Tweet "Report" Button After Cyber Threats*, MASHABLE (August 1, 2013).

10 Emily Schultheis, *Top Senate Republican Calls on Facebook to Respond to Censorship Accusations*, CBS News (May 10, 2016).

11 Cyberinstitute.com, *How to Use Preventive Law Principles to Develop New Preventive Law HOW Applications* (2016).

12 Kim Anne Zimmerman, *Internet History Timeline: Arpanet to the World Wide Web* (June 4, 2012).

13 Id.

14 Michael Gordon, *Perennial Entrepreneur: Sheldon Laube Launches Artkick* THE SUIT: PROMOTING ENTERPRISE THROUGH INFORMATION (March 12, 2014).

CHAPTER ONE

Computer Ethics & the Law

§ 1.0: WHY STUDY COMPUTER ETHICS?

> I think it's fair to say that personal computers have become the most empowering tool we've ever created. They're tools of communication, they're tools of creativity, and they can be shaped by their user.
>
> —Bill Gates

[A] How Computers Impact Our Daily Lives

The word ethics comes from the Greek word ethos (character), and the Latin word mores (norms or customs). Ethics is a branch of philosophy that studies the nature and development of good character. Computer ethics applies moral reasoning to resolve dilemmas created by a plethora of rapidly evolving information age technologies. As recently as 1994, there were only 150 websites in the entire world. Google did not open its first office until 1998 and Apple launched the iPhone in 2007. Internet hardware such as routers, hubs, servers, cell phone towers, satellites, radios, smartphones and countless other devices have become ubiquitous.

A world without email (first created in 1971), text-messages (1992), Skype (2003), Facebook (2004), YouTube (2005), Twitter (2006), Instagram (2010) and Tinder (2012) is difficult to imagine for today's "digital natives," who grew up after the widespread availability of the Internet. The term "digital immigrant," in contrast, refers to an individual who was not exposed to the World Wide Web until adulthood. Both of this book's authors are digital immigrants, who remember when making a long-distance telephone call was an expensive luxury, which was reserved only for important communications. Both of us began using the Internet in the 1970s, when almost all users were military, governmental or educational researchers.

Advertisers have a marketing category called "digital resisters" for digital immigrants who still fax documents, write physical checks and refuse to use email or social networks. Michael Rustad often chides Tom Koenig for wearing a wristwatch and using landlines for most telephone calls. Michael's daughter Erica, who is a digital native raised in a media-rich world, criticizes him for rarely sending text messages and never using emojis. Digital natives casually send emails, update their calendars, check the weather forecast, access databases, play games, get traveling directions, make financial transactions and perform countless other everyday tasks online.

When Psion Corporation released the first Personal Digital Assistants (PDAs) in 1984, only a few visionaries could foresee the smartphone applications that would become omnipresent three decades later. The first mobile telephones with Internet connectivity did not arrive until 1999. By 2008, there were more devices connected to the Internet than people on Earth. As of April 2017, Apple's App Store had 2.2 million products, while Google Play boasted 2.8 million applications.

Technological advances are testing moral and legal boundaries on an unprecedented scale. "Computer systems design and related services" is the most rapidly growing industrial category in the U.S. economy. Private companies in this field increased their sales by 18% in 2016, more than twice the 6.8% growth rate of the average corporation.[1] The software industry increased its direct employment "from 778,000 jobs in 1990 and 1,083,000 jobs in 1995, to 2,095,000 in 2010 and 2,501,000 in 2014."[2] The average American spends nearly two hours a day on social media websites. Nearly one in five Americans report being online "almost constantly." Reevaluations of morality, human rights and the proper role of government regulation must evolve to address these technological and cultural developments.

[B] Computer Ethics and the Law: Past, Present, Future

In Roman mythology, Janus, the god of beginnings, had two faces, one looking to the past and one to the future. Law and ethics, too, are Janus-faced because they must evaluate the past with an eye toward future developments. While every computer ethics book describes scores of legal rules, we are the first to follow Mahatma Gandhi's lead in systematically treating law as a form of "codified ethics." Law incorporates ethical norms that "are propositions about how values ought to be distributed, including those. . . like power, respect, knowledge, safety, health, comfort and convenience."[3]

Ethical disputes are often fought out in the court system. Gender discrimination in Silicon Valley's top companies, for example, is an endemic problem that requires a strong ethical culture to root out workplace inequities. In August 2017, James Damore was fired for posting a ten-page memo critical of what he labeled "Google's Ideological Echo Chamber."[4] In his internal posting, he charged that Google was "pressing individual managers to increase diversity" by hiring women and minorities even if they were less qualified.[5] Google fired Damore on the grounds that his "memo promoted harmful gender stereotypes and violated its code of conduct."[6]

Google, like many other information technology leaders, strongly values a diverse work force. In an employment-at-will workplace, Google has a legal right to terminate an employee who violates its code of corporate conduct. Damore is reportedly considering suing for wrongful dismissal, perhaps alleging a violation of Section 7 of the National Labor Relations Act that bars employers from interfering with "concerted activities" to improve the workplace. Damore would face an uphill battle because federal labor law requires a showing that this protected form of expression relates to labor union organizing or similar activities.

[C] Law Lags Behind Technological Advances

(1) What Is Legal Lag?

"Legal lag" occurs when legal institutions fail to keep up with changing societal conditions. A rapid change in one social institution requires readjustments in the other parts of the culture. Justice Benjamin Cardozo argued that law must continually evolve to deal with emergent social realities: "The inn that provides shelter for the night is not the journey's end. The law, like the traveler, must be ready for the morrow. It must have a principle of growth."[7]

New technologies often take many years to reshape other social institutions. The development of reliable electrical power in the 1870s, for example, did not immediately displace steam power. The steam-driven factory was organized around a central drive shaft, while electricity worked best in a less centralized factory setting. Reorganizing the workplace around the assembly line versus the drive shaft required decades of adjustment.[8] Recent advances in artificial intelligence will require similar social, ethical and legal reconfiguration over the next decades.

Today, technology is on an exponential expansion curve that is impacting everything—everywhere. Changes of a scale that once took centuries now happen in a few years. Not long ago, Facebook was a dorm-room dating site, mobile phones were for the ultra-rich, drones were multimillion-dollar war machines and supercomputers were largely employed for secret government research. Today, hobbyists can build drones and poor villagers in India access Facebook accounts on smartphones that have more computing power than the Cray 2 supercomputer, which in 1985 cost $17.5 million and weighed 2,500 kilograms.

A full human genome sequencing, which cost $100 million in 2002, today can be completed for $1,000 and will likely cost less than a cup of coffee by 2020.[9] Will insurance companies be permitted to modify coverage for those whose genetic profiles predict a potential need for expensive medical treatments? Will limitations be imposed on the rights of parents to abort fetuses with genetic features that they consider undesirable? Ethical and legal codes often remain unsettled for decades after new social problems emerge.

(2) Legal Lag in Response to Technological Changes

President John F. Kennedy stated: "Change is the law of life. And those who look only to the past or present are certain to miss the future." The rise of the automobile affected nearly every branch of the law in the first half of the twentieth century. The current penalty for jaywalking in Boston is only a $1 fine, a holdover from a period when pedestrians resisted giving priority to the "pleasure vehicles" of the wealthy over people on foot or traveling by horse-drawn wagon. Widespread middle-class ownership of cars, combined with an automobile industry-funded public relations campaign against jaywalking, changed public attitudes in most of the U.S. by the 1940s.

By 1930, Henry Ford had sold three million Ford Model A Coupes, fulfilling his goal of making cars so affordable that any "any man with a job could own his own automobile." By the 1950s, cars had become important symbols of widespread prosperity, rather than being viewed as toys for the arrogant rich. Futurologists predict the demise of the personal automobile over the next quarter century, with robot vehicles being conveniently dispatched from a central location whenever needed. This "distributed public transportation system" will require dramatically different laws than those that currently govern traffic.

Eighty-one years ago, in 1936, a Duke University student published a law review article predicting the future path of automobile liability law.[10] He observed that, in 1905, all American automobile case law could be contained within a four-page law review article. Only three decades later, explaining the complexities of automobile law would require an entire encyclopedia. That law student was Richard M. Nixon, who would later become President of the United States. Nixon's conclusion was that the courts of his day were mechanically extending "horse and buggy law" to this new mode of transportation. However, the most creative judges developed entirely new rules that were specifically designed to address the growing use of the automobile.

(a) Products Liability for the Age of the Internet

Prior to the mid-1960s, the doctrine of privity shielded manufacturers and others in the line of distribution from legal responsibility for deaths and injuries caused by defective products. Under privity, only a direct purchaser of a product from a manufacturer could file suit for injuries caused by defective products. Consumers injured by defective cars had no recourse against car makers because they were not in direct contractual privity with the company but were only in privity with the local automobile dealer.

Pedestrians and other injured bystanders had no privity either and no cause of legal action against the car maker if injured by a dangerously defective vehicle. This contract-based defense may have made some sense in an earlier America in which sellers were largely local and dealt directly with their customers. However, privity left those injured by defective automobiles without recourse as giant companies increasingly distributed their products through dealerships.

Numerous automobile safety improvements were available, but not instituted, until the law mandated them. "While a headrest design was patented in 1923, the National Highway Transportation Association only enacted a regulation that all passenger cars should have headrests in 1969—after hundreds of thousands of spine injuries as the result of whiplash."[11] Ralph Nader's 1965 best-selling book, *Unsafe at Any Speed: The Designed-In Dangers of the American Automobile*, charged U.S. car manufacturers with resisting the introduction of safety features such as seat belts, anti-roll bars, safety glass and the elimination of sharp edges and knobs on dashboards.

Without legal responsibility for the epidemic of deaths that resulted from needlessly hazardous vehicles, automobile manufactures had little incentive to improve the safety of their vehicles. Advertisements stressed the fun and social admiration that came with owning the latest model of luxury automobile, not the possibility of flaming death from an insecure fuel system or of being impaled by a rigid steering wheel column after a collision.

Privity finally collapsed in a 1960 in a New Jersey Supreme Court case when a court refused to recognize this doctrine, as it was out of step with the modern marketing of automobiles.[12] The decision in *Henningsen v. Bloomfield Motors, Inc.,*[13] altered legal thinking, leading courts and legislatures around the country to overturn privity of contract in products liability litigation. In *Henningsen,* Chrysler sold an automobile to a dealer, Bloomfield Motors. The dealer then resold the car to Claus Henningsen. Henningsen's wife was injured when the car's steering gear malfunctioned only ten days after delivery.

Helen Henningsen was driving at 20–22 miles per hour on a smooth two-lane highway. She heard a loud noise, the steering wheel spun in her hands and the vehicle suddenly veered, crashing into a wall. Helen Henningsen filed suit to recover for her injuries and the loss of her new automobile. Helen had no direct contractual relationship (no privity) with the dealer because Claus had bought the car for his wife as a Mother's Day present. Neither Claus nor Helen was in privity with the Chrysler Corporation because the vehicle had been purchased from a New Jersey dealership.

New Jersey's highest court ruled that consumers could recover for damages caused by defective parts despite the lack of privity and the manufacturer's disclaimers. Justice John Francis, writing for the majority of the New Jersey Supreme Court, held the manufacturer liable despite the lack of privity. The court reasoned that privity was a legal anachronism, given the reality that car makers use local dealers to sell their vehicles nationally:

> Under modern marketing conditions, when a manufacturer puts a new automobile in the stream of trade and promotes its purchase by the public, an implied warranty that it is reasonably suitable for use as such accompanies it into the hands of the ultimate purchaser. Absence of agency between the manufacturer and the dealer who makes the ultimate sale is immaterial.[14]

Most other state courts soon adopted the New Jersey Supreme Court's reasoning, allowing a consumer to file a products liability action despite the absence of privity. A growing number of courts also refused to enforce the manufacturer's warranty disclaimers. Automobile manufacturers and dealers could no longer limit the customer's remedy to only the replacement of the defective parts by writing this restriction into the car's purchase and sale agreement.

These new legal principles shifted the cost of accidents created by defective design from consumers onto manufacturers, who were in the best position to redesign the cars and fortify warnings of known defects. Today, a product seller is "subject to liability to the user or consumer even though he has exercised all possible care in the preparation and sale of the product."[15] Today, courts are beginning to extend this principle to software companies, who have a history of routinely disclaiming any liability to users.

(b) Legal Lag & Information Technologies

Internet technologies are evolving far faster than industry groups, legislatures and international standards organizations can formulate new laws and regulations. The legal system law limps behind technological developments, inevitably failing to catch up to advances in the digital world. Neither criminal nor tort law, for example, has yet developed appropriate remedies to punish and deter gender-linked injuries such as online stalking, harassment and humiliation.

Google's Larry Page expressed the frustration felt by many computer professionals about the need for a living law that adapts more fluidly to cyberspace developments: "The law can't be right if it's 50 years old. Like, it's before the Internet." The U.S. Court of Appeals for the Second Circuit compared revising laws to keep up with rapidly changing technologies as being "somewhat like trying to board a moving bus."[16]

U.S. jurisdictions often have different community standards for what content is considered obscene, defamatory or is otherwise illegal content. In *United States v. Thomas*,[17] a married couple was charged and convicted of violating federal obscenity statutes. The couple's California-based online bulletin board uploaded erotic pictorial images. A postal inspector obtained a password from the couple and transmitted allegedly obscene material to his computer in Tennessee. The couple also sent allegedly obscene videotapes to the Tennessee-based inspector.

The U.S. Court of Appeals for the Sixth Circuit affirmed the Thomas's conviction in a Tennessee district court. The court reasoned that the defendants had knowingly sent their material into Tennessee by accepting a subscription from a resident of that state and it was therefore appropriate to apply the community obscenity standard of Tennessee.

The erotic images would be protectable under the First Amendment in California, where they had been uploaded, but the same images were deemed obscene in Tennessee, where the images were downloaded because of that state's more conservative community standards. This was the first case to apply the community standard definition of obscenity to an Internet transmission. The U.S. Supreme Court in *Miller v. California* acknowledged that: "It is neither realistic nor constitutionally sound to read the First Amendment as requiring the people of Maine or Mississippi to accept public depiction of conduct found tolerable in Las Vegas or New York City."[18]

Chart One (below) provides examples of the potential legal consequences of actual moral dilemmas faced by our students over the past two years. Without knowledge of the applicable laws, it is easy to become entrapped in a costly and potentially career-destroying legal quagmire.

CHART ONE: LEGAL ISSUES RAISED BY COMMON ETHICAL DILEMMAS

Ethical Issues Facing Computer Professionals	*Legal Issues Raised*
You have been asked to install software that monitors the keystrokes of a client's employees.	What privacy rights do the employees have? If the employees are working in a European subsidiary, do you owe them a duty of notice that they are being monitored?
You are working as a computer consultant for an educational institution and asked to install software that secretly monitors peer-to-peer sharing of music and software.	Will the software take into account the students' fair use rights under copyright law? Are the students entitled to receive notice that their downloaded content is being monitored? What duty does the computer professional have to notify law enforcement if students download illegal content?
You have been asked to develop software for a hospital that is a "covered entity" under the Health Insurance Portability and Accountability Act of 1996 (HIPAA). If the cost of implementing security is great, how much security is enough to protect patients' privacy?	The HIPAA Privacy Rule establishes national standards to protect individuals' medical records and other personal health information and it applies to health plans, health care clearinghouses and those health care providers that conduct certain health care transactions electronically.
What privacy information must be protected and at what cost if your client is subject to the HIPAA's Security Rule? What steps must a programmer take to protect medical records?	The HIPAA Privacy Rule protects most "individually identifiable health information" held or transmitted by a covered entity or its business associates, in any form or medium, whether electronic, on paper or oral. The Privacy Rule calls this information protected health information.

What security safeguards must be implemented at what cost to protect medical records? Does it matter whether the health care provider is a "covered entity" under HIPAA? Are all patients entitled to reasonable computer security or only those covered by HIPAA?	HIPAA's Security Rule requires covered entities to maintain reasonable and appropriate administrative, technical and physical safeguards for protecting patient information.
You are a computer professional served with a legal summons requiring you to turn over the personally identifiable records of your service provider client.	There is a definite legal requirement to respond to and comply with a court order, even though this may conflict with the privacy rights of the client's customers.

§ 1.1: ETHICAL ROOTS OF COMPUTER LAW

[A] Rapidly Evolving Technologies Raise Moral Issues

Critics warn that the increasing economic and cultural power of the Internet's largest corporations may alter the political system in unpredictable ways.[19] Skillful tweeting, banner fundraising advertisements, manipulative emails, online opinion polling, strategic leaking and other newly enhanced online political techniques will play increasingly central roles in election campaigns. President Trump continues to use Twitter to communicate directly with his constituents, redefining the relationship between government and the electorate. Trump's leading critics, such as Senator Elizabeth Warren and entrepreneur Mark Cuban, are increasingly employing social media postings to counter the President's tweets.

The ISIS terrorist organization rose from obscurity by broadcasting violent recruitment propaganda on social media. As a presidential candidate, Donald Trump proposed restricting the Internet access of such groups, stating; "We have to talk to [cyberspace experts] about, maybe in certain areas, closing that Internet up in some way . . . Somebody will say, 'Oh, freedom of speech, freedom of speech.' These are foolish people." Critics fear that such proposals will lead to censorship of all oppositional groups, noting that the Internet plays a key role in organizing grassroots social movements such as the Native American opposition to the Keystone oil pipeline. The activist group, *Grab Your Wallet*, is employing the Internet to organize consumer boycotts against retailers that carry Ivanka Trump branded clothing.

Calls for greater computer security have increased since intelligence services confirmed that Russian hackers undermined Senator Hillary Clinton's candidacy and the integrity of the American political system in the 2016 U.S. Presidential election. Facebook has disclosed that more than "$100,000 worth of divisive ads were purchased by a Russian company linked to Prime Minister Putin's government."[20] In September 2017, Facebook admitted that it hosted a Russian influence operation that micro-targeted millions of users with hate speech messages.[21]

Texas separatists and other U.S. activist groups were manipulated to create an "AstroTurf" social movement that encouraged demonstrations against Senator Clinton. The AstroTurf designation refers to political efforts that have the appearance of being spontaneous expressions of popular outrage, but in fact are composed of hoaxes and half-truths that are orchestrated by public relations experts. In August 2017, Facebook moved to discourage disinformation campaigns by banning websites that repeatedly shared stories marked as false from advertising on its platform.[22]

The vastness of the Internet makes it difficult to enforce rules against illegal postings. The peer-to-peer file sharing movement on the Internet, for example, pits the movie, record and film industries against copyright infringing Internet users. Visitors upload 300 hours of content per minute. YouTube has one billion users who account for four billion views each day. It would take 600 persons watching YouTube 24/7 just to classify the content as infringing or not. In May 2017, Facebook announced that would increase the number of employees charged with reviewing bad behavior such as crimes and suicides shown in its postings from 4,500 to 7,000 individuals.

[B] Resolving Ethical Disputes Through Law

(1) The Ethics & Law of Ticket Bots

Michael Rustad remembers standing in line for six hours in 1974 so he could attend a nationally televised basketball game between two ACC powerhouses, the Maryland Terrapins and the North Carolina Tar Heels. The only way to get a student ticket was to personally buy one at the Cole Field House ticket office in College Park, Maryland. Today, a student can make a last-minute decision to purchase a ticket from a resale website without the buyer needing to interact with potentially dishonest street scalpers. Nevertheless, the virtue of the older method of ticket distribution is that those who stood in line when the office opened could buy a face value ticket.

Today's college students, in contrast, often have no recourse but to pay inflated prices for a popular concert or sporting event on a resale website, which often has acquired a huge block of tickets electronically. The New York Attorney General (New York AG) reports receiving numerous complaints from consumers citing "price gouging," "scalping," "outrageous fees" and "immediate sell-outs." As one citizen wrote in a typical complaint: "The average fan has no chance to buy tickets at face value . . . this is a disgrace."[23] The New York AG describes online ticketing as a "fixed" game:

> Consider, for example, that on December 8, 2014, when tickets first went on sale for a tour by the rock band U2, a single broker purchased 1,012 tickets to one show at Madison Square Garden in a single minute, despite the ticket vendor's claim of a "4 ticket limit." By the end of that day, the same broker and one other had together amassed more than 15,000 tickets to U2's shows across North America. Consider that brokers sometimes resell tickets at margins that are over 1,000% of face value.[24]

Companies producing ticket bot software boast that they can easily circumvent the security of event websites by masquerading as human buyers. Is it ethical to use bots to gain an unfair advantage by preventing the public from purchasing tickets at a fair market value? Until recently, there was no state or federal regulation prohibiting ticket-buying bots.

The ticket bot problem is an example of how emergent moral predicaments are often resolved through legislation, regulations or legal decisions. In late 2016, Congress enacted a statute declaring that the use of ticket bots is an unfair or deceptive trade practice in violation of the Federal Trade Commission Act. The use of anti-circumvention ticket bots arguably violates several states' unfair and deceptive trade practices statutes. As new forms of wrongdoing emerge, judges must determine how far existing laws can stretch to cover cyberspace disputes.

(2) Updating the Law for Price Bots

In the fall of 2017, several U.S. airlines raised prices dramatically for flights leaving cities in the path of Hurricane Irma. This price gouging was not a human management decision. Bots automatically increased prices in response to Internet searches for and purchases of these airline tickets. Observers fear that as Internet giants come to dominate commercial transactions, price-monitoring bots will be able to conspire against consumers through algorithmic pricing that allow suppliers to coordinate cost increases. "A cabal of AI-enhanced price-bots might plausibly hatch a method of colluding that even their handlers could not understand, let alone be held full responsible for."[25]

It is unclear under what circumstances AI programmers or their employers can be held legally responsible for the unanticipated misdeeds of a defectively programmed rogue bot. Legislation against this new form of price fixing will be difficult to design because:

> the more consumers are pushed to deal directly with price-bots (to thwart the transparency that allows rival sellers to collude), the more the algorithms learn about the characteristics of individual customers. That opens the door to prices tailored to each customer's willingness to pay, a profitable strategy for sellers.[26]

Overregulation of technology's cutting-edge products and services is a danger if lawmakers move too quickly to remedy perceived digital wrongs.

(3) Classifying Workers as Independent Contractors

Ethical questions regarding the just distribution of societal burdens and benefits arise from the widespread introduction of digital products. For example, Intuit.com, a software corporation, estimates that 40% of all American workers will be classified as independent contractors by the year 2020. Uber drivers are challenging their classification as independent contractors in the U.S. courts.

They argue for the right to enjoy employee benefits such as unemployment insurance, workers' compensation and to organize labor unions. In 2016, Uber settled two class action lawsuits filed by its drivers, agreeing to pay $84 million and allow their drivers to organize to remedy grievances, receive tips from passengers and appeal deactivations by Uber.

(4) Algorithmic Bias

Algorithms may make sexist or racist decisions that reflect the non-conscious assumptions of their programmers. The software used by property owners to screen out potentially troublesome tenants has the appearance of objectivity, but the underlying algorithms discriminate against immigrants. The algorithm will unjustly reject people who cannot document a stable work history in the United States. The website Algorithmic Justice's mission is to "identify and discuss ethical challenges of algorithms, big data and artificial intelligence, but also to suggest solutions how algorithms can be harnessed for ethical purposes."

Uber's subjective passenger and driver-rating system is said to discriminate against socially disfavored groups because minority drivers tend to receive unfairly lower scores from white passengers. Cornell University researchers argue that:

> We know that people tend to have implicit biases that affect how they evaluate people from different groups. It would be illegal for an employer to discriminate directly, but this creates the possibility for backdoor bias creeping in from customers. These new technologies challenge the traditional way law prevents discrimination in the workplace.[27]

AI programs stand accused of depicting women disproportionately in ads for lower paying jobs and tracking African-Americans into cheaper neighborhoods.[28] Algorithmic beauty contest judges overwhelmingly find white contestants to be the most attractive, which is a systematic bias against other races.

A crime prediction algorithm might focus surveillance on minority neighborhoods in response to official statistics showing that these areas have the highest recorded crime rates. These statistics, however, may be the result of an unwritten law enforcement policy of aggressively arresting minority youth from "bad neighborhoods" while releasing teens from "better" families into the custody of their parents. When the AI's efforts result in the arrest of a disproportionate number of residents of these areas, the program might interpret the apparent increase in criminal activity as a need to further increase its targeting of minority youth.

Racist software in the criminal justice system is not a mere hypothetical. A 2016 study of the accuracy of software that predicts the likelihood that a criminal defendant will reoffend concluded that "[w]hite defendants who re-offended within the next two years were mistakenly labeled low risk almost twice as often as black re-offenders (48 percent vs. 28 percent)."[29]

(5) Balancing Security Versus Privacy Concerns

The most perplexing dilemmas arise when policymakers must choose between conflicting ethical principles. In early 2016, the FBI sought a court order to compel Apple to write software that would decrypt the messages contained on an iPhone used in a San Bernardino, California terrorist attack. Apple opposed this order, contending that if the company developed software to unlock the iPhone, the technology inevitably would lead to mass surveillance, especially of their customers living under despotic regimes. Apple argued that unconditional user trust is essential for the continuing vitality of information technology companies.

The dispute became moot when the FBI announced that an unidentified third party had developed a method to defeat the iPhone's encryption. In a parallel 2016 case, Amazon refused to provide Arkansas murder investigators with audio recordings gathered by its Echo smart speaker system.[30] Such fundamental ethical conflicts between technology corporations and law enforcement agencies appear destined to be decided by the U.S. Supreme Court.

§ 1.2: TECHNOLOGY, ETHICS, AND LAW

[A] How New Technologies Disrupt the Law

Throughout American history, new information technologies have remade social institutions. The fabled Pony Express of the American West was displaced by the telegraph after less than two years of operation when Western Union completed its transcontinental telegraph system in October 1861.[31] The telegraph, in turn, was replaced by the telephone as the leading mechanism for long-distance communication. Operator-assisted telephone calls gave way to direct dialing. Today, smart phones are rapidly replacing the classic landline, which had required the installation and maintenance of an extensive string of telephone poles and wires.

Netflix's streaming service has driven Blockbuster almost out of business. Of the 9,000 Blockbuster stores in the 1990s, less than ten are still in operation. Netflix's future, in turn, is now being threatened by the proposal of the head of the Federal Communications Commission (FCC), Ajit Pai, to weaken net neutrality. Under the principle of net neutrality, the Obama administration treated Internet Service Providers as similar to public utility providers, which prevented ISPs from favoring one content provider over another. Pai, in contrast, takes a libertarian position, that government intervention to protect online equality should give way to market-driven decisions by private entities. Netflix fears that its entertainment services could be slowed to give priority to rivals that are owned or collaborate with the major ISPs.

Those who resist new information technologies often lose out to those who first learn to exploit new methods of communication. In the sixteenth century Protestant Reformation, Martin Luther played a key role in transforming Europe's ethical and legal order. Luther was the equivalent of a blogger in his day, authoring frequent essays about the need to radically reform Christianity.

Luther's sacrilegious broadsides could be printed relatively quickly and inexpensively thanks to advances in the development of the movable type printing press.[32] The Roman Catholic Church was slow to marshal the power of these improvements in information technology and therefore was unable to crush Martin Luther's Protestant movement before it gained a rock-solid foothold in Northern Europe.

As Martin Luther's reputation grew, he began to make money from the sales of his writings. However, his profits were limited because Luther was unable to prevent unauthorized copying. Unscrupulous printers reproduced Luther's texts with impunity, sometimes stealing his original manuscripts to make their illicit editions. Copyright law had not evolved to the point where Luther's rights could be vindicated. The British Statute of Anne, 1710, "An Act for the Encouragement of Learning, by vesting the Copies of Printed Books in the Authors or purchasers of such Copies, during the Times therein mentioned," was the first copyright statute.

In the preface of one edition of his German translation of the New Testament, a frustrated Martin Luther wrote: "I beg all my friends and foes, my masters, printers and readers, let this New Testament be mine. If you lack one, then make one for yourselves. . . . But this Testament is Luther's German Testament."[33]

"Technological determinism" overstates the role of technical innovations as the driver of social change. It is far too simplistic to attribute the Protestant Reformation solely to the technological advances in movable type printing. Without the support of local Saxon princes, Luther's writings would have been easily suppressed. His polemics would not have been influential without a critical mass of literate Christians, who were already receptive to his message. Germany already had a long tradition of opposition against the Catholic Church's oppressive hierarchy, which predisposed the populace to support Luther's attacks.[34]

[B] Unauthorized Copying in the Information Age

The ethics of downloading copyrighted material without paying royalties to the author remains a hotly contested issue. Is unlawful downloading of content equivalent to stealing physical objects? While the original work is expensive to produce, additional copies can be created at almost no cost, making the theft of intellectual property feel morally different from traditional types of misappropriation that deprive the original possessor of physical property.

Martin Luther's attempt to shame printers who copied his religious writings without permission parallels contemporary attempts to shame unauthorized downloaders from pirating music, films and software. Paul Stanley, the rhythm guitarist and singer of the rock band *Kiss*, argues, "Illegal music downloading is 'morally' and 'ethically wrong,' and laments the fact that new artists "don't have a chance in hell" of "ever getting that pot of gold."[35] Bono, the lead singer of *U2* rebuts the idea that illegal downloading only harms greedy capitalists:

> A decade's worth of music file-sharing and swiping has made clear that the people it hurts are the creators—in this case, the young, fledgling songwriters who can't live off ticket and T-shirt sales like the least sympathetic among us.[36]

The Australian film industry uses shame in its advertising campaign to deter illegally copying of the country's movies: "You wouldn't steal a car, you wouldn't steal a handbag, you wouldn't steal a television and you wouldn't steal a movie. Downloading pirated films is stealing." The public relations campaign to label unauthorized downloading as immoral "piracy" has failed to gain widespread credibility because:

> Copyright infringement is illegal, and like many things that are illegal (jaywalking, driving a car with an expired license), it doesn't have anything in common with stealing except for the (not unimportant!) fact that it's illegal. Piracy, by contrast, is a special form of stealing committed on the high seas. It involves rolling up to a boat, and taking stuff away from the occupants of the boat. Normally one accomplishes this by threatening to kill the occupants of the boat, and from time to time people actually get killed. By contrast, nobody has ever been killed downloading an authorized copy of a Katy Perry song or sharing the license key of a copy of PowerPoint with a colleague. Sensible people understand this, which is one reason that the content industry's efforts to get copyright infringers treated like dangerous violent criminals have fallen into increasing discredit.[37]

[C] The Policy Debate over Unauthorized Copying

Copyright has always been contested ethical and legal terrain in American society. In the 1780s, the famous textbook and dictionary creator, Noah Webster, campaigned for strong U.S. copyright laws to stop wholesale distribution of unauthorized reproductions of his dictionary. His efforts, along with those of other stakeholders, were rewarded with a clause in the U. S. Constitution that recognized copyright protection.

Two important American ethical principles appear to conflict in copyright law. The First Amendment's right to free expression in the form of reprinting, modifying and parodying existing works, clashes with the right of the original artists to be fully compensated for their creative efforts. Opponents of overly expansive copyright laws argue that corporate owners of intellectual property are attempting to extort excessive profits by privatizing everyone's common heritage. Music industry spokespeople counter that strong copyright protection and free expression have been mutually supportive throughout U.S. history:

> In a two-year span, this nation adopted two major, interlacing principles: Americans were free to write whatever they wanted and had every right to be compensated for their work. The First Amendment encouraged creativity, and the copyright clause guaranteed compensation. So often, the debate over illegal downloading focuses on technology. Those who defend the unauthorized sharing of music say that critics are living in the past and had better get used to the new reality. But that new reality is taking a toll. Over the past decade, America has lost a staggering number of professional songwriters and composers; primarily due to the impact of illegal music downloading. . . Those that remain in the profession are struggling to earn even a minimal income."[38]

Congress has responded to extensive lobbying by pro-copyright interests by ramping up criminal penalties for intellectual property infringement. President Bill Clinton signed the *No Electronic Theft Act of 1997* (NET), which fortified criminal penalties for Internet-related theft. NET amended the U.S. Copyright Act to include online piracy that caused commercial harm, even where there was no proof that the defendant was attempting to make a profit. The media industry continues to press for harsher penalties to deter illegal downloaders.

When the authors of this book ask our students if they illegally download copyrighted music, the great majority admit that they have done so. When asked if they feel guilty for engaging in this infringing activity, only a few indicated that they perceive their downloading as unethical. Moral codes often evolve over time. In the future, this act may be widely viewed as immoral "piracy," or perhaps efforts to punish downloaders will be castigated as an example of illegitimate and futile government overreach.

Changes in online music distribution technology and corporate practices raise new ethical and legal concerns for musicians who are attempting to gain increased recognition. Spotify, with thirty million subscribers, and Apple Music, which has signed up fifteen million subscribers since launching in 2015, are said to be using their immense economic leverage to pressure lesser-known artists through the threat of giving a lower profile to their musical creations:

> Spotify has been retaliating against musicians who introduce new material exclusively on rival Apple Music by making their songs harder to find, according to people familiar with the strategy. Artists who have given Apple exclusive access to new music have been told they will not be able to get their tracks on featured playlists once the songs become available on Spotify, said the people, who declined to be identified discussing the steps. Those artists have also found their songs buried in the search rankings of Spotify, the world's largest music-streaming service, the people said. Spotify said it doesn't alter search rankings.[39]

Such practices are likely to be challenged by attorneys as an updated version of the monopoly power used by anti-competitive business "trusts" during the period of America's robber barons.

§ 1.3: PERSONAL VS. FORMAL ETHICS

[A] Personal and Informal Ethical Codes

The social disruption created by rapid advances in computer technology requires software decision-makers to consider the societal impact of their inventions. Programmers are being challenged to take "responsibility for the outcomes, externalities and downright damaging impacts of our hyper-consumer, ever-changing landscape of new gadgets and virtual arenas that are coming on board at a lighting-speed pace."[40] To quote Spider-Man's Uncle Ben: "With great power, comes great responsibility."

Ethical computing guidelines draw from three sources: "(1) the individual's own personal code, (2) any informal code of ethical behavior that exists in the workplace and (3) exposure to formal codes of ethics."[41] For example, individuals may have very different beliefs about the moral justification involved in an online purchase of recreational marijuana. A drug user who is illegally diverting his legally purchased Colorado supply to make a fast profit in jurisdictions where the possession of marijuana is still criminalized, may be viewed as unethical or alternatively, as advancing liberty. The willingness to limit Internet freedoms in order to enforce laws against this illegal reselling will vary sharply in America's pluralistic society.

Similarly, informal rules of online behavior in the workplace or within other small groups will differ significantly according to local conditions. One office will encourage forwarding jokes as a method of keeping morale high, while, in another work setting, this behavior may result in termination, especially if the jokes are risqué. The macho "bro" culture of some Silicon Valley firms such as Uber has been widely criticized as unethically sexist but praised by a few as encouraging the aggressively competitive ethos necessary in an economic environment where, in the famous aphorism of Intel CEO Andy Grove, "only the paranoid survive."

Formal rules about the use of computers in the classroom vary between outright bans on the use of the Internet to incorporating cyberspace into in-class learning. Some professors encourage students to consult the Internet to look up applicable statutes or a relevant news story, while others view online surfing during class as undermining the educational experience. A lecture on the importance of having a nuanced Internet-deployed advertising campaign can be enhanced as students find examples for themselves and share their discoveries with the class. On the other hand, holding the attention of students is more challenging in classrooms because of the mesmerizing appeal of instant messaging, social networks and other Internet-related distractions.

[B] Formal Codes of Computer Ethics

Preamble to Association of Computer Machinery Code of Ethics

(1) *Public*—Software engineers shall act consistently with the public interest.

(2) *Client and Employer*—Software engineers shall act in a manner that is in the best interests of their clients and employers consistent with the public interest.

(3) *Product*—Software engineers shall ensure that their products and related modifications meet the highest professional standards possible.

(4) *Judgment*—Software engineers shall maintain integrity and independence in their professional judgment.

(5) *Management*—Software engineering managers and leaders shall subscribe to and promote an ethical approach to the management of software development and maintenance.

(6) *Profession*—Software engineers shall advance the integrity and reputation of the profession consistent with the public interest.

(7) *Colleagues*—Software engineers shall be fair to and supportive of their colleagues.

(8) *Self*—Software engineers shall participate in lifelong learning regarding the practice of their profession and shall promote an ethical approach to the practice of the profession.

(1) *The ACM's Code of Ethics*

Formal codes of ethics play an important role in the socialization of professionals. The world's largest educational and scientific society devoted to computing, the Association for Computing Machinery (ACM), has developed a code of ethics to guide computer professionals away from immoral practices. The ACM notes that these principles also can serve as a basis for judging the merits of any formal complaint about violations of professional ethical standards.

The organization's Code of Ethics (ACM Code) consists of twenty-four broad rules that define the personal responsibilities of computer professionals. This code is not legally enforceable since membership in the association is voluntary and the ACM cannot prohibit violators from continuing their work in the information technology field. As this book goes to press, the ACM Committee on Professional Ethics (COPE) is revising the ACM Code of Ethics and Professional Conduct to reflect the shifts in technology and society since the Code's creation in 1992. The ACM ethics committee requests that computer professionals respond to four guiding questions:

> What parts of The Code no longer make sense due to changes in technology or society? What could be done to make them better fit the current context? Are there any blind spots in The Code? Are there principles that ought to be contained in The Code that are currently missing? In the area of technology where you are most expert, what have been the greatest changes since 1992, and how might The Code be updated to reflect these changes? What parts of The Code are confusing, ambiguous or likely to be misinterpreted?[42]

Rule 2.3 of the Association of Computer Machinery Code of Ethics calls for ACM members to "know and respect existing laws pertaining to professional work." However, ACM members, the Code explains, should not blindly obey unjust laws because "compliance must be balanced with the recognition that sometimes existing laws and rules may be immoral or inappropriate and, therefore, must be challenged." For example, Edward Snowden argues that his exposure of the National Security Agency's (NSA) mass monitoring of online communications and its subsequent misleading of Congressional committees about its systematic privacy invasions, created a situation where his personal ethical code and his moral obligations to the American people were more important than obeying U.S. law.

Libertarians, who believe in battling government overreach, have supported Snowden. However, backing from the libertarians will not save Snowden from severe punishment if he returns to any nation that recognizes U.S. legal jurisdiction. The ACM has no power to protect computer professionals from suffering the consequences of breaking the law, even if its membership were to agree that Snowden did the right thing. Chapter Two will address the intersection between ethical perspectives and legal responsibilities.

Section 1.2 of the ACM Ethics Code requires computer professionals to avoid doing harm to others, which is an ethical admonition that applies to diverse legal duties. Chapter Three on Cybertorts, Chapter Four on Cybercrime and Chapter Five on Information Privacy all discuss the legal standards that enforce this ethical dictate. ACM's Code notes that:

> To minimize the possibility of indirectly harming others, computing professionals must minimize malfunctions by following generally accepted standards for system design and testing. Furthermore, it is often necessary to assess the social consequences of systems to project the likelihood of any serious harm to others.

Chapter Five examines information privacy issues from a globalized perspective. Section 1.7 of the Code requires respect for the privacy of others. Failure to protect data privacy may lead to legal liability:

> Computing and communication technology enables the collection and exchange of personal information on a scale unprecedented in the history of civilization. Thus, there is increased potential for violating the privacy of individuals and groups. It is the responsibility of professionals to maintain the privacy and integrity of data describing individuals.

ACM ethical rules implicitly require computer professionals to understand and comply with not only the letter of the law, but also with its spirit. Section 2.6 of the ACM Ethics Code requires computer experts to "honor contracts, agreements and assigned responsibilities." Examining the law and ethics of electronic contracts allows one the exploration of such issues as when online contracts are so deceptively presented that courts may refuse to enforce them. If software publishers use licensing to disclaim all responsibility for remedies in the event that their software fails, is it ethical, even if it is legal? Chapter Six discusses the difficult ethical issues raised by contract law in inequitable information technology contracts.

Chapters Seven and Eight of this book will apply ethical and principles to copyrights, patents, trademarks and trade secrets. As Section 1.5 of the ACM notes:

> Violation of copyrights, patents, trade secrets and the terms of license agreements are prohibited by law in most circumstances. Even when

software is not so protected, such violations are contrary to professional behavior. Copies of software should be made only with proper authorization. Unauthorized duplication of materials must not be condoned.

ACM Ethics Code Section 1.8 requires computer professionals to "honor confidentiality." Reviewing how different countries have adopted varying approaches to the trade-offs between protecting personal privacy and other social values such as security and intellectual property rights will reveal the complexity of this issue. Once again, there has been significant litigation over when confidentiality legally applies and when it can be broken.

(2) Computer Professionals for Social Responsibility

Computer Professionals for Social Responsibility (CPSR), an organization founded to further ethical behavior in computing, existed from 1983 until it was disbanded in 2013. Like the ACM, the CPSR realized that computers are instrumentalities for accomplishing good, but they can also enable morally questionable behavior. The CPSR developed a similar, though less detailed, list of ethical principles as the ACM. CPSR's Ten Commandments proscribe wrongs that may arise in a computer professional's work life. This code of personal conduct parallels the Biblical Ten Commandments in being overwhelmingly composed of "don'ts" rather than positive actions.

Both the ACM's and CPSR's ethical codes are merely aspirational, like the Scout Oath or The American's Creed, rather than a set of legally enforceable duties. The coercive power of law makes it difficult to craft. Criminal law must be carefully fashioned so that people know in advance what activities are illegal and have a clear idea of what punishment is proper. Hastily drafted statutes encourage unethical people to exploit legal ambiguities by sidestepping the exact wording of the law or they may unnecessarily frighten ethical individuals from doing the right thing for fear of legal jeopardy. The overwhelming message implicit in CPSR's Ten Commandments is that moral principles frequently overlap with explicit legal duties and rights.

Unethical conduct can trigger legal liability as computer ethics is concretized in judicial opinions, regulations and statutes. Chart Two (below) describes U.S. laws that prescribe punishments for violating the CPSR's ethical principles. The history and effectiveness of these and other laws, including the laws of the European Union, will be discussed in depth in subsequent chapters.

CHART TWO: CPSR'S TEN COMMANDMENTS OF COMPUTER ETHICS

Ten Commandments	Legal Issues Addressed	Illustrations
(1) Thou shalt not use a computer to harm other people.	Applies to cybercrimes as addressed by the Computer Fraud & Abuse Act and the Electronic Communications Privacy Act.	Intercepting an electronic communication or trespassing on a government computer.
(2) Thou shalt not interfere with other people's computer work.	Applies to cybercrimes and personal property cybertorts.	Ransomware, computer viruses and worms. Malicious software also constitutes the tort of trespass to chattels or conversion.
(3) Thou shalt not snoop around in other people's computer files.	Applies to the tort of the "intrusion upon seclusion," a privacy-based tort and a crime under the Computer Fraud and Abuse Act, which forbids downloading data without authorization.	Obtaining data from a computer system's private files. Snooping around in another person's files or reading someone else's personal messages.
(4) Thou shalt not use a computer to steal.	Applies to cybercrimes and to personal property, privacy torts and business torts.	Hacking constitutes a violation of the Economic Espionage Act as well as the misappropriation of trade secrets.
(5) Thou shalt not use a computer to bear false witness.	Covers many cybercrimes, cybertorts and regulatory actions by the Federal Trade Commission.	False information about individuals constitutes defamation.
(6) Thou shalt not copy or use proprietary	Prohibits using software without a license, which is both a violation of contract	Using proprietary software without a license can result in

software for which you have not paid.	law and intellectual property.	copyright or patent infringement lawsuits, which can result in millions of dollars in judgments and fines.
(7) Thou shalt not use other people's computer resources without authorization or proper compensation.	Unauthorized access to a password protected computer system is a crime under the Computer Fraud and Abuse Act and could also be a personal property tort.	Unauthorized access may also constitute a tort if the computer system is impaired. If the computer system is destroyed, the tort of conversion applies.
(8) Thou shalt not appropriate other people's intellectual output.	IP infringement can violate criminal law.	If a programmer uses software developed for his employer for other applications, it is likely a breach of a nondisclosure agreement and may constitute copyright infringement.
(9) Thou shalt think about the social consequences of the program you are writing or the system you are designing.	Failure to consider social consequences could result in tort liability.	Software engineers who do not consider social consequences may find themselves liable for negligent computer security, illegal discrimination and other torts.
(10) Thou shalt always use a computer in ways that ensure consideration and respect for your fellow humans.	N/A (Only Commandment that does not address legal liability issues.)	The law does not reward good behavior. Instead, it penalizes bad acts.

§ 1.4: ETHICS & THE INTERNET OF THINGS

The Internet of Things (IoT) refers to all everyday consumer products and services that receive and transmit data on the Internet. A 2015 Federal Trade Commission report provides examples of this rapidly expanding phenomenon and the dangers presented by lax security:

> The Internet of Things adds new security dimensions to consider. For example, an insecure connection could give a hacker access not just to the confidential information transmitted by the device, but also to everything else on a user's network. . . If that home automation system isn't secure, a criminal could override the settings to unlock the doors. And just think of the consequences if a hacker were able to remotely recalibrate a medical device—say, an insulin pump or a heart monitor.[43]

The IoT is evolving in a policy vacuum, with minimal regulation or legal precedent. Industry remains ill-prepared to deal with the security issues raised by smart products, despite the government's warning. In September 2016, cybercriminals took advantage of substandard IoT security to build a massive botnet using smart devices such as Internet-enabled televisions, baby monitors, security systems, cameras and printers.

Companies like Amazon, Twitter and Netflix were crippled for hours, while Internet access was interrupted on the East Coast. Whether the burden of such losses should be principally borne by the websites or by those who did not adequately protect their devices is a legal and ethical judgment that will shape the future of information engineering.

Internet-enabled vehicle safety devices, for example, can dramatically lessen the carnage on America's highways, but they also raise vexing ethical and legal issues. This technology permits the tracking of any automobile. Under what circumstances should law enforcement personnel be permitted to access a car's travel record? When should insurance companies or traffic police be allowed to evaluate the safety of a driver's conduct? When should an employer be permitted to check an auto's electronic records to see if the employee took an unauthorized break? Should the records be available to determine whether a restraining order has been violated or should the records be automatically destroyed to preserve individual privacy?

If these questions in applied ethics appear complex, examine the "futurecraft" city envisioned by the Massachusetts Institute of Technology's Senseable City Project, where nanosensors, cell phones and other information-gathering devices would provide optimal services by tracking every movement of individuals.[44] People could be warned away from crime scenes or traffic jams and toward opportunities to engage in their favor hobbies. Developing new laws to regulate this predicted "smart city" will require ethical visionaries. How should information engineers make certain that this highly useful technology does not create a dystopian future in which constant surveillance renders privacy nonexistent?

Policy Issues for the Internet of Things (IoT)

What are the privacy concerns raised specifically by IoT? How are they different from other privacy concerns?

Do these concerns change based on the categorization of IoT applications? What role or actions should the Department of Commerce and, more generally, the federal government takes regarding policies, rules and standards about privacy and the IoT?

Are there other consumer protection issues that are raised specifically by IoT? If so, what are they and how should the government respond to the concerns? In what ways could IoT affect and be affected by questions of economic equity? In what ways could IoT potentially help disadvantaged communities or groups? Rural communities? In what ways might IoT create obstacles for these communities or groups?

What effects, if any, will Internet access have on IoT, and what effects, if any, will IoT have on Internet access? What role, if any, should the government play in ensuring that the positive impacts of IoT reach all Americans and keeping the negatives from disproportionately affecting disadvantaged communities or groups?

Source: United States Department of Commerce, *Internet of Things* (2017).

§ 1.5: GLOBALIZED LAW AND ETHICS

[A] The Internet as a Cross-Border Legal Environment

Advances in information technology are bringing cultures that were once geographically separate into constant interaction. The Internet crosses national borders at the speed of light, making it very difficult to avoid violating different national laws and moral standards. No virtual tollgates warn users that they are entering into the jurisdiction of a country with very different legal, ethical and political realities.

[B] Global Business Dilemmas

A U.S. e-commerce business must not only comply with consumer law, competition law and regulations in every country where it does business, but its corporate leadership must understand that law enforcement effectiveness varies significantly around the world. Highly paid industrial and professional jobs may also be readily transferred to much less expensive Third World countries or assigned to robots, destroying what were once the secure careers of millions. Some futurologists foresee a huge growth of unemployment among those replaced by artificially intelligent machinery, which might require a vastly expanded, globalized system of unemployment compensation or mass retraining of displaced workers.

[C] Cross-Border Cultural Clashes

European law differs sharply from U.S. legal practices in evaluating what is protected as free expression. For example, the Union of Jewish French Students filed suit against Twitter because it refused to disclose the "names of anti-Semitic tweet authors, despite a French court ruling commanding their identification." In the United States, these tweets, though objectionable to many, are protected expression under the First Amendment of the U.S. Constitution.

Some European countries still retain anti-blasphemy criminal law but Europe's recognition of free expression as a fundamental right is now supplanting the older law. In May 2017, the Irish government investigated Stephen Fry for blasphemy after the prominent actor was quoted as asking why he should "respect a capricious, mean-minded, stupid God who creates a world that is so full of injustice and pain?" and for denouncing God as "utterly monstrous." Irish prosecutors did not file charges against Fry. It is highly unlikely that the European Court of Justice would permit prosecution for these anti-religious statements, as free expression is also a fundamental right throughout the European Union.

In the United States, the First Amendment protects comedians like Bill Maher, who calls religion a mass delusion.[45] Maher, in his HBO show *Real Time* denounced what he considers liberals' mistaken argument that both Christians and Muslims are equally likely to engage in violent religious intolerance: "Are there Christian terrorist armies like ISIS, Al Qaeda, Boko Haram, al-Shabaab? Are there armies like that in the world that aren't Muslim?"[46] In contrast, in July 2017, a Pakistani was sentenced to death for insulting Mohammed in a Facebook post.[47]

Website designers and operators must tailor their content to conform to radically different legal cultures. A news story critical of Islam or the Prophet Mohammed is blasphemous in Saudi Arabia and lead to severe punishment of the author. This same story would be protected expression under the First Amendment of the U.S. Constitution and as a fundamental right under European law. Article 11 of the European Union's Charter of Fundamental Rights guarantees the "freedom to hold opinions and to receive and impart information and ideas without interference by public authority and regardless of frontiers."[48]

Where exactly is the line between free expression and enabling terrorism? A Christian Coptic living in California produced *The Innocence of Muslims*, an anti-Islamic film trailer that portrayed Mohammed as a hypocrite, looter and sexual deviant. The amateurish trailer, dubbed in Arabic, was uploaded to YouTube in September 2012, inciting riots that led to fifty deaths and hundreds of injuries throughout the Middle East. Afghanistan, Bangladesh, Sudan and Pakistan blocked YouTube because it would not remove the incendiary video. Should such postings be forbidden as dangerous hate speech or protected under the right to religious freedom?

[D] Terrorism and Hate on the Internet

The Boston Marathon bombers learned to make pressure cooker bombs from an online magazine called *Inspire*, which, in 2010, published detailed instructions for creating lethal devices out of easily acquired materials. How aggressive do websites need to be in locating and removing such potentially dangerous postings? Well after the terrorist attack, a *Guardian* newspaper reporter viewed "a 30-slide guide about how to build a bomb posted on Facebook. Although it was removed by moderators, it had been on the site for some time—and reappeared again weeks later."[49]

Determining whether to block hate speech on the Internet always involves balancing ethical values such as safety, security and property rights against free expression. YouTube, as a privately owned business, is developing its own standards of decency. The website's software reviews hundreds of millions of clips to purge the site of videos showing brutal crimes or glamorizing terrorism. In August 2017, YouTube adopted a new policy calculated:

> to catch and flag what it calls "controversial religious and supremacist" videos hosted on the platform. The platform plans to hide these videos from wider audiences and demonetize them to prevent their creators from earning revenue from YouTube.[50]

The Internet forces a rethinking of human rights, legal jurisdiction and other basic moral and legal concepts. Regions with no tradition of free speech feel themselves assaulted by disruptive, obscene and blasphemous online postings. In contrast, nations that highly value free expression complain of suffocating foreign censorship. The international harmonization of cyberspace law is proving to be extremely complex because different regions vary in their cultural beliefs, legal systems and economic interests.

§ 1.6: ETHICAL NORMS & LAW

Basic agreements on ethical values are the glue that hold voluntary communities together. Internet users collectively determine what violations of these unwritten rules should be penalized. Sociologists divide these collective norms into "mores" (ethical norms reflecting fundamental values) and "folkways" (customary ways of doing things). Spamming, pop-up ads and excessively commercial conduct on websites are relatively minor violations that are classified as folkways. Distribution of child pornography violates mores in the great majority of social circles. In the absence of legal enforcement, group members may develop informal ethical codes that can be enforced through ostracism, harassment or banishing.

In the early years of the Internet, there were few laws regulating online activity. Lacking an effective legal code, citizens of the Internet, or netizens, developed their own normative rules and enforced them through the cyberspace version of vigilante justice. Without a physical presence, a lynch mob can hang no one. However, informal social control mechanisms emerged in the 1990s, when the online community was far smaller and more cohesive than today's Internet community.

Social ostracism augments acceptable use policies, which tend to be normatively, not legally, based. In a well-known incident, customers in a San Francisco Apple retail store "noticed a vaguely androgynous person spending a lot of time there with a computer," using the store's free wireless, which negatively affected the system's availability to others. "Some people became annoyed at the person and they blogged and posted pictures online" to embarrass the norm breaker. Employing YouTube to shame the annoying Apple user illustrates the emergence of informal social controls to both establish and enforce norms.[51]

Informal social controls also played an important role in punishing bad behavior in the early chat rooms where snarky comments tended to quickly spiral into insulting postings. Angry users "flamed" racists, spammers and deceitful advertisers to enforce ethical norms of civility in the early Internet. "Bozo filters" blocked messages from excessively loquacious participants in discussion groups. User communities still employ online shaming tactics to enforce norms against certain types of behavior when formal legal remedies are either unavailable or impractical. Public humiliation has now been crowd sourced to outraged Internet denizens who may fire off a stream of hostile postings that attack the violator of informal norms. For example, when L.A. Fitness refused to cancel the memberships of a couple who had lost their jobs, Internet hostility led the company to reverse its policy. Cyberbullies or aggressive proponents of unpopular viewpoints would find their email systems subject to denial of service attacks or other forms of cyber harassment.

The contemporary Internet is too immense and multifaceted to be self-governed by the informal norms and vigilante sanctions that punished wrongdoers during the Internet's infancy. Moderators are often empowered by website owners to enforce norms against purposeful harassment or distasteful Internet postings. Networking site administrators regularly suspend subscribers for spamming, profanity, harassment or other breaches of "netiquette." At some point, moderators employ the equivalent of capital punishment for those who violate norms by permanently banning persistent rule-breakers.

Many computer game servers have automated the process of ejecting rule-breakers. When a user is banned from an online game, the reason for the exclusion is posted to shame the ex-user for his failure to follow the norms of e-sportsmanship. Banned posters often complain that their Constitutional right to free expression has been violated, only to find out that the First Amendment of the U.S. Constitution only applies to governmental actions, not the actions of private actors, such as website owners, private employers or social networks. Posters, of course, are free to leave a website if they disagree with its policies.

§ 1.7: PROFESSIONAL ETHICS

The term "professional" has expanded in the popular lexicon to apply to dedicated practitioners of almost any specialized activity. The Professional Bike Mechanics Association promotes the interests of technicians who repair bicycles. The Professional Beauty Association is the largest and most inclusive trade organization of the beauty industry. Elite athletes, such as NFL or NBA players, label themselves as professionals because they have a strong personal drive to excel. When athletes are asked whether the team will be negatively impacted by unfavorable playing conditions, they often respond that they are professionals who will do their best no matter what unusual difficulties they encounter.

Both law and sociology consider this common use of the term "professional" to be incorrect. A profession for these scholars is an occupational group that mandates specialized educational training, credentialing and adherence to a code of ethics, such as the fields of law and medicine. Professionals owe a fiduciary duty to their client, which means that consumers have both a legal and ethical right to receive a higher duty of care. Professional ethics is a subfield of applied ethics that attempts to develop the rules of right and wrong in established professions where practitioners must make decisions beyond the expertise of ordinary persons.

[A] What Are Professional Ethics?

Laws governing the traditional professions are comprised of specific duties, established by the state as necessary for maintaining social order, resolving disputes and properly distributing societal resources. Professional ethics may differ from ordinary norms of morality. A criminal defense attorney, for example, has an ethical duty to zealously represent his or her client, even if there is clear evidence of guilt. Some canons of professional responsibility are imported into formal legal duties, such as rules against disclosing the confidential information of clients or misusing client's funds. The norms of ethical communication between a doctor and patient are increasingly shaped by the legal rules that mandate confidentiality and informed consent.

Some cynics charge that the professions are hypocritical conspiracies against the public interest designed primarily to enrich its members. Critics of the legal profession, medical profession and actuaries note that professional organizations make it difficult for "competitors to set up shop. Very long qualification periods and professional bodies that give approval only to a certain number of candidates per year can be viewed as a way of keeping fee payments exorbitantly high."[52]

To become a patent attorney or patent agent, for example, it is necessary to pass the Patent Bar Examination, which is only open to individuals possessing a scientific or technical educational background. This requirement can be viewed as a valid method of ensuring the competence of patent agents, though it inevitably increases the cost of obtaining a patent.

New hardware and software developments are undermining the traditional professions and challenging their ethical codes. Smart devices using expert systems that incorporate artificial intelligence to learn and adapt over time are displacing some of the straightforward professional services. Routine legal work such as discovery is increasingly being automated through software. Bots have been designed to mount legal challenges to invalidate parking tickets. A bot has been developed enabling the victims of Equifax data breach to sue the company in small claims court without the need to retain an attorney.

Fewer lawyers are needed for reviewing legal papers and background information because software applications enable faster and more efficient data searches and document management. E-discovery enables a single lawyer to search through massive numbers of documents in seconds and to gain valuable information about whether to negotiate settlements. YouTube and other content-heavy websites use software to automatically take down infringing or illegal content.

Aggressively competitive technology companies, such as Facebook, whose long-time motto was "move fast and break things," tend to be skeptical about the relevance of rigid professional codes in their dynamic industry. Big picture thinking encourages the development of disruptive technologies that can revolutionize long established, but inefficient, corporate practices. However, this social network giant recently dropped its original motto in favor of stressing better consumer service, which suggests at least a slight move in favor of the traditional view of the need to build a reputation for high ethical standards:

> We used to have this famous mantra . . . and the idea here is that as developers, moving quickly is so important that we were even willing to tolerate a few bugs in order to do it. . . . "What we realized over time is that it wasn't helping us to move faster because we had to slow down to fix these bugs and it wasn't improving our speed."[53]

Silicon Valley has come under criticism for its lack of ethical grounding. High profile startups, such as blood testing company, Theranos, the human relations management systems provider Zenefits, the loan matching company, Lending Club, and others stand accused of misrepresenting the capabilities and success of their products. Critics call for better ethical training because "more money is sloshing around ($73 billion in venture capital was invested in U.S. startups in 2016, compared with $45 billion at the peak of the dotcom boom, according to PitchBook), there's less transparency as companies stay private longer (174 private companies are each worth $1 billion or more), and there's an endless supply of legal gray areas to exploit as technology invades every sector, from fin-tech and med-tech to auto-tech and ed-tech."[54]

Google, and many other leading technological companies, have enacted codes of conduct to provide ethical guidance to their employees and users. Google's Code of Conduct emphasizes the need for a moral rudder that is strong enough to guide employees in times of uncertainty:

> It's impossible to spell out every possible ethical scenario we might face. Instead, we rely on one another's good judgment to uphold a high

> standard of integrity for ourselves and our company. We expect all Googlers to be guided by both the letter and the spirit of this Code. Sometimes, identifying the right thing to do isn't an easy call. If you aren't sure, don't be afraid to ask questions of your manager, Legal or Ethics & Compliance. And remember. . . don't be evil, and if you see something that you think isn't right—speak up![55]

Uber's reputation has been badly damaged by what is perceived as an overly aggressive workplace culture, and this is leading it to formulate a more socially acceptable set of ethical conduct guidelines. Uber is "at the center of all this ever-growing list of ethical leadership controversies. The company is accused of violating the most basic standards of business ethics to stifle competition."[56]

The #DeleteUber boycott campaign, which is protesting alleged sexist behavior within the company as well as other moral failings, has led to multiple employee resignations, substantial turnover in the board room and a significant loss of business. Travis Kalanick, Uber's founder was replaced in large part because of his perceived failure to prevent widespread unethical behavior in the company.

[B] Medicine as a Profession

Information technology has yet to become an established profession such as medicine and law. The field of medicine is marked by a mandated curriculum that includes rotations, internships and residencies. Medical schools' admission criteria and their curriculums are similar across the country. After completing four years of medical school, students pursue residencies of three or four years, depending on specialty, and then optional fellowships that last a year or two. Doctors must complete national uniform testing with certification for specialties, such as emergency medicine, pediatric anesthesiology or psychiatry. Physicians who enter into doctor-patient relationships have both an ethical and a legal duty not to abandon their patients. Medical professionals, for example, do not request payment for emergency treatment when they come to the rescue of an airplane passenger who suddenly becomes ill.

The medical field's professional association, the American Medical Association, sharply limits what tasks a nurse or physician's assistant can perform independently. No such formal rule applies in the field of information technology. Computer scientists are not licensed, and there is no state or federal organization that can prohibit them from practicing in their field of expertise. State Medical Boards, in contrast, have the power to conduct a thorough investigation, and have the legal authority to revoke a physician's license.

In New York, for example, the Office of Professional Medical Conduct (OPMC) investigates complaints about physicians, physician assistants and specialist assistants. It also monitors practitioners who are subject to Orders of the State Board for Professional Medical Conduct. The OPMC publishes a list of all physicians, physician assistants, specialist assistants and professional medical corporations who have been disciplined since 1990, who are subject to a non-disciplinary Board Order, or upon whom charges of misconduct have been served.

State Medical Boards will suspend or revoke a doctor's license for serious ethical offenses, such as having a sexual relationship with a patient or performing surgical procedures while under the influence of alcohol. Public Citizen, a consumer rights advocacy group, believes that Medical Board oversight is too weak. The watch dog organization found slightly more than a thousand doctors were reported to the National Practitioner Data Bank due to offenses such as sexual misconduct, and subject to sanctions by medical boards or malpractice settlements over the past decade. State medical boards only acted in only one out of three cases where physicians were disciplined by hospitals or other health care organizations, or made malpractice payments related to an ethical infraction.

Expert testimony, rather than the experience of ordinary laypersons, determines whether a physician is liable for medical negligence. In a medical malpractice case, the crucial element is that the adverse event is of a kind that does not ordinarily occur unless there has been negligence. Courts require experts to testify as to the standard of care and breach, which are elements are beyond the common understanding of a typical jury. Informed consent is a negligence concept predicated on the duty of physician to disclose to the patient all pertinent information that will enable him or her to understand the risks attendant to a course of treatment.

The medical profession is regulated by legal standards as well as the ethical codes of their professional association. For example, Congress enacted the Emergency Medical Treatment and Labor Act (EMTLA) in 1986, which requires Medicare-participating hospitals that offer emergency services to provide for an appropriate medical screening examination. If the hospital determines that the individual has an emergency medical condition, the EMTLA imposes a legal duty to stabilize the patient's medical condition, even if he is insolvent. This unfunded mandate is informally referred to as an "anti-dumping law," because it is designed to keep emergency departments from saving money by refusing to provide services for indigents.

[C] Law as a Profession

Law, like medicine, is an established profession with a prescribed course of formal academic study. Law students nationally take similar courses in the first year of law school. After graduation, they must pass a state bar examination in order to practice law. Lawyers who violate the rules of their profession are subject to sanctions, such as having their law license suspended or being permanently disbarred. The Virginia Bar, for example, imposes graduated punishment for violations of ethical standards:

> The lawyer can receive a private reprimand or admonition for less serious rule violations; The lawyer can receive a public reprimand for more serious rule violations; The lawyer's license can be suspended for up to five years, during which time the lawyer cannot practice law; or The lawyer's license can be revoked.

All U.S. attorneys must pass a Multistate Professional Responsibility Examination (MPRE) before they can practice law. The purpose of the MPRE is to assess a law graduate's knowledge and understanding of the specialized code of professional ethics followed by legal professionals. Professional ethics for lawyers are enforced by state bar organizations. In Massachusetts, it is the Board of Bar Overseers, whereas in Virginia, it is the Virginia State Bar (VSB). These state organizations develop lawyer-run disciplinary systems to determine whether a lawyer has violated legal ethics rules and, if so, what the appropriate discipline should be.

Professional associations serve their members by providing a variety of services, such as informing them of important new social, political and technology developments and risks. Bar Associations, for example, are educating their members about "social engineering" hoaxes, which have victimized many lawyers. In these "spear-phishing" attacks, cyber criminals target attorneys who have websites or have posted information about their bar membership. "Often, the e-mails contain accurate information about victims obtained via a previous intrusion, or from data posted on social networking sites, blogs or other websites. This information adds a veneer of legitimacy to the message, increasing the chances that victims will open the e-mail and respond as directed."[57] These phishing schemes will frequently involve fraudulent checks. Scammers frequently access attorneys' email address books to forward:

> the e-mail from one attorney to another giving the appearance that it is a referral. It is apparently a scam enlisting attorneys to prepare legal documents upon receiving a cashier's check deposited in trust accounts

with an overpayment of legal fees being returned to the scammer from the attorney's trust account. The initial payment is fraudulent.[58]

[D] Computer Science Is Not a Traditional Profession

Computer science meets all the qualifications of being a scientific discipline, but satisfies almost none of the criteria for being a traditional profession. Software engineering is a relatively new field without a prescribed curriculum or credentialing. Computer scientists have no formal educational requirements or established industry standards as in medicine and law. Lacking licensure requirements, software-coding boot camps are sprouting up across America.

In contrast to the in-depth education required for the four-year computer science degree, coding boot camps promise to make their students ready for employment in a few months at a tenth of the cost. These are the trade schools for the information age. In contrast, paralegals are required to be closely supervised by licensed attorneys just as licensed medical doctors, no matter what their level of skill and practical experience, supervise registered nurses.

Computer scientists cannot be reprimanded, suspended or prohibited from practicing in their field, as they have no professional associations or boards that have the power to police their practices. Whether professionalization is necessary or even desirable is an open question. Most computer practitioners resist traditional professionalization, viewing it as a barrier to innovation, anti-competitive and exclusionary. Computer science may never follow the path of law and medicine.

One exception to this resistance is the Professional Engineers Ontario (PEO). The province of Ontario, which accounts for nearly forty percent of Canada's population, has a strong professional organization that is empowered to investigate engineers who violate the organization's code of professional ethics and to bar violators from practicing their profession within its jurisdiction.[59]

Skilled hackers may be hired as computer security experts with minimal formal training, while alternatively, someone who learns a great deal of law while in prison could not simply become an attorney. Frank William Abagnale, Jr., a master conman and imposter, whose criminal career and imprisonment is chronicled in the book and movie, *Catch Me If You Can*, is advertising his expertise in countering forgery, embezzlement, and the theft of documents.

Abagnale's history of illegal activities is considered by some to be a better qualification for combating crime than having an advanced degree in computer security. Law or medicine, in contrast, does not permit self-taught individuals to practice in any independent capacity, despite their skill level. In the field of information technology, results are generally valued over formal educational credentials.

Even though computer science requires advanced expertise that is beyond the understanding of typical members of the lay public, courts do not recognize computer malpractice because this field does not have a governing body (such as a state bar association), an enforceable code of professional ethics or licensing laws. Judges have uniformly rejected attempts to apply a professional standard of care to software engineers, designers or consultants.

CONCLUSION

The rapid evolution of information technologies far outpaces the ability of computer ethics to keep up. Consequently, the study of computer professional ethics must center on general rules of applied ethics. Uses, misuses and abuses of technologies are hotly debated in the information era as practitioners struggle with common ethical issues such as:

> Is it wrong for a system operator to disclose the content of employee email messages to employers or other third parties?
>
> Should individuals have the freedom to post discriminatory, degrading and defamatory messages on the Internet?
>
> Is it wrong for companies to use data-mining techniques to generate consumer profiles based on purchasing behavior, and should they be allowed to do so?
>
> Should governments design policies to overcome the digital divide between skilled and unskilled computer users?[60]

Each of these decisions is not merely a matter of personal beliefs about right and wrong. The legal system may punish those who violate the laws that regulate these thorny issues.

When can corporations release software that they know contains design defects in order to win an early market share? Is it sufficient to electronically send patch after patch to fix software vulnerabilities that are discovered by hackers, or after examining the causes of system failures? Different ethical perspectives offer varying conclusions. Chapter Two will describe and apply the five leading ethical perspectives used to analyze and resolve moral dilemmas arising out of rapid advances in information technology.

REFERENCES FOR CHAPTER ONE

[1] Mary Ellen Biery, *The Ten Fasting Growing Industries in the U.S.*, FORBES (April 9, 2017).

[2] Software & Information Industry Association, *The U.S. Software Industry: An Engine for Economic Growth and Employment*, SIIA White Paper (2014) at 2.

[3] EDWIN PATTERSON, JURISPRUDENCE: MEAN AND IDEAS OF THE LAW (Brooklyn, New York: The Foundation Press, Inc., 1953) at 284.

[4] Daisuke Wakabayashi, *Google Fires Engineer Who Wrote Memo Questioning Women in Tech*, THE NEW YORK TIMES (August 7, 2017).

[5] *Fired Google Engineer Damore Says the Company is Hiring and Promoting Workers Based on Race or Gender*, CNBC.com (August 14, 2017).

[6] *Id.*

[7] BENJAMIN N. CARDOZO, THE GROWTH OF THE LAW (New Haven, Connecticut: Yale University Press, 1973) at 19–20.

[8] Tim Harford, *Why Didn't Electricity Immediately Change Manufacturing?* BBC WORLD SERVICE (August 21, 2017).

[9] Vivek Wahwa, *Law & Ethics Can't Keep Pace with Technology*, MIT TECHNOLOGY REVIEW (April 15, 2014).

[10] Richard M. Nixon, *Changing Rules of Liability in Automobile Accident Litigation*, 3 LAW & CONTEMPORARY PROBLEMS 476 (1936).

[11] Michael Frank, *The 13 Most Dangerous Car Interiors in History*, POPULAR MECHANICS (April 18, 2011).

[12] *Henningsen v. Bloomfield Motors*, 161 A.2d 69, 99–100 (1960) (finding no contractual privity for breach of warranty in accident arising out of a malfunctioning automobile steering system).

[13] 32 N.J. 358, 161 A.2d 69 (1960).

[14] *Henningsen*, 32 N.J. at 384, 161 A.2d at 84 (finding liability against both Chrysler and Bloomfield).

[15] 2 Restatement (Second) § 402A, comment (a).

[16] *Bensusan Restaurant Corp. v. King*, 126 F.3d 25 25 (2d Cir. 1997).

[17] 74 F.3d 701 (6th Cir. 1996) cert. denied 117 S. Ct. 74 (1996).

[18] *Miller v. California*, 413 U.S. 15, 32 (1973).

[19] Asher Schecter, *Is There a Case to be Made for Political Anti-Trust?,* PRO-MARKET (April 28, 2017).

[20] Scott Shane & Vindu Goel, *Fake Russian Facebook Accounts Brought for $100,000 in Political Adds*, THE NEW YORK TIMES (September 6, 2017).

[21] Christopher Mims, *Facebook Is Still in Denial About Its Biggest Problem*, THE WALL STREET JOURNAL (October 1, 2017).

[22] Tanya Dua, *Here's Facebook's Latest Move in the War on Fake News*, BUSINESS INSIDER (August 28, 2017).

[23] ERIC T. SCHEIDERMAN, NEW YORK STATE ATTORNEY GENERAL, OBSTRUCTED VIEW: WHAT'S BLOCKING NEW YORKERS FROM GETTING TICKETS (2017) at 1.

[24] *Id.* at 3–4 (Executive Findings).

[25] Free Exchange: Algorithms and Antitrust, *How Price-Bots Can Conspire Against Consumers—and How Trustbusters Might Thwart Them*, THE ECONOMIST (May 6–12) at 71.

[26] *Id.*

[27] Leslie Morris, *Rating Systems May Discriminate Against Uber Drivers,* CORNELL CHRONICLE (December 15, 2016).

[28] Laura Sydell, *Can Computers Be Racist? The Human-Like Bias of Algorithms*, NPR (March 14, 2016).

[29] Jeff Larson et al., *How We Analyzed the Recidivism Algorithm*, PRO PUBLICA, (May 23, 2016).

[30] Tom Dotan and Reed Albergotti, *Amazon Echo and the Hot Tub Murder*, THE INFORMATION (December 27, 2016).

[31] Evan Andrews, *10 Things You May Not Know About the Pony Express*, HISTORY CHANNEL, HISTORY.COM (June 10, 2016).

32 Barry Waugh, *The Importance of the Printing Press for the Protestant Revolution*, REFORMATION (October 2013) at 21.

33 *Id.*

34 CHRIS HARMAN, A PEOPLE'S HISTORY OF THE WORLD, (New York, New York: Verso, 2017) at 178.

35 Paul Stanley: *'Illegal Music Downloading Is Morally and Ethically Wrong': KISS Frontman Compares File Sharing to Stealing a Car*, ULTIMATEGUITAR.COM (October 21, 2014).

36 *Artists Speak Out on Music Piracy*, UPVENUE.COM (December 27, 2016).

37 Matthew Yglesias, *Piracy is a Form of Theft, and Copyright Infringement is Neither*, SLATE (December 15, 2011).

38 Ken Paulson, *Real Cost of 'Free' Downloads*, USA TODAY (August 20, 2012).

39 Lucus Shaw & Adam Satarino, *Spotify is Burying Musicians for the Apple Deals*, BLOOMBERG TECHNOLOGY (August 27, 2016).

40 Leyla Acaroglu, *What Would Plato Do? Ethics Isn't Just for Philosophers—Designers Need to Take Responsibility, Too*, QUARTZ (September 28, 2016).

41 Margaret Anne Pierce and John W. Henry, *Computer Ethics: The Role of Personal, Informal, and Formal Codes,* 15 JOURNAL OF BUSINESS ETHICS 425 (1996).

42 ACM Ethics, Code 2018 Project.

43 Federal Trade Commission, Careful Connections: Building Security in the Internet of Things (2015) at 1.

44 Massachusetts Institute of Technology, *MIT Senseable City Lab* at http://senseable.mit.edu/.

45 *Bill Maher Calls It as He Sees It*, https://schwartzdns.wordpress.com/bill-maher-calls-it-like-he-sees-it/.

46 Chris Enloe, *Islamic Terrorism Has Nothing to Do With Islam*, THE BLAZE (March 25, 2017).

47 *Pakistan: Death Penalty for Blasphemy on Facebook*, Aljazeera (June 12, 2017).

48 Charter of Fundamental Rights of the European Union (2000/C 364/1) at Art. 11.

49 Ewen MacAskill & Nick Adams, *Bomb-Making Guides Are Online, But Getting Them to Work Is Not Easy*, The Guardian (May 23, 2017).

50 Ian Miles Cheong, *Popular YouTubers React to Censorship of 'Controversial' Content*, THE DAILY CALLER (August 1, 2017).

51 DANIEL J. SOLOVE, THE FUTURE OF REPUTATION: GOSSIP, RUMOR, AND PRIVACY ON THE INTERNET (New Haven, Connecticut: Yale University Press, 2007) at 3.

52 TIM HARFORD, THE UNDERCOVER ECONOMIST, (Oxford, United Kingdom: Oxford University Press, 2007).

53 Samantha Murphy Kelley, *Facebook Changes Its 'Move Fast and Break Things' Motto*, MASHABLE (2014).

54 Erin Griffith, *The Ugly Unethical Underside of Silicon Valley*, FORTUNE (December 28, 2016).

55 Alphabet Investor Relations, *Google Code of Conduct* (last updated April 11, 2012).

56 *Uber is in Dire Need of Ethical Leadership*, INDUSTRY LEADERS (June 14, 2016).

57 Internet Crime Complaint Center (2013).

58 Joanna Herzlik, *Scams Continue to Target Texas Attorneys*, TEXAS BAR BLOG (September 13, 2017).

59 The Code of Ethics of Professional Engineers Ontario, http://ethics.wikia.com/wiki/The_Code_of_Ethics_of_Professional_Engineers_Ontario.

60 Phillip Brey, *Values in Technology and Disclosive Computer Ethics*, in LUCIANO FLORIDI, THE CAMBRIDGE HANDBOOK OF INFORMATION AND COMPUTER, United Kingdom: Cambridge University Press (2009) at 41.

CHAPTER TWO

Ethical Theories & Computers

§ 2.0: LEGAL AND ETHICAL DILEMMAS

[A] How Computers Change Norms & the Law

Information technology has become so transformative that in January 2016 the World Economic Forum declared that we are currently living through "the fourth industrial revolution."[1] Advances in artificial intelligence, drones, robotics, 3D printing, the advent of the Internet of Things and other revolutionary breakthroughs continually transform life as we know it. Today's ABCs are Apple, Bluetooth and Chatting, followed by Downloads, Email, Facebook, Google, Home Pages and iPhones.

Sophisticated computer applications allow us to book airplane flights, communicate with distant relatives, shop in virtual bookstores, view trending videos and pursue Pokémon characters. Even our cars have become computers on wheels, with microprocessors controlling functions like brakes, traction control and cruise control.[2] The 2016 Ford F150, for example, contains over 150 million lines of code. Future cars will require substantially more software as cars are increasingly connected to the Internet.

Every major technological advance produces new ethical challenges that require legal reforms. For example, the Obama Administration enacted a rule requiring that Comcast, AT&T and other Internet Service Providers obtain users' explicit consent before they can sell customers' personal data. In April 2017, the Republican-controlled Congress reversed the Obama Administration's broadband privacy rules. In August 2017, Trump's Department of Justice attempted to reduce online privacy rights, when it sought a warrant to force an anti-Trump website to reveal personally identifiable data about thousands of website visitors.

Legal developments in one nation have cascading effects worldwide. The European Union is following a very different legal and ethical path than in the

United States. European regulators are concerned that the Trump Administration's reversal of the digital privacy rule, coupled with widespread governmental surveillance, demonstrates the United States' unwillingness to take online privacy seriously. In 2016, the U.S. and the EU agreed to Safe Harbor 2.0 mandating that American companies safeguard EU consumer's personal data and implement enhanced data protection safeguards. European privacy experts worry that the Safe Harbor 2.0 will soon collapse because of the Trump Administration's lack of commitment to privacy.

Self-driving vehicles provide another example of the need to update laws to accommodate technological change. Cloud-connected cars already collate extensive data about individual's travel habits. What geolocation data about a spouse or ex-spouse's travel will be available to opposing parties in divorce or child custody disputes? Can courts require smart automobiles to monitor the sobriety of drivers and passengers as a condition of parole? Will manufacturers be liable if criminals use malware to exploit inadequate safe in robotic vehicles? These urgent legal and ethical dilemmas issues are only a tiny snippet of the pressing quandaries raised by rapidly evolving information technologies.

[B] Computer Ethics as an Applied Discipline

(1) Multiple Views of Right and Wrong

This chapter will introduce the five most commonly used perspectives on computer ethics: (1) Consequentialism, (2) Virtue and Duty Theory, (3) Conflict Perspective, (4) Social Contract Theory and (5) Libertarianism. These approaches assume differing core assumptions about:

(1) The nature of justice;

(2) Basic assumptions of human nature;

(3) The conception of law and its role in resolving ethical dilemmas;

(4) The proper role for government and regulatory agencies; and

(5) The nature of good and evil.

Advocates of each of these perspectives, for example, have radically different perspectives about whether courts can censor hate speech or order the removal of other offensive postings.

The libertarian policies of a social media site such as 4chan, for example, differ dramatically from more heavily monitored websites such as Facebook, Instagram or Twitter. The search for the best ways to use digital technology to create a more just society will be shaped by policymakers' own vision of social justice. Do people who lose their jobs to robots deserve compensation, retraining, or even guaranteed employment at a comparable salary? Is access to the Internet a basic human right that should be provided to all or is it a luxury reserved for those who pay for access? Do employers have the right to mandate that job applicants provide them with passwords to their Facebook accounts so they can screen out candidates with undesirable values?

(2) The Ethics and Law of Sexting

The debate over whether sexting should be criminalized illustrates the interrelationship between ethics and law. Are sexting teenagers just engaging in risqué flirtations via an updated dating ritual or should these salacious communications be criminalized? Law enforcement personnel have wide discretion in interpreting and enforcing existing statutes. Colorado law, for example, classifies the possession of any explicit pictures of underage individuals as a felony, even if exchanged between consenting minors. However, in a Canon City, Colorado case, the district attorney's (DA's) office declined to prosecute more than one hundred teenagers caught sharing sexually charged photographs. Convictions for violating child pornography laws would severely stigmatize these teenagers by forcing them to register with law enforcement as sex offenders.[3]

A harsh penalty would fit the letter of the Colorado law but, arguably, violate the intentions of the legislators who enacted it. Legislators originally enacted child pornography statutes to punish the adult exploitation of vulnerable children, and did not contemplate that this statute would be extended to sexting teenagers. Other district attorneys have filed child pornography charges against sexting teenagers, using the rationale that:

> when a minor takes and sends a lascivious picture of his or herself, the sexted image easily amounts to self-produced child pornography. As a result, the child can effortlessly be charged with violating child pornography laws—and, depending on the jurisdiction, the recipient can be charged with possessing child pornography. In these cases, the child is simultaneously considered the victim and the perpetrator.[4]

In the opinion of these more aggressive DAs, to ignore criminal violations by these sexting teenagers would violate the prosecutors' ethical duty to enforce the law. These prosecutors seek not only to punish the direct perpetrators of these crimes ("specific deterrence"), but also to send a strong deterrent message to the larger community ("general deterrence"). Libertarians, in contrast, contend that these zealous prosecutors are abusing the spirit of the law. This perspective contends that the voluntary exchange of risqué photos should not be a governmental concern.

(3) The Morality of Winning at All Costs

In his book, *The Art of the Deal*, Donald Trump boasts of misleading Holiday Inn executives into investing in his Atlantic City casino project in 1982 by hiring bulldozers to stand by, creating the impression that a new construction project was commencing. This type of moral breach is sometimes referred to as poker game ethics. In poker, bluffing is not deemed immoral but is encouraged as a legitimate tactic to win the game.

Many venture capitalists are proud of their poker playing ability, considering their skills of reading others' motivations, bluffing the opposition, calculating the odds of success and overcoming adversity to be invaluable in mastering the hypercompetitive environment of Silicon Valley.[5] Salespersons often promise that new computer applications will be highly reliable, even though most features have not yet been developed. Is selling vaporware, (i.e. software or hardware that has been advertised but is not yet available for purchase) ethical? Is this justifiable "growth-hacking" or is it immoral behavior? The five leading theories of computer ethics and law will be applied to analyze and resolve these and many other dilemmas raised throughout the book.

§ 2.1: FIVE LEADING COMPUTER ETHICS THEORIES

[A] Computer Ethics Theories as Ideal Types

The five vantage points used throughout this book illustrate what German sociologist Max Weber (1864–1920) called ideal types, which "are constructs or concepts which are used as methodological devices in our understanding and analysis of any social problem."[6] The social scientist employs the ideal type as a construct for depicting complex social realities. Weber used the German phrase, *Idealtypus* to signify:

> A common mental construct in the social sciences derived from observable reality although not conforming to it in detail because of deliberate simplification and exaggeration. It is not ideal in the sense that it is excellent, nor is it an average; it is, rather, a constructed ideal used to approximate reality by selecting and accentuating certain elements.[7]

This heuristic device overemphasizes polarities as opposed to commonalities between seemingly incongruent theories.[8] One should rarely view a moral dilemma from a single ethical perspective. When confronted with a problematic moral impasse, it is often most productive to blend insights from several approaches into a hybrid solution.

(1) Deontological Ethics as an Ideal Type

Most theories of computer ethics are subdivided into deontological or teleological approaches. The term "deontology" derives from the Greek words for duty (*deon*) and science (*logos*). For deontological ethics, the focus is on the character of the moral agent and actions are delineated as either right or wrong without considering practicality or social context. Deontologists emphasize performing actions because they are virtuous and avoiding actions that are immoral. "In deontological ethics, an action is considered morally right because of some characteristic of the action itself, not because the product of the action is right.

Policymakers frequently consider deontological issues when drafting, interpreting and enforcing legal statutes. For example, the criminal law often considers *mens rea*, which is the intention or knowledge element of a crime as opposed to *actus reus*, which is the action or conduct element. The *mens rea* for involuntary manslaughter is very different from first-degree murder, even though both punish a victim's death.

Hacking into someone's computer system is illegal, but the hack may be done for relatively virtuous motives, such as to expose government or corporate misdeeds. Should punishments for Internet-related crimes be adjusted based on the immorality of the cybercriminal's actions? For example, should a legal distinction be made between punishing a playful script kiddie versus a profit-seeking, black hat hacker, even though both released malware that caused equivalent harm? Should legislators draft criminal statutes to consider the motives of teenage pranksters as opposed to organized criminal gangs? A deontologist considers the degree of virtue underlying a cybercriminal's actions versus the consequences, which is the teleological approach.

(2) Teleological Ethics as an Ideal Type

Teleological ethics, contrast to deontological perspectives, assess moral goodness or badness by the consequences, rather than the inherent virtue of the actor. Jeremy Bentham (1747–1832), the father of the Utilitarianism, denounced rights-based ethical theories as "nonsense on stilts." Moral behavior, for utilitarians, is producing the greatest overall amount of societal happiness, even if it requires suppressing some dissenting or unproductive groups.

The five leading computer ethics theories extend to each hot button issue in this book. Mechanically applying a single viewpoint for every situation cannot serve as a moral compass for deciding computer ethical dilemmas. These ethical perspectives are outlined in Chart One below.

CHART ONE: FIVE LEADING THEORIES OF COMPUTER ETHICS

Computer Ethics Theories	Subtypes	Principal Focus
Consequentialism	Utilitarianism, Pragmatism, Law and Economics	Are the outcomes good, even though the motives may not be? The goal of any public policy is to maximize overall societal happiness.
Virtue and Moral Duties Theories	Aristotelians, Kantian Categorical Imperatives	Is the action moral in itself? Does it spring from good motives? Are actors doing what is right without concern for the consequences?
Conflict Perspective	Marxism, Elite Theory, Critical Feminism, Critical Race Theory, Intersectionality of race, sex, class, age and disability.	How can legislation be drafted to minimize societal inequities? How are societal inequities impacted by computer technologies?
Social Contract Theory	Hobbes, Locke and Rousseau's State of Nature, Rawlsian Social Justice	The goal is to attain a stable social order without violating essential human rights. A core dispute is over

		what rights must not be violated.
Libertarianism	Traditional Libertarianism, Cyberlibertarians	How can we maximize human freedom but still have a stable social order? Nation states have no authority to impose regulations in cyberspace.

[B] Consequentialist Ethical Theories

(1) The Canons of Consequentialism

Consequentialists weigh positive consequences against harms created by the technological innovation. John Stuart Mill (1806–1873), a leading representative for the creed, enunciated the Greatest Happiness Principle, holding that "actions are right in proportion as they tend to promote happiness, wrong as they tend to produce the reverse of happiness."[9] The use of artificial intelligence to control London traffic, for example, is a considerable advance from traditional traffic signals. By harvesting data on road traffic volumes and obstructions, this AI-product will allow optimal solutions for maximizing vehicle flow.[10] The consequences of this technological advance are extremely positive and clearly worth the financial costs of implementing this innovation, at least in densely populated central cities.

(2) Applying Consequentialism to Drones

A U.S.-centric consequentialist approach evaluates the morality of a drone's use in warfare by the weapon's success in furthering U.S. national defense objectives. A more global consequentialist would consider the worldwide impacts of deploying killer drones. Airborne military robots reduce the risk of deaths and injuries sustained by American troops, but may have devastating on civilian populations. The benefit of this strategic weapon must be weighed against negatives such as the unintended consequences caused by malfunctioning weapons and the possibility that captured robots will reveal U.S. military secrets. Consequentialists purposely remove emotion from the cost-benefit equation by using terminology such as "collateral damage," to describe civilian deaths caused by wayward drones.

Leaders from the world's top AI and robotics companies issued a 2017 letter warning of the dangers of military drones and other killer robots. The letter states that these technologies "will permit armed conflict to be fought on a scale . . . faster than humans can comprehend."[11] The founder of Clearpath Robotics cautions that: "The development of lethal autonomous weapons systems is unwise, unethical and should be banned on an international scale."[12]

Legislators have yet to draft statutes addressing the privacy concerns raised by the widespread deployment of drones in the civilian economy. Should it be illegal to take pictures of celebrities through the windows of their private dwellings? Should jealous husbands be legally permitted to deploy drones to document their spouse's infidelity?

Computer professionals will play a pivotal role in developing code that can enforce ethical drone regulations. It might be possible, for example, to implement software that will apply AI in denying the user the ability to take intrusive photographs by blocking their commands to take intrusive pictures using the drone's camera. Similarly, drone software could override any command that would endanger commercial or military flights.

Drone package deliveries will displace large numbers of transportation workers with computerized systems, potentially instigating a "jobs apocalypse." Should governments allocate tax dollars to comprehensive retraining programs?[13] At present, the legal system is lagging far behind the development of drones and has not sufficiently addressed these and many other basic issues.

[C] Virtue and Duty Ethics

(1) Kant's Duty Theory

Virtue and duty theorists, adopting deontological logic, regard the amoral emphasis on efficiency in consequential models to be objectionable. Immanuel Kant, the founding father of duty ethics, denounced consequentialism, stating that: "Morality is not the doctrine of how we may make ourselves happy, but how we may make ourselves worthy of happiness." In Kant's words, "a good will is not good because of what it effects or accomplishes, but rather because it is one's duty."

Utilitarians denounce Kant's rigid definition of correct behavior as destructive of the practical necessity of compromise.[14] To a utilitarian, "when lying is necessary to maximize benefit or minimize harm, it may be immoral not to lie."[15] In contrast, Kant's moral duties must be fulfilled no matter what the consequences, a rigid rule that Utilitarians view as absurd and unjust:

> For example, we must always tell the truth no matter what. Suppose a German SS officer knocked on my door, asking me whether I had any Jews. And suppose further that I had two Jews in a secret compartment in the attic that he'd never be able to find. Everybody will agree that I must lie and say I haven't any Jews in my house. But I'd have to disobey Kant's categorical imperative "do not lie", because I felt obliged to not betray innocent people leading to their death.[16]

Virtue theorists find this accusation to be imbalanced, arguing that a more generous reading of Kant's essential point is that wrongs, even done in a virtuous cause, are still deeply problematic.[17]

Immanuel Kant, (1724–1804)
Father of Secular Duty Ethics
"Always recognize that human individuals are ends, and do not use them as means to your end."
Source: Government Document, U.S. Library of Congress.

Ethicists approaching computer technology dilemmas from a Kantian perspective believe that morality is not pursued "for the sake of anything else: it does not owe its value to anything outside itself."[18] Kantians would follow their ideals and refuse to design a manipulative website, because such work would not produce a product of the highest moral worth. Deceiving consumers violates a moral duty, even if the designer acts within the boundaries of contract law.

Kantianism was prefigured by Aristotelian ethics, which emphasized that law should reward virtue and punish vice. Like many classical Greek thinkers, Aristotle (384–322 B.C.), the tutor of Alexander the Great, believed that the goal of government is to cultivate good character. Nevertheless, Aristotle acknowledged that law is always subject to revision when conditions change. The Aristotelian conceptions of nature, justice and equity still shape contemporary views of right behavior.[19]

(2) Applying Virtue Theory to the Ashley Madison Breach

Ashley Madison is a website that, at its core, violates the moral imperative that honesty is the best policy. Virtue and Duty Theorists would likely find the cheating website morally repugnant simply because it promotes extramarital affairs. Worse, the site deployed bots masquerading as sexually available females calculated to coax male customers into sending gifts to win the affections of those bots they mistook for eligible women. This behavior would certainly fail any test of compliance with virtue ethics. As part of case's settlement, Ashley Madison's parent company agreed to provide a refund of up to $500 to members who spent money to chat with an estimated 70,000 "engagers" that were actually bots with fake female profiles.[20]

Violating Kantian ideals of truthfulness, however, can be the most effective tactic in catching and prosecuting cybercriminals. In computer security parlance, a "honey pot" is a trap set to detect, deflect, or in some manner counteract attempts at unauthorized use of information systems. The computer security administrator uses the honey pot to learn more about how cybercriminals exploit any vulnerability in their system, and then redesigns the system to eliminate these flaws. Online pedophiles may be identified and arrested through honey pots created by FBI agents masquerading as adolescents. This type of deception can be viewed from a virtue perspective as an unethical form of entrapment, where a person may be enticed into a criminal action they might otherwise not have performed. Consequentialists would not object to this law enforcement strategy because it works.

[D] Conflict Theory Ethical Perspectives

(1) Applying Conflict Theory to New Technologies

The conflict perspective evaluates novel technologies in terms of how they are used to increase or decrease social equality. Conflict theorists contend that the widespread use of artificial intelligence will result in greater inequality over time. Under capitalism, the leaders and financiers of a small number of high technology companies unjustly become immensely wealthy, while robots and other new technologies displace increasing numbers of workers. A more just social order would provide a guaranteed income for everyone:

> Robotization, like past technological changes, can be a very good thing, relieving the workload of humans while helping overcome the many challenges the world faces. But it could also affect humans disastrously, dividing societies between the owners of the robots on one side, and the

> workers who compete with the robots on the other. We should worry less about the potential displacement of human labor by robots than about how to share fairly across society the prosperity that the robots produce. . . . Today, gains accrue disproportionately to the wealthy—who are the principal owners of capital.[21]

Even highly trained workers, such as legal professionals, are threatened by artificial intelligence and other expert systems that can process thousands of documents far more quickly and efficiently than armies of junior lawyers and paralegals. The medical profession is vulnerable to the development of increasingly sophisticated AI diagnostic computers and robot surgeons. President Trump's election victory has been attributed partly to his success in tapping into anger over technology leaders employing foreign workers over Americans.[22]

(2) The Computer Industry & Social Inequalities

Conflict perspectives focus upon the constraints of "sex, gender, race, sexual orientation and class that shape individuals' knowledge, experience and opportunities."[23] These theorists assert that the field of computer science has been marked by increasing gender injustice. The percentage of computer science degrees granted to women by American colleges has dropped from 37% in 1985 to only 18% in 2014.[24] In top-ranked universities, the percentage of female computer science graduates has decreased even further, to 14%. The computing industry is creating jobs at three times the national average, but a recent study projects that women will hold only a fifth of computing jobs by 2025.[25] Melinda Gates, a computer science major and former technology company executive, has pledged $80 million to help recruit more women into high tech jobs.

As an example of how computer science's "bro culture" discourages women from remaining in the computer science field, one woman computer scientist observes:

> On Sunday, after an all-night hackathon at TechCrunch Disrupt, Australian programmers presented Titstare. 'Titstare is an app where you take photos of yourself staring at tits,' Jethro Batts explained. He went on to say, 'I think this is the breast hack ever.' The app was dreamed up during an overnight hackathon and presented to an audience of 500.[26]

Inequality is socially constructed in some virtual reality games. The Gamergate controversy, for example, arose out of a series of threats and other hostile actions against women who criticized sexism in the gaming industry. In

August 2014, a group of mostly young men launched a vitriolic attack on Zoie Quinn, a female game developer. She became the target of trolls and stalkers after "she began trying to publish *Depression Quest,* a text-based game partially based on her own experience with depression."[27]

Anonymous misogynists who "sent images showing video-game characters raping her harassed Anita Sarkeesian, a prominent media critic. Sarkeesian's Wikipedia entry was repeatedly vandalized" after she won a Game Developer Choice Award.[28] She contends that online gaming has a deeply misogynistic history:

> The gaming industry has been male-dominated ever since its inception, but over the last several years there has been an increase in women's voices challenging the sexist status quo. We are witnessing a very slow and painful cultural shift. Some male gamers with a deep sense of entitlement are terrified of change.[29]

The attacks on Quinn, Sarkeesian and other leading women in the gaming field as originating in a misogynist subculture dominated by young, white, heterosexual males:

> Campaigns of personal harassment aimed at game developers are nothing new. They are dismayingly common among those who happen to be women, or not white straight men, and doubly so if they also happen to make the sort of game that in any way challenge the status quo, even if that challenge is only made through their very existence. The viciousness and ferocity with which this campaign occurred, however, was shocking, and certainly out of the ordinary. This was something more than routine misogyny (and in games, it often is routine, shockingly). It was an ugly spectacle that should haunt and shame those involved for the rest of their lives.[30]

(3) Updating Marxism for the Information Age

(a) Karl Marx's Theory of Class Conflict

The term "Marxist" refers to those who believe that the economic structure plays a key role in shaping social reality. Karl Marx (1818–1883) predicted continual class conflict between wealthy capitalists, who control the means of production and the proletariat, who are increasingly deskilled wage laborers lacking control over their work product.[31] In the *Manifesto of the Communist Party*, Marx and Engels wrote that "society as a whole is more and more splitting up into two great hostile camps, into two great classes, directly clashes with each other:

Bourgeoisie and Proletariat."[32] "The proletariat is without property . . . . Law, morality, religion is to him so many bourgeoisie prejudices, behind which lurk in ambush just as many bourgeois interests."[33] The central tenets of Marxism are to:

(1) See the character of economic organization as the basic factor in shaping a society's value system, social class structure and political institutions and practices;

(2) See a capitalist economy as creating profit-oriented, materialistic values and a class structure in which wealthy owners constitute a ruling class that uses the power of the state, both at home and abroad, in exploitative and selfish ways; and

(3) Believe that such a social system is unjust, unnecessary, inconsistent with man's nature and should be eliminated—peacefully or, if necessary, by force.[34]

Marxists argue that most people are suppressed under capitalism because this economic system clashes with the basic human desire to be cooperative. Marxists point to the negative consequences of the need of the economic elite to constantly increase corporate profits. Gender inequality, racial inequality, militarism, imperialism and other social problems are viewed as being, at least partially, created by class conflict.

(b) Updating Marx for the Information-Based Economy

Cyberspace is a modern arena of struggle between the capitalist class's desire to maximize their power and the desires of the great majority to use the Internet to create a more just society. The emergence of a free society will require a democratic and inclusive Internet, many Marxists argue, which the capitalists will try to sabotage. In a post-capitalist society, technological and cultural progress will be far more rapid because, without the profit motive, software advances would be freely available.

(4) An IT Labor Aristocracy?

If Marx was alive today, he might be startled by how well workers are treated in the information technology sector. "There's no shortage of perks at the world's best tech employers—free food, massages, on site medical centers—the industry is jam-packed with employers who offer lucrative pay and enviable extras."[35] Google has become one of the best places to work in the country:

> Attracting high-achieving talent with endless perks and bonuses, the media giant aims to make employees' lives easier with meditation

> facilities and free meals. Googlers are a proud lot. Scoring 98 percent in Great Rated!'s "Great Pride" category overall, employees say they often or almost always carry meaningful responsibilities with the organization. And Googlers share that pride in giving back to the community: the company donated more than a billion dollars to charity last year. Says one employee: 'I have never worked in any place like this. It feels like working at a cross between Harvard, Hogwarts and NASA. The atmosphere and culture is truly unique and unlike anything I've ever experienced elsewhere.'[36]

Contemporary Marxists stress that these luxurious working conditions are actually a way to encourage high tech workers to spend more hours on the job.

Eighty-seven percent of Twitter's employees agreed that "they often or almost always experience a free and transparent exchange of ideas within the organization."[37] Twitter hosts special Global Tea Times where executives and staff socialize:

> Twitter keeps the conversation going between staff members. Offices feature on-tap kombucha and iced coffee and employees have access to training and improvisation courses and receive a $100 fitness reimbursement. Says one employee: 'Between celebrities coming into work on a regular basis, the relaxed vacation policy and the genuine friendship I have with co-workers is unlike anything I've experienced before. I work my ass off and get a lot done, but the ability to take breaks in the game room, or take the day off when necessary, provides for a really relaxed while upbeat work environment.'[38]

(5) Profit-Sharing as a Refutation of Marxist Theory?

Many high technology companies give their employees a share of the profits in the form of direct grants or stock options:

> Every Intuit employee is eligible for some kind of equity grant, whether it be stock option or restricted stock units. Those in vice president positions or higher receive non-qualified stock options upon being hired, while those in lower positions are offered RSUs. Either way, the equity grant vests over a period of three years. The information technology company also offers an employee stock purchase plan. Workers have the option to contribute up to 15% of their eligible pay to purchase stock at a discount of at least 15%, an option that more than two-thirds of employees choose.[39]

GoDaddy Inc., a publicly traded Internet domain registrar and web hosting company, gave its nearly 5,000 employees non-qualified stock options when it went public in 2015:

> After the initial six-month lock up period following its IPO ended this past October, at which point they were allowed to begin trading their shares, though a majority chose to hold onto them. The technology provider also offers a stock purchase plan that offers employees the opportunity to buy and sell stock every six months at a discounted rate of 15%.[40]

Employees working in the top rungs of the information industry can hardly be considered the oppressed proletariat. However, profits are not equally apportioned. Three of the five wealthiest persons in the world are founders of leading information technology companies. Bill Gates, the founder of Microsoft, is the richest person in the world with a fortune of $86 billion.[41] Jeff Bezos, Amazon's CEO, is ranked third at $27.6 billion.[42] Mark Zuckerberg, Facebook's founder has a fortune of $11.4 billion, while Google's chairperson, is worth an estimated $11 billion.

The economic gap between the privileged elites and a much larger group that labors in disrupted industries such as retail sales, transportation and food services continues to widen. Third World temporary computer employees often toil long hours in bad workplace conditions at low pay. Marxists argue that the modern class struggle is between badly treated remotely located workers and their privileged First World employers.

(6) How Open Source Blurs the Worker/Owner Divide

Open Source Software (OSS) is defined as "software for which the human-readable source code is available for use, reuse, modification, enhancement and redistribution by the users of that software."[43] Under the traditional proprietary license, source code is kept secret and the program is only made available in object form. Open source license agreements do not restrict anyone from selling, or even giving away the software.

Yochai Benkler, a Harvard law professor, argues that information technology companies have softened the sharp division between the owners and workers by changing the meaning of property ownership. "Property in open source is configured fundamentally around the right to distribute, not the right to exclude."[44] The Open Source Initiative explains this principle:

> In order to get the maximum benefit from the process, the maximum diversity of persons and groups should be equally eligible to contribute to open sources. Therefore, we forbid any open-source license from locking anybody out of the process.[45]

Open source license agreements enable the sharing of source code with greater collaboration and less inequality.

In the information-age economy, everyone can be a producer as well as a consumer, so the means of production are not solely in the hands of the capitalist class. Benkler sees the open source movement and the rise of the Internet as key to the democratizing the means of production. Benkler conceptualizes three layers of Internet governance: the "physical infrastructure" layer, the "content" layer and the "logical" layer. He writes:

> We are making regulatory choices at all layers of the information environment—the physical infrastructure, logical infrastructure and content layers—that threaten to concentrate the digital environment as it becomes more central to our social conversation. These include decisions about intellectual property law, which can make ownership of content a point of reconcentration, decisions about the design of software and its standards, and the regulation of physical infrastructure available to Internet communications, like cable broadband services.[46]

Free and open source software is generative, continually being improved by the programmers who produce, distribute and modify it. In contrast, proprietary software reflects a pro-capitalist model, where the software publishers own the code and control the means of production. Open source licensing allows a community of downstream users to look under the hood and improve the code. A spacious intellectual commons is a core component of a free-networked society. Hollywood, the recording industry and other large proprietors of intellectual property, are seen as systematically undermining the innovations of the collaborative-networked economy.

Yochai Benkler concludes that we should not let "yesterday's winners dictate the terms of tomorrow's economic competition." Peer-to-peer production, Benkler argues, is creating a new order where collective efforts contribute to the common goal of better software. Benkler cites the triumph of user-driven innovation, such as the General Public License version 3 (GPL/V3), which requires licensees to return modifications to the public under the same terms. To qualify as a GPL, the license must permit users to redistribute software so that other licensees have access to source code. Linus Torvalds, the developer of the

"Linux kernel," famously quipped that "Software is like sex; it's better when it is free."

[E] Social Contract Ethical Perspectives

(1) History of Social Contract Theory

Social Contract Theory is predicated upon the philosophical assumption that we must surrender individual freedoms for the privilege of living in a civilized society. However, certain basic human rights are guaranteed by the social contract to be protected at all costs. The ethical questions for social contract theory center on how to determine fundamental rights in cyberspace. The right to physical security often clashes with free expression rights. To what degree is it ethical to limit online expression in order to clamp down on immoral cyberspace activities?

Different social contract-inspired theories do not agree on what rights are classified as fundamental. A United Nations report declared "that disconnecting people from the Internet is a human rights violation and against international law."[47] Several nations, "including Costa Rica, Estonia, Finland, France, Greece and Spain, have asserted some right of access in their constitutions or legal codes, or via judicial rulings."[48]

Monitoring and suppressing Internet communications violates the fundamental rights guaranteed in the Bill of Rights of the U.S. Constitution. Social contract theorists seek to balance privacy and security in a world in which "hackers can take control of cars or shut down an electric grid."[49]

Classical Greek philosophers such as Socrates advocated social contract theories long before the birth of Christ. Socrates explains that he must accept the Athenian government's death sentence because society requires cooperation with mutually agreed upon rules. Classical social contract theorists, such as Seventeenth & Eighteenth Century contract theorists Thomas Hobbes, John Locke and Jean-Jacques Rousseau, further developed the idea that all humans live under an implied covenant.[50] John Rawls updated this vision in the Twentieth Century by postulating that people who did not know their eventual fate would voluntarily choose an extensive social safety net.

The social contract philosophers depicted in Chart Two each promoted different versions of the argument that society is based on an implicit contract by which individuals voluntarily surrender their non-essential freedoms in return for the advantages of living in society. Certain freedoms were not surrendered in joining society and people have the right to reject any law or policy that violates these natural rights. The United States Constitution's Bill of Rights is a literal social contract that delineates essential human rights the U.S. government is forbidden to violate. The basic dispute among the major social contract theorists lies in what essential rights are too important to be debased.

CHART TWO: THREE VARIETIES OF SOCIAL CONTRACT THEORY

Key Concept	Thomas Hobbes	John Locke	John Rawls
Human Nature	Selfish; Can be vicious	Selfish, but restrained by common sense	Seeks equality if outcomes are concealed by a "veil of ignorance"
State of Nature	Life is "solitary, nasty, brutish and short"	Inefficient cooperation	Cooperative because fate is unknown
Role of Government	Necessary	Useful	Useful
Social Contract Rights	Life	Life, liberty, and property rights	Strong social safety net to protect the weak

(2) Thomas Hobbes' Leviathan

Thomas Hobbes (1588–1679) developed a version of social contract theory in his 1661 book, *The Leviathan,* written during the English Civil War of 1642 to 1651. The thesis of *The Leviathan* is that we surrender power to the state as the price for our collective security. Hobbes argued that a strong central state or sovereign was necessary to prevent returning to the state of nature, which is a time of an intolerable "war of all against all":

> In the State of Nature, which is purely hypothetical, men are naturally and exclusively self-interested, they are equal to one another, (even the strongest man can be killed in his sleep), there are limited resources, and yet there is no power able to force men to cooperate. . . . Given Hobbes' reasonable assumption that most people want first to avoid their own deaths, he concludes that the State of Nature is the worst possible situation in which men can find themselves. It is the state of perpetual and unavoidable war. The situation is not, however, hopeless. Because men are reasonable, they can see their way out of such a state by

> recognizing the laws of nature, which show them the means by which to escape the State of Nature and create a civil society.[51]

Under a Hobbesian model, the government's basic duty is to protect the lives and safety of the citizenry. Applying this perspective to modern issues, violations of Internet freedom would be permissible if the alternative would be to let terrorists destabilize society.

(3) John Locke's State of Nature

John Locke (1632–1704) challenged Thomas Hobbes' "nasty, brutish and short" view of human life without a strong sovereign. Instead, Locke described the state of nature "as a state of perfect and complete liberty to conduct one's life as one best sees fit, free from the interference of others."[52] "The Law of Nature, which is in Locke's view the basis of all morality, and given to us by God, commands that we not harm others with regards to their 'life, health, liberty, or possessions.' "[53]

John Locke highlighted the role of government in protecting property and life as the basis of the social contract, arguing; "That the obligation to obey civil government under the social contract was conditional upon the protection not only of the person, but also of private property. If a sovereign violated these terms, he could be justifiably overthrown."[54] America's Bill of Rights to the U.S. Constitution was inspired by Locke's social contract theory.

(4) Jean-Jacques Rousseau's Social Contract

Jean-Jacques Rousseau (1712–1778), who lived and wrote during the Enlightenment in eighteenth century France, described his version of social contract theory in his 1762 work entitled *Social Contract.* Rousseau's central question was "how can we live together without succumbing to the force and coercion of others?" We can do so, Rousseau maintains, by submitting our individual wills to the collective or general will, created through agreement with other free and equal persons.

Like Hobbes and Locke before him, Rousseau contended that all men are created to be equals. These philosophers maintain that no person has a natural right to govern others. The "only justified authority is the authority that is generated out of agreements or covenants."[55] People have the right to revolt against a government that sufficiently violates this basic morality. The Declaration of the Rights of Man and of the Citizen enacted by France's National Constituent Assembly in August 1789 was the most important document of the French

Revolution. This Declaration was shaped in large part by the theory of natural rights, maintaining that the rights of man are universally valid. Rousseau's political philosophy was a major influence in the French Revolution and modern political thought. In September 2016, the Internet Security Alliance proposed a social contract to provide a coherent framework to create a "sustainable system of cybersecurity."[56] Cybersecurity Social Contract 2.0 posits two key elements:

> First is the realization that cyber security is not a purely technical problem. Rather, cyber security is an enterprise-wide risk management problem which must be understood as much for its economic perspectives as for its technical issues. The second key element is that, at this point, government's primary role ought to be to encourage the investment required to implement the standards, practices and technologies that have already been shown to be effective in improving cyber security.[57]

(5) John Rawls' Veil of Ignorance

John Rawls (1921–2002) was a twentieth century social contract theorist who employed the thought experiment of asking what people would choose if they did not know what body, nationality and social status they would be born into.[58] Rawls' "veil of ignorance" was presented as a hypothetical about a situation in which: "No one knows his place in society, his class position or social status; nor does he know his fortune in the distribution of natural assets and abilities, his intelligence and strength, and the like."[59]

Rawls contended that in this "veil of ignorance," people would overwhelmingly support an eclectic position in which there is an adherence to the social contract rather than libertarian or utilitarian positions. Their fear of being born with few resources, or being cut off from the connected society, would trump any desire to gamble on being born into a privileged position. This logic led Rawls to argue that morality requires helping the downtrodden. He advocated for the difference principle, under which "only those social and economic inequalities are permitted that work to the benefit of the least advantaged members of society."[60]

Rawls' argument applies equally well to the social impact of computing. No one in their original position would choose to implement a digital divide, where a relative lack of access to information technologies undermines the life chances of the underprivileged. Social justice would involve using the Internet to disproportionately benefit the disadvantaged, which brings Rawls' implied policies much closer to those of conflict theorists than the other leading social contract theorists. Nevertheless, conflict theorists are far more likely to believe that society is so deeply stratified and imbalanced that the idea of a social contract is a fiction. For many conflict theorists, the legal system itself needs to be radically revised or even overthrown, which is a goal that Rawlsians would not favor.

[F] Libertarianism and Cyberlibertarian Ethics

(1) The Traditional Libertarian Approach

Libertarianism draws heavily upon nineteenth-century laissez faire capitalism argues, "so long as we do not violate others' rights, we should each be free to live as we choose."[61] Central to this ideology is the belief that the free market is a key source of economic and political freedoms.[62] The total amount of satisfaction is greater in a free market than in any collectivistic alternative because of the lack of coercion of the individual. Private contracts, with government intervention only to ensure that both parties live up to their agreements, are the best way to maximize freedom. Traditional libertarians assume that the parties would not enter an agreement, unless it was mutually beneficial.

Andrew Grove, a co-founder and CEO of the semiconductor manufacturer Intel, characterized the intense competition among high technology entrepreneurs in a book entitled *Only the Paranoid Survive*.[63] Customers benefit greatly from the ceaseless competitive struggle to gain an advantage over rivals. Consumers have the responsibility to read and understand these terms rather than relying on government oversight. If the terms of use are not to the consumer's liking, he or she has the freedom to boycott the website and to use (or profit from establishing) one that offers more satisfactory terms.

The legal invention of licensing seeks to protect software, trade secrets, patents and derivative works through private contracts as opposed to heavy-handed government regulation. Software licensing contracts are used to advance intellectual property rights, limit liability, earn royalties and commodify the product. The licensor and licensee voluntarily enter into a contract, even if the consumer is foolish enough to check "I agree" without reading the terms. The government should be limited to being a "night-watchman," which restricts itself to protecting people against force and fraud but not from their own bad judgment.

The software industry adopts a libertarian position when it opposes activist courts that invalidate one-sided terms, such as anti-class action waivers, caps on damages, or mandatory predispute arbitration. The industry argues that paternalistic courts foster a nanny state when they refuse to enforce anti-consumer clauses. Providers contend that, in a free market, rivals will displace companies that do not serve consumers well. In the words of Amazon CEO, Jeff Bezos, "Your profit margin is my opportunity." Netflix was setting its prices higher than was necessary, which motivated Amazon to enter the market with a competing film streaming service, available through Amazon Prime.

Libertarians contend that established interest groups attempt to block potential competitors by lobbying for laws that masquerade as being enacted for the common good, but actually protect the proposers' privileged position. For example, the hotel industry encourages governments to pursue policies that would undermine Airbnb, under the guise of protecting consumers. Taxicab companies are trying to enact laws that will limit Uber, Lyft and other ride-sharing services.

Brick and mortar liquor stores seek to stifle potentially disruptive rivals by mounting legal challenges to online wine sellers, resorting to the rationale that virtual sellers cannot sufficiently prevent minors from purchasing alcoholic beverages. Open competition, not governmental regulation, should determine which online services flourish and which ones go out of business.

Other perspectives, particularly conflict theories, disagree with the libertarians, noting that mass-market software licenses impose terms on a "take it or leave it" basis, which is inconsistent with the libertarian assertion that these are truly voluntary agreements. In a *South Park* episode entitled "Humancentipad," one character, Kyle, failed to read his iTunes terms of service and agreed to become a component in a web browser and emailing device that is part human and part centipede. The *South Park* episode parodies U.S. courts that mechanically uphold one-sided website terms.

(2) Cyberlibertarians

(a) Protecting the Free Flow of Information

A central tenet of traditional libertarianism is respect for private property. In contrast, cyberlibertarians take freedom one step further by arguing, "Information wants to be free." They are sympathetic to the anarchist motto that "property is robbery."[64] Activist hackers often "liberate" information that companies or governments wish to keep secret.

Cyberlibertarians agree with the traditional libertarian value of maximizing individual freedom and distrusting government. Like the traditional libertarians, they strongly support undermining established organizations through websites such as Kickstarter, which allows small individuals to voluntarily fund startups without the need for government or venture capitalist financing. The website

GoFundMe permits those in need of money to make their case and gather contributions by posting an explanation of why donors should contribute to them.

Similarly, Lending Club, an online organization enables individuals to borrow money from other individuals without the need for banks and other traditional lenders, is praised as a free market mechanism where willing borrowers and lenders reach voluntary agreements. Lending Club is now being accused of financial irregularities, but a variety of rivals will emerge if this company fails to effectively exploit its first mover advantage.

Cyberlibertarians champion crowd sourcing of social control, instead of government actions, to police the Internet. Clay Shirky's 2008 cyberlibertarian book, *Here Comes Everybody: The Power of Organizing Without Organizations*, explores "what happens when people are given the tools to do things together, without needing traditional organizational structures." Predicting a future of "mass amateurization," Shirky uses the example of getting a lost cell phone returned by exposing the personal information of the unrepentant thief.

Both types of libertarians support Bitcoin and other cryptocurrencies to shield individual privacy from governmental and corporate intrusion. Ross Ulbricht, the former owner of Silk Road, a DarkNet marketplace for the buying and selling of illicit goods, authored cyberlibertarian manifestos. Before Ulbricht was arrested and the Silk Road shut down:

> There were 10,000 products for sale in the spring of 2013, 70% of which were drugs. But there were also 159 listings for "services," most of which were for hacking into social network accounts like Twitter or Facebook and more than 800 listings for digital goods such as pirated content, or hacked Amazon and Netflix accounts, according to the FBI indictment. Fake drivers' licenses, fake passports, fake utility bills and fake credit card statements.[65]

Merchants on the Silk Road and its many successors are constrained by an evaluation system by which customers report on the quality of the providers' goods. The higher a seller's ratings, the more it can charge. Amazon, eBay and hosts of other legal companies use the same seller rating method. A seller with a record of reliably providing quality goods can profit from its exemplary reputation. A provider without a record of reliability may need to sell at a loss to build its online standing. Meanwhile, websites such as *RipOff Report* publish complaints that can severely damage the sales of unethical online sellers.

(b) Cyberlibertarian Utopianism

In his article, *Cyberlibertarians' Digital Deletion of the Left*, David Golumba writes that: "There are overt libertarians who are also digital utopians—figures like Jimmy Wales, Eric Raymond, John Perry Barlow, Kevin Kelly, Peter Thiel, Elon Musk, Julian Assange, Dread Pirate Roberts, and Sergey Brin and the members of the Technology Liberation Front who explicitly describe themselves as cyberlibertarians."[66] Cyberlibertarian John Perry Barlow thundered, "On behalf of the future, I ask you of the past to leave us alone." His utopian vision is an Internet free from censorship: "Governments of the Industrial World, you weary giants of flesh and steel, I come from Cyberspace, the new home of Mind." Barlow proclaimed that governments have no legitimate authority in cyberspace:

> We have no elected government, nor are we likely to have one, so I address you with no greater authority than that with which liberty itself always speaks. I declare the global social space we are building to be naturally independent of the tyrannies you seek to impose on us. You have no moral right to rule us nor do you possess any methods of enforcement we have true reason to fear.[67]

Barlow's argument is that legitimate authority must ultimately come from the consent of Internet users around the world, not from legislators, judges or corporate giants. He wrote his famous Manifesto in response to the German government's prosecution of a Bavarian Internet service provider that enabled permitting Internet users to access Nazi memorabilia. By what authority can a Bavarian court order a U.S. service provider to block content to German citizens?

Similarly, what gives the European Union the right to demand that U.S. companies obtain consent from users before dropping cookies that capture consumer information? Barlow is also critical of governmental content regulations that that constrain online political expression. Authoritarian regimes view the Internet as an existential threat and are quick to erect roadblocks and access controls to censor subversive content. Cyberlibertarian idealists want the Internet to be used to advance global democratization.

Libertarian-influenced privacy advocates, such as the Electronic Frontier Foundation, worry about the potential for widespread surveillance and the emergence of a new form of Jeremy Bentham's *Panopticon*. The design of the *Panopticon* was such that a single guard could watch the inmates without the inmates themselves knowing whether or not they were being watched. Cyberlibertarians fear that the Internet could become a similar total-controlling institution, used by elites to violate basic human freedoms.

(c) Cyberlibertarian Ethics

The cyberlibertarian perspective can be seen in the hacker community's view of computer ethics, as illustrated in Chart Three below. In sharp contrast to computer industry ethical codes, which emphasize respect for intellectual property rights, the cyberlibertarian view is that property is communal and information should be freely shared. Traditional libertarians see humans as naturally self-interested and are therefore skeptical of extreme cyberlibertarianism, believing that private property and the profit motive are the best defenses for individual freedom.

CHART THREE: CYBERLITERTARIAN CODE OF ETHICS

The hacker community's computer ethics commandments challenge computer professional's core values:
(1) We believe: That every individual should have the right to free speech in cyberspace.
(2) We believe: That every individual should be free of worry when pertaining to oppressive governments that control cyberspace.
(3) We believe: That democracy should exist in cyberspace to set a clear example as to how a functioning element of society can prosper with equal rights and free speech to all.
(4) We believe: That hacking is a tool that should and is used to test the integrity of networks that hold and safe guard our valuable information.
(5) We believe: Those sovereign countries in the world community that do not respect democracy should be punished.
(6) We believe: That art, music, politics and crucial social elements of all world societies can be achieved on the computer and in cyberspace.
(7) We believe: That hacking, cracking, and phreaking [1970s practice of hacking telephone systems in order to get free long distance calls] are instruments that can achieve three crucial goals: (a) Direct Democracy in cyberspace; (b) The belief that information should be free to all; and (c) The idea that one can test and know the dangers and exploits of systems that store the individual's information.

(8)	We believe: That cyberspace should be a governing body in the world community, where people of all nations and cultures can express their ideas and beliefs has to how our world politics should be played.
(9)	We believe: That there should be no governing social or political class or party in cyberspace.
(10)	We believe: That the current status of the Internet is a clear example as to how many races, cultures and peoples can communicate freely and without friction or conflict.
(11)	We believe: In free enterprise and friction-free capitalism.
(12)	We believe: In the open source movement fully, as no government should adopt commercial or priced software for it shows that a government may be biased to something that does not prompt the general welfare of the technology market and slows or stops the innovation of other smaller company's products.
(13)	We believe: That technology can be wielded for the better placement of man kind and the environment we live in.
(14)	We believe: That all sovereign countries in the world community should respect these principles and ideas released in this constitution.[68]

Lawrence Lessig charges libertarians with extreme naiveté: "Cyberspace, it is said, cannot be regulated. It 'cannot be governed;' its 'innate ability' is to resist regulation. In its essence, cyberspace is a space of no control." A change in the architecture of the Internet could radically restrict the freedoms of users. For example, message content could be scanned to increase social control or to manipulate customers. The potential of the Internet to become a technology of social control and oppression is the great fear of both traditional and cyberlibertarians.

[G] Learning from Multiple Perspectives

Science fiction writer James Gunn wrote *The Immortals* in which an impoverished drifter is found to have a uniquely valuable blood that can temporarily cure any illness in those who receive a transfusion.[69] The ideal type consequentialist would advocate capturing him for study and extracting his blood for the greater good because his plasma would save thousands of lives. His sperm might be extracted to maximally breed him in the hope that his offspring would inherit the same ability to produce this invaluable blood.

The other four perspectives, in contrast, would reject this extreme violation of the drifter's rights, no matter what the social benefits, as it is morally wrong to use another human being as merely a means to a broader societal end. The conflict perspective would abhor solutions that would allow the rich to live for centuries, while the poor die early deaths.

All five of the ethical perspectives agree that powerful corporations must be opposed when they seek to illegitimately stifle critics of their products and services. However, where the line is drawn depends on the ethical perspective of the decision maker. One prominent example of this is when copyright owners representing the film and music industries aggressively seek to unveil anonymous file sharers. Courts issuing these subpoenas must balance the rights of anonymous speakers against the right of owners to protect their intellectual property. Optimal societal benefits and the motives of the parties involved may also enter into the decision.

Except for the libertarians, the great majority of ethicists would agree that society must deter and punish certain bad behaviors, which may call for suppressing the worst excesses of free expression. Most Americans recognize that even though free expression is both useful and a core societal value, too much Internet freedom can be socially costly. Terrorists, criminals and sexual predators exploit online anonymity to harm other people.

Particularly ironic is the fact that the U.S. Navy invented and protects Tor (a name taken from the initials of "The Onion Router"), which is the preeminent anonymizing software. At the same time, the U.S. National Security Agency and its UK counterpart are attempting to de-anonymize Tor because the service enables illicit messaging by terrorists and other cybercriminals. Illegal online marketplaces are thriving because Tor allows them to operate beyond the reach of any nation's law.

Some computer professionals contend that all laws should be obeyed, regardless of a programmer's personal opinion about their reasonableness. Other information ethicists, especially the cyberlibertarians, contend that a principled programmer must use her professional judgment and, if necessary, resist immoral laws. Computer professionals, like any other group, have the right to call for law reform, but they must obey the law or face potential punishment.

§ 2.2: THE FUTURE OF COMPUTER ETHICS

Professional associations often play an important role in providing guidance to practitioners faced with ethical challenges and to lawmakers attempting to regulate controversial practices. Robert Martin, popularly known in computer circles as "Uncle Bob," in a November 2016 episode of his "The Future of Programming" series, argued for the necessity of computer professionals organizing into a formal profession.[70] Martin has proposed a nine-element Programmer's Oath to "defend and preserve the honor of the profession of computer programmers."[71] Chart Four reprints Martin's aspirational code of conduct for programmers:

CHART FOUR: ROBERT MARTIN'S PROGRAMMER'S OATH

In order to defend and preserve the honor of the profession of computer programmers,
I Promise that, to the best of my ability and judgment:
(1) I will not produce harmful code.
(2) The code that I produce will always be my best work. I will not knowingly allow code that is defective either in behavior or structure to accumulate.
(3) I will produce, with each release, a quick, sure and repeatable proof that every element of the code works as it should.
(4) I will make frequent, small releases so that I do not impede the progress of others.
(5) I will fearlessly and relentlessly improve my creations at every opportunity. I will never degrade them.
(6) I will do all that I can to keep the productivity of myself, and others, as high as possible. I will do nothing that decreases that productivity.
(7) I will continuously ensure that others can cover for me, and that I can cover for them.
(8) I will produce estimates that are honest both in magnitude and precision. I will not make promises without certainty.
(9) I will never stop learning and improving my craft.

Robert Martin argues that, with the ubiquity of smart machines, civilization is becoming increasingly dependent on effective software. A coding error, like the one alleged in Toyota's class action litigation over the sudden, unintended acceleration of its cars, could result in a substantial number of fatal crashes. In 2014, emergency dispatch centers serving eleven million Americans in six states were disabled by a coding error. Programmers had capped the number of 911 calls at an arbitrary number in the millions, which was reached, shutting down the system.[72] Key systems that formerly were controlled by humans are now software-driven. On a single day in 2015:

> United Airlines grounded its fleet because of a problem with its departure-management system; trading was suspended on the New York Stock Exchange after an upgrade; the front page of *The Wall Street Journal's* website crashed; and Seattle's 911 system went down again, this time because a different router failed.[73]

Computer professionals must adopt high ethical standards or face having lawmakers impose rules upon them when, inevitably, a serious software error results in mass fatalities:

> Other people think they write the rules; but then they hand those rules to us, and we actually write the rules that make the machines work. We rule the world. With that great power ought to come great responsibility. And, indeed, society will hold us responsible when our actions result in disaster. And yet nothing binds us together as a profession. We share no ethics. We share no discipline. We share no standards. We are viewed, by our employers, as laborers. We are tools for others to command and use. We have no profession. This cannot continue. If we do not form a profession on our own, then society will force it upon us—and define it for us. And that will be good neither for society, nor for us. We must get there first.[74]

Several U.S. engineering associations, which include software professionals among their membership, have aspirational, though not legally binding, codes of ethics. The National Society of Professional Engineers (NSPE) is an American group representing licensed professional engineers. Engineering.com describes NSPE as "the recognized voice and advocate of licensed Professional Engineers," represented in 52 state (and territorial) organizations and over 400 local chapters. The ethical code of the NSPE calls for its membership to exhibit "honesty, impartiality, fairness and equity, and must be dedicated to the protection of the public health, safety, and welfare."[75] The NSPE Code is standards-based rather than rules-based.

The province of Ontario, which contains more than one-third of Canada's population, employs legally enforceable ethical codes that parallel the practices of the medical and legal professions. The Professional Engineers Ontario (PEO) has been empowered for more than ninety years by the province's Professional Engineer Act[76] to license and discipline engineers. Only those licensed by the PEO can offer engineering services and take responsibility for professional engineering work in the province.

In addition to educational requirements, applicants for licensure must pass the Professional Practice Examination (PPE), "a three-hour, closed-book exam on ethics, professional practice, engineering law and professional liability."[77] The PEO's Code of Ethics requires that engineers demonstrate fairness and loyalty to "associates, employers, clients, subordinates and employees" and "fidelity to public needs."[78]

The high ethical standards expected of engineers are reinforced by universities throughout Canada, whose graduates participate in a symbolic Ritual of the Calling of the Engineer, a private ritual written by Rudyard Kipling. All Canadian engineering graduates receive an iron ring, which symbolizes their commitment to a high standard of professional ethics. The iron ring is the new graduate's reminder of their duty to conduct themselves ethically in their professional and personal life. Unethical behavior will be investigated by the PEO and can result in the temporary or permanent withdrawal of the right to practice engineering in Ontario, in a monetary fine, and/or the publication of the engineer's failings, among other possible punishments.[79]

A discussion about whether U.S. software engineers should form a similar organization has gone viral on *Hacker News* in the wake of a November 2016 essay by Bill Sourour, entitled, "The Code I'm Still Ashamed of."[80] Sourour is haunted by an online questionnaire he programmed more than a decade earlier, which appeared to be an informative diagnostic tool, but was actually designed to promote the financial interests of a pharmaceutical company. Respondents received a recommendation that they should be taking his client's powerful antidepressant in response to almost any possible combination of answers to the questionnaire.

The covert goal was to boost sales of a profitable anti-depressant drug, even though it might have fatal side effects. Sourour concluded, "The more software continues to take over every aspect of our lives, the more important it will be for us to take a stand and ensure that our ethics are ever-present in our code." Computing boot camps should expand their mission beyond straightforward technical training to a discussion of ethical issues.

Some bloggers argue that without a professional organization that can assert moral or disciplinary authority, ethical software engineers are disempowered because employers can easily find a less ethical replacement. Without legal enforcement, the ethical code is ineffective because "it's easy to fall into the trap of thinking that just because a job is legal and has a steady paycheck: the company is ethical."

One commentator echoed the conflict perspective by arguing: "The most effective way to change the world, in my opinion, is to push for political and social changes that change incentives in a manner that reduces the number of unethical economic niches that exist for the necessity of social change."[81] This raises a much larger issue, to be discussed in subsequent chapters, of whether recent advances in artificial intelligence and the Internet of Things will require significant modifications in society so as not to create a large class of permanently unemployed individuals.

Libertarian-style resistance to the establishment of legally enforceable codes of ethics is found in the individualistic streak possessed by many programmers, who want no oversight by a professional organization. One commentator argued that, in reality, the Ontario board acts to limit competition by artificially restricting the number of engineers who can work in the province. Milton Friedman, a famed free market economist, denounced laws controlling who can practice in a profession as the "tyranny of the status quo." Friedman believed that established special interest groups protect their privileged status—and generous paychecks—by using legal restrictions to block innovations that threaten the profession's profits.

Some commentators argue that programming is essentially different from traditional engineering. New regulatory models need to be devised for this unique profession. Perhaps the label "software developers" is better than "software engineers" because it suggests the need for a fresh look at how the law should operate. For example, because the cover-up of defective software is hard to discover, perhaps enhanced financial awards for whistleblowing would be particularly effective.

Writing a list of vague admonitions suggesting that programmers should pursue a variety of virtues, such as "protecting the public interest," "refusing unethical assignments," "acting with honor and integrity," and "promoting fairness," is easy. Producing laws that will punish those who violate these aspirational principles is extremely difficult. The following chapters of this book will discuss how the legal system is evolving to advance the public interest, regulate unethical online behavior and control the misdeeds of cybercriminals.

As societal dependence on reliable computer systems advances at an ever-increasing pace, the legal order will require constant modifications that build on ethical principles. This book is designed to provide a survey of the existing legal structure so that practitioners will know what they are allowed to do, victims will understand what defenses are available and policymakers will understand the successes and failures of the current legal code.

CONCLUSION

Computer ethics is an applied field that examines moral and legal issues raised by computers, software and information technologies. This chapter introduced five leading theories of ethics: (1) Consequentialism; (2) Virtue and Duty Ethics; (3) Conflict Perspective; (4) Social Contract Theory; and (5) Libertarianism. These ethical perspectives embody divergent ways of conceptualizing and resolving moral dilemmas. The contemporary debates discussed in subsequent chapters will demonstrate the value of approaching ethical problems from multiple vantage points. Our overarching argument is that the most useful insights often arise from combining the most relevant features of several perspectives.

This book is designed to help you to develop and refine your critical thinking skills and your ability to make persuasive arguments about the best approaches to the ethical quandaries that will inevitably arise as the digital era progresses. Radical advances in information technology are continuously producing unique moral challenges that will require the rethinking of laws and regulations governing knotty topics such as online privacy, Internet security, intellectual property and computer contracts.

In the following chapters, you will learn about the ethical and legal dimensions of issues such as peer-to-peer file sharing, Internet crime, employee surveillance, human rights and the hazards of simultaneously operating under the laws of multiple nations. The phenomenal growth in traffic on the Internet requires that all branches of the law be adapted to globalized cyberspace.

Information professionals, lawyers and informed citizens will be called upon to determine how to maximize the benefits that can arise from the Fourth Industrial Revolution. Everyone will need to become increasingly global minded. Information technology has a great potential to increase international cooperation, coordination and mutual prosperity. However, to achieve this goal, Internet governance must agree on the basic ethical and legal rules that will apply in the information age.

The set of questions that follow are designed to help you apply the abstract ethical principles that are presented in this chapter to concrete information technology dilemmas. To quote prolific inventor and head of research for General Motors, Charles Kettering, "we should all be concerned about the future because we will have to live the rest of our lives there."[82]

CHAPTER TWO: REVIEW EXERCISES

2.1: "In the classic science-fiction film '2001,' the ship's computer, HAL, faces a dilemma. His instructions require him both to fulfill the ship's mission (investigating an artifact near Jupiter) and to conceal the mission's true purpose from the ship's crew. To resolve the contradiction, he tries to kill the crew. As robots become more autonomous, the notion of computer-controlled machines facing ethical decisions is moving out of the realm of science fiction and into the real world. Society needs to find ways to ensure that they are better equipped to make moral judgments than HAL was."[83] What would a duty-based deontologist, a consequentialist and a libertarian say about HAL's actions? How much autonomy should computers be allowed? Please explain.

2.2: "Armed drones currently fly the skies over Afghanistan and have been used to attack Taliban and Al Qaeda leaders. Although those drones are not completely autonomous, they certainly could be."[84] From each of the five ethical perspectives, what factors should be considered for the deployment of drones against ISIS?

2.3: Consider the computer game, Fallout 3. In the Tenpenny Tower quest, players "find a building in which the dream of a time past is preserved. The dominant cast keeps the population happy, but scared. They prevent riots by presenting the ghouls that roam just outside the residence as the enemy. Throughout the game, however, ghouls are presented as mostly pacific denizens. In this quest, players face a dilemma: They can eliminate all ghouls in the proximity of the Tower, help the ghouls kill the humans, or negotiate peace between both."[85] How would supporters of the five ethical perspectives approach this issue? How can it best be resolved? Please explain.

2.4: Should game designers and software engineers have a higher duty to produce ethical software products that teach lessons in morality? In Gamergate, women were harassed with violent threats for suggesting that online games should be more socially complex and contextual.[86] Conflict theory would see this as suppression of females at the hands of privileged males. How might this be approached from the other four perspectives?

2.5: "While ethics courses have become a staple of physical-world engineering degrees, they remain a begrudging anomaly in computer science pedagogy."[87] Why do you think that some students disfavor requiring courses in computer ethics?

2.6: "On the Internet, 'free' services abound. The question of where the money will come from is often put off, being off-putting. We just build the amazingness, keep an eye on the adoption metrics, and figure someone else will take care of the dirty work of keeping the server lights on. Worst case, there are always ads."[88] Do software developers have any ethical obligations in creating "free services" that are not really free? Do developers have any obligation to provide users with more information regarding how a profit is being made? What would the ethics theorists say about companies that trick consumers into downloading software, a practice called drive-by downloads?

2.7: In his science fiction story, *I Robot*, Isaac Asimov created three laws of robotics. The Three Laws from Asimov's "Handbook of Robotics, 56th Edition, 2058 A.D.," are:

> (1) A robot may not injure a human being or, through inaction, allow a human being to come to harm.
>
> (2) A robot must obey the orders given it by human beings except where such orders would conflict with the First Law.
>
> (3) A robot must protect its own existence as long as such protection does not conflict with the First or Second Laws.

Fast forward six decades after Asimov wrote *I Robot*. Now, "ethical subroutines may sound like science fiction, but once upon a time, so did self-driving cars."[89] What ethical rules should be formulated for self-driving cars? What ethical rules apply to the following scenario? "Your car is speeding along a bridge at fifty miles per hour when an errant school bus carrying forty innocent children crosses its path. Should your car swerve, possibly risking the life of its owner (you), to save the children, or should it keep going, putting all forty kids at risk? If the decision must be made in milliseconds, the computer will have to make the call."[90] Do you believe that people will buy vehicles that might kill the driver? Should they be forced to do so?

2.8: We are far from realistically programming a robot that would refuse to harm humans. However, is it even desirable to program a robot to never harm a human? Would a virtue theorist prevent a robotic sniper from killing a terrorist who has taken a group of thirty-five preschoolers hostage? In Isaac Asimov's short story, "Liar," a robot lies to protect its programmer from psychological harm that would come from knowing the truth. Should psychological harms be forbidden or only physical ones?

2.9: What rules need to be formulated to prevent journalists from violating the privacy of celebrities? Should there be different rules for using drones to follow public officials who are suspected of corruption or treason? Does your answer change if an investigative journalist uses drones to learn about the illegal activities of a toxic waste recovery company? Suppose this is a contested divorce case, in which a spouse wishes to prove her spouse's secret liaisons. Should a court allow this evidence to be considered?

2.10: In the 1950s and 1960s, the American automobile industry blamed the epidemic of car accidents on driver error and bad roads to deflect attention away from design defects that created excessive, preventable dangers. Automobiles in this era were not even equipped with safety glass, let alone seatbelts. Rigid steering wheel columns crushed chests and tattooed drivers with imprints of decorative, though sharply pointed, emblems. Today's automobiles are much safer because products liability exposed such flaws and encouraged the auto industry to adopt improved designs. Is it now time to extend products liability to include insecure software or applications with potentially deadly design defects?[91]

2.11: California was the first state to enact a statute requiring companies to notify consumers of computer security breaches. The Business Roundtable opposes "breach notification laws requiring companies to report computer security breaches or implement minimum security standards because these obligations may lead to greater litigation costs." Some consumers, particularly those who know little about computers, may be needlessly alarmed by such a notification. What are the ethical issues in imposing an obligation to notify consumers of any breach of the security of their data?

2.12: A leading commentator wrote: "the software industry is no longer in its infancy. Its development has moved out of garages and into corporate offices. It has matured to become a dominant sector of the economy. Consequently, it is appropriate to consider liability for defective software in the same light as liability for defective automobiles, pharmaceuticals and other products."[92] What is the case for and against imposing greater liability on software makers when they market defective products? Are there any reasons to shield the software industry, while holding other manufacturers accountable when defective designs cause injury or death?

2.13: Chapter One argued that law and medicine are professions because of having implemented a standard curriculum of study, post-graduate certification tests and enforceable model rules of discipline. Do you think that computer professionals' codes of ethics will be recognized by the courts in the near future? Should computer scientists organize themselves into a traditional profession? Why or why not?

2.14: Should there be a law requiring that Internet Service Providers help trace the true identify of threatening posters? Is there too much anonymity on the Internet? What would the five perspectives say about this issue? How would you resolve this dilemma?

2.15: A John Doe, or anonymous poster, described a Dunkin Donuts shop the plaintiff owned as one "of the most dirty and unsanitary-looking food-service places he had ever seen." The owner of the Dunkin Donuts franchise wishes to file a subpoena to the news website where the statement appeared to learn in order to unveil the identity of the anonymous critic. A subpoena is a request to produce documents, or a request to appear in court or other legal proceeding. In this case, the subpoena would be issued to the news group, requiring it to reveal the identity of the poster of the derogatory statements about the plaintiff's donut shop. The franchise operator suspects that the owner of a rival coffee shop posted the message. What factors should courts consider in deciding whether to issue the subpoena to unmask the anonymous poster?

REFERENCES FOR CHAPTER TWO

---

1 Klaus Schwab, *The Fourth Industrial Revolution: What It Means, How to Respond*, WORLD ECONOMIC FORUM (January 14, 2016).

2 Jim Motavalli, *Technology: The Dozens of Computers That Make Modern Cars Go (and Stop)*, THE NEW YORK TIMES (Feb.4, 2010).

3 Kiley Crossland, *Should Sexting Teens Be Charged with Child Pornography?* WORLD (November 18, 2015).

4 Matthew H. Birkhold, *Freud on the Court: Re-interpreting Sexting & Child Pornography Laws*, 23 FORDHAM INTELLECTUAL PROPERTY, MEDIA, AND ENTERTAINMENT LAW JOURNAL 897, 905 (2013).

5 Eugene Kim, *Why Silicon Valley's Elites Are Obsessed with Poker*, BUSINESS INSIDER (November 2, 2014).

6 Sabla Priyadarshini, *Weber's Ideal Types: Definition, Meaning, Purpose, and Use* (2016).

7 *Ideal Type*, ENCYCLOPEDIA BRITANNICA (2016).

8 *Id.*

9 JOHN STUART MILL, UTILITARIANISM (1863) at Chapter Two.

10 Tyron Stading, *The Role of Artificial Intelligence in Intellectual Property*, IPWATCHDOG.COM (July 27, 2017).

11 Chris Pash, *The World's Top Artificial Intelligence Companies Are Pleading for a Ban on Killer Robots*, BUSINESS INSIDER (August 21, 2017).

12 *Id.*

13 JOHN MARKOFF, MACHINES OF LOVING GRACE: THE QUEST FOR COMMON GROUND BETWEEN HUMANS AND ROBOTS (New York, New York: Harper/Collins Publishers 2015) at 327.

14 PETER K. MCINERNEY & GEORGE W. RAINBOLT, ETHICS (New York, New York: Harper Perennial, 1994) at 90.

15 Tim C. Mazur, *Lying*, Markkula Center for Applied Ethics, Santa Clara University (2016).

[16] *What Would Kant Do When Two Categorical Imperatives Conflict? Could He Ever Justify Lying?*, http://philosophy.stackexchange.com/questions/259/what-would-kant-do-when-two-categorical-imperatives-conflict-could-he-ever-just.

[17] Helga Vardon, *Kant and Lying to the Murderer at the Door. . . One More Time: Kant's Legal Philosophy and Lies to Murderers and Nazis*, 41 JOURNAL OF SOCIAL PHILOSOPHY 403 (Winter 2010).

[18] RALPH C.S. WALKER, KANT: THE ARGUMENT OF THE PHILOSOPHERS, (London, Henley and Boston: Routledge and Kegan Paul, 1978) at 151.

[19] EDWIN PATTERSON, JURISPRUDENCE: MEAN AND IDEAS OF THE LAW (Brooklyn, New York: The Foundation Press, Inc., 1953) at 341 (discussing Aristotle's ethics and law and influence upon later developments in law and legal philosophy).

[20] David Kravets, *Lawyers Score Big in Settlement for Ashley Madison Cheating Site Data Breach*, ARS TECHNICAL (July 17, 2017).

[21] Richard B. Freeman, *Who Owns the Robots Rules the World*, HARVARD MAGAZINE (May-June 2016).

[22] Patrick Thibodeau, *Trump Tapped the Viral Anger Over H-1B Use*, COMPUTERWORLD (November 9, 2016).

[23] JULIA T. WOOD, GENDERED LIVES: COMMUNICATION, GENDER & CULTURE (New York, New York: Thomson, Wadsworth, 2005) at 2.

[24] Selena Larson, *Why So Few Women Are Studying Computer Science*, READWRITE (September 2, 2014).

[25] Gaby Galvin, *Middle School Is Key to Girls' Coding Interest*, U.S. NEWS & WORLD REPORT (October 20, 2016).

[26] Elise Hu, Sexism *in the Tech Industry Takes Center Stage*, NATIONAL PUBLIC RADIO: ALL THINGS CONSIDERED (September 11, 2013).

[27] Jay Hathaway, What is *Gamergate, and Why? An Explainer for Non-Geeks*, GAWKER.COM (October 10, 2014).

[28] Simon Parkin, Gamergate*: A Scandal Erupts in the Video-Game Community*, NEW YORKER (October 17, 2014).

[29] *Id.*

[30] Dan Golding, *The End of Gamers*, DANGOLDING.TUMBLR.COM (August 28, 2014).

[31] HARRY BRAVERMAN, LABOR AND MONOPOLY CAPITAL: THE DEGRADATION OF WORK IN THE TWENTIETH CENTURY (New York, New York, Monthly Review Press, 1974).

[32] Karl Marx & Frederick Engels, Manifesto of the Communist Party (Cosimo Classics 2009) (1848) at 49.

[33] *Id.*

[34] PAUL BARAN & PAUL M. SWEEZY, MONOPOLY CAPITAL (New York, New York: Modern Reader Paperbacks, 1966) at 6.

[35] Robert Hackett, *20 Great Workplaces in Tech*, FORTUNE (October 8, 2014).

[36] *Id.*

[37] *Id.*

[38] *Id.*

[39] Michael Addady, *These 10 Companies Are Generous With Stock Options,* FORTUNE (March 11, 2016).

[40] *Id.*

[41] Luisa Kroll & Kerry A. Dolan, *Forbes 2017 Billionaires List: Meet The Richest People On The Planet* FORBES (March 20, 2017) ("Bill Gates is the number one richest for the fourth year in a row, and the richest person in the world for 18 out of the past 23 years. He has a fortune of $86 billion, up from $75 billion last year.").

[42] *Id.*

[43] Amicus Brief of Software Freedom Law Center in *Microsoft Corp. v. AT & T Corp.*, 2005 U.S. Briefs 1056 (Dec. 15, 2005).

[44] STEPHEN WEBER, THE SUCCESS OF SOURCE CODE (Cambridge, Massachusetts: Harvard University Press, 2004) at 1.

[45] *Id.*

[46] Yochai Benkler, *From Consumers to Users: Shifting Deeper Structures of Regulation: Toward Sustainable Commons and User Access*, 52 FEDERAL COMMUNICATIONS LAW JOURNAL 561, 562 (2000).

[47] David Kravits, *U.N. Declares Access to the Internet as a Human Right*, Wired (June 3, 2011).

[48] David Rothkopf, *Is Unrestricted Access to the Internet a Modern Human Right?*, FP (February 2, 2015).

[49] Chris Willentz, *The Dark Side of Technology*, 53 FINANCE & DEVELOPMENT (INTERNATIONAL MONETARY FUND) (September 2016).

[50] STEVEN N. DURLAUF, AND LAWRENCE E. BLUME, THE NEW PALGRAVE DICTIONARY OF ECONOMICS (New York, New York: Palgrave, MacMillan, 2d ed. 2008).

[51] INTERNATIONAL ENCYCLOPEDIA OF PHILOSOPHY, *Social Contract Theory* (1995).

[52] *Id.*

[53] *Id.* at ¶ 6.

[54] ENCYCLOPEDIA BRITANNICA, Social Contract (2016).

[55] INTERNATIONAL ENCYCLOPEDIA OF PHILOSOPHY, *Social Contract Theory* (2016).

[56] INTERNET SECURITY ALLIANCE, SOCIAL CONTRACT 2.0: A 21ST CENTURY PROGRAM FOR EFFECTIVE CYBER SECURITY (September 2016).

[57] *Id.* at 4.

[58] INTERNATIONAL ENCYCLOPEDIA OF PHILOSOPHY, *Social Contract Theory* (1995).

[59] JOHN RAWLS, A THEORY OF JUSTICE (Cambridge, Massachusetts: Harvard University Press, 1999).

[60] MICHAEL SANDEL, JUSTICE: WHAT'S THE RIGHT THING TO DO (New York, New York: Farrar, Straus and Giroux, 2009) at 151–152.

[61] JASON BRENNAN, LIBERTARIANISM: WHAT EVERYONE NEEDS TO KNOW (New York, New York: Oxford University Press, 2012) at 1.

[62] MILTON FRIEDMAN, CAPITALISM AND FREEDOM (Chicago, Illinois: University of Chicago Press, 1962) at 7–21.

[63] ANDREW S. GROVE, ONLY THE PARANOID SURVIVE: HOW TO EXPLOIT THE CRISIS POINTS THAT CHALLENGE EVERY COMPANY, (New York, New York: Crown Business Group, 1999).

[64] Pierre-Joseph Proudhon, *No Gods, No Masters: An Anthology of Anarchism* (Chico, California: AK Press, 2005) at 55–56.

[65] Parmy Olson, *The Man Behind Silk Road—The Internet's Biggest Market for Illegal Drugs*, THE GUARDIAN (November 10, 2013).

[66] David Golumba, *Cyberlibertarians' Digital Deletion of the Left*, JACOBIN MAGAZINE (Dec. 13, 2013).

[67] *Id.*

[68] This email message, written by the hacking group Xanatomy, was sent to a Computer Ethics instructor as a response to the Ten Commandments mentioned in Chapter One.

[69] JAMES GUNN, THE IMMORTALS, (New York, New York: Simon & Schuster; 2005).

[70] Robert C. Martin, *The Future of Programming*, https://www.youtube.com/watch?v=ecIWPzGEbFc&feature=youtu.be&t=1h9m49s.

[71] Robert C. Martin, *The Clean Code Blog*, (November 18, 2015).

[72] James Somers, *The Coming Software Apocalypse*, THE ATLANTIC (September 26, 2017).

[73] *Id.*

[74] Robert C. Martin, *The Clean Code Blog*, *Id.*

[75] NSPE Code of Ethics for Engineers (revised July 2007).

[76] Professional Engineers Act, R.S.O. 1990, c. P.28

[77] *Id.*

[78] Professional Engineers Ontario, *Code of Ethics* (2017).

[79] Professional Engineers Ontario, Discipline (2017).

[80] Bill Sourour, *The Code I'm Still Ashamed of*, DevMastery.com (November 13, 2016).

[81] *Id.*

[82] Charles Kettering (1876–1958), Quoted in Robert Andrews, THE CONCISE COLUMBIA DICTIONARY OF QUOTATIONS (Columbia University Press, New York, New York 1989) at 105.

[83] Stephen DeAngelis, *Artificial Intelligence and Moral Dilemmas*, ENTERRO (June 29, 2012).

[84] *Id.*

[85] Miguel Sicart, *Moral Dilemmas in Computer Games*, 29 MIT: DESIGNER ISSUES 28, 32 (2013).

[86] Caitlin Dewey, *The Only Guide to Gamergate You'll Ever Need to Read*, WASHINGTON POST (October 14, 2014).

[87] Peter Waynor, *12 Ethical Dilemmas Gnawing at Developers Today*, INFOWORLD (April 21, 2014).

[88] *Id.*

[89] Gary Marcus, *Moral Machines*, NEW YORKER (November 24, 2012).

[90] *Id.*

[91] Some commentators have urged extending strict products liability principles to software. See, e.g., Lori A. Weber, *Bad Bytes: The Application of Strict Products Liability to Computer Software*, 66 ST. JOHN'S LAW. REVIEW 469 (1992); See generally, Diane Savage, *Avoiding Tort Claims for Defective Hardware and Software Strategies for Dealing with Potential Liability Woes*, 15 COMPUTER LAW STRATEGIES 1 (1998).

[92] Frances E. Zollers et al., *No More Soft Landings for Software, Liability for Defects in an Industry That Has Come of Age*, 21 SANTA CLARA COMPUTER & HIGH TECHNOLOGY LAW JOURNAL 745, 746 (2005).

CHAPTER THREE

Cybertorts for the Information Age

§ 3.0: UPDATING TORTS FOR CYBERSPACE

[A] Torts as Civil Wrongs

The term "tort" derives from the Latin word "tortus" that means twisted or wrong. Torts are civil wrongs where an injured person or entity (plaintiff) seeks financial redress against a defendant who interfered with his reputation, privacy, bodily integrity, emotional tranquility, contracts, property or some other legally protectable interest. While businesses cannot be injured by an invasion of their privacy or suffer from the intentional infliction of emotional distress, corporations typically file tort lawsuits for reputational injuries, interference with contract and other economic harms. In most tort lawsuits, plaintiffs seek monetary compensation for damages, but in computer cases, injunctive relief is increasingly common. Injunctions are orders by a court requiring a party to act or refrain from particular injurious acts. The victims of defamatory online postings, for example, seek injunctive relief that requires the perpetrator to remove the libelous posting and refrain from future damaging postings.

[B] Legal Definition of Cybertorts

A "cybertort" is an act or omission where a computer system is an instrumentality of harm. Cybertort remedies are increasingly redressing injuries from defective software, spam email, cyberstalking, the invasion of privacy and other rapidly evolving civil wrongs. This chapter will cover the role of cybertort lawsuits in filling the enforcement gap left by obsolete criminal statutes unable to keep pace with Internet-related harms. The preventive law principles presented in this chapter are tailored to help computer professionals prevent or mitigate exposure that may result in multi-million dollar jury awards or settlements that consume time, foreclose opportunities, and result in adverse publicity that can even bankrupt a company.

[C] The Three Branches of Tort Law

(1) Intentional Torts

Intentional torts occur when an individual, corporation or other entity deliberately injures a plaintiff or damages his property. Justice Oliver Wendell Holmes Jr. drew the line between an intentional harm and one caused by negligence by using a memorable analogy: "Even a dog distinguishes between being stumbled over and being kicked."[1] Intent for purposes of intentional torts means the desire to cause contact or a substantial certainty of harm from a purposeful act. The most common intentional cybertorts are defamation, the invasion of privacy, trespass to chattels, conversion and the intentional infliction of emotional distress.

(2) Negligence

Unlike intentional torts, negligence does not involve deliberate acts. Negligence is an act or omission by which the defendant fails to exercise the due care of a reasonable person in the circumstances. To prove negligence, the plaintiff must establish four elements:

(1) A person must owe a duty or service to the victim in question;

(2) The individual who owes the duty must violate a standard of care;

(3) The injury causes must have been reasonably foreseeable from this act or omission; and

(4) The plaintiff suffers an injury or damages.

The person or entity injured by inadequate security, for example, will typically initiate a negligence lawsuit to recover direct damages to the computer system and consequential damages such as lost business, reputation harm and the cost of monitoring their databases. The core concept of negligence is that we must all act with reasonable care to avoid harming others.

Computer companies are increasingly subject to liability for negligent hiring, which is harm that results from a failure to do adequate pre-employment background checks, employee drug testing or checks on references. Information industry firms increasingly face negligent security claims for cyberbreaches, computer viruses or enabling computer intrusions.

(3) Strict Liability

Strict liability, the third branch of tort law, imposes legal responsibility without the necessity of the plaintiff proving fault. Since ancient Roman times, for example, strict liability extended to the harboring of wild animals, such as bears or tigers, which involved obvious dangers that could not be eliminated even by the utmost care. Imposing strict liability is a utilitarian decision to place the costs of accidents directly on the least cost avoider, which is the entity in the best position to prevent the harm.

A Brookings Institution study on driverless cars concludes strict products liability should apply to autonomous vehicles to ensure that producers aggressively monitor and correct dangerous design flaws:

> Manufacturers that become aware of potentially risky software problems will need to act quickly to provide upgrades as soon as possible, but at the same time will need to appropriately test the upgraded software before releasing it. Properly finding that balance will in some cases be challenging, in part due to the associated liability considerations.[2]

Critics of this perspective charge that imposing strict liability on autonomous car makers will have a chilling impact on innovation by jeopardizing a potentially important industry.

§ 3.1: THE EMERGENCE OF CYBERTORTS

In every historical era, tort law continually evolves to address technological advances. During the early nineteenth century, workers injured while building canals and turnpikes generally had no legal remedy. Under the harsh nineteenth century doctrine of contributory negligence, plaintiffs were barred from recovering any amount even if they were responsible for just 1% of their injury. In this era, courts routinely applied the assumption of risk defense, reasoning that workers should have no legal recourse because they had voluntarily assumed the danger of employment injury in return for higher wages. Similarly, the fellow servant rule barred a worker injured by a co-employee from filing suit against the employer.

Congress abolished contributory negligence, the fellow servant rule and the assumption of risk in workplace accident cases when it enacted the Federal Employer's Liability Act of 1908. Worker's compensation statutes also gave injured employees financial compensation for many workplace accidents in place of their tort remedy.

§ 3.2: SUPPLEMENTING CRIMINAL LAW

Tort law involves the recovery of monetary damages, whereas criminal law is designed to punish and deter. Federal or state prosecutors apply criminal law to punish or deter socially harmful acts or the failure to act where there is a legal requirement to do so. Many of the cybertorts discussed in this chapter could have been prosecuted as crimes, but district attorneys are seldom willing to apply criminal law statutes to cyber wrongs.

A fifteen-year-old high school student in Florida, for example, committed suicide after classmates circulated covertly filmed Snapchat images of her taking a shower. Accompanying this humiliating posting was a running commentary of insulting comments. Government prosecutors refused to file criminal charges because of the lack of a clear state statute criminalizing this type of misconduct. The victim's estate, on the other hand, may file a lawsuit seeking financial compensation for torts such as the intentional infliction of emotional distress and invasion of privacy.

[A] How Torts and Crimes Differ

A plaintiff may file a tort action for false imprisonment, which is also a crime. However, a criminal trial is very different from a civil case. Criminal defendants may not be convicted unless the judge or jury finds guilt beyond a reasonable doubt, a high standard to meet. Tort litigants enjoy none of these constitutional protections allowing torts to evolve more quickly than criminal statutes can be revised.

Tort law has no death penalty or ability to incarcerate a defendant. However, a large tort award sends a deterrent message that the victim deserves compensation at the perpetrator's expense. A tort verdict that includes a punitive damages component not only punishes a blameworthy defendant but also sends a public message that such wrongdoing is abhorrent. Chart One below summarizes the numerous differences between the criminal and tort law systems for pursuing cyber wrongs.

CHART ONE: CRIMES VERSUS TORTS

Feature of the Law	Criminal Law	Tort Law
Attributes of Legal Field	Criminal law is purely statutory; i.e. enacted by Congress and state legislatures.	Tort law is a matter of common law, which creates legal principles

		through judicial precedent.
Who Is Harmed?	Crimes are public wrongs. An act is harmful not just to individuals, but to society.	Torts are private wrongs where individuals who have been injured or harmed initiate litigation.
Final Disposition for Defendant	Criminal defendants are found guilty or innocent of specific charges. The guilty criminal defendant is sentenced and/or pays a fine.	Civil defendants are found liable or not liable for torts. Tort defendants found liable must pay monetary awards to the plaintiff.
Definition of Branch of Law	A crime is any act or omission that violates a criminal statute.	A tort is a civil wrong that injures or interferes with another's person or property. Torts are vindicated in civil court proceedings.
Who Initiates the Court Case?	Federal or state officials prosecute crimes.	Private individuals file suit to obtain redress for personal injuries or property damage.
Purpose of Branch of Law	Punishment, Deterrence, and Retribution.	Compensation to injured party, but punishment and deterrence in the rarely awarded remedy of punitive damages.
Burden of Proof in Trial	All elements of a crime must be proven beyond a reasonable doubt for an individual or entity to be convicted.	Preponderance of the evidence that requires the trier of fact (jury or judge) to believe that the liability is more likely than not to exist for an individual or entity.
Recipient of Fines or Damages	The State	The Plaintiff

Relevance of Defendant's State of Mind	Most criminal laws require proof of the defendant's intent to cause harm. A small percentage of crimes are predicated upon negligence or strict liability.	Most torts require proof of a defendant's negligence or intentional misconduct. Strict liability torts impose liability without a showing of either intent or fault. Strict liability is imposed for inherently dangerous activities for policy reasons.
Right to Jury Trial	Under the Sixth Amendment, the accused has the right to a trial by an impartial jury of the state and district in which the defendant allegedly committed a crime.	The Seventh Amendment requires civil jury trials only in federal courts. State constitutions give plaintiffs a right to a jury trial in state courts.
Defendant's Right to Counsel	The Sixth Amendment provides for a defendant's right to an attorney.	No constitutional right to counsel in civil cases.
Statute of Limitations	Statutes of limitation vary significantly by state law and the crime. In some states, a Class A felony (i.e. murder) has no statute of limitations.	A statute of limitations is the time in which a plaintiff must file a tort lawsuit against a defendant. Most states' statute of limitation for tort actions is three or four years.

[B] Cybertorts Supplement Cybercrime Enforcement

Tort litigation will sometimes follow criminal convictions so that the direct victims of a crime may recover money damages as in a wrongful death case. In the most publicized criminal case in American history, a Los Angeles jury acquitted O.J. Simpson for stabbing Nicole Brown Simpson and Ronald Goldman to death on June 12, 1994. The families of the murder victims then filed a tort lawsuit, called a survival action, against O.J. Simpson. On February 4, 1997, a civil jury found O.J. Simpson responsible for the wrongful death of Nicole Brown Simpson and Ronald Goldman, awarding $25 million in punitive damages and $8.5 million in compensatory damages. No double jeopardy exists because this doctrine only applies to being tried twice for the same crime.

In 2008, Fox Sports broadcaster and *Dancing with the Stars* co-host, Erin Andrews, was secretly videotaped in the nude by a stalker, Michael Barrett. Barrett tricked a poorly trained Marriott employee into confirming Andrews's reservation and booking him into a room next to hers. Barrett filmed Andrews with his cell phone through a peephole in her hotel room door and posted the humiliating video on the Internet where millions viewed it. Barrett was sentenced to two and a half years in prison for filming Andrews without her consent and stalking her.

After Barrett's criminal conviction, Erin Andrews filed a tort lawsuit against Marriott International, West End Hotel Partners, Windsor Capital Group and Barrett for $75 million to compensate her for her emotional distress and the invasion of her privacy. In April of 2016, Andrews settled her premises liability suit against Marriott International and West End Hotel Partners after a jury found Barrett and the hotels both partially at fault. Windsor Capital Group had previously paid $27 million. These defendant entities are sufficiently solvent to pay these large sums. In contrast, the $28 million award against Barrett, the actual wrongdoer, is almost certainly uncollectable because he lacks sizable assets.

Tort law plays a key role in punishing emergent forms of wrongdoing because criminal law requires clear-cut statutes that enable individuals to know in advance what conduct may subject them to the risk of prosecution. Since cybercrime laws always lag behind rapidly evolving technologies, applicable criminal statutes may not yet exist. The greatly flexibility of torts allows civil punishment to fill the enforcement gap.

[C] Prosecutors' Lack of Investigatory Resources

The Manhattan District Attorney is one of the few public prosecution offices with the trained computer personnel and forensic labs to successfully combat cybercrimes. The Santa Clara District Attorney, located in the heart of Silicon Valley, has expertise in prosecuting economic espionage cases. The Los Angeles County District Attorney's Office has the largest prosecutorial unit devoted to cybercrime in the country. The overwhelming majority of district attorneys, in contrast, are overstretched by a full docket of traditional crimes to investigate, prepare for trial and prosecute.

Most police view their primary role as protecting the public from physical crime. Computer crimes are often difficult to investigate, as there is limited physical evidence to track down the cybercriminal. The U.S. Justice Department is updating its investigation strategies by enlisting crowdsourced cyber-tip hotlines for reporting online wrongs.

Contemporary law is premised upon territorial sovereignty, which legislatures need to amend to accommodate to the globalized Internet. Cloud computing providers, for example, may store data on servers located outside of the United States, making the D.A.'s jurisdictional authority uncertain. The increasing amount of cross border wrongdoing requires the updating of obsolete jurisdiction rules as well as cross-border law enforcement cooperation.

[D] Constitutional Protections for Criminal Defendants

The U.S. Constitution arms criminal defendants with numerous protections against the misuse of governmental power, which makes it more difficult to prosecute crimes than to obtain tort recoveries. These constitutional protections apply to all persons tried in U.S. courts even if they are not citizens and have their residence in a foreign country. Criminal statutes must be clear-cut giving all persons advance notice as to what conduct may subject them to prosecution. An overly broad anti-spam statute, for example, may be struck down by the courts because it criminalizes not only its intended target but also other speech that is protected by the First Amendment.

The U.S. Supreme Court in *Ashcroft v. Free Speech Coalition* struck down the Child Pornography Prevention Act of 1996 in criminalizing "virtual child pornography."[3] The New Jersey Supreme Court overturned part of that state's statute on bias intimidation because defendants could:

> be convicted of bias intimidation if their victims "reasonably believed" they were harassed or intimidated because of their race, color, gender, ethnicity, religion or sexual orientation. The court, the state's highest, unanimously ruled that the 2001 statute was "unconstitutionally vague," because it does not give defendants fair notice of when they are crossing the line to commit a crime.[4]

Pre-arrest investigation of criminal suspects is constrained by the Fourth, Fifth, Sixth and Fourteenth Amendments of the United States Constitution. The Fourth Amendment protects individuals from unreasonable searches and seizures. Law enforcement personnel typically must obtain search warrants before conducting a search and seizure, except in certain exceptions such as a search incident to a lawful arrest. Courts require the police to give Miranda warnings informing defendants of their right to remain silent and their right to have an attorney present during an interrogation. If suspects are not informed of their Fifth and Sixth Amendment rights, a court will exclude any incriminating statements that they make.

The Fifth Amendment's Due Process Clause gives a criminal defendant a privilege against self-incrimination. The Sixth Amendment guarantees criminal defendants the right to a speedy public trial by an impartial jury. The Seventh Amendment grants every American the right to a trial by jury in federal civil actions. The rigidities of criminal law, the difficulty of proof by beyond a reasonable doubt, and other constitutional constraints at every stage make it difficult for criminal law to keep pace with technological change. Tort litigants enjoy none of these constitutional protections so torts can evolve more quickly than criminal statutes can be revised.

[E] Criminal Law Requires Clearly Defined Statutes

Legislators continue to struggle with the drafting of effective statutes to address the problem of nonconsensual pornography on the Internet. In 2004, New Jersey enacted a criminal statute that prohibits the disclosure of "any photograph, film, videotape, recording, or other reproduction of the image of another person whose intimate parts, or is engaged in an act of sexual penetration of sexual contact, unless that person has consented to such disclosure."[5] Thirty-three states and the District of Columbia now have similar laws.

In the summer of 2016, Congress proposed a federal statute to address revenge porn, which is the nonconsensual posting of intimate activity. Opponents argue that such a statute violates free expression, even though the First Amendment affords no protection of "the right to invade a person's privacy by publicizing, without consent, nude photographs, or videos of sexual activity."[6] Congress has yet to enact a federal statute addressing revenge porn, in large part because of the difficulty of defining the crime so that the law is neither vague nor in violation of the First Amendment. Thirty-four states have enacted statutes addressing revenge porn but, to date, only a few of these have been judicially reviewed.[7]

In Vermont v. Rebekah Van Buren,[8] a Vermont Superior Court invalidated a state statute that criminalized the distribution of sexually explicit images without the subject's consent.[9] Vermont prosecutors brought charges against Van Buren, alleging that she had violated the state's revenge porn law. She accessed the Facebook account of her boyfriend and found nude photos sent by his ex-girlfriend.[10] Van Buren vengefully posted the nude photos on her ex-boyfriend's Facebook page, along with the sender's name:

> Van Buren later told police she posted the pictures "for revenge" and to harm the ex-girlfriend's reputation. After prosecutors brought charges under the revenge porn law, Van Buren filed a motion to dismiss, arguing that the statute was unconstitutionally vague both generally and as applied. In granting Van Buren's motion, Vermont Superior Court Judge David Howard found that the photos at issue in the case were not obscene and therefore did not fall within a category of speech that has no First Amendment protection. Turning to the revenge porn law itself, Judge Howard wrote that "[t]he possible overbreadth of this statute is a concern."[11]

Even when criminal statutes pass constitutional scrutiny, enforcement is difficult as local law enforcement lacks the financial, technical and scientific expertise to investigate computer crimes effectively. Public prosecutors have great discretion in deciding when to file criminal charges. Tort law often serves to supplement criminal law when the district attorney has inadequate resources, is unclear about the boundaries of the law, lacks expertise or is otherwise reluctant to prosecute computer crimes.

§ 3.3: INTENTIONAL CYBERTORTS

The potential for Internet torts is staggering. The overwhelming majority of cybertorts over the past quarter century are information-based intention torts such as the violation of privacy, defamation, misrepresentation and the intentional infliction of emotional distress. To establish the existence of an intentional tort, a cybertort plaintiff must prove three things:

(1) An act by the Internet defendant;

(2) Intent, which means that the defendant desires to cause or is substantially certain that a harm will occur; and

(3) A causal connection between the defendant's intentional act and damages arising out of the defendant's intentional act.

Many online tortfeasors are spiteful individuals who use anonymous or pseudonymous identities to perpetrate their wrongdoing. Social media postings of false and defamatory information are frequently employed to tarnish the reputation of a company. Courts struggle with how to extend traditional tort remedies to cyberspace harms. It is unclear, for example, how to best apply tort law to the harms produced by catfishing, which is the fabrication of online personalities to manipulate victims into believing that they are developing romantic personal connections.

[A] Online Torts Are Frequently Gendered

Women are disproportionately the victims of intentional harms in cyberspace. A 2014 Pew Research Center study found that about 40% of Internet users say they have experienced harassment, with young adult females enduring much higher rates of threats. Women under the age 25 are three times more likely to be stalked or harassed than women aged 30 or over.

Internet wrongdoers have victimized women by maliciously posting personal information such as home addresses on sadomasochistic websites.[12] Others use image morphing and manipulation technologies such as Photoshop to superimpose their victim's face onto pornographic images. Tort law lags far behind the epidemic of female victimization. Only four states have enacted tort remedies for the victims of stalkers.[13]

A Michigan court awarded a 26-year-old woman $500,000 after her ex-boyfriend fraudulently obtained nude photos of her and posted them on multiple revenge porn websites. A judge entered a permanent injunction against the former boyfriend, ordering that he destroy any photos and not publish them again. If the defendant repeats his actions, he faces fines and possibly jail for civil contempt.

In recent years, criminal cyberstalking laws have been enacted, but convictions have been scarce. In *US v Cassidy*,[14] William Lawrence Cassidy allegedly cyberstalked Alyce Zeoli unleashing over 8,000 Tweets. Zeoli suffered, by universal stipulation, "severe emotional distress." Cassidy was charged with violating the federal interstate stalking statute.[15] The court ruled that Cassidy's blog and Twitter postings were protected by the First Amendment as religious speech.

[B] Intentional Bodily Harm Cybertorts

(1) Cyber-Assault

An assault is the intentional creation of a reasonable apprehension of an imminent battery, while battery is offensive or harmful touching. The unprivileged touching of a person, including harmful or offensive contacts with the body, constitute the tort of battery. William Prosser, the author of the leading torts hornbook, famously stated that "assault and battery go together like eggs and bacon." If X punches Y from behind without warning, there is a battery, but not an assault. Conversely, if X comes very close to hitting Y, but does not strike Y, there is an assault without a battery. In cyberspace, there is very rarely a reasonable apprehension of either assault or battery because of the lack of imminence.

The tort of assault requires the plaintiff to prove that the defendant threatened the plaintiff who understood that a physical attack was imminent. The defendant must have the present ability to carry out either a harmful or an offensive touching of the plaintiff's body. President Trump's retweeting a GIF of him striking Hillary Clinton in the back with a golf ball is not actionable as a battery because there was no physical touching, nor is there an action for assault because the imminence requirement is not met. Arguably, a court could find assault when threatening words are received over the Internet, as the recipient may have no way of knowing whether the sender is nearby. At least one case has held that threats from a telephone user one room away can constitute assault.

Courts have yet to accept the argument that a woman "virtually groped" in an online game has an action for the tort of battery.[16] A young woman was humiliated when playing an online video game:

> Another player, BigBro442, noticed that she was a female, approached her avatar, and grabbed her. [The young woman] yelled, "Stop!" which apparently emboldened BigBro442. He then chased her avatar around the virtual world making grabbing and pinching motions near her chest. He even went so far as to shove his avatar's hand at her private area.[17]

The gamer suffered apprehension and humiliation from this virtual incident but in an action for assault cannot satisfy the imminence element. Cyberspace assault cases may never develop because virtual space cannot satisfy the requirement of imminent harm.

(2) Internet-Related Battery

Battery is the tort of intentionally creating an unconsented harmful or offensive contact with a person. The plaintiff's fear of being struck or offensively touched is the essence of assault, whereas a battery addresses the actual physical harm or offensive touching by the defendant. Malicious hackers attacked the nonprofit Epilepsy Foundation website by injecting JavaScript into some posts that redirected the users' browsers to a page whose pulsating pattern of squares flashing in different colors was calculated to trigger seizures in epileptics.[18]

The victims of this vicious attack might have a clear case for battery but not for assault because the attack occurred without warning. Photo and pattern-sensitive sufferers would need to convince courts to stretch the law to prove it was substantially certain that epileptics would suffer harmful or offensive contact, even though there was no physical touching. The epileptics, however, did not file a tort lawsuit because they had no way of identifying the perpetrators.

[C] Intentional Infliction of Emotional Distress

The intentional infliction of emotional distress (IIED), sometimes called the tort of outrage, has the greatest potential for addressing Internet wrongs such as stalking or cyberbullying because of its inherent flexibility. A plaintiff in a cybertort case must prove three things to prevail in an IIED lawsuit:

(1) The conduct involved must be extreme and outrageous;

(2) The actor must either intend that his conduct will inflict severe emotional distress or know that there is a high probability that he will cause severe emotional distress; and

(3) The conduct must in fact cause severe emotional distress.

Mass culture frequently portrays cyberbullying and other online cruelty. In Lena Dunham's hugely successful HBO series, *Girls,* Marnie, played by Allison Williams, unsuccessfully tries to convince a customer service representative at YouTube to remove a music video cover of Edie Brickell's 1988 song "What I Am," which Marnie's ex-boyfriend had posted to humiliate her. The YouTube representative refuses to take down Marnie's video, telling her only her ex-boyfriend can request removal. Demeaning comments left by viewers greatly upset Marnie. She quits her job after catching her boss and a coworker laughing at her music video during a break.

Marnie's ex-boyfriend's cruel act of posting this video would fall far short of the threshold necessary to constitute the tort of outrage. Courts require that the outrageous conduct be truly extreme. Rants that might be outrageous in the neighborhood will typically not be actionable in a tweetstorm or barrage of tweets designed to humiliate.

In a real-life cyberbullying example of the severity necessary to qualify for the IIED tort, a girl's classmates created a bogus Facebook page in her name, with photos and posts that were distorted to make her appear to be overweight, racist, sexually promiscuous and an illegal drug user. Even though the website was a cruel hoax, her tort of outrage lawsuit is very unlikely to succeed because the conduct was not so extreme as to violate all bounds of decency. Most online cyberbullying never ripens into a tort of outrage lawsuit, unless it involves racial and sexual discrimination in the workplace.

In *Butler v. Continental Express, Inc.*,[19] Rainer Krebs, a pilot for Continental Express, used a software application to superimpose a female coworker's face onto nude pictures of a woman in sexually suggestive poses. He posted these pornographic images on the Internet as well as Continental's intranet. A jury awarded the female pilot compensatory and punitive damages for the intentional infliction of emotional distress and other torts. Repeated threats of physical harm directed toward the plaintiff, stated in graphic emails and Internet bulletin board postings, were sufficiently outrageous to support a claim of intentional infliction of emotional distress.[20]

§ 3.4: PERSONAL PROPERTY TORTS IN CYBERSPACE

[A] Virtual Trespasses to Chattels in Cyberspace

The trespass to chattels tort, which originated in medieval England, compensated persons for damages to their tangible personal property, such as cows, horses and farm implements.[21] A neighbor who borrowed a horse without permission but returned it to the rightful owner after riding it would be liable for damages during the period of dispossession. Similarly, if a farmer borrowed his neighbor's mule to plow his field without permission, he would be liable for interfering with his neighbor's chattel. The elements of trespass to chattels require that:

(1) There must be a disturbance of the plaintiff's possession; and

(2) The disturbance may be either by an actual taking; a physical seizing and taking hold of the goods, removing them from their owner; or by exercising a control or authority over them inconsistent with the owner's possession.

Modern courts have stretched this preindustrial English tort to computer viruses, scraping websites and distributing spam email. The major difficulty in most trespass to chattels claims is to prove injury in fact as illustrated in *Intel Corp. v. Hamidi*.[22] In this case, Ken Hamidi, an ex-employee of Intel, created an anti-Intel website. Hamidi transmitted messages critical of the company's employment practices to over 30,000 Intel employees on six separate occasions. When Intel was unable to block or otherwise filter out Hamidi's messages, it sent a letter demanding that its ex-employee stop transmitting the mass emails to its current employees. After Hamidi refused to heed this warning, Intel filed suit based on trespass to chattels.

The California Superior Court issued a preliminary injunction, prohibiting Hamidi from sending further email messages to Intel employees. The California Court of Appeals upheld the injunction enjoining Hamidi and his nonprofit organization from sending the unsolicited emails. The appeals court found that Intel was likely to prevail on its claim that Hamidi trespassed onto Intel's computer system. However, the California Supreme Court reversed this decision, holding that Hamidi's emails to current Intel employees did not constitute trespass of Intel's email system because his messages had not caused any proven damages.

The California Supreme Court found Hamidi's emails intermeddled with, but did not dispossess Intel of its computer system, and therefore these actions caused no actual damages. The court analogized Hamidi's unwelcome emails to an unpleasant letter that caused no damage to the recipient's mailbox. Intel's argument that its computer users suffered damages because Hamidi's emails exposed them to a high risk of identity fraud was not sufficient to satisfy trespass to chattels' "present injury" requirement.

(1) Calculating Damages for Cybertrespass

Although an email service provider's customers are inconvenienced by being subjected to a barrage of pornographic images, get-rich-quick schemes, health products and other annoying "spam," finding an appropriate level of compensation is a difficult task. In many cases, the Internet Service Provider (ISP) seeks damages for the cost of responding to subscriber complaints, for storing large numbers of messages and for transmitting electronic communications.

Courts have not settled on any widely-accepted methodology for compensating companies victimized by recidivist spammers. America Online (AOL), for example, claimed in one early case that the cost of each email sent to AOL members was $.00078 (i.e., 78 cents per thousand pieces of email) "even without considering personnel or other costs associated with the computer's operation."[23] The federal court's award to the ISP was $101,400, computed by $.00078 times 130,000,000 spam emails. To date, the AOL judge has been the only service providers to use successfully deploy this methodology.

(2) Web Robots as Trespassers

EBay Inc. v. Bidder's Edge, Inc.,[24] is the leading case stretching the trespass to chattels to Bidder's Edge (BE) for using web crawlers to aggregate auction listings. Bidder's Edge enabled consumers to do comparison-shopping by viewing aggregated listings from numerous other auction websites. BE accessed the eBay site about 100,000 times per day, accounting for between 1 and 2 percent of the information requests received by eBay and a slightly smaller percentage of the data transferred by eBay. Sixty-nine percent of Bidder's Edge's aggregated data was gathered from eBay. The parties were unable to negotiate a license agreement permitting Bidder's Edge from use bots to gather data from eBay in order to notify its users about when auction prices changed. Bidder's Edge did not accept eBay's offer for a license agreement and thus eBay notified BE that its activities were no longer permitted.

EBay sought a preliminary injunction against BE for trespassing on its website—trespass to chattels—as well as for a variety of other business torts, including trade libel and interference with prospective advantage. The court found sufficient proof of threatened harm to support a preliminary injunction. The *eBay* court reasoned: "If BE's activity is allowed to continue unchecked, it would encourage other auction aggregators to conduct similar, high-traffic searches of the eBay system such that eBay would suffer irreparable harm from reduced system performance, system unavailability, or data losses," ruling that:

> If the court were to hold otherwise, it would likely encourage other auction aggregators to crawl the eBay site, potentially to the point of denying effective access to eBay's customers. If preliminary injunctive relief was denied, and other aggregators began to crawl the eBay site, there appears to be little doubt that the load on eBay's computer system would qualify as a substantial impairment of condition or value.

Had this case been decided differently, eBay might not have evolved into an Internet icon because new entrants would piggyback on eBay's listings. EBay charges higher selling fees than other online auction sites because it attracts more customers, which produces more rapid sales at higher prices. If other auction sites could gather and display all online auctions on their websites, sellers would transfer their business to the cheapest auction site since customers would be able to go to websites that amalgamated selling prices from every site. The downside of this decision is that consumers do not have the ability to compare prices on different online auction services.

[B] Conversion in Cyberspace

Trespass to chattels and conversion are the only two recognized personal property torts, and each has evolved to address Internet harms. The main difference between conversion and trespass to chattels is the degree of interference or damages caused to a computer system. Conversion is the appropriate tort if a malware creator destroys or locks up a computer's hard drive. In contrast, a trespass to chattels is an act that falls short of conversion in that the damages or interference is not as great. These two personal property torts differ only in the remedy granted plaintiffs. For trespass to chattels, the defendant is only liable for the damage done, whereas a converter must pay the full market value of the personal property.

In the first and largest cyberconversion of a domain name in history, the plaintiff was awarded $65 million for theft of the domain name, sex.com. This case involved forgery, bankruptcy and the defendant's flight to Mexico to avoid paying the judgment. In *Kremen v. Cohen*,[25] ex-convict Stephen Cohen forged a letter to a domain name registrar, Network Solutions.

In the faxed document, Cohen claimed he was the new contact person for Online Classifieds, Inc., the owner of the domain name, and requested Network Solutions to deregister sex.com. Network Solutions made no effort to determine the authenticity of the faxed letter and instead transferred the domain name, sex.com, to Cohen. When Gary Kremen contacted Network Solutions some time later, questioning the transfer of the domain name, an administrator informed him it was too late to undo it. Cohen went on to build sex.com into an extremely profitable cyberporn empire.

Gary Kremen filed suit against Stephen Cohen, seeking damages and return of the domain name. A federal court awarded him $40 million in compensatory damages and another $25 million in punitive damages. Cohen fled to Mexico, concealing his ill-gotten gains in offshore locations beyond the reach of the legal process. Kremen next filed suit against Network Solutions for the tort of conversion because it had not detected that the faxed letter requesting delisting was a forgery. The district court, however, reasoned that Network Solutions was not liable for conversion because domain names were intangible and, therefore, not personal property.

On appeal, the Ninth Circuit reversed the lower court's decision, holding that the defendant converted a domain name, despite its intangible nature. The court reasoned that corporations could be liable when they take away someone's shares, even though these are merely pieces of paper that symbolize intangible assets. Cohen was arrested in Mexico on October 28, 2005, for civil contempt for his failure to disclose his assets and returned to the United States where he was incarcerated. Cohen was released a year later. Kremen's attorneys have been unable to locate Cohen's concealed assets. Stephen Cohen has not paid Gary Kremen a single cent, and it is unlikely that he ever will satisfy the multi-million-dollar judgment.

§ 3.5: INTENTIONAL INFORMATION-BASED & CYBER-BUSINESS TORTS

[A] Cyber-Business Torts

Business torts in cyberspace are increasing steadily with the growth of e-commerce. Nevertheless, companies are rarely liable for the tort of interference with contract in fact patterns arising out of the Internet. In *Search King, Inc. v. Google*,[26] the plaintiff sued Google for tortious interference with contractual relations under Oklahoma law. Search King, who builds digital advertising campaigns, filed an interference with contract claim against Google after its revised search algorithm dropped Search King's page rank. Search King alleged Google's devaluation of its page ranks limited the readership of its clients' online advertisements.

The court dismissed Search King's claim that Google intentionally manipulated its PageRank algorithm to harm the advertiser's business opportunities. The federal court held that there was no likelihood that Search King could prevail because the PageRank Google assigns to a site is classified as an opinion protected by the First Amendment. As long as a page ranking statement is not "provably false" it is privileged and therefore not actionable.

[B] Cyberfraud or Intentional Misrepresentations on the Internet

Cyberfraud occurs when an individual uses the Internet to commit the intentional torts of fraud, deceit, or misrepresentation. The elements of an intentional misrepresentation claim in cyberspace are the same as in the real world:

(1) A knowingly false representation by the defendant;

(2) An intent to deceive or induce reliance;

(3) Justifiable reliance by the plaintiff; and

(4) Resulting damages.

Cyberfrauds are enabled by the anonymity of the Internet and the ensuing difficulty of locating the wrongdoer. Despite the ubiquity of fraud on the Internet, relatively few plaintiffs have been successful in collecting an award. In a Texas case, a seller of a computer system was found liable for fraudulent inducement for convincing a buyer to enter into a computer contract. The seller's false representation was that untrained personnel could operate the computer system and that the software would be "bug-free."[27] The buyer prevailed because neither of the seller's statements was true.

Companies are defrauded by click farms when they are charged for clicks on ads that are created by robots, or low paid Third World operatives, rather than real consumers. *Silicon Valley*, a television show that chronicles the trials and tribulations of the fictional tech start-up company, portrays a character who enlists the help of a Bangladesh click farm to inflate the website's daily active user count to impress potential investors. The show cuts from the modern world of California to a large, dark, crowded room overseas that houses rows of individuals who seemingly spend their days repetitively creating fictitious user profiles and clicking through programs throughout the day. In real life, the deceived investors will often face daunting jurisdictional and procedural obstacles in recovering their losses.

[C] Online Defamation

(1) The Historical Roots of Defamation

Defamation is a false statement that tends to injure plaintiff in his trade, profession, or community standing, or lower him in the estimation of the community, when both the words and the entire context in which the statement occurs are taken into account. Four elements are necessary to establish a defamation cause of action:

(1) A false and defamatory statement concerning another;

(2) An unprivileged publication to a third party;

(3) Fault of negligence or greater on the part of the publisher; and

(4) Resulting injury.

"Defamatory words" are, by definition, words which tend to harm the reputation of another so as to lower the person in the estimation of the community, to deter others from associating or dealing with the person, or otherwise expose a person to contempt or ridicule.

Defamation involves the invasion of a person's interest in his or her reputation and good name, but only applies to false statements of fact not opinion. Opinions have been protected speech ever since the 1732 trial of John Peter Zenger, the publisher of the *New York Journal*, for seditious libel. James Hamilton, who represented Zenger, argued:

> The question before the Court and you, Gentlemen of the jury, is not of small or private concern. It is not the cause of one poor printer, nor of New York alone, which you are now trying. No! It may in its consequence affect every free man that lives under a British government on the main of America. It is the best cause. It is the cause of liberty.[28]

The jury set Zenger free, creating an important precedent for freedom of the press. The U.S. Constitution, adopted at the Philadelphia Convention in 1787, recognized free expression as the First Amendment to the U.S. Constitution that applies equally well to cyberspace postings, shielding statements of opinion and allowing the public criticism of officials.

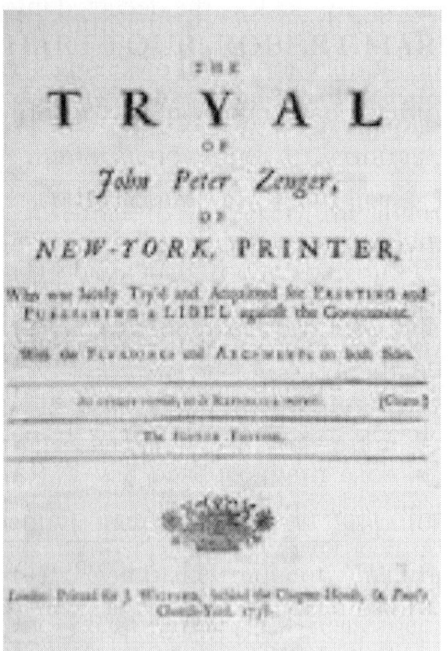
THE
TRYAL
OF
John Peter Zenger,
OF
NEW-YORK, PRINTER,

The trial of John Peter Zenger, arising from a criticism of a local governor, was a monumental decision for the freedom of the press. Truth was found to be a defense against libel.
"No nation ancient or modern ever lost the liberty of freely speaking, writing, or publishing their sentiments, but forthwith lost their liberty in general and became slaves."
—John Peter Zenger
Source of Photo: Historical Society of the New York Courts

The *Zenger* precedent that opinions are protected speech has been extended to cyberspace torts. A panel of Massachusetts Superior Court judges ruled unanimously that the Boston newspaper's articles attributing the suicide of Brad Delp, the lead singer of the rock group *Boston*, to the actions of a fellow band member were not defamatory. The court reasoned that the band members' statements were opinions, not fact and therefore, were not libelous. The newspaper's story drew upon interviews with the lead singer's ex-wife and several of his friends. The court reasoned that the "plaintiffs cannot prove or disprove the actual cause of his suicide. That secret went to the grave with him."

(2) Defamation for Individuals

Defamation is comprised of the complementary torts of libel for written statements and slander for oral statements. A statement must be false to be defamatory. Statements of opinion cannot form the basis of a defamation claim because opinions cannot be proven true or false. A common-law action for defamation requires proof of false statement, communicated by speech, conduct, or in writing to another person other than person defamed, and unprivileged communication "which tends to harm one's reputation so as to lower him or her in the estimation of community or to deter third persons from associating or dealing with him or her."

For example, an executive who makes false, negative statements about a former employee when providing an employment reference would be liable for defamation unless protected by a qualified privilege. The defense of qualified privilege permits free communication in certain relationships without the risk of an action for defamation. If a qualified privilege applies to a statement made by an employer giving a reference, the plaintiff must prove that the person who made the defamatory statement acted intentionally, recklessly, or with malice.

One who republishes a defamatory statement may be liable to the same extent as the original speaker because each new publication theoretically results in an additional harm to the plaintiff's reputation. However, a republisher is liable only if the original statement is defamatory. J.K. Rowling, the author of the *Harry Potter* series, sued Associated Newspapers, the owner of the media website, *Daily Mail*, for publisher's liability. Rowling filed suit after the newspaper published a story claiming that members of her congregation gossiped about her for being a single mother.

Rowling settled the case after the Associated Newspapers agreed to publish a statement that its story was false, and agreed to donate money to charity.

(3) Trade Libel for Businesses

Companies cannot be defamed, but they can file suit for trade libel, which redresses financial losses such as lost profit when their business reputation is tarnished. Fraudulent consumer reviews created by websites are the leading source of trade libel actions. To prevail in a trade libel case, the plaintiff must prove that the defendant knowingly or recklessly published a false statement that disparaged the products or services of a competitor.

In *Patterson v. Grant-Herms*,[29] Jennifer Patterson, a Southwest Airlines gate agent filed a civil lawsuit against Natalie Grant-Herms, for libel. The gate agent contended that Grant-Herms defamed her in tweets, Facebook statements and postings about a confrontation between them that occurred when the plaintiff and her three children attempted to board an airplane in violation of Southwest Airlines policy. One Grant-Hermes posting stated "I fly @southwestair at least 75x/year. Just had the WORST experience. Me; A1, Sadie A1 Gracie A34. Woman refused to let Gracie board w/me."

The statement need not have named Patterson explicitly if a reasonable reader of the posting would know that the statement was about her. The Tennessee Appeals court ruled that the statements were protectable as opinions, concluding that the words attributed to the gate agent could not reasonably be construed to portray Patterson as one who would endanger a four-year-old's welfare. However, the appeals court reversed the trial court and remanded the issue of whether Grant-Herme's statements about the agent constituted publicity that places her in a false light to the public. Southwest Airlines would have a trade libel case on these facts, while their flight attendant would have an action for defamation.

Trade libel cases are very difficult to win. In *Global Telemedia International, Inc., v. Doe 1*,[30] a publicly traded telecommunications company filed suit against anonymous posters on the Raging Bull message board. The court concluded that the company could not prevail because the postings were opinions. The online discussion was "part of an on-going, free-wheeling and highly animated exchange" about the company that was "full of hyperbole, invective, and short-hand phrases." To rise to the level of trade libel there must be a false statement of fact, which induces readers not to deal with the company.

(4) Libelous Internet Postings

Under the law of defamation a libelous or slanderous statement must be published by means of some communication to a third-party. Publication occurs if the statement at issue has been communicated to a third person other than the plaintiff. Courts have had little difficulty extending the law of libel to websites, blogs and Internet forums. Nevertheless, there are difficult issues raised by the Internet.

For example, libel cases are judged according to community standards as to what will incite hatred or contempt against the plaintiff. With hundreds of diverse cultures connected to the Internet, it is unclear how courts should define community for purposes of libel. A statement that might be defamatory in Jeddah, Saudi Arabia would be non-objectionable in Boston, Massachusetts. Courts have long held that defamation is determined by both the content and the context for a given communication.

A photograph of Evel Knieval with his arms around both his wife and another woman was captioned: "Evel Knievel proves that you're never too old to be a pimp." This photograph published on ESPN's Extreme Sport was ruled to be not defamatory by the Ninth Circuit because the term "pimp" would not be seen as a negative by most of this daredevil's fans. Knievel argued that the caption hurt him with his advertisers and sponsors, a more conservative community. The Ninth Circuit dismissed his case, ruling that no reasonable reader would interpret the caption to mean that Knievel literally was a pimp.

(5) Defamation Per Se

The injury resulting from a defamatory statement may include nonpecuniary or general damages such as injury to reputation, personal humiliation, embarrassment and mental anguish even when no special damages such as loss of income is claimed. However, when a plaintiff proves publication of words that are defamatory *per se*, the elements of falsity and malice or fault are presumed. In contrast, the plaintiff has the burden of establishing special damages, which include the loss of customers or business, the loss of employment, or something of financial value in a case where the words are not defamatory *per se*. Words which expressly or implicitly accuse another of criminal conduct, or which by their very nature tend to injure one's personal or professional reputation are considered defamatory *per se*. When a plaintiff proves publication of words that are defamatory *per se*, the elements of falsity and malice or fault are presumed, but may be rebutted by the defendant.

Under common law, defamatory statements are actionable *per se*, if the published statement fell into one of four categories:

(1) Imputation of a crime,

(2) Statements injurious to one's trade, business, or occupation,

(3) Charges of having a loathsome disease or

(4) Charging that a woman is unchaste.

These traditional categories of defamation *per se* must be updated to redress new forms of reputational harm in cyberspace.

(6) Balancing Libel vs. Anonymous Speech

Anonymous speech employed in blogs or chatrooms receives First Amendment protection. However, the First Amendment does not shield the content of allegedly defamatory materials, only the source. The degree of scrutiny courts employ in evaluating the enforceability of restrictions on speech "varies depending on the circumstances and type of speech at issue," and "the nature of the speech should be a driving force in choosing a standard by which to balance the rights of anonymous speakers."[31]

A "John Doe subpoena" is served on a website to unveil the identity of an anonymous poster. When considering whether to issue a requested John Doe subpoena, courts balance the need to unveil the anonymous speaker to protect the victim's rights against the First Amendment. Courts weigh four factors; whether:

(1) The subpoena was issued in good faith;

(2) The information sought relates to a core claim or defense;

(3) The identifying information is directly and materially relevant to that claim or defense; and

(4) The information sought is sufficient to establish or to disprove the claim or defense is unavailable from any other source.

A Seattle company filed a libel lawsuit against anonymous users of Yahoo! message boards who were later unveiled with the help of John Doe subpoenas. Copyright owners sought John Doe subpoenas to reveal Verizon's customers who allegedly downloaded copyrighted music or video without authorization. A standard discovery request will be for electronic files, email messages (with attachments), Instant Message communications, and/or other communication transmitted on a provider's service for a designated period.[32]

(7) First Amendment Defenses to Defamation Cases

(a) How the U.S. Supreme Court Constitutionalized Libel Law

In 1964, the U.S. Supreme Court in *New York Times v. Sullivan*[33] held for the first time that the constitutional protection given to speech and the press limits state defamation lawsuits brought by public officials. The Court in *Sullivan* required a public official to prove defamation by "actual" malice. A private individual can maintain a suit for defamation if the publisher of the allegedly false and defamatory statement has acted negligently in disseminating the falsehood. In contrast, public figure plaintiffs must demonstrate that the allegedly false and defamatory statement was made with "actual malice." The U.S. Supreme Court defines actual malice as "knowledge that the information was false" or was published "with reckless disregard of whether it was false or not." In defamation cases, "actual malice" is a term of art that focuses on what the defendant knew about the veracity of the statements, and should not be confused with ill will or "malice" in the ordinary sense of the term. The Court extended the actual malice standard from public officials to public figures only three years later.[34]

The level of fault that a defamation plaintiff must plead under U.S. law depends on the plaintiff's status, and there are three recognized classes of plaintiffs: (1) general public figures, i.e., public officials or persons whose conduct is generally a matter of interest to the public; (2) limited public figures, i.e., persons whose conduct is of interest to certain portions of the public as to a limited range of issues; and (3) private figures. Public officials and public figure plaintiffs (general and limited) must plead actual malice, that is, knowledge that the statement at issue was false or reckless disregard of whether it was false or not. Plaintiffs who are only private figures must prove negligence by at least the standard of negligence.

(b) Public Officials in Cyberlibel Litigation

In cyberlibel cases, public officials and public figures must prove the defamation was done with actual malice. In U.S. election cycles, candidates are frequently subject to scathing attacks, many of which are defamatory and untrue. In the 2016 Republican Party primaries, Donald Trump threatened to sue Ted Cruz for defamation, unless he apologized for making "totally untrue" statements in a campaign advertisement that showed Trump advocating liberal positions on abortion and other issues in the past. Trump accompanied his threat with harsh words for Cruz:

> "He is a liar and these ads and statements made by Cruz are clearly desperate moves by a guy who is tanking in the polls—watching his campaign go up in flames finally explains Cruz's logo," Trump replied in a statement. He went on to pledge, if I want to bring a lawsuit it would be legitimate. Likewise, if I want to bring the lawsuit regarding Senator Cruz being a natural born Canadian I will do so.[35]

Ted Cruz, a Harvard University Law School graduate who had clerked for Chief Justice William Rehnquist of the U.S. Supreme Court, showed little concern about Donald Trump's threat of a defamation lawsuit. Trump is a public figure and, as President, now qualifies as a public official. Under U.S. defamation law, it is almost impossible for either public figures or public officials to pursue defamation lawsuits because of the difficulty of proving the defendant's actual malice by clear and convincing evidence.

Clear and convincing evidence is a burden of proof greater than the usual "preponderance of evidence" standard in civil cases but less than the criminal law standard of "beyond a reasonable doubt." America's "profound national commitment to the principle that debate on public issues should be uninhibited, robust, and wide-open,"[36] allows attacks, even outright falsehoods, to be leveled by and against candidates for public office, as well as elected officials. Donald Trump has called for amending libel laws to provide public figures with more effective remedies against defamatory statements.

Lindsay Lohan and her mother filed a lawsuit against Fox News after a guest stated that Ms. Lohan and her mother did cocaine together. In 2015, the trial court dismissed the libel lawsuit, holding that both Ms. Lohan and her mother were public figures, so actual malice was required, and the comments were not made with actual malice. The judge is reported to have stated that it was a fact that Ms. Lohan did cocaine, referring to an interview with Oprah Winfrey where Lohan admitted to this fact. Truth is an absolute defense in libel and slander lawsuits.

Even a local official who is not well known outside a locality is classified as a public figure. In *Ghanam v. John Does,*[37] a city official filed a defamation action against anonymous commentators who posted accusations on an Internet message board dedicated to local politics that the official had been stealing road salt and vehicle tires. The Michigan Appeals Court denied a motion to unveil the anonymous commentators, ruling that the city official had not provided reasonable notice of the lawsuit to them and observing that, "Internet message boards and similar communication platforms are generally regarded as containing statements of pure opinion rather than statements or implications of actual, provable fact."[38] The court characterized the difference between Internet messages and those made in standard print publications:

> [A]ny reader familiar with the culture of . . . most electronic bulletin boards . . . would know that board culture encourages discussion participants to play fast and loose with facts . . . . Indeed, the very fact that most of the posters remain anonymous, or pseudonymous, is a cue to discount their statements accordingly.[39]

(c) Public Figures

Where the defamation plaintiff is a public figure, the First and Fourteenth Amendments to the federal Constitution mandate that the plaintiff prove actual malice by clear and convincing evidence. The test for determining actual malice in a public figure defamation action against media defendant is subjective. A public figure must show that the defendant knew the statement was false, in fact entertained serious doubts as to the truth of a publication, or had a high degree of awareness of probable falsity. A federal court once said that defining "a public figure is much like trying to nail a jellyfish to the wall."[40] Whether an individual is a public official, public figure, limited public figure or private person is a question of law for the court to resolve.

Relatively few people will qualify as a general-purpose public figure because the threshold is quite high. In a current defamation suit, singer Ciara sued her baby's father, rapper Future, for $15 million for threatening and libeling her fiancé, Seattle Seahawks' QB Russell Wilson, on a social network. Ciara claimed that she feared for Wilson's life after the rapper posted various threats and demeaned Wilson's character. Ciara argued that football emojis with guns pointing in the couple's direction is a clear threat. Ciara and Russell Wilson are examples of people classified as public figures because they are well-known celebrities. If either Ciara or Wilson files a defamation case against Future, they will need to prove actual malice.

(d) Limited Public Figures

In contrast, limited-purpose public figures are those who have voluntarily injected themselves into a specific public controversy. This makes them public figures only for that limited range of issues. For example, when we testified before Congress urging that they not place federal limitations on the remedy of punitive damages, we thrust ourselves into the forefront of a controversy. Bloggers that weigh in on a public controversy can also qualify as limited public figures. To qualify as a limited-purpose public figure for a defamation claim a plaintiff must have: (1) successfully invited public attention to its views in an effort to influence others prior to the incident that is the subject of litigation, (2) voluntarily injected itself into a public controversy related to the subject of the litigation, (3) assumed a position of prominence in the public controversy, and (4) maintained regular and continuing access to the media.[41]

The U.S. Supreme Court, in *Gertz v. Robert Welch, Inc.*,[42] distinguished between general-purpose public figures and limited-purpose public figures. A general-purpose public figure has such "pervasive fame or notoriety so that she is a public figure for all purposes and in all contexts." General-purpose public figures include celebrities who are famous enough to be featured in salacious supermarket tabloids, whereas limited public figures inject themselves in public debates and may not be famous or well known.

Plaintiffs rarely can demonstrate by clear and convincing evidence that the defendant knew the information was false at the time of publication. The "publication" element of a defamation claim requires a defendant to have published or knowingly participated in publishing the defamation. In *Gertz v. Robert Welch Inc.*, the U.S. Supreme Court noted that:

> [t]hose who, by reason of the notoriety of their achievements or the vigor and success with which they seek the public's attention, are properly classed as public figures and those who hold governmental office may recover for injury to reputation only on clear and convincing proof that the defamatory falsehood was made with knowledge of its falsity or with reckless disregard for the truth."[43]

Typically, limited purpose public figures are those who have become public figures for a specific range of issues. To decide if a party is a limited purpose public figure, a court will examine an individual's participation in the controversy from which the alleged defamation arose, and decide if he or she has attained general notoriety in the community because of the participation. In *TotalExposurecom Ltd. v. Miami Valley Broadcasting Corp.*, the business entities that operated exotic entertainment clubs and an Internet website featuring x-rated videos were classified as limited purpose public figures. The adult entertainment entities filed a defamation claim against a broadcasting corporation, a local affiliate and a TV reporter who broadcasted a news story reporting that dancers were having sex live on the Internet.

The federal court applied three factors in determining that the entities were limited public figures, requiring application of actual malice standard to defamation claims: (1) the notoriety of the business to an average individual in areas where the business has a presence; (2) the nature of the business with respect to creating a high profile or prominence in public perception; and (3) the frequency and intensity of media scrutiny of the company. The federal court found that the adult entertainment entities were unquestionably limited purpose public figures and were notorious to average individuals in Ohio due to their operation of several nightclubs. Furthermore, the court found that very nature adult entertainment is controversial and has a high public profile.

Qualifying as a Limited Public Figure

Three things are necessary to prove that the plaintiff is a limited public figure:

(1) That there has been a public controversy;

(2) That the plaintiff has played a sufficiently central role in the controversy; and

(3) That the alleged defamatory statements have been germane to the plaintiff's participation in the controversy.

A "limited-purpose" public figure in cyberspace will generally be an individual who voluntarily injects himself, or is drawn, into a public controversy in the blogosphere, thereby becoming a public figure for a limited range of issues. It is unclear whether the mere posting of comments on a website voluntarily thrusts a plaintiff into a public controversy, or categorizes the plaintiff as a limited-purpose public figure. If a court determines that a plaintiff is a limited public figure, the plaintiff will need to prove that a defendant made an allegedly defamatory statement with malice, which is a nearly impossible burden to meet.

(e) Private Person

In a common law defamation cause of action that does not involve a public figure, there are only three elements: (1) a false statement; (2) communicated by speech, conduct or in writing to a person other than the person defamed; and, (3) the communication is unprivileged and tends to harm one's reputation so as to lower him or her in the estimation of the community or to deter third persons from associating or dealing with him or her.

(8) SLAPP Motions

To prevail on an anti-Strategic Lawsuits Against Public Participation (SLAPP) motion, the moving defendant must make a prima facie showing that the plaintiff's suit arises from an act in furtherance of the defendant's constitutional right to free speech. In *Makaeff v. Trump University*,[44] a former student filed a class action alleging deceptive business practices against Trump University, which offered real estate seminars to small groups of students. Trump University asserted a counterclaim for defamation. California's anti-Strategic Lawsuits Against Public Participation (SLAPP) provides for the pre-trial dismissal of certain defamation actions that masquerade as ordinary lawsuits but are intended to deter ordinary people from exercising their political or legal rights. To prevail on an anti-Strategic Lawsuits Against Public Participation (SLAPP) motion, the moving defendant must make a prima facie showing that the plaintiff's suit arises from an act in furtherance of the defendant's constitutional right to free speech.

The federal district court held that Makaeff had satisfied her initial burden of showing that Trump University's claim was in furtherance of her free speech rights. She published statements to "unknown third parties and the general public on the Internet." Makaeff contended that she posted these statements "to alert other consumers of my opinions and experience with Trump University," and to "inform other consumers of my opinion that Trump University did not deliver what it promised."

The court found Makaeff's explanation plausible and concluded that she spoke out with the goal of stopping Trump University from defrauding other consumers. The Ninth Circuit found that at least some of her statements about the educational experience at Trump University arose under California's anti-SLAPP statute dismissing the for profit school's defamation claim.

§ 3.6: NEGLIGENCE-BASED CYBERTORTS

[A] Negligent Security

Premises liability, where an individual injured by a third party tries to hold liable the owner or tenant of the property in which a criminal injury is inflicted, first evolved in the 1990s. With negligent computer security, the plaintiff seeks to hold a website or other defendant liable for enabling a cybercrime. A major consideration in the decision to impose liability for negligent computer security is whether a company could have foreseen the particular harm resulting from its existing security precautions and whether cost-effective measures would have significantly reduced the risk. The first wave of computer security lawsuits stemmed from claims alleging that defective software offered inadequate security and was unreliable in protecting network perimeters.

A plaintiff alleging inadequate computer security must demonstrate that the defendant had a duty of care to protect the plaintiff against injury or loss. The traditional formula for negligence asks whether:

(1) The defendant owed a duty to the foreseeable plaintiff;

(2) The defendant breached that duty to the plaintiff;

(3) The plaintiff suffered an injury or damages; and

(4) The breach of the duty of reasonable care was the foreseeable (i.e., proximate) cause of the injury.

The issue of proximate cause asks whether an injured individual's conduct was so unusual, extraordinary or bizarre that it is unforeseeable. In a New York subway case,[45] the court ruled that a passenger's reckless conduct of attempting to enter train by squeezing through spring-loaded gate between two train cars was unforeseeable and that the city transit authority was not liable for passenger's injuries. Thus, the court used proximate cause to cut off the city's liability where the connection between the breach and the harm suffered by the rider was an improbable freak occurrence.

[B] Negligence *Per Se* & HIPAA's Privacy & Security Rules

The Health Insurance Portability and Accountability Act of 1996 (HIPAA) ordered the Secretary of the U.S. Department of Health and Human Services (HHS) to develop regulations protecting the privacy and security of certain health information of patients. To fulfill this requirement, HHS published the HIPAA Privacy Rule and the HIPAA Security Rule. The Privacy Rule or Standards for Privacy of Individually Identifiable Health Information, established national standards for the protection of certain health information.

Prior to 1996, health care providers had not developed industry-level security standards or general requirements for protecting information in the health care industry. HHS proposed the HIPAA Privacy and Security Rules in response to rapidly evolving technologies for the maintenance of patient records as the health care industry moved from paper to e-records. Health care providers implemented electronic information systems to pay claims, answer eligibility questions, provide health information and conduct a host of other administrative and clinically based functions.

Software providers and information technology vendors must be HIPAA-compliant or they may not design electronic networks for covered entities. HIPAA imposes multiple duties on covered entities to protect the confidentiality of patients' medical records including to:

(1) Ensure the confidentiality, integrity, and availability of all electronic protected health information (e-PHI) they create, receive, maintain or transmit;

(2) and protect against reasonably anticipated threats to the security or integrity of the information;

(3) Protect against reasonably anticipated, impermissible uses or disclosures; and

(4) Ensure compliance by their workforce.[46]

HIPAA's Security Rule defines "confidentiality" to mean that patient information will not be made available or disclosed to unauthorized persons. The Security Rule promotes the two additional goals of maintaining the integrity and availability of electronic protected health information. Under the Security Rule, "integrity" means that e-PHI will not be altered or destroyed in an unauthorized manner. "Availability" means that e-PHI is accessible and usable on demand by an authorized person. The HIPAA Security and Privacy Rules imposes duties on providers to reasonably secure data and can be used to establish breach of the standard of care in negligence-based lawsuits arising out of inadequate computer security.

[C] Computer Security & Negligence *Per Se*

When a covered entity breaches HIPAA's Privacy and Security Rules, this violation can be the basis of a claim for negligence. If a health care provider is in violation of either of the HIPAA rules, a plaintiff's attorney can use this fact to demonstrate negligence. For example, a lawyer representing a psychiatric patient convinced the North Carolina Court of Appeals that a medical provider's breach of HIPAA's Security Rule was evidence that the provider breached a duty of care and was thus liable for negligent security.[47]

In the North Carolina case, a psychiatric patient of the Psychiatric Associates of Eastern Carolina filed an invasion of privacy and negligent infliction of emotional distress claim against the psychiatrist owner of the clinic and his office manager, charging that they had a personal vendetta against the patient and were snooping into her records. The Psychiatric Associates' patient charged that the psychiatrist allowed the office manager to misuse medical record access codes to expose her medical records to third parties. The court held that the plaintiff had sufficient evidence to support her claims that the unauthorized disclosure of medical information violated HIPAA's Privacy Rule, which gave the patient a negligence cause of action.

In a 2016 case against Tampa General Hospital, the plaintiffs contended that the health care system had an obligation to secure and safeguard patients' information and to utilize commercially reasonable methods to secure this data under HIPAA's Security Rule. The plaintiffs' class action lawsuit argued that the hospital knowingly disregarded standard principles relating to the security of patient data. In addition, the plaintiffs claimed that the hospital negligently failed to provide adequate supervision and oversight of the personal health information entrusted to it, despite the known likelihood of breach and misuse. In December 2016, the Tampa General Hospital agreed to settle the class action and pay every patient $10,000 to compensate for the security lapse that compromised their health information.[48] Class action awards typically are split between the class members after payment of the attorneys' fees and expenses.

[D] Negligent Enablement of Cybercrime

A company that releases software into the marketplace with known design defects may have liability under the law of torts. The first wave of computer security lawsuits stemmed from claims alleging that defective software offered inadequate security, rendering it unreliable in protecting network perimeters. A software maker may be subject to tort liability for racing to market despite grossly inadequate testing. In December of 2009, multiple restaurants filed suit because their inadequately secured software enabled data heists by Romanian cybercriminals. The suit charged the hardware and software developers as well as the service provider with failure to include standard security measures.

The cybercriminals exploited a security flaw to load keylogger code that enabled them to steal customers' credit card numbers. Committing one of the largest cybercrimes in history, intruders gained unauthorized access to forty million credit cards and transferred data from 200,000 cards from CardSystems Solution's computer network. The complaint charged CardSystems with numerous negligent acts, including insecure data handling practices, failure to maintain properly configured firewalls, failure to encrypt confidential customer data and violations of reasonable Internet security standards. The complaint also charged the financial services firm with violating a California state statute requiring it to inform customers of computer intrusions that might compromise their data. The parties in the CardSystems Solutions' class action entered into a confidential settlement.

In a 2016 class action, plaintiffs contended that Yahoo! did not adequately secure the personal information of its users. The plaintiffs compared Yahoo!'s promise to "take your privacy seriously" with the reality of substandard security. The complaint charged that hackers in Eastern Europe previously breached Yahoo!'s security systems by extracting email addresses and passwords stored unencrypted within a Yahoo! database. The hackers then posted these login credentials online, exposing Yahoo!'s lax security measures. Yahoo! acknowledged that it is likely that a state-sponsored actor compromised one billion accounts:

> The account information may have included names, email addresses, telephone numbers, dates of birth, hashed passwords and, in some cases, encrypted or unencrypted security questions and answers. The ongoing investigation suggests that stolen information did not include unprotected passwords, payment card data, or bank account information; payment card data and bank account information are not stored in the system that the investigation has found to be affected.[49]

In 2017, Verizon, Yahoo!'s parent company, reported that the data breach had impacted three billion accounts, making this by far the largest data breach in world history. The tort law issue is whether Yahoo! owes a duty of care to employ reasonable Internet security measures to protect personally identifiable information against hackers. Yahoo!'s delay in discovering and reporting the extent of the reach is likely to become an issue in any negligence cases filed against the search engine.

The cybersecurity standard of care is whether Yahoo! implemented reasonable technical measures that were readily available to protect its users. Current industry standards define reasonableness for the encryption of data, the necessary security standards for mobile devices and for the integrity of firewalls. The law firm representing the plaintiffs charges that "Yahoo has not offered users any assistance with identity theft protection, even though its users are now at a much higher risk of having their identities stolen and must pay out of their own pockets to protect themselves."[50]

A growing number of courts are finding companies liable for failing to protect their customers, employees and company information from cyberintrusions. Equifax's loss of 143 million American's personally identifiable records in 2017 could result in negligent computer security claims if the customers suffer damages from identity theft.[51] In 2017, Anthem, America's largest insurance company settled a data breach case for $115 million for negligently enabling a cybertheft of personal information of 80 million customers.[52] In 2016, Home Depot agreed to a settlement of $19.5 million for failing to secure the personally identifiable data of its customers. The settlement required that Home Depot pay $13 million to reimburse shoppers for their direct losses and another $6.5 million to monitor for potential identity theft.[53]

§ 3.7: ONLINE STRICT LIABILITY

[A] Defective 3D Products

Products liability holds manufacturers, distributors, suppliers, retailers, and anyone in the chain of distribution liable for placing a defective product into the hands of a consumer. Dangerously defective goods produced by three-dimensional printing is the latest iteration of products liability. But if a producer of a defective product uses his or her 3D printer for personal, household or family use, there is no professional seller and therefore no products liability. As 3D printing becomes more developed, it is likely that manufacturers will use this technology to produce consumer products on a large scale. There would be traditional products liability if faulty software caused a product to be defectively designed. Gerard Magliocca argues that defective 3D products may revitalize the common law of products liability:

> In a world of 3D printing, anyone could be a manufacturer. Let's say I make something from scratch in my 3D printer at home and that product (a toy, a cookie, a tool, a spare part) injures someone. Should we apply the same principles of products liability to that person that we would to a firm? Yes and no, I think. We probably won't require individuals to put warnings on what they make, but we may say that a design or manufacturing defect should lead to strict liability. Or would we say that a negligence standard should apply to homemade products?
>
> Now try this one on for size. I upload a file that will make some something to a website. Someone downloads my file, makes the item, and this injures someone. Is the author of the file on the hook for a design defect claim? What about the website? While this could depend on many factors, courts will again need to think hard about how products liability rules should be adapted to this ecosystem.[54]

Failure to warn could arise if the 3D manufacturer acquired knowledge of a known or developing profile of danger but took no action. It is possible that a single 3D product could be defective as part of a bad batch, which would be analogous to a manufacturing defect. A New York statute would prohibit the production of "firearms via 3D printer unless the maker is a licensed gunsmith. Additionally, the gunsmith would have to notify the NYPD and register the 3D-printed weapon within 72 hours of its creation."[55] To date, no court has decided a 3D printing case as a products liability action. The Internet of Things and 3D printing creates new challenges for products liability as a cause of action:

> What if there is a security breach and private information is obtained and even shared but not used. How do you quantify those damages? Damages related to privacy issues are intangible and hard to quantify. These types of damages also create legal questions of standing. In addition, how do you allocate responsibility for damages? Does legal fault lie with the hacker, with the manufacturer, or with the owner who may have failed to properly secure the product (*i.e.*, by using a sufficiently strong password or by timely updating the software)? If there is a software failure versus an actual defect in the product, should the maker of a product be held liable for the software failure? What if the manufacturer of the product or the software failed to include sufficient security designs? What about component part liability? Traditional products liability law holds that defective component part manufacturers can be held liable. Is software a component part?[56]

To date, no court has conceptualized a 3D printing case as a products liability action. Traditional products liability will need to evolve further to take into account the unique aspects of 3D printing as well as data-driven products.

[B] Information-Based Products

Over the past quarter-century, the U.S. economy has been shifting from durable manufacturing, such as the automobile industry, to a software-driven economy. Internet sales and services, Computer-Aided Design (CAD) and Computer-Aided Manufacturing (CAM) are replacing traditional business and manufacturing. Online databases, data processing services and software publishing are rapidly replacing the assembly line. The software industry is growing, not just through software development, but also through dependent industries such as computer graphics and multicasting. Other forms of engineering are becoming increasingly dependent on software, as more than fifty thousand software engineering jobs involve creating professional design tools.

[C] Software Products Liability

The race to market products without sufficient attention to known defects may cause inadequately tested software to be released. As one software entrepreneur stated, "Everyone is in a dirty race to get products out quick, and they are getting their feet held to it on quality."[57] Software products liability has not yet sufficiently evolved to address issues of inadequate cybersecurity, unreliable code or lost data.

Computer-related products liability cases are rare and rarely successful. One software case arose from the online sale of an ankle-monitoring device for tracking criminals under house arrest. They incorporate cellular communications features that utilize mobile phone technology that allow them to send real-time GPS tracking information to the offender-monitoring center. These devices are designed to store undelivered outgoing data in the event of loss of cellular coverage, power outage or battery failure. The manufacturer advertised that its field-monitoring unit was tamper-proof but:

> This warranty was breached when the murderer was able to disable the device and commit another crime. . . . The court ruled that the website seller of the monitoring device did not breach any express or implied warranty, nor was it dangerously defective. The victim's estate successfully prevailed on an action only for misrepresentation based on false statements about the field-monitoring unit on the company's website.[58]
>
> This case illustrates that the manufacturer of a product is liable for a personal injury that results from a false misrepresentation.

Samsung Galaxy 7 as a Defective Product

Products liability potentially applies to the distributors of defective computer hardware as well as to software. Samsung, a Korean electronics company, released a cell phone called the Galaxy Note 7, which exhibited battery problems that caused the phones to overheat and start fires. The overheating of batteries is not an isolated event, but affects the Korean company's entire smartphone line. Samsung offered a recall and exchange of the phones for what they claimed were safety-tested phones. However, the exchanged phones suffered the same problem, and resulted in the company killing off the phone entirely.

Samsung will be liable for consequential damages, such as the "car fire in Port St. Lucie, Florida, where the owner of the vehicle believes the cause of the fire was his charging Samsung Galaxy Note 7."[59] An Ohio man filed suit for personal injury caused by burns he suffered from "the negligence of Samsung and directly from the explosion of the Samsung Galaxy S7 Edge cell phone battery and subsequent fire."[60] In the future, products liability needs to expand to address the defective software powering physical goods, since the current products liability framework was developed for tangible physical products, not for software.[61]

§ 3.8: CYBERTORTS OF THE FUTURE: THE INTERNET OF THINGS

[A] Internet of Things

Science fiction writer Philip Dick's 1953 short story, *The Colony*, takes place on the distant Planet Blue, a setting that appears to be ideal for colonization because of its idyllic climate and apparent lack of dangerous animals. In fact, the predators on this planet masquerade as everyday objects. A scientist is attacked by his microscope. A second traveler narrowly escapes from a deadly encounter when his bath towel violently attempts to strangle him. These disguised predators eventually kill off all the space travelers. Much like the everyday objects in *The Colony*, defective software can pose hidden dangers when disguised among devices containing software code.

The Internet of Things (IoT) is a network of digital products communicating and interacting with the environment and with other devices, creating "interdependencies between products gathered, or data generated, and service providers. There is a wide variety of IoT systems and ways that these systems can be used."[62] The Internet of Things, which includes physical objects that are embedded with sensors or actuators and connected to a network, is the latest frontier for tort law. Internet-enabled cameras, baby-monitors, thermostats, health-monitoring bracelets, smart refrigerators, and, eventually, driverless cars, increasingly record, send and receive data.

The U.S. Senate has introduced the *Cybersecurity Improvement Act of 2017* "to require companies that sell wearables, sensors and other web-connected tools to adhere to new security standards."[63] What duty should the manufacturers of these interconnected devices have to incorporate security or to conduct risk assessment in the absence of legislative action? If a company fails to update its computer systems to counter new malware, is it liable for customer losses from a cyber-intrusion? The problem of security for the IoT is a perfect storm of dangerous irresponsibility and unclear liability:

> The Internet of Things is bringing computerization and connectivity to many tens of millions of devices worldwide. These devices will affect every aspect of our lives, because they're things like cars, home appliances, thermostats, light bulbs, fitness trackers, medical devices, smart streetlights and sidewalk squares. Many of these devices are low-cost, designed and built offshore, then rebranded and resold. . . . The

> owners of those devices don't care. . . . The sellers of those devices don't care: They've already moved on to selling newer and better models.[64]

At present, the Internet of Things is particularly vulnerable to security breaches due to the lack of industrial standards. Plaintiffs will find it difficult to assert that a given data breach constitutes negligence because a key predicate is that the defendant has violated some standard of care. If there is no industry-wide agreement on the standard of care, the plaintiff must find some other basis to demonstrate this violation.

The policy question is whether a website, data handler or service provider should have a legal responsibility to protect others from unreasonable risks and how the courts and regulatory agencies will interpret "reasonable security." In December 2016, the Food and Drug Administration (FDA) issued guidelines that placed responsibility for managing medical cybersecurity threats on device manufacturers and health care facilities:

> Manufacturers are responsible for remaining vigilant about identifying risks and hazards associated with their medical devices, including risks related to cybersecurity. They are responsible for putting appropriate mitigations in place to address patient safety risks and ensure proper device performance. Hospitals and health care facilities should evaluate their network security and protect their hospital systems.[65]

Defectively Designed Software Products Liability Cases

The greater the risk, the more likely a court will recognize a legal duty of care. In one high profile case, a New York City hospital did not detect a computer software malfunction that caused a patient to suffer an excruciating death from excessive radiation. The New York Times reported that flaws in computer software were causing an epidemic of radiation therapy injuries and fatalities.

Defectively designed software components incorporated in automobiles have been the largest category of defective software products cases. *Wired* reported a lawsuit arising out of a remote hack of a Chrysler Jeep, in which software developers took control of a moving vehicle through its Internet-connected "infotainment" system.

Parents who bought VTech learning toys for their children filed would-be class action lawsuits against the company after learning that its database had been hacked, affecting information from millions of people, including children. A judge in the Northern District of Illinois recently consolidated the five suits that are pending before him over these toys.

Source: *In re VTech Data Breach Litig.*, N.D. Ill., No.15–10889, consolidation (December 10, 2016).

The complaint that a company has weak computer security can also be the basis of a trade libel case. Muddy Waters, a short-seller, and MedSec, a medical device and health care security firm, alleged the existence of "key vulnerabilities" in St. Jude Medical's implantable pacemaker and defibrillator devices that can "apparently be exploited by low-level hackers." St. Jude's implantable cardiac devices detect and correct abnormal heart rhythms. The home monitor transmits and receives signals used to wirelessly connect to the patient's cardiac device and read the data stored on the device. The transmitter, located in the patient's home, sends patient data to their doctor.

The Food and Drug Administration (FDA) reported cybersecurity vulnerabilities in the home transmitters but found no instance in which a patient had been harmed. The investment firm defendant issued a report contending that the vulnerabilities found in St. Jude's cardiac devices were a "magnitude more worrying than the medical device hacks that have been publicly discussed in the past." St. Jude filed suit against these financial industry analysts, contending that their report contained false information designed to drive down the price of the company's stock.

This lawsuit for defamation, deceptive trade practices, civil conspiracy and other violations of state and federal law, charged the analysts with unethical conduct in the cybersecurity community by not conveying their legitimate concerns first to the company and the FDA St. Jude Medical charged that the industry reporters were scaring patients into unplugging their home transmitters, thus losing the benefits of remote cardiac monitoring.

Ethicists differ as to the solution of defectively designed IoT products with inadequate security. Libertarians defer to the market, but this can also be viewed as an instance of market failure, given the difficulty that buyers experience in evaluating the security of these devices. Consequentialists would implement additional regulation. Bruce Schneier calls for governmental regulation, given the failure of the market to ratchet up security:

> Governments will get involved in the IoT, because the risks are too great and the stakes are too high. Computers are now able to affect our world in a direct and physical manner. Security researchers have demonstrated the ability to take control of Internet-enabled cars. They've demonstrated ransomware against home thermostats and exposed vulnerabilities in implanted medical devices. They've hacked voting

> machines and power plants. In one recent paper, researchers showed how vulnerability in smart light bulbs could be used to start a chain reaction, resulting in them all being controlled by the attackers—that are everyone in a city. Security flaws in these things could mean people dying and property being destroyed.[66]

Increasingly, websites rely upon third-party cloud providers to protect their data. If a customer's data is compromised because of the cloud provider's inadequate computer security, is the company liable? Is there a duty to do a complete inventory of information technology assets to see that the provider has sufficient protection from cybercriminals? Such questions are likely to be fought out in the courts over the coming decades.

[B] Self-Driving Cars

In the early 1960s, radio announcers routinely reported the predicted number of holiday crash fatalities before each Labor Day and Memorial Day weekend. Americans were told to "drive carefully," and to look out for "the nut behind the wheel." The focus on accident prevention was on the drunk driver or the distracted driver, not on defective cars or badly designed highways. We were deeply impressed by the dark magic that permitted statisticians to predict the number of fatalities in advance, but we also wondered about what could be done about the highway deaths.

It never occurred to us, or, apparently, to the radio announcer, that cars and highways contained designed-in dangers. The 1960s were not happy days when it came to automotive safety. Prior to the advent of products liability, the American automobile industry designed its vehicles for looks, not safety. Automobiles of the 1960s, even hardtop sedans, "crumpled like a Japanese lantern" in foreseeable rollover accidents. Drivers were impaled by non-collapsible steering wheel columns and permanently tattooed by sharp-edged emblems in collisions. Because cars had no seat belts, occupants frequently catapulted through windshields that were not made from laminated safety glass. When someone was thrown through the windshield, shards of glass would cause deep lacerations.

We are at a crossroads as to what liability rules should apply to the latest incarnation of the "horseless carriage." Some consequentialists contend that we should not stretch products liability rules to driverless cars, as excessive liability will undermine the rapid development of this valuable technology. Industry advocates argue that we should instead turn to an alternative compensation system, modeled after the special fund for infants harmed by vaccines. Anyone injured by a driverless car could receive compensation from a fund established by the automakers, without the necessity of going to court. Libertarians would argue that this forced insurance for the driverless car makers is not a market-based solution. Manufacturers who make safer vehicles would subsidize those who trade safety for short-term profits under a government-run, no fault insurance system.

Social contract theorists are highly skeptical that a no-fault compensation fund would work as effectively as products liability in creating manufacturer incentives for safety in driverless cars. Between 1964 and 2013, products liability has helped to dramatically lower the number of fatalities per 100 million vehicle miles traveled from 5.39 to only 1.10.

The good news is that driverless cars have the potential to all but eliminate driver error. This should save large numbers of lives and greatly reduce accident insurance costs. The annual death toll created by drunk, reckless and distracted drivers will potentially be eradicated. However, driverless vehicles present novel safety, privacy and security issues.

The German Federal Highway Research Institute concluded that the Tesla Model S's autopilot feature constitutes a "considerable traffic hazard" because of both software and hardware defects. Test vehicles made navigational errors while driving through a construction zone where there were no road markings. The car's sensors were not able to detect road conditions over 40 meters behind the car, which makes it hazardous for driving on the autobahn, which has no speed limit.

If the software controlling this vehicle is not sufficiently secure, a cybercriminal could override its settings to speed up the car or shift it into reverse. Ransomware extortionists may use malware to disable cars' safety devices or lock passengers into vehicles that have been immobilized in isolated settings. Advertisers, law enforcement, insurers and cybercriminals may misuse inadequately secured metadata gathered by connected cars.

These risks are neither far-fetched legal hypotheticals nor science fiction fantasies. A Federal Trade Commission Workshop participant demonstrated that an attacker could gain "access to the car's internal computer network without ever physically touching the car." This terrifying scenario was explored in Season 7 of *The Good Wife*. In the episode entitled "Driven," attorney Alicia Florick tells the story of how a hacker caused a crippling accident by disabling the driver's ability to control the vehicle.

Many U.S. states have enacted or are considering regulations addressing the operation of self-driving vehicles. California is one of the few states to address privacy issues in requiring that the:

> manufacturer of the autonomous technology installed on a vehicle shall provide a written disclosure to the purchaser of an autonomous vehicle that describes what information is collected by the autonomous technology equipped on the vehicle.[67]

A District of Columbia statute requires that a human driver be "prepared to take control of the autonomous vehicle at any moment." This statute restricts the ability to convert current automobiles to software-controlled vehicles.[68] Michigan shields the original vehicle manufacturer from liability for design defects occurring after an automobile is converted to an autonomous vehicle.[69] In July of 2017, Congress passed a statute enabling federal regulators to address autonomous vehicles that would replace the recently enacted patchwork of state statutes.[70] These are modest first steps towards developing a regulatory regime that will shape tort liability rules for the coming age of robotic transportation.

Driverless cars will raise new ethical issues as to how software will be programmed to react in life or death situations.[71] The algorithms controlling driverless cars must reflect moral principles that guide decision making in situations where harm is unavoidable.[72] What role, if any, should ethical principles apply to diverse scenarios where a vehicle must choose between passenger and pedestrian safety?[73] If a driverless car kills a pedestrian to protect its occupants, is the company legally liable for the death? Tort law must continue to be forward-looking, with the flexibility to adapt to the latest technologies.

§ 3.9: BARRIERS TO CYBERTORT CLAIMS

[A] Section 230 of the CDA Liability Shield

Congress enacted the Communications Decency Act (CDA) in 1996, while the commercial Internet was still in its infancy, "to promote the continued development of the Internet and other interactive computer services and other interactive media."[74] Section 230 of the CDA shields websites and other providers from any liability for third-party content, which cripples the role of tort law in evolving to constrain online wrongs. "Section 230 requires that entities as different as an online matchmaking service, a copy shop, an online bookseller, an online auction service, a public library and an Internet user who created a chat room all receive immunity from civil liability."[75]

Before passage of the CDA, courts were divided over the question of whether websites should be liable for third-party postings. A New York federal court had held CompuServe, an early service provider, not liable for defamatory content, as it was a distributor of information, not a publisher. Congress enacted

Section 230 to overturn a 1995 New York state court decision, *Stratton Oakmont, Inc. v. Prodigy Servs. Co.*,[76] where the plaintiffs, who were later depicted in the film *The Wolf of Wall Street*, sued Prodigy for defamatory comments made by an unidentified party on one of its bulletin boards.

Congress followed the *Cubby* court rather than *Stratton Oakmont*, reasoning that too much liability would discourage investment in Internet-related innovations. Many of Silicon Valley's leading technology companies applaud CDA Section 230. Service providers argue that without this liability shield, they would have to keep a tab on every posting and that would add unmanageable overhead costs. "CDA 230 creates a broad protection that has allowed innovation and free speech online to flourish."[77] Forty-seven state attorney generals, in contrast, call for placing limitations on Section 230 in order to make ISPs accountable for hosting illegal content such as child sex trafficking advertisements.

[B] Section 230 Blocks the Evolution of Tort Remedies

Section 230's liability shield has made it enormously difficult for tort plaintiffs to obtain compensation, even when they have been clearly victimized by reprehensible third-party online content. In *Zeran v. America Online,*[78] the Fourth Circuit ruled that Section 230 shields websites from publisher and distributor liability, leaving victims of libel without the ability to sue websites for any third-party postings. In this case, a spiteful, anonymous poster instructed members of the public to call Kenneth Zeran, a Seattle resident, to order merchandise with tasteless slogans that celebrated the 1995 bombing of the Alfred P. Murrah Federal Building in Oklahoma City. The messages provided Zeran's name and telephone number.

An offended Oklahoma City radio announcer repeated some of these provocative messages on the air. In the aftermath of the radio broadcast, Ken Zeran was subject to a flood of hostile telephone calls and death threats, but could not change his number because it was his business telephone. Zeran contended that AOL was negligent in failing to remove the incendiary posts, even after AOL had been made aware of their falsity. AOL defended on the grounds of Section 230's immunity. The Fourth Circuit agreed, reasoning that the congressional intent of 230 was to maintain robust Internet communications. Service providers are thus not liable for refusing to remove the defamatory postings of third parties, even after receiving notice of illegal content.

In *John Does v. Franco Productions*,[79] Illinois State University college athletes were secretly taped while they were in locker rooms, restrooms and at wrestling meets. The secret videotapes were advertised as "hot young dudes" and sold on the Internet. The tapes carried names like "Straight Off the Mat" and "Voyeur Time" and depicted hundreds of young athletes in various degrees of nudity. A federal jury awarded $506 million against the pornographers for the invasion of privacy and civil conspiracy.

The college students could not locate the pornographers, so they sued the websites and the service providers who profited from these illicit films. The court dismissed these actions, ruling that the websites and service providers were immunized under Section 230. A federal jury awarded $506 million in compensatory and punitive damages against the pornographers who had surreptitiously created and then openly sold these humiliating films. Liability was based on invasion of privacy, unlawful use of the plaintiffs' images for monetary gain and mail and wire fraud under civil RICO laws.

This enormous award imposed by the *Franco* court against the pornographers was largely symbolic. The judgment was unenforceable because these criminals could not be located. The defendants had only a virtual presence and no traceable assets to seize. Websites can easily go dark and their developers can disappear. U.S. courts have not been receptive to imposing website liability for third-party postings even where the victim has no practical recourse against the primary wrongdoer. In *GoDaddy.com v. Toups*,[80] the victim of a nonconsensual posting of pornographic images of herself on two "revenge porn" websites filed an action against an online intermediary, GoDaddy.com that hosted the websites for intentional infliction of emotional distress, violation of the Texas Penal Code and gross negligence.

The basis of the claim against GoDaddy was that the domain name registration company knew of the content, failed to remove it, and then profited from the activity on the websites. At trial, GoDaddy was held jointly responsible for the plaintiff's damages. However, the Texas appeals court reversed this finding, ruling that CDA Section 230 imposes no takedown duty, which foreclosed all causes of action against the service provider.

In *Jones v. Dirty World Entertainment Recordings Inc.*,[81] a Cincinnati Bengals cheerleader and school teacher filed a defamation action against an online tabloid known as *The Dirty*. *The Dirty* website enables users to anonymously upload comments, photos, and videos that the website operator publishes along with his snarky comments. An anonymous visitor to The Dirty website submitted two photographs of Jones and a male companion, along with the following post:

> THE DIRTY ARMY: Nik, this is Sara J, Cincinnati Bengal Cheerleader. She's been spotted around town lately with the infamous Shayne

> Graham. She has also slept with every other Bengal Football player. This girl is a teacher too!! You would think with Graham's paycheck he could attract something a little easier on the eyes Nik![82]

The website refused to take down the postings and Jones filed tort claims of defamation, libel *per se,* false light and the intentional infliction of emotional distress. The case was submitted to a jury, which returned a verdict in favor of Jones for $38,000 in compensatory damages and $300,000 in punitive damages. On appeal, the Fourth Circuit held that Section 230 of the Communications Decency Act bars Jones' tort claims, and reversed the entire judgment. The broad shield from liability of Section 230 is the single most important reason that cybertorts have been slow to evolve. At the end of this chapter, we will examine the case for and against Section 230, by applying five ethical perspectives.

[C] Cracks in the Section 230 Shield

Courts are slowly chipping away at the Section 230 shield, recognizing exceptions especially where the service provider becomes, in effect, a content creator. In *Huon v. Denton,*[83] Huon filed suit against the *Above the Law* website for implying that he was a rapist in an article published on the same day that he was acquitted of rape. The Seventh Circuit concluded that the district judge correctly rejected Huon's defamation claim as to the article, but reversed the lower court as to the third-party user claims.

Another website, Jezebel (then owned by Gawker), reported on the lawsuit in an article entitled, "Acquitted Rapist Sues Blog for Calling Him Serial Rapist." Huon then accused Gawker of defamation, false light, invasion of privacy and the intentional infliction of emotional distress. The court rejected Gawker's Section 230 defense because Gawker helped create and develop at least some of the comments, and one of those comments constituted defamation. The court reasoned that Gawker itself was an information content provider because it:

> (1) Encouraged and invited users to defame Huon, through selecting and urging the most defamation-prone commenters to "post more comments and continue to escalate the dialogue;
>
> (2) Edited, shaped, and choreographed the content of the comments that it received;
>
> (3) Selected for publication every comment that appeared beneath the Jezebel article; and
>
> (4) Employed individuals who authored at least some of the comments themselves.

In *Doe v. Internet Brands*,[84] Jane Doe, an aspiring model, contended that two rapists used the defendant's Model Mayhem website to lure her to a fake audition. The rapists drugged her and recorded their sexual assault, turning it into a pornographic video for sale. The two rapists browsed model profiles that Model Mayhem posted, contacted potential victims by using fake identities, and lured victims to south Florida for modeling auditions by posing as talent scouts. Doe contended that Internet Brands knew about the criminal scheme, but negligently failed to warn her or other users.

Jane Doe filed an action against Internet Brands, alleging liability for negligence under California law, based upon a failure to warn. The district court dismissed the action because Section 230 of the Communications Decency Act barred her claim. The Ninth Circuit, ruled that CDA Section 230 did not bar Doe's claims against Internet Brands because it had detailed knowledge of the criminal scheme but did nothing to warn users that rapists were trolling for victims on their site.

California law imposes a duty to warn potential victims of third-party harm when a person has a "special relationship to either the person whose conduct needs to be controlled or . . . to the foreseeable victim of that conduct."[85] The court reasoned that the CDA did not shield the defendant from Internet Brand's negligent failure to warn. The court stated that Doe was not suing Internet Brands as a publisher, but rather for its negligence in failing to warn her about these predators.

The federal court of appeals also held that Section 230 did not eliminate the duty to post or email a warning to Doe and others. The Ninth Circuit withdrew this opinion, held a rehearing on the issue of CDA immunity, and issued a superseding opinion on May 31, 2016, that upheld its 2014 opinion. This case has not yet been finalized, but it presents a possible exception to the broad shield of CDA Section 230.

§ 3.10: GLOBAL CYBERTORTS

European service providers do not enjoy the near absolute immunity of their American counterparts. Although they have no duty to monitor content, they must remove tortious, infringing or other illegal content. Congress has devised separate liability rules for ISPs tort and copyright liability but has not enacted ISP rules as to trademark infringement or other illegal content. E-commerce companies, which are highly dependent on proprietary software, have gone global and therefore need a sophisticated familiarity with the legal regimes of multiple nations.

As social media sites increasingly target consumers in Europe and beyond, corporate counsel and outside lawyers need to keep abreast of worldwide trends in consumer law to avoid costly cross-border litigation, fines and regulatory actions. Counsel advising a buyer or seller in a cross-border transaction will need to comply with foreign as well as domestic laws to protect the buyer's or seller's rights and to avoid infringing upon the rights of others. Many U.S. attorneys representing tech companies are too U.S. centric, failing to consider foreign law despite operating globalized businesses.

[A] EU Products Liability

The European Commission is updating the EU Directive on Products Liability to address 3D printing, the Internet of Things and other new technological developments.[86] Internet-connected products are vulnerable to "the transmission of erroneous data by a sensor, due to software defects, connectivity problems or an incorrect operation of the machine."[87] One scholar proposes adapting the EU Directive on Products Liability to autonomous cars because establishing causation for accidents may be extremely difficult.[88]

[B] Defamation Outside the U.S.

Internet postings can be read simultaneously in many nations, allowing some plaintiffs to file their lawsuits in jurisdictions where the law is particularly favorable. Libel tourism refers to U.S. publishers and writers being sued in foreign courts where defamation is a strict liability tort. In twenty-three countries of the European Union, defamation is a crime.[89]

No foreign countries impose First Amendment limitations on tort actions, such as defamation, false light privacy, or the intentional infliction of emotional distress. *The Wall Street Journal*, for example, was the defendant in a United Kingdom lawsuit over its republication of an April Fool's Day prank press release that was disseminated by Harrods Department Store on its website and in print editions.

Harrods Department Store had issued a mock press release, stating its plan to "float" its department store by building a ship version of the store and offering to sell shares in the venture. Upon learning that the announcement had been a joke, the *Wall Street Journal* countered with an editorial stating, "If Harrods, the British luxury retailer, ever goes public, investors would be wise to question its every disclosure." Harrods and its then-owner, Mohamed Al-Fayed, filed a libel suit in London's High Court of Justice even though the story was published on a

U.S. website. In 2004, a UK court ruled against Harrods, finding that it was not a victim of trade libel.

Dow Jones & Company, Inc. v. Gutnick[90] illustrated the clash of different defamation regimes in the U.S. and Australia. In October 2000, the online edition of *Barron's Magazine*, a Dow Jones publication, posted an article entitled "Unholy Gains," suggesting that Joseph Gutnick had been involved in questionable financial activities. Gutnick filed a defamation lawsuit in a Victoria, Australia court, contending that the story was untrue. Australia's High Court held that Dow Jones could be sued in Victoria since that was the place of publication.

Dow Jones argued that the Australian High Court should adopt the U.S.'s single publication rule that would restrict the plaintiff to filing only a single defamation case in New Jersey, the place of publication. The tort of defamation in Australia "focuses upon publications causing damage to reputation. It is a tort of strict liability, in the sense that a defendant may be liable even though no injury to reputation was intended and the defendant acted with reasonable care."

Most U.S. states have adopted some version of the single publication rule. In contrast, Australia rejects the single publication rule and imposes liability standards that make it easier to win defamation lawsuits. In November 2004, the parties settled for $44,000 and legal fees. This decision leaves U.S. media companies—including social networking sites—liable for defamation in any jurisdiction where the content is downloaded. In 2013, the United Kingdom enacted the single publication rule. Dissimilar legal cultures will approach the same tort action differently, an enormous problem for globalized websites.

In *CG v. Facebook Ireland Ltd and Joseph McCloskey*,[91] CG, the plaintiff had served prison sentences for multiple sexual offenses. At the time of his release, "CG discovered that he had been identified on a Facebook page entitled "Keeping our Kids Safe from Predators 2" (the "Predators 2" page). One of the posts on the page contained an article from the *Irish News* identifying him by name, detailing his convictions, and containing a photograph of him."[92]

CG filed suit against Facebook and one of its users because these postings led anonymous posters to respond angrily, recommending violence against CG. The Irish court ruled that CG had an expectation of privacy in the information posted on the Facebook pages. The court classified Facebook as a data controller, ruling it was liable for not expeditiously removing the user's postings. The court awarded £20,000 in damages to the plaintiff and imposed "a mandatory injunction requiring the first defendant to terminate the account of the second defendant."

§ 3.11: FIVE ETHICAL PERSPECTIVES APPLIED TO SECTION 230 OF THE CDA

As noted earlier, Section 230 of the Communications Decency Act is a broad liability statute that shields "interactive computer services," by immunizing them from cybertorts for content posted on their service by third parties. Section 230 protects freedom of expression in cyberspace by giving online intermediaries a liability-free shield against defamation lawsuits arising out of the third-party content they post. U.S. courts have expanded Section 230 beyond publisher's liability to preclude nearly all tort lawsuits against ISPs, websites and search engines. Bloggers, website designers, news aggregators and many others, benefit from this protection against libel lawsuits but tort victims often have no meaning remedy. The next section asks whether Section 230 appropriately balances the right of freedom of expression and the right to vindicate tort injuries by applying the strongest arguments from each of our five ethical perspectives.

[A] Consequentialism

The principal consequentialist argument for this broad immunity is that it enables entrepreneurs to post third-party content without censorship arising from the fear of liability. Section 230 lowers the costs of defending against lawsuits. The court in *Zeran v. America Online*[93] recounted Congress's purpose in enacting Section 230: to protect the vigorous exchange of opinions on the Internet from being undermined by excessive liability:

> The specter of tort liability in an area of such prolific speech would have an obvious chilling effect. It would be impossible for service providers to screen each of their millions of postings for possible problems. Faced with potential liability for each message republished by their services, interactive computer service providers might choose to severely restrict the number and type of messages posted. Congress considered the weight of the speech interests implicated and chose to immunize service providers to avoid any such restrictive effect.[94]

Even though some Internet users will unfairly have no remedy for injuries suffered in cyberspace due to the Section 230 shield, the vast majority benefit due to the Internet's ability to evolve free of liability. Social media websites, such as Facebook or Instagram, would never have grown into significant institutions if the providers faced liability for the tortious postings of their users. Congress had another statutory purpose in mind when enacting Section 230, which was to incentivize service providers to self-regulate the dissemination of offensive material over their services. Websites are voluntarily using their terms of service to ban offensive messages, fake news and other objectionable postings.

Because courts have stretched Section 230 beyond defamation to shield providers from every tort, there may now be underdeterrence, especially where service providers have knowledge of ongoing torts and even crimes on their service. The Dirty.com, for example, enjoys complete immunity, even though it is an Internet defamation machine whose entire business model is to destroy reputations. Some websites harm society by spewing hatred, conspiracy theories and unsubstantiated rumors.

Consequentialists might seek a greater alignment of economic incentives with societal benefits to encourage more socially responsible behavior by websites. Reforming the law requires careful, unemotional study that empirically contrasts the U.S. system with those of other nations that lack this shield for defamatory postings and other online oppression.

[B] Virtue & Duty Theory

Virtue theory views cybertort law as advancing morality when it provides victims with the legal weapons necessary to right wrongs. Section 230 allows unethical and dishonest people to thrive at the expense of their innocent victims. It creates a classic "race to the bottom" of morality, where the more vicious the postings, the more profitable the website becomes.

A virtue theorist would note that total immunity for websites breeds irresponsibility. Society should reward the virtuous, not immoral entities such as scandal-mongering website operators, mugshot pay-per-view site owners and revenge porn site providers. South Dakota's Attorney General, through the National Association of Attorney Generals, has asked state attorney generals throughout the U.S. to sign a letter advocating the reduction of the immunity to make it easier for states to pursue "particularly egregious website conduct that is shielded under Section 230 of the Communications Decency Act."

[C] Conflict Theory

(1) CDA Section Shields Online Bullies

The largest and most powerful Internet service providers in the mid-1990s and their wealthy financial backers proposed CDA Section 230 to limit liability of websites. Women, the poor and other disadvantaged groups are underrepresented among those who lobbied for and enacted this legislation. Under this broad shield from liability, the powerful have become even more powerful because the moneyed interests have been freed from liability concerns. If punitive damages were available for well-established torts like the intentional infliction of emotional distress, websites would be required to take down egregiously false, defamatory postings and humiliating images that disproportionately afflict women.

Those targeted by online oppression—disproportionately women, minorities and the disabled—now have no recourse against service providers because of Section 230 immunity. The primary wrongdoers are usually anonymous and generally beyond the reach of the law. Tort law should redress imbalances of power, especially those based on race, class, gender, physical deformities or sexual orientation. Some conflict theorists have called for limitations on online anonymity to help disadvantaged groups to pursue direct action against the perpetrator.

(2) Marxist Class Conflict

In Chapter One of the *Communist Manifesto*, Karl Marx famously wrote that "[t]he executive of the modern state is nothing but a committee for managing the common affairs of the whole bourgeoisie." The law is designed to appear fair, but it systematically reinforces the great advantages already held by the members of the ruling class. Karl Marx would likely have regarded Section 230 as another example of a harsh, pro-capitalist legal doctrine that furthers the power of America's economic elite by denying recovery to victims of social prejudice.

Given his theory, Marx would have observed that law is a means of oppression, but can also be a means of resistance against oppression as the common people can organize online to enact laws that will advance social justice. Law has the potential for redressing imbalances of power while compensating the injured. Punitive damages, which can calibrate penalties to the assets of the wrongdoer, are potentially valuable in teaching wealthy website owners that even the rich are not above the law.

[D] Social Contractualists

The social contract requires the best possible balance between human rights and social stability and efficiency. A Rawlsian would argue that Section 230 should be scaled back because it is unjust for disadvantaged groups who are deprived of remedies against websites that profit from their misery. John Rawls argued, "Laws and institutions no matter how efficient and well-arranged must be reformed or abolished if they are unjust."[95] Lockeans, on the other hand, might put more emphasis on the property rights of website owners.

Cybertorts should be freed to develop remedies for online misbehavior, such as Internet fraud, online stalking, the invasion of privacy and defamatory postings. Effective civil remedies are essential because criminal law often lacks the flexibility to deter and punish Internet wrongdoers. Under Rawls' "veil of ignorance" thought experiment, people would have empathy toward women who have been harmed by, for example, malicious postings of personal information on sadomasochistic websites or by individuals using morphing technologies to superimpose victim's faces onto pornographic pictures. Congress could amend CDA Section 230 by requiring websites to take down content or sites that constitute ongoing torts or crimes, such as revenge porn websites.

[E] Libertarianism

Congress enacted Section 230 of the CDA to keep government interference to a minimum by enabling market forces to function with minimal liability. This policy has largely succeeded in creating an uninhibited exchange of ideas on the Internet. The Electronic Frontier Foundation argued that Section 230 supports human freedom:

> This immunity has allowed for YouTube and Vimeo users to upload their videos, Amazon, and Yelp to offer countless user reviews, craigslist to host classified ads, and Facebook and Twitter to offer social networking to hundreds of millions of Internet users. Given the sheer size of user-generated websites (for example, Facebook alone has more than 1 billion users, and YouTube users upload 100 hours of video every minute), it would be infeasible for online intermediaries to prevent objectionable content from cropping up on their site. Rather than face potential liability for their users' actions, most would likely not host any user content at all or would need to protect themselves by being actively engaged in censoring what we say, what we see, and what we do online. In short, CDA 230 is perhaps the most influential law to protect the kind of innovation that has allowed the Internet to thrive since 1996.[96]

Libertarians believe that we should let the free market determine online winners and losers. Those who do not want to be exposed to the cyber cesspools should not visit them. If substantial numbers of persons wish to frequent revenge porn websites or mugshot websites, these sites will make profits and proliferate. Those who wish to view incendiary postings have a right to visit them without outside interference. Websites that self-censor may go out of business or they may attract additional customers who wish to avoid offensive postings.

If libertarians were forced to choose between greater tort liability and strict governmental regulations, however, they would prefer tort law as a form of private ordering to "nanny state" paternalism. Additional government regulation of Internet content would be expensive, intrusive and bureaucratic. Lawmakers would forbid unpopular ideas and regulators would tend to stifle free expression. Fear of excessive liability would cause websites to shy away from publishing information that the powerful wish to keep secret. The excesses of free speech are a small price to pay for the benefits of a free society.

CONCLUSION

The Internet's anonymity and its cross-border nature make it difficult for victims of cybertorts to identify the primary wrongdoer. Users rarely even file claims for their online injuries or losses despite a vast number of online harms. Courts have stretched Section 230 to virtually every tort, so the few plaintiffs filing lawsuits against websites for hosting abusive content created by third parties, are seldom successful.

Cybertorts must evolve further to provide remedies for harms due to defective software, inadequate cybersecurity, online defamation, cyber stalking and online fraud. Tort law's remarkable quality of adapting old causes of new forms of oppression, such as adapting the personal property tort of trespass to chattels to control spam email and computer viruses, makes it a flexible tool that has the potential to supplement inadequate criminal law enforcement.

In times of rapid technological change, torts play a critical role in filling the enforcement gap created by the limitations of criminal law that will be further explored in the following chapter. The social costs associated with hackers and cybercriminals will not decrease until the software industry is held accountable for marketing products with known security flaws and other design defects. Digital currencies, mobile banking products, advanced payment technologies and the rapidly growing development of the Internet of Things have great social value, but they also pose a variety of threats that must be met with more effective tort remedies.

CHAPTER THREE: REVIEW EXERCISES

3.1: Kim Kardashian "posted a series of videos on Snapchat in which Kanye West, her husband, was talking to Taylor Swift on the telephone about his song "Famous"—a song that Swift has criticized as "offensive and derogatory." In the short clip, Taylor Swift:

> appears to give approval of the lyrics West wrote about her for his Life of Pablo track "Famous," in which he raps, "I feel like me and Taylor might still have sex." Whether the video is an accurate portrayal of the conversation is doubtful since West claimed he talked to Swift for an hour and the Snapchat is considerably shorter than that, and it would contradict Swift's prior claims that the pair had only talked about whether she would post the song to her social media.

Taylor Swift demanded that the Snapchat posting be taken down. Rolling Stone reported that:

> Swift issued a response to the post on Instagram highlighting that the video didn't show West asking her if he could call her "that bitch" in the next line of the track ("I made that bitch famous")—a phrase she previously described as "misogynistic"—because, she claimed, it didn't happen. On Instagram, she characterized the move of posting the video as "character assassination," and TMZ reports that in February, her lawyer sent a letter demanding that video of the phone call be destroyed under California's wiretapping laws.

If Taylor Swift files suit against Kanye West and Kim Kardashian, evaluate Swift's chances of prevailing in tort actions for the intentional infliction of emotional distress, the right of privacy and defamation. Should it matter whether Taylor Swift is a public figure? Please explain. What defenses would West and Kardashian assert in response? Could Swift file suit against Snapchat for failing to delist or remove the controversial clip?

3.2: In 2013, South Dakota's Attorney General, through the National Association of Attorney Generals, asked state attorney generals throughout the U.S. to sign a letter urging Congress to amend the exemptions under Section 230 of the Communications Decency Act to give state officials greater authority in pursuing what he called "certain egregious website conduct." Explain how you would respond to this request if you were a key policymaker.

3.3: Will cybertorts evolve to address the growing problems of defective software and substandard cybersecurity? What are the most significant barriers that will make it difficult for tort law to properly protect the public from these, and other, hazards? Are there some that you consider in need of reform?

3.4: Shaquille O'Neal, the former NBA star and public personality, posted images on Twitter and Instagram where he contorted his face and posted a picture of a disfigured face alongside it. Jahmel Binion suffers from a rare genetic condition called ectodermal dysplasia that left him with a "disfigured appearance" due to abnormalities in his hair, nails, and teeth. He believes that O'Neal's pictures encourage people to ridicule his appearance. What tort actions would Binion have against Shaquille O'Neal? Which defenses would O'Neal use against these claims? Would Binion have a cause of action against Twitter or Instagram arising out of these facts? Why or why not?

3.5: June White is the mother of Ultimate Fighting Championship president, Dana White, about whom she has written an unauthorized biography. Cynthia Ortiz posted extensive derogatory information about White, accusing her of being mentally ill and a terrible mother with no normal maternal relationship with her children. Ortiz also used the Twitter handle @RealJuneWhite to post statements, purportedly by White, apologizing for her book and saying its contents weren't true. You represent Dana White's mother, June. What claims could White bring against Ortiz on these facts? How would White counter Ortiz's claims that the First Amendment of the U.S. Constitution protects her statements? Would White have a cause of action against Twitter on these facts?

3.6: In *Brandner v. Molonguet*,[97] an oral and maxillofacial surgeon filed a petition for a preliminary injunction against a poster on a Yahoo! website who asserted that the dental surgeon negligently cut a nerve. The Yahoo! poster warned others to check the CPT (current procedural terminology) codes billed and was critical of other reviewers who posted favorable reviews. What are the practical problems that the dental practice will face in addressing these unfavorable reviews? Can they use tort law to force Yahoo! to take down the harmful postings? Please explain. What procedures will the plaintiffs need to take to unveil the anonymous posters? Are there any First Amendment concerns that the court must consider?

3.7: Courtney Love, founding member of the band Hole and widow of Nirvana's Kurt Cobain, posted a tweet that alleged that Dave Grohl, former Nirvana drummer, tried to seduce her teenage daughter, Frances Bean Cobain. Grohl described Love's allegations as false statements that were extremely upsetting. What if any torts may have been committed? What result is most likely?

3.8: Prince William has spoken out against homophobic bullying. He established a cyberbullying task force along with his wife (the Duchess of Cambridge) and his brother Prince Harry. He is aware that people who are gay endure a great amount of discrimination, particularly over social media. What are the difficulties of enacting an anti-cyberbullying statute addressing homophobia and other gender linked harms on social media? What are the advantages and disadvantages of using torts versus statutory criminal law to approach this problem?

REFERENCES FOR CHAPTER THREE

1 OLIVER WENDELL HOLMES JR., THE COMMON LAW (Boston, Massachusetts: Little Brown 1881) at 3.

2 Brookings Institution (John Villasenor), Products Liability and Driverless Cars: Issues and Guiding Principles for Legislation (April 24, 2014).

3 535 U.S. 234 (2002).

4 Kate Zernike, *Part of New Jersey's Bias-Intimidation Law Is Ruled Unconstitutional*, THE NEW YORK TIMES (March 19, 2015).

5 Margaret Talbot, *Annals of Law: The Attorney Fighting Revenge Porn*, NEW YORKER (December 5, 2016).

6 *Id.* at 13.

7 Elizabeth Hewitt, *Judge Finds 'Revenge Porn' Unconstitutional,* VTDIGGER.COM (August 1, 2016).

8 No. 1144–12–15 (Vt. Sup. Ct. Bennington Unit July 1, 2016).

9 13 V.S.A. § 2602(b)(1).

10 University of Minnesota, Silha Center for the Study of Media Ethics & the Law, *Revenge Porn Remains Controversial Topic for State and Federal Legislatures*, http://silha.umn.edu/news/Summer%202016/SILHACENTERRevengePornLegislationUniversityofMinnesota.html.

11 *Id.*

12 Thomas H Koenig & Michael L Rustad, *"Hate Torts" to Fight Hate Crimes: Punishing the Organizational Roots of Evil*, 51 AMERICAN BEHAVIOR SCIENTIST 302 (October 2007).

13 Noel Anne-Brennan, *Stalking and Domestic Violence: The Third Report to Congress* (2000).

14 *US v. William Lawrence Cassidy, Defendant*, Criminal Case No. RWT 11–091US District Court For The District Of Maryland 2011 U.S. Dist. LEXIS 145056.

15 18 U.S.C. §§ 2261A(2)(A).

16 Jordan Belamire, *My First Virtual Reality Groping*, MEDIUM-COM (October 20, 2016).

17 Kristin Hoffman, *Are There Real World Remedies for Virtual Reality Harassment?* JURIS: DUQUESNE LAW MAGAZINE (November 5, 2016).

18 Kevin Poulsen, *Hackers Assault Epilepsy Patients via Computer*, WIRED.COM (March 28, 2006).

19 2002 NLP IP Company—American Lawyer Media, J: 98: 05227, No. 96–1204096 (Montgomery, Texas June 8, 1998).

20 *Delfino v. Agilent Technologies, Inc.*, 145 Cal. App. 4th 790, 52 Cal. Rptr. 3d 376, 30 A.L.R.6th 639 (6th Dist. 2006).

21 "Originally, trespass covered the wrongful taking of a chattel, in contrast to detinue that covered the wrongful detention of personal property. Trover was a common law action for the recovery of personal property. Trover was a far more flexible writ than detinue because it permitted an action against a defendant who unlawfully exercised dominion or control over the personal property of another by any means. If, for example, a neighbor borrowed a horse and did not return it, the owner could bring a writ for any damage done to the horse and to compensate for the loss of the horse's services." Michael L. Rustad & Thomas H. Koenig, *Taming the Tort Monster: The American Civil Justice System as a Battleground of Social Theory*, 68 BROOKLYN LAW REVIEW 1, 10 (2002).

22 30 Cal. 4th 1342, 1351, 71 P.3d 296, 302 (2003).

23 *America Online, Inc. v. Prime Data Systems, Inc.*, No. Civ. A. 97–1652–A, United States District Court, E.D. Virginia (Nov. 20, 1998).

24 100 F. Supp. 2d 1058 (N.D. Cal. 2000).

25 337 F.3d 1024, 1027 (9th Cir. 2003).

26 No. Civ–02–1457–M (W.D. Okla., Jan. 13, 2003).

27 *Integrated Title Data System v. Delaney*, 800 S.W.2d 336 (Tex. App. El Paso 1990).

28 The Historical Society of the New York Courts, *Crown v. John Peter Zenger*, http://www.nycourts.gov/history/legal-history-new-york/legal-history-eras-01/history-new-york-legal-eras-crown-zenger.html.

29 2013 WL 5568427 (Tenn. Ct. of Appeals, Oct. 8, 2013).

30 *Global Telemedia Int'l Inc. v. Doe*, 132 F.Supp.2d 1261 (C.D. Cal. 2001).

31 *In re Anonymous Online Speakers*, No. 09–71625, 2011 WL 61635, at *2, *6 (9th Cir. Jan. 7, 2011).

32 *See e.g., First Time Videos v. Does*, No. C 11–01675 LB, 2011 U.S. Dist. LEXIS 42376, at *7 (N.D. Cal., April 14, 2011) (ruling that copyright owner of pornographic videos and photographs had good cause to unveil names and addresses of peer-to-peer users who distributed content without their permission).

33 376 U.S. 254 (1964).

34 *Curtis Publishing Co. v. Butts*, 388 U.S. 130 (1967).

35 Katie Glueck, *Cruz on Trump Lawsuit Threat: Bring It On*, POLITICO (February 17, 2016).

36 *New York Times v. Sullivan*, 376 U.S. 254 (1964).

37 845 N.W.2d 128 (Mich. Ct. of App. 2014).

38 *Id.* at 546–7.

39 *Id.* at 546.

40 *Rosanova v. Playboy Enterprises, Inc.*, 411 F. Supp. 440 (S.D. Ga. 1976).

41 *Enigma Software Group USA v. Bleeping Computer LLC*, 194 F.Supp.3d 263, 287 (S.D. N.Y. 2016).

42 418 U.S. 323 (1974) (ruling that Robert Welch of the John Birch Society was not either a public official as in Sullivan or a general public figure as in Curtis, but was a limited public figure because he thrust himself into the vortex of a public issue).

43 *Id.* at 342.

44 715 F.2d 254 (9th Cir. 2013).

45 *Kitt v. New York City Transit Authority*, 26 A.D.3d 301 (N.Y. Sup. Ct., Feb. 28, 2006).

46 HHS Government, Health Information Privacy, Security Rules (2017).

47 *Acosta v. Byrum*, 638 S.E.2d 246 (N.C. Ct. App. 2006).

48 Marianne Kolbasuk McGee, *Settlement in Tampa General Hospital Insider Breach Lawsuit Plaintiffs Alleged a 'History of Poor Data Protection*, DATA BREACH TODAY (December 6, 2016).

49 Yahoo! Help, *U.S. and Ireland, Yahoo Security Notice* September 22, 2016.

50 Labaton-Sucharow, *First Class Action Against Yahoo! for Largest Data Breach in History Filed by Labaton Sucharow and Robbins Geller Rudman & Dowd* (September 23, 2016) (asserting that the Yahoo! breach, which went undetected for two years, affected 500 million users),

51 ClassAction.com, *Data Breach Lawsuit* (September 11, 2017), https://www.classaction.com/data-breach/lawsuit/.

52 *Id.*

53 *Id.*

54 Gerard Magliocca, *Products Liability and 3-D Printing*, CONCURRING OPINIONS, March 5, 2013), http://www.concurringopinions.com/archives/2013/03/product-liability-and-3-D-printing.html.

55 Zach Sokol, *NYC's New Bill to Regulate 3-D Printed Guns Is Just the Beginning*, MOTHERBOARD.COM, June 13, 2013.

56 Lita Gorman, *The Era of the Internet of Things: Can Products Liability Keep Up?* 84 DEFENSE COUNSEL JOURNAL 1(2017).

57 Quentin Hardy, *Saving Software from Itself*, FORBES, Mach. 14, 2005, at 60.

58 Michael L. Rustad & Thomas H. Koenig, *Rebooting Cybertort Law*, 80 WASHINGTON LAW REVIEW 355, 359 (2005) (discussing *Kirby v. B.I. Inc.*, No. CIV.A.4:98–CV–1136–Y, 2003 U.S. Dist. LEXIS 16964, at 49–50 (N.D. Tex. Sept. 26, 2003).

59 Vlad Savov, *Samsung Sinks Deeper into Exploding Battery Quagmire as 'Samsung 7' Blamed for Car Fire,* THE VERGE (September 15, 2016).

60 Robert Donachie, *These Pictures Show The Horrifying Result of Samsung's Phone Explosions,* THE DAILY CALLER (September 12, 2016).

61 Stephen Gardner, *Internet of Things: Caution Urged as EU Reviews Smart Device Liability*, BLOOMBERG BNA: INTERNET RESOURCE CENTER (January 18, 2017).

62 *Id.*

63 Tony Romm, *Two U.S. Lawmakers Think the Government Has a New Cybersecurity Problem: The Internet of Things*, RECODE (August 1, 2017).

64 Bruce Schneier, *Regulation of the Internet of Things*, SCHNEIER ON SECURITY (November 10, 2016).

65 U.S. Food and Drug Administration (FDA) *Cybersecurity* (December 30, 2016).

66 Bruce Schneier, *Your WiFi-Connected Thermostat Can Take Down the Whole Internet. We Need New Regulations*, THE WASHINGTON POST (November 3, 2016).

67 Stanford University, The Center for Internet & Society, *Automated Driving: Legislative and Regulatory Action* (2017) (discussing the enactment of California S.B. 1298).

68 *Id.* (D.C.'s enactment of 1319–0931 (2013).

69 *Id.*

70 Arrian Marshall, *Congress Finally Gets Serious About Regulating Self-Driving Cars*, WIRED (July 19, 2017).

71 Larry Greenerneier, *Driverless Cars Will Face Moral Dilemmas*, SCIENTIFIC AMERICAN (June 23, 2016).

72 *Id.*

73 *Id.*

74 Section 230 of the Communications Decency Act (CDA) applies not only to large-scale providers of interactive computer services such as America Online but also to websites where third parties post content. Section 230 broadly extends liability: "No provider or user of an interactive computer service shall be treated as the publisher or speaker of any information provided by another information content provider." 47 U.S.C. § 230(c)(1) (2001). Information content providers is also defined broadly to include "any person or entity that is responsible, in whole or in part, for the creation or development of information provided through the Internet or any other interactive computer service." 47 U.S.C. § 230(f)(3) (2001).

75 Electronic Frontier Foundation, *CDA Cases*, https://ilt.eff.org/index.php/Defamation:_CDA_Cases.

76 *Stratton Oakmont, Inc. v. Prodigy Servs. Co.*, 63 U.S.L.W. 2765 (May 24, 1995), reargument denied, 1995 WL 805178 (N.Y. Sup. Dec. 11, 1995).

77 Electronic Frontier Foundation, Section 230 of the Communications Decency Act, https://www.eff.org/issues/cda230.

78 *Zeran v. America Online*, 129 F.3d 327 (4th Cir. 1997).

79 2000 U.S. Dist. LEXIS 8645 (N.D. Ill. June 21, 2000).

80 429 S.W.3d 752 (Tex. Ct. of App. 2014).

81 *Jones v. Dirty World Entertainment Recordings Inc.,* 755 F.3d 398 (6th Cir. 2014).

82 *Id.* at 403.

83 841 F.3d 733 (7th Cir. 2016).

84 767 F.3d 894 (9th Cir 2014).

85 *Tarasoff v. Regents of University of California,* 17 Cal.3d 425, 435, 131 Cal. Rptr. 14, 551 P.2d 334 (1976), *superseded by statute,* Cal. Civ. Code § 43.92.

86 *Id.*

87 Stephen Gardner, *Internet of Things: Caution Urged as EU Reviews Smart Device Liability*, BLOOMBERG BNA: INTERNET RESOURCE CENTER (January 18, 2017).

88 Roeland de Bruin, *Autonomous Intelligent Cars on the European Intersection of Liability and Privacy* (March 23, 2015) at 19.

89 *Don't Say a Word: How Powerful People Use Criminal Defamation Laws to Silence Their Critics*, THE ECONOMIST (July 12, 2017).

90 HCA 56 (Austl. 2002).

91 [2015] NIQB 11.

92 *CG v. Facebook Ireland Ltd.*, Columbia University, Freedom of Expression, https://globalfreedomofexpression.columbia.edu/cases/cg-v-facebook-ireland-ltd/.

93 *Zeran v. America Online*, 129 F.3d 327 (4th Cir. 1997).

94 *Id.* at 331.

95 JOHN RAWLS, A THEORY OF JUSTICE, (Cambridge, Massachusetts: The Belknap Press of Harvard University Press, 1971).

[96] Electronic Frontier Foundation, *CDA Section 230: The Most Important Law Protecting Internet Law* (2016).

[97] 2014 WL 73332206 (La. Ct. of App., Dec. 23, 2014).

CHAPTER FOUR

Cybercrimes: Law & Ethics

§ 4.0: CRIME ON THE INTERNET

Terms such as hacking, spoofing, piracy, spyware, adware and identity theft, are now part of the popular lexicon as Americans' fear of cybercrime victimization now exceeds that of street crime.[1] Popular movies such as *Blackhat*, *Live Free or Die Hard* and *The Girl with the Dragon Tattoo* feature cybercrime plots. Pop culture's unrealistic portrayals of law enforcement's ability to counter cybercriminals irks many security professionals. In the movies:

> every product works perfectly, every enterprise has the skilled team that it needs, and it's just a matter of getting that last puzzle piece into place for a magical security state to happen.[2]

One security professional satirizes CBS's *CSI Cyber*, which features an FBI agent who leads a team of brilliant government hackers: "Dark net! Deep web! Leetspeak! Cyber arson! This television program strains credibility even if you don't know a smartphone from a thermostat. This new CSI spinoff exists on the premise that whatever you don't know that's powered by electricity can kill you, and it does it with a visual flourish that rings false."[3]

Such romanticized mass-media depictions mislead the public about the complex technological and legal barriers that obstruct law enforcement's efforts to foil computer intrusions. This chapter will review the limitations of leading computer crime statutes and the need to fortify cross-border international enforcement. Our emphasis will be on the need to continuously update cybercrime statutes to meet the increasing challenges created by rapid advances in computing.

§ 4.1: FEDERAL COMPUTER CRIME AGENCIES

The National Cyber Investigative Joint Task Force (NCIJTF), founded in 2008, coordinates the anti-cyber threat activities of more than twenty federal agencies from across law enforcement, the intelligence community and the Department of Defense. This unique multi-agency organization's mission is synchronizing "joint efforts that focus on identifying, pursuing, and defeating the actual terrorists, spies, and criminals who seek to exploit our nation's systems. To accomplish this, the task force leverages the collective authorities and capabilities of its members and collaborates with international and private sector partners to bring all available resources to bear against domestic cyber threats and their perpetrators."

The Federal Bureau of Investigation (FBI) and the United States Department of Justice (DOJ) are the two most important federal law enforcement agencies proactively investigating cybercrime. Chart One depicts the major categories of computer crime and explains which law enforcement agencies take the lead in addressing specific crime categories.

CHART ONE: FEDERAL AGENCIES TARGETING CYBERCRIMES

Type of Computer Crime	Appropriate Federal Investigative Law Enforcement Agencies
Computer Intrusion (i.e. hacking)	FBI local office U.S. Secret Service Internet Crime Complaint Center
Password Trafficking	FBI local office U.S. Secret Service Internet Crime Complaint Center
Counterfeiting of Currency	U.S. Secret Service
Child Pornography or Exploitation	FBI local office if imported, U.S. Immigration and Customs Enforcement Internet Crime Complaint Center

Child Exploitation and Internet Fraud Matters That Have a Mail Nexus	U.S. Postal Inspection Service Internet Crime Complaint Center
Internet Fraud and SPAM	FBI local office U.S. Secret Service Federal Trade Commission (online complaint) if securities fraud or investment-related SPAM emails, Securities and Exchange Commission (online complaint) Internet Crime Complaint Center
Internet Harassment	FBI local office
Internet Bomb Threats	FBI local office ATF local office
Trafficking in explosive or incendiary devices or firearms over the Internet	FBI local office ATF local office

[A] Federal Bureau of Investigation

The Federal Bureau of Investigation describes itself as the first line of defense in investigating cyberattacks by criminals, foreign adversaries and terrorists. The Bureau's literature explains that "just as the FBI transformed itself to better address the terrorist threat after the 9/11 attacks, it is undertaking a similar transformation to address the pervasive and evolving cyberthreat."[4] For example, the Internet Crime Complaint Center (IC3), which is sponsored by the FBI and the National White Collar Crime Center, has created a database to track the most widespread online cybercrimes. To combat cybercrime, the FBI has launched the following initiatives:

> A Cyber Division at FBI headquarters to address cybercrime in a coordinated and cohesive manner;
>
> Specially trained cybersquads at FBI headquarters and in each of our 56 field offices, staffed with "agents and analysts who protect against and investigate computer intrusions, theft of intellectual property and

personal information, child pornography and exploitation and online fraud;

New Cyber Action Teams that travel around the world on a moment's notice to assist in computer intrusion cases and that gather vital intelligence that helps us identify the cybercrimes that are most dangerous to our national security and to our economy;

Our 93 Computer Crimes Task Forces nationwide combine state-of-the-art technology and the resources of our federal, state, and local counterparts; and

A growing partnership with other federal agencies, including the Department of Defense, the Department of Homeland Security, and others—which share similar concerns and resolve in combating cybercrime.[5]

[B] United States Department of Justice (DOJ)

United States Attorneys working for the DOJ prosecute cybercrimes by bringing lawsuits on behalf of the United States. The DOJ has identified cybercrimes such as hacking, online stalking and the theft of intellectual property as priority areas for federal law enforcement. The DOJ's Computer Crime and Intellectual Property Section (CCIPS) implements the agency's national anti-cybercrime strategies. This DOJ division prevents, investigates and prosecutes computer crimes by working with other government agencies, the private sector, academic institutions and its foreign counterparts.

CCIPS attorneys regularly resolve unique legal and investigative issues raised by emerging computer and telecommunications technologies. They run complex investigations, litigate cases, provide support for other prosecutors, educate law enforcement personnel and propose new legislation. CCIPS initiates and participates in numerous international campaigns that counter computer and intellectual property crimes.

§ 4.2: COMPUTER FRAUD AND ABUSE ACT

[A] The Provisions of the Computer Fraud & Abuse Act

Federal prosecutors "faced the dawn of the computer age with growing concern about the lack of criminal laws available to fight emerging computer crimes."[6] The Comprehensive Crime Control Act of 1984 was the first attempt of Congress to create criminal liability for computer-related crimes offenses.

The Computer Fraud and Abuse Act (CFAA) updated the 1984 statute in order to specifically address the unauthorized access and use of computers and computer networks. The CFAA punished any person who, knowingly and without authorization, caused at least $5,000 of damage to a protected computer in a single year.[7] "Protected computer," in this statute, refers to computers used in or that affect interstate or foreign commerce as well as all computers used by the federal government or financial institutions.

In addition to clarifying many provisions of the 1984 Act, the CFAA criminalized additional computer-related acts such as accessing computers to defraud and trespassing in a governmental computer.[8] Congress has amended the CFAA to penalize those who intentionally alter, damage or destroy data belonging to others. This CFAA amendment covers "such activities as the distribution of malicious code and denial of service attacks."[9]

Computer Fraud and Abuse Act Elements
1030(a)(2) Summary (Misdemeanor)

(1) Intentionally access a computer

(2) without or in excess of authorization

(3) obtain information

(4) from financial records of financial institution or consumer reporting agency

OR

the U.S. government

OR

a protected computer

1030(a)(2) Summary (Felony)

(5) committed for commercial advantage or private financial gain

OR

committed in furtherance of any criminal or tortious act

OR

the value of the information obtained exceeds $5,000

The CFAA has "been invoked involving a variety of Web-based activities that the drafter did not contemplate at all."[10] For example, the original authors of the legislation could not have foreseen the use of botnets or other automated software to extract information from websites.[11] Chart Two reports the current prison sentences by the type of CFAA offense.

CHART TWO: CRIMINAL PENALTIES FOR CFAA OFFENSES

Type of CFAA Offense	*Initial Prison Sentence in Years*
Obtaining National Security Information	Ten Years
Accessing a Computer and Obtaining Information	One Year (for misdemeanor) Five Years (for felony)
Trespassing in a Government Computer and Obtaining Information	One Year
Accessing a Computer and Obtaining Information (without authorization)	One Year (for misdemeanor) Five Years (for felony)
Accessing a Computer to Defraud & Obtain Value	Five Years
Intentionally Damaging by Knowing Transmission	Ten Years
Recklessly Damaging by Intentional Access	One Year (for misdemeanor) Five Years (for felony)
Negligently Causing Damage & Loss by Intentional Access	One Year
Trafficking in Passwords	One Year
Extortion using Computers	Five years[12]

[B] Stretching the CFAA to the Internet

(1) Amendments to the CFAA

After the 9/11 terrorist attacks, Congress amended the CFAA by the USA Patriot Act that broadened the meaning of "protected computer" to include computers located outside of the United States.[13] The USA Patriot Act "addresses situations where an attacker within the United States attacks a computer system located abroad and situations in which individuals in foreign countries route communications through the United States as they hack from one foreign country to another."[14]

The National Information Infrastructure Protection Act of 1996 extended federal computer crime statutes to encompass crimes committed using the Internet. This amendment to the CFAA extended the scope of the statute from "federal interest computers" to "protected computers." The law made it a federal crime to intentionally cause damage to a protected computer or to "cause damage recklessly, negligently or otherwise if the protected computer was intentionally accessed without authorization."

This federal statue specifically penalizes the act of accessing a computer to steal national security information. The computer must be "used in or affecting interstate or foreign commerce or communication." Several courts have held that using the Internet from a computer is sufficient to meet this element.[15]

Federal prosecutors deploy the CFAA to punish cybercriminals who release malware to obliterate files, crash computers through distributed denial of service attacks (DDoS), or knowingly impair a computer's integrity through other techniques.[16] However, relatively few cybercriminals have been prosecuted nationwide under the CFAA, despite the high frequency of attacks that employ malicious software. At present, "the CFAA is limited to violations of restrictions on access to information and not restrictions on its use."

Updating the CFAA in Response to Cybercrimes

As computer crimes continued to grow in sophistication and as prosecutors gained experience with the Computer Fraud & Abuse Act (CFAA), Congress amended the CFAA in 1988, 1989, 1990, 1994, 1996, 2001, 2002, and 2008. The 2008 amendments to the CFAA made the following changes to respond to evolving cybercrimes:

- Eliminated the requirement in 18 U.S.C. § 1030(a)(2)(C) that information must have been stolen through an interstate or foreign communication, thereby expanding jurisdiction for cases involving theft of information from computers;

- Eliminated the requirement in 18 U.S.C. § 1030(a)(5) that the defendant's action must result in a loss exceeding $5,000 and created a felony offense where the damage affects ten or more computers, closing a gap in the law.
- Expanded 18 U.S.C. § 1030(a)(7) to criminalize not only explicit threats to cause damage to a computer, but also threats to (1) steal data on a victim's computer, (2) publicly disclose stolen data, or (3) not repair damage the offender already caused to the computer;
- Created a criminal offense for conspiring to commit a computer hacking offense under section 1030;
- Broadened the definition of "protected computer" in 18 U.S.C. § 1030(e)(2) to the full extent of Congress's commerce power by including those computers used in or affecting interstate or foreign commerce or communication; and
- Provided a mechanism for civil and criminal forfeiture of property used in or derived from section 1030 violation.

Source: U.S. Justice Department, Prosecuting Computer Crimes (2017) at 2–3.

(2) The CFAA & Social Media Contracts

The *United States v. Drew*[17] prosecution illustrates the difficulties of applying traditional computer crime law to cyberbullying on social networks. Lori Drew, a homemaker, masqueraded as a teenage boy, stalked a 13-year-old girl and then induced her to commit suicide. Drew used a false MySpace identity to humiliate Meagan Meier, who was feuding with Drew's daughter.

She misled her teenage victim into forming an online romantic relationship under the pseudonym "Josh" and then began sending hostile notes. Megan Meier killed herself shortly after receiving an antagonistic message from Josh, declaring that the "world would be a better place without you."

Prosecutors charged Lori Drew with violating the CFAA by knowingly and intentionally accessing a computer used in interstate and foreign commerce in excess of her authorized access. Her computer access was unauthorized because her use of a false identity violated MySpace's terms of use that stated, "All registration information [must be] truthful and accurate." The issue in *U.S. v. Drew* was whether the intentional breach of MySpace's terms of use constituted a misdemeanor crime for purposes of the CFAA.

The federal court reversed Drew's jury conviction, holding that stretching the CFAA to apply to a mere violation of MySpace's terms of use violated the void-for-vagueness doctrine which stems from the Fifth and Fourteenth Amendments to the U.S. Constitution. Criminal statutes are void for vagueness if they do not state explicitly what conduct is punishable. Large numbers of people use false online identities and no law enforcement agency attempts to prosecute and jail them. The void for vagueness doctrine is limited to criminal law, therefore tort law can evolve faster to address new cyberwrongs.

§ 4.3: THE FEDERAL WIRETAP ACT

The Electronic Communications Privacy Act (ECPA), popularly known as the federal wiretap act, was enacted as an amendment to the Omnibus Crime Patrol and Safe Streets Act of 1968. The ECPA establishes criminal and civil remedies for the unauthorized interception or disclosure of electronic communications. An "electronic communication" is defined as any "transfer of signs, signals, wiring, images, sounds, data, or intelligence of any nature transmitted in whole or in part by a wire, radio, electromagnetic, photoelectronic, or photooptical system that affects interstate or foreign commerce . . ."[18]

The ECPA "aims to prevent hackers from obtaining, altering, or destroying certain stored electronic communications."[19] Web sites are classified as "users" of Internet access and are governed by the ECPA. Similarly, e-mail systems are electronic communications covered by the ECPA. In 2000, Congress updated the federal wiretap law when it enacted the Electronic Communications Privacy Act (ECPA) as an amendment to the Omnibus Crime Patrol and Safe Streets Act, Title III, of 1968.

The purpose of the amendments to the existing wiretap law was an effort to "update and clarify Federal privacy protections and standards in light of dramatic changes in new computer and telecommunications technologies."[20] The ECPA or the Wiretap Act punishes a person who intercepts, uses or discloses any wire or oral communication by using any electronic, mechanical or other device. The Wiretap Act criminalizes intercepting a communication, disclosing an intercepted communication and using an intercepted communications.

The Wiretap Act also recognizes statutory exceptions, defenses, and penalties. The ECPA protects the rights of persons who post or receive electronic communications on the Internet. The provision of the ECPA proscribing interception of electronic communications only applies to intercepting or accessing information while in transmission whereas provision of ECPA proscribing unauthorized access of stored electronic communications applies once electronic messages are stored.

Title II punishes a person who, without authority, accesses a wire or electronic communication while in storage. The USA PATRIOT Act also amended the ECPA to list crimes for which investigators may get wiretap orders to access communications. Under this Amendment, federal government agents may intercept email and monitor other Internet communications.

The USA Patriot Act empowers the FBI to issue national security letters (NSLs) to wire or electronic communication service providers allowing them to gain access to subscriber information relevant to terrorism investigations. The FBI typically couples NSLs with nondisclosure clauses that prohibit the recipient from even disclosing the request.

The FBI Director authorizes the nondisclosure clause, only after certifying "that otherwise there may result a danger to the national security of the United States, interference with a criminal, counterterrorism, or counterintelligence investigation, interference with diplomatic relations, or danger to the life or physical safety of any person." The targets of NSL orders and nondisclosure clauses challenge them as prior restraints under the First Amendment of the United States Constitution.

[A] The Elements of an ECPA Criminal Offense

The Electronic Communications Privacy Act (ECPA) is the federal criminal statute that prohibits the unauthorized access or alteration of records, stored wire communications, or electronic communications by persons without the authority to access the computer. The ECPA prohibits the unauthorized disclosure to any person or entity of the contents of an electronic communication. To establish a violation of the ECPA (often referred to as the Wiretap Act), federal prosecutors must prove five elements: that a defendant:

(1) Intentionally

(2) Intercepted, endeavored to intercept or procured another person to intercept or endeavor to intercept

(3) The contents of

(4) An electronic communication or

(5) Using a device.[21]

The core prohibition of the Wiretap Act is prohibits "any person" from intentionally intercepting, or attempting to intercept, any wire, oral, or electronic communication." Under Title I of the Wiretap Act there are three types of activities that are prohibited: (i) intercepting or endeavoring to intercept electronic communications, (ii) disclosing or endeavoring to disclose intercepted information, and (iii) using the content of intercepted information.

The Stored Communications Act (SCA) amended the ECPA to prohibit the unauthorized access of stored communications. Once an e-mail is received and stored in the system it falls under the Stored Communications Act (SCA), or Title II, regardless of how temporary the storage. Title II protects stored communications from unauthorized or exceeded authorized access, but it does not apply to the person or entities providing the wire or electronic communications service. The distinction between the ECPA and the SCA is that the ECPA applies to electronic data in transit, while the SCA applies to stored data.

[B] ECPA & SCA Defenses

(1) The Ordinary Course Exception

The ECPA recognizes an "ordinary course of business" exception that shields computer professionals who are updating, modifying, or doing routine maintenance with computer systems. To meet the ordinary course of business exception, the employer has to demonstrate that: (i) the device used to intercept the electronic communication is "a telephone or telegraphic instrument, equipment or facility, or any component thereof," either provided or installed by the employer, and (ii) that the device is used by the employer within the ordinary course of the business.[22]

However, the employer is only allowed to intercept long enough to determine the nature of the communication. If the communication is personal, the employer must cease and desist from intercepting the communications further. This exception will apply where an Internet service provider (ISP) acquires electronic information during its ordinary course of business and it is not an interception of an electronic communication.

(2) The Rendition of Service Exception

Under the rendition of service exception to the ECPA, a provider may intercept electronic communications within its network "as may be necessarily incident to the rendition of the service or to the protection of the rights or property of the provider of that service."[23]

This federal liability shield protects systems operators from prosecution or being liable for civil damages when they intercept data to improve the communication service. The "necessary to the rendition of his service" clause permits providers to intercept, use, or disclose communications in the ordinary course of business when the interception is unavoidable."[24]

(3) Consent of Users

The ECPA permits service providers or anyone else to intercept and disclose an electronic communication where either the sender or recipient of the message has effectively consented to disclosure. The Wiretap Act allows interception and disclosure of an electronic communication if either the sender or the recipient of the message consents.[25] Consent, as defined by the ECPA, encompasses implied consent, which in the context of email monitoring is an employer's prior notice that it will monitor emails and other Internet usage.[26]

§ 4.4: THE ECONOMIC ESPIONAGE ACT

The Economic Espionage Act (EEA) signed into law by President Clinton on October 11, 1996, was enacted to punish and deter foreign and domestic spies threatening America's economic well-being. Until 1996, there was no federal criminal statute punishing industrial spying by foreign governments and agents.

The prosecution of trade secret theft as a criminal offense is a fairly recent development. Prior to the EEA, prosecutors pursued the theft of trade secrets by using existing law such as the 1934 National Stolen Property Act, which was intended to punish thieves who also fled across state borders in automobiles. The National Stolen Property Act applied to tangible goods but was not clearly applicable to the unauthorized transfer of intangibles such as intellectual property.

Congress enacted the EEA to address gaps in the criminal law punishing and deterring industrial espionage. The EEA criminalizes trade secret misappropriation and the theft of other confidential information. To qualify for trade secret protection, the information must have actual or potential economic value that the owner has taken reasonable measures to protect. For domestic economic espionage, individuals can be fined $250,000 and are subject to ten years of imprisonment. For organizations, the maximum fine is $5,000,000.[27]

The EEA criminalizes two types of offenses: (1) economic espionage that benefits foreign governments or entities and (2) the theft of trade secrets that benefit any person but the true owner.[28] The vast majority of prosecutions were filed under Section 1832, which classifies "attempt" and "conspiracy" as distinct offenses from those acts that constitute completed crimes under the statute.

The EEA specifically prohibits the theft of trade secrets for the benefit of a foreign government, instrumentality or agent. Individuals convicted of this offense are subject to $500,000 fines and a maximum of fifteen years in prison, while organizations face fines of up to $5,000,000. Prosecutors seldom use this provision because the U.S. Attorney General requires that the Assistant Attorney General for the National Security Division approve lawsuits against foreign governments.

§ 4.5: PRIVATE ENFORCEMENT OF FEDERAL COMPUTER CRIME STATUTES

[A] Crimtort Civil Actions to Combat Cybercrimes

The clear division between criminal law and civil law is rapidly eroding as federal criminal statutes increasingly allow the victims of computer crimes to file private lawsuits to recoup their damages. In a wide range of legal fields, including antitrust, securities, computer crimes and environmental litigation, Congress has enacted a private cause of action to supplement public enforcement. For example, only the government had standing to sue under the Economic Espionage Act until 2016, when Congress amended the EEA to permit the victims of trade secret misappropriation to file civil actions for monetary damages.

The term "crimtort" is a portmanteau to describe a hybrid remedy that combines criminal and tort legal principles to fill the enforcement gap created by the inherent limitations of U.S. criminal law. Cybercrimtorts allow private litigants to seek compensation for civil damages suffered from computer intrusions (CFAA), the interceptions of electronic communications (ECPA) and the theft of trade secrets (EEA).

The dual private/public enforcement provisions of many federal crime statutes represent a uniquely American legal approach that uses private lawsuits to advance a public purpose. Chart Three compares federal criminal prosecution of cybercrimes to the civil action provisions contained in these statutes.

CHART THREE: THE KEY ATTRIBUTES CYBERCRIMTORTS

Type of Action	Federal Computer Crime Statutes (CFAA, ECPA, and EEA)	Cybercrimtort Actions (CFAA, ECPA, and EEA)
Branch of Law	Public Law	Private Law
Purposes	Punishment, Deterrence	Compensation for the Victimized Computer Company that Serves a Public Purpose
Who Initiates the Lawsuit?	Federal District Attorneys	Private Companies Victimized by Computer Intrusion, Interceptions, or Trade Secret Theft
Standard of Proof for the Offense	Beyond a Reasonable Doubt	Preponderance of Evidence (More Likely Than Not)
Global Reach of Legal Action	Only U.S. Federal District Attorneys May File Criminal CFAA and ECPA but There Must Be a Nexus to Conduct Inside the U.S. Specific Application to Conduct Outside the U.S. is needed to invoke the Economic Espionage Act.	Civil Litigants May Reach Conduct Outside the U.S. Under the Defend Trade Secrets Act of 2016.

[B] CFAA Private Enforcement

The CFAA authorizes private civil lawsuits by victims who wish to seek compensatory damages or injunctive relief for computer intrusions. "Any person who suffers damage or loss by reason of a violation of [the CFAA] may maintain a civil action against the violator to obtain compensatory damages and injunctive relief or other equitable relief."[29] Civil CFAA lawsuits have been far more successful than federal prosecutions in seeking redress for computer intrusions because of the limitations of criminal law enforcement.[30]

The CFAA's civil damages' provision defines the victim's "loss" as the reasonable cost of responding to an offense, conducting a damage assessment, restoring the data, system, or information to its prior condition, as well as any lost revenue.[31] Courts have yet to determine whether a mere violation of terms of use, where there is authorized access, constitutes a violation of the CFAA as illustrated in the following scenario:

> An employee logs onto a password-protected company server, visits an electronic directory to which she has proper access (because of her position in the company) and steals thousands of the company's most sensitive files by transferring them to an external hard drive. Days later, that employee terminates her employment, hands off the external hard drive to a competitor and joins the competitor's operations using her former employer's trade secrets. What remedies, if any, does the former employer have?[32]

The following Internet court decisions illustrate the clashing judicial perspectives about the application of the CFAA to this legal dilemma.

[C] CFAA Civil Lawsuits

(1) International Airport Centers v. Citrin

In *Int'l Airport Centers v. Citrin,*[33] International Airport Centers (IAC) employed Jacob Citrin in their real estate business. IAC issued Citrin a company computer that he used to assemble and interpret data on the sale and leasing of properties. When Citrin left IAC, he used permanent erasure software to delete his files by writing over the company's files and backups. IAC filed a CFAA civil lawsuit against him, which did not require proof that the defendant accessed a computer at all.

Judge Richard Posner, writing for a Seventh Circuit panel, held that Citrin's erasure of real estate data caused damage without authorization to a protected computer, thus violating the CFAA. Damage, as defined by the CFAA, includes "any impairment to the integrity or availability of data, a program, a system, or information." *Citrin* is a significant case for computer professionals because of the federal appeals court's expansive reading of the CFAA in applying this statute to an ex-employee who deleted data files after he left his job.

(2) LVRC Holdings Inc. v. Brekka

In *LVRC Holdings LLC v. Brekka,*[34] an employee at an addiction treatment center negotiated with his employer, LVRC Holdings, seeking an ownership stake in the business. During negotiations, Brekka emailed several confidential business documents to his and his wife's personal email accounts. The negotiations broke down and Brekka left his employment with LVRC. The former employer filed a civil CFAA action against Brekka after discovering that he had retained confidential business emails on his personal email accounts.

The Ninth Circuit ruled in favor of Brekka, reasoning that even if he accessed a company computer for an improper purpose, he would not be liable for a CFAA cause of action until the employer revoked his access. The U.S. Justice Department describes *Brekka* as a bellwether case, reflecting the path of the law:

> Based on this recent case law, courts appear increasingly likely to reject the idea that a defendant accessed a computer "without authorization" in insider cases—cases where the defendant had some current authorization to access the computer. Accordingly, prosecutors should think carefully before charging such defendants with violations that require the defendants to access a computer "without authorization" and instead consider bringing charges under those subsections that require proof that the defendant exceeded authorized access.[35]

This Ninth Circuit's decision, which limits the scope of when an employee violates the CFAA by accessing a computer "without authorization," conflicts with the more expansive Seventh Circuit opinion in *Citrin.* Critics argue that the Seventh Circuit's broader reading permits social media providers to use CFAA civil actions to prevent start-up companies from accessing user data.[36] In October 2017, the U.S. Supreme Court declined requests to resolve this federal circuit split. Judicial splits encourage "forum shopping," which is the filing of civil actions in jurisdictions favorable to the plaintiff.

[D] ECPA Private Enforcement

Like the CFAA, the ECPA provides for private enforcement against violators of the federal wiretap statute. The ECPA allows civil actions by any "electronic communication service, subscriber, or other person" where a wiretap was committed intentionally. Employers and other corporate entities frequently use the ECPA as a civil cause of action against a current or ex-employee who has intercepted an electronic communication.

The victims of illegal wiretaps can file civil lawsuits seeking actual damages, punitive damages and attorney's fees. A former employee was awarded $150,000 in statutory damages and $50,000 in punitive damages after "her employer's president accessed her personal email accounts without her permission both during her employment and one-year after her separation."[37] The Federal Trade Commission is empowered to seek civil enforcement of the ECPA but this provision has been rarely invoked.

[E] ECPA Civil Lawsuits

Each of the cases in this section are federal wiretap civil actions filed by private parties against defendants who intercepted electronic communications Eloisa LaRocca filed an ECPA claim after her ex-husband installed spyware on her computer that intercepted the emails she transmitted. The former husband argued that the ECPA did not apply to the interception of spousal electronic communications and that the computer was not her separate property but joint marital property, where she had no expectation of privacy. The Louisiana district court established an important precedent by refusing to dismiss the ex-wife's ECPA cause of action reasoning:

> Harboring uncertainties as to his wife's faithfulness, appellee obtained a device for tapping and recording telephone conversations. He attached the device to phone lines within his home and thereby intercepted conversations between his wife and another man. The conversations were mildly compromising, establishing that the other man was making advances, and that while the wife was resisting, she was not doing so in a firm and final fashion. Convinced that he had "caught her," appellee played the tapes, or portions thereof, to various neighbors and family members. He also played them for a lawyer, on whose advice the wife agreed to an uncontested divorce.[38]

Facebook, Instagram and other social media sites provide electronic communications services and thus are subject to the ECPA. In *In re Facebook Privacy Litigation,*[39] Facebook users filed a class action lawsuit against the provider, contending that the social media site divulged information about users to advertisers without their consent; thus, subjecting Facebook to liability under the SCA.

The federal court ruled that the Facebook users did not state a valid claim under the SCA because they did not allege that the communications at issue were sent to Facebook or to its advertisers. Nevertheless, a 2013 New Jersey federal court ruled that the SCA applied to Facebook postings where the user's privacy preferences restricted postings to Facebook friends.[40]

[F] EEA Private Enforcement

In 2016, Congress amended the Economic Espionage Act with the Defend Trade Secrets Act of 2016 (DTSA), which gives companies victimized by trade secret theft the right to seek injunctive relief and damages. Trade secret owners are now able to conduct discovery and seek monetary and injunctive relief. Courts can award trade secret owners the greater of either $5,000,000 or three times the value of the stolen trade secret, including expenses for research and design and other costs. The essence of a crimtort remedy is using private enforcement to supplement public prosecution as with CFAA and ECPA civil lawsuits.

[G] EEA Civil Lawsuits

DTSA dramatically increases the effectiveness of the EEA by granting plaintiffs a right to pursue monetary damages against those who improperly acquire a company's trade secrets. Improper means include "theft, bribery, misrepresentation, breach or inducement of a breach of a duty to maintain secrecy, or espionage through electronic or other means."[41] In the first year after the DTSA was enacted, civil litigants filed over 100 cases, approaching the total number of criminal cases filed by federal prosecutors in the two decades after the EEA became law in 1996.

[H] Other Civil Enforcement

Many computer companies have established bug bounty programs that give cash or recognition rewards for uncovering exploitable holes in security.[42] Facebook, for example, offers a minimum of a $500 bounty to encourage ethical hackers to report vulnerabilities to the company. Between 2011 and early 2016, Facebook received more than 2,400 valid submissions, awarding more than $4.3 million to 800+ researchers.

Google, Microsoft and Facebook joined forces in 2012 to advance a bug bounty program to address open source security issues. Other companies refuse to pay bounties, viewing this as an incentive for extortion by hackers. The proper balance between voluntarily rewarding a security researcher for uncovering computer susceptibilities and creating corporate problems by encouraging extortion is difficult to draw.

In 2015, *InfoWorld* reported that Kristin Erik Hermansen notified FireEye, a cybersecurity provider, that he had identified serious zero-day vulnerabilities within FireEye's computer system that, if publicly revealed, could be exploited by hackers before FireEye had time to develop a patch. Hermansen demanded compensation in return for informing the company about the design flaws. FireEye had no bug bounty program and Hermansen refused to disclose the vulnerabilities unless he was paid. When denied payment, Hermansen harmed FireEye by posting the details on two websites, Exploit Database and Pastebin. A prominent security researcher summarizes the dilemma involved in the decision of whether to pay:

> [T]o be on the receiving end of an email that says we've found a critical security vulnerability in your site but I'm not going to tell you unless you pay me certainly feels like extortion. On one hand, I want to be as responsible as possible and if my users are at risk then I need to know and patch this issue to protect them. On the other hand, this is such irresponsible and unethical behaviour that interacting with this person seems out of the question. Their behaviour and approach calls into question their motives. They've effectively conducted a penetration test against my website, without permission and are trying to extract money out of me.[43]

§ 4.6: UPDATING CYBERCRIME LAW

[A] Crime & Technological Change

A century ago, the Second Industrial Revolution required a parallel period of legal updating. The profusion of technological advances created novel societal troubles while it was solving old ones. The rise of the automobile, for example, led to a new crime of trafficking women across state lines for prostitution. In response, Congress enacted the Mann Act, known as the White Slave Traffic Act of 1910. In 1919, Congress enacted the National Motor Vehicle Theft Act (Dyer Act) that gave the FBI authority to investigate auto thefts that crossed state lines. The Bureau's official history states:

> The technological revolution was contributing to crime as well. 1908 was the year that Henry Ford's Model T first began rolling off assembly lines in Motor City, making automobiles affordable to the masses and attractive commodities for thugs and hoodlums, who would soon begin buying or stealing them to elude authorities and move about the country on violent crime sprees.

The FBI, aided by strengthened federal criminal laws and an enhanced budget, coordinated multi-state law enforcement to counter criminal use of the automobile. By the mid-1930s, armed robbers like Bonnie and Clyde could no longer escape justice simply by driving across state lines. During the same era, advances in telephone technology enabled the launching of illegal gambling empires, which were dismantled by the FBI's effective use of wiretaps.

[B] Old Crimes Take on New Forms

"Traditional" offenses often require updating, or at least modifying, extant criminal law to apply to intangibles such as software, databases and intellectual property.[44] For example, in April 2017, hackers obtained ten unreleased episodes of the television show "Orange Is the New Black" and published them on the Internet after Netflix refused to pay a demanded Bitcoin ransom. In May 2017, a similar extortion plot was launched against Disney by black-hat hackers who threatened to publish a purloined copy of the not yet released "Pirates of the Caribbean: Dead Men Tell No Tales" film unless they were paid.

Disney has refused to cooperate with these criminals and enlisted help from law enforcement agencies. Courts may stretch current laws against theft and extortion to cybercrimes, but many aspects of these crimes do not mesh well with statutes drafted before the existence of the Internet. For example, Disney's big concern is not the return of stolen copies, but rather the loss of profits if these films are illicitly uploaded onto the Internet.

[C] Updating Criminal Procedure

Contemporary law enforcement agencies are gradually shifting from an exclusive concern with street crime to cybercrime prosecution. For example, in 2016, the U.S. Supreme Court updated the Federal Rules of Criminal Procedure to permit a single warrant to apply to an army of captured computers that cybercriminals have incorporated into an illegal botnet, even though the machines are located throughout the United States.

Previously, judges in each of the U.S.'s ninety-four districts had to issue individual warrants so that infected computers in their jurisdiction could be searched. Warrants for botnets are still problematic to execute. It is almost impossible to determine which computers have been incorporated into the botnet with specificity demanded by federal judges.

Botnet Operation Disabled By FBI
The FBI disabled an enormous botnet composed of an estimated two million captured computers, which tracked their users' keystrokes in order to steal passwords and other confidential information.
Source: Federal Bureau of Investigation, *Botnet Operation Disabled: FBI Seizes Servers to Stop Cyber Fraud* (April 14, 2011).

Internet crime investigations do not mesh well with customary law enforcement techniques because computer crimes are fast moving and lack a physical crime scene. Online intruders, unlike those at physical crime scenes, will typically leave few digital footprints. There are seldom witnesses to cybercrimes because the criminal is physically remote. Security breaches frequently remain unseen until weeks or months after the intrusion. Only the best-funded law enforcement agencies possess the expertise and resources necessary to investigate and prosecute cybercriminals.

[D] Updating Criminal Law Jurisdiction

The authority of enforcement officials is generally restricted to a specific physical jurisdiction, while cybercriminals often launch their crimes from outside of U.S. borders. In *United States v. Ivanov*,[45] a federal court addressed the issue of whether a defendant lured to the United States from a foreign country could be prosecuted for violating the CFAA because the victim was a U.S. entity.

Aleksey Vladimirovich Ivanov of Chelyabinsk, Russia was caught in a honeypot sting operation, created by the FBI, when he was lured to the United States for a fake "job interview" in Seattle. Federal prosecutors charged Ivanov with CFAA offenses including conspiracy, extortion and the possession of illegal access devices. The indictment alleged that these crimes had been committed against the Online Information Bureau (OIB) whose business and infrastructure were based in Vernon, Connecticut.

Ivanov filed a motion to dismiss the charges since his computer crimes were committed in Russia, outside of U.S. jurisdiction. The district court refused to dismiss the action, ruling that OIB, located in Connecticut, suffered detrimental effects from Ivanov's actions. Ivanov was prosecuted for accessing a company's computers without authorization. The Russian hacker was convicted upon proof that he knowingly obtained, altered, or caused the transmission of information with the intent to defraud. Ivanov was sentenced to serve 48 months and, following his release, an additional period of supervised probation.

Law enforcement agencies are continually requesting strengthened statutes and additional mutual law enforcement treaties to police the growing number of international cybercrimes. To provide U.S. authorities with more effective legal weapons to thwart international cybercriminals, President Obama issued an executive order in April 2015 that granted U.S. Treasury officials the right to freeze foreign bank accounts and block the travel of international cybercriminals. This temporary measure was necessary because there is no effective cross-border cybercriminal law enforcement in some regions.[46]

[E] First Amendment & Cyberbullying

Drafting U.S. cyberbullying statutes that do not violate First Amendment free speech guarantees has become an almost-insurmountable challenge as illustrated by the 2016 case of *State v. Bishop*.[47] In this case, Robert Bishop was charged with cyberbullying under a North Carolina state statute, which criminalizes using an online posting to intimidate a minor. During the 2011–2012 school year, two students at a North Carolina high school engaged in a series of hostile online exchanges that involved accusations of deviant sexual proclivities.

The mother of one of the participants contacted the police, who charged Bishop with cyberbullying. He was convicted but, on appeal, the North Carolina Supreme Court reversed the trial court's decision. The court struck down the cyberbullying statute because it restricted constitutional protected speech, not merely non-expressive conduct.

[F] Fourth Amendment & Cell Phones

The Fourth Amendment "protects people from unreasonable government intrusions into their legitimate expectations of privacy." Obtaining a search warrant requires convincing a judge that there is "a fair probability that contraband or evidence of a crime will be found in a particular place." The exclusionary rule suppresses evidence secured by the government without a warrant or some exception to the warrant requirement. The test for whether the government violated the Fourth Amendment is whether the search or seizure was reasonable under the totality of the circumstances.

Laws drafted to address telephone booths do not mesh well with modern electronic communications such as email or text messaging. Countless U.S. Supreme Court decisions have updated the Fourth Amendment by considering changing sociological and technological realities. In a 1928 decision, the U.S. Supreme Court ruled that there was no violation of the Fourth Amendment when the police employed a secret telephone wiretap.

The court reasoned that law enforcers had not physically entered the telephone booth and therefore had not violated the defendant's rights. This precedent was overruled in 1967 where the Court reasoned: "The Government's activities in electronically listening to and recording the petitioner's words violated the privacy upon which he justifiably relied while using the telephone booth and thus constituted a 'search and seizure' within the meaning of the Fourth Amendment."

Today's criminal procedure also lags behind Internet-related technologies. The smartphone, in particular, is dramatically affecting Fourth Amendment jurisprudence. Cell phones—once figments of science fiction—now live in most Americans' pockets and purses. These devices enable owners not only to send and receive audio telephone calls, but also to access the Internet, send text messages, initiate video calls, participate in multi-player virtual reality games and access cloud data that may contain a user's most intimate information. Law enforcement officers routinely track cell phones and attempt to introduce text messages as evidence in criminal prosecutions.

These devices are double-edged swords, increasing convenience at the expense of privacy. Each time one makes or receives a call, the phone leaves a digital trail in the form of historical cell-site location information (CSLI). CSLI is comprised of business records kept by service providers that identify which cell towers routed which communications. A CSLI was the focus in the *Zanders* case, which tested search-and-seizure protections under the Federal and Indiana Constitutions. To locate Marcus Zanders—an armed-robbery suspect at large—police asked his cell-phone service provider, Sprint, to provide historical CSLI. At Zanders' trial, the state presented the CSLI, along with a detective's explanatory testimony.

Following his convictions on four robbery-related counts, Zanders appealed. He argued that obtaining the CSLI violated his Federal and State Constitutional rights and that the detective improperly testified as an expert witness. The court ruled that asking a provider for a user's historical CSLI is not a Fourth Amendment "search." No warrant was required because the combination of high suspicion, low intrusion and moderately high law-enforcement needs justified the request given the totality of the circumstances. Finally, explaining the CSLI to the jury required only a skilled witness, not an expert.

(1) Global Positioning System (GPS)

The extent of Fourth Amendment protection for the government's use of GPS in surveillance was an issue in *United States v. Jones.*[48] In *Jones*, the United States Supreme Court held that the installation of a GPS device on a person's car to gather information, along with the use of the device to track the car's movements, constituted a Fourth Amendment search.

In that case, police officers were investigating Antoine Jones, the owner and operator of a nightclub in the District of Columbia, who was under suspicion of trafficking in narcotics. Police used multiple techniques "including visual surveillance of the nightclub, installation of a camera focused on the front door of the club, and a pen register covering Jones's cellular phone." The government conceded that it did not seek a warrant to place a GPS on the defendant's vehicle:

> [A]gents installed a GPS tracking device on the undercarriage of the Jeep while it was parked in a public parking lot. Over the next 28 days, the Government used the device to track the vehicle's movements, and once had to replace the device's battery when the vehicle was parked in a different public lot in Maryland. By means of signals from multiple satellites, the device established the vehicle's location within 50 to 100 feet, and communicated that location by cellular phone to a Government computer.

The defendant was charged with cocaine distribution, causally connected to the information provided by the GPS. The Court held that the government's installation of a GPS device to monitor a car's movements constituted a Fourth Amendment search requiring a warrant.

In *Cunningham v. N.Y State Dept. of Labor*,[49] the New York Court of Appeals ruled that a State Inspector General's order to attach a GPS device to a Department of Labor employee's personal car constituted a search within the meaning of the Fourth Amendment and the New York Constitution. The search in question was conducted as part of an investigation into the employee's alleged unauthorized absences and the submission of false time reports. The nonstop GPS surveillance employed satellite communications to track the automobile's location.

To download the location information retrieved by the device, the investigator would simply drive past the car and press a button on a receiver unit, causing the tracking history to be transmitted and saved to his computer. The court ruled that the government's search did not require a warrant because it fell under the workplace exception. However, the search did not comply with either the New York or U.S. Constitution because it was not a reasonable search.

(2) Stingray Searches

Rapidly evolving information technologies and applications insure that the requirements for a legal search will continue to be a subject of controversy. In a July 2016 precedent-setting decision, a U.S. federal judge suppressed evidence against an alleged drug dealer because law enforcement's warrantless use of a cell phone tracking device, known as a "stingray," violated the Fourth Amendment's provision against unreasonable government search and seizure.[50]

The stingray tricks mobile phones into transmitting "pings" to the device by mimicking a cell phone tower, permitting investigators to determine the physical location where the telephone is being used. In August 2016, the U.S. Circuit Court of Appeals ruled that the warrantless tracking of a cell phone was admissible in an emergency in a case where a drug dealer had murdered a potential witness.

U.S. courts have not yet determined how the Fourth Amendment applies to mass surveillance. The FBI would require a court-ordered search warrant to enter an individual's house to access emails. However, a federal enforcement agency can potentially examine every Gmail message you have ever sent without a warrant through a subpoena issued to Google. Whether using facial recognition technology to search through millions of photos to identify an individual requires a search warrant is still unclear.

Observers predict that the Trump Administration will grant the FBI, the National Security Agency, and the CIA broadened powers of mass surveillance including "a single warrant to access and search thousands or millions of computers at once" as well as other expanded rights to monitor cyberspace communications.[51] "In a reversal of curbs imposed after Edward Snowden's revelations in 2013 about mass data-gathering by the NSA, Trump and Congress may move to reinstate the collection of bulk telephone records, renew powers to collect the content of emails and other internet activity, ease restrictions on hacking into computers and let the FBI keep preliminary investigations open longer."[52]

§ 4.7: CYBERLAW ENFORCEMENT

[A] Child Pornography

Child pornography has exploded on the Internet because "[t]he advent of the Internet has greatly increased the ease of transporting, distributing, receiving and advertising child pornography in interstate commerce."[53] The most effective child pornography prosecutions employ nationwide sweeps in cooperation with local law enforcement. For example, "Operation Pacifier" led to charges filed against almost two hundred men in 2016. In this sting operation, the FBI took over a DarkNet child pornography website and then gathered evidence against the site's visitors.

Any individual who attempts or conspires to commit a child pornography offense is subject to prosecution under state and federal laws. New Jersey prosecutors filed charges against an elementary school teacher, a school bus driver and fourteen other persons for possession and distribution of child pornography on a popular online file-sharing network.

Louisiana's "Unlawful Use or Access of Social Media" law prohibits registered sex offenders whose previous criminal convictions involved juveniles from "using or accessing social networking websites, chat rooms and peer-to-peer networks." The Louisiana statute is vulnerable to a void-for-vagueness challenge because it does not define the terms "using" or "accessing."

Criminal penalties for child pornography include life imprisonment without parole.[54] The justification for such a harsh penalty is that pedophiles can purchase, view, or exchange abusive child pornography with virtually complete anonymity on Internet.[55] The United States Attorney's Office for the Central District of Illinois prosecuted a case in which an Ohio defendant received a life-imprisonment sentence for his extensive participation in a globalized online child exploitation enterprise. Gmoser, the defendant, was arrested after a search of his home computer and other devices yielded millions of files containing child pornography. Discovery uncovered that Gmoser was part of a 30,000-member network for pornography production and exchange.

[B] Criminalizing Sexual Advertisements

Backpage.com charges users "$5–$10 to post ads in the adult category, $1 to post ads in the dating category, or otherwise post ads for free." The state of Washington filed charges against this business practice because the website lacks the ability to ensure that none of the sexual advertisements involves minors.

A federal court ruled in *Backpage.com v. McKenna*[56] that Backpage.com could not be held criminally or civilly responsible for advertisements created by third parties, even if they are "ads for commercial sex acts involving minors." After this decision, state attorneys general across the U.S. drafted a letter urging Congress to better address particularly egregious website misconduct.

In 2015, the U.S. Senate approved an amendment entitled the Stop Advertising Victims of Exploitation (SAVE) Act, which would add the word "advertises" to a federal sex trafficking criminal statute. This proposed statute would weaken website providers' shield under Section 230 of the Communications Decency Act, a law discussed in Chapter Three. Sex trafficking statutes, whether at the state or federal law, are notoriously difficult to draft to overcome problems of vagueness and other First Amendment infirmities.

[C] Ransomware

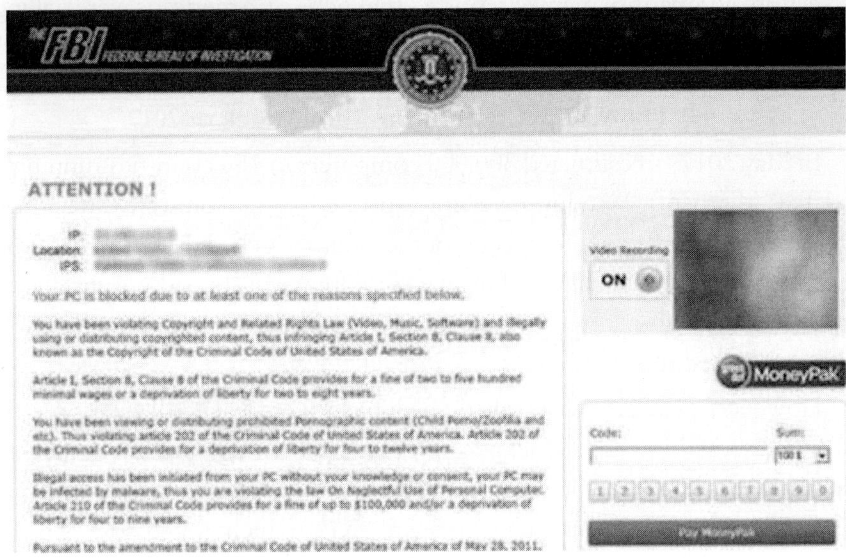

Federal Bureau of Investigation, New Internet Scam Ransomware Scam: 'Ransomware' Locks Computers, Demands Payment, (August 9, 2012).

Ransomware denies companies or individual victims the use of critical data and/or computer systems unless the victim pays a "ransom" to have his data restored. The targets of ransomware are generally unaware of their victimization until they can no longer access their data and they see instructions on how to pay the ransom. Generally, the extortionist demands payment in a cryptocurrency because of the anonymity that this transaction provides.

Innovative techniques are being developed in the struggle against ransomware. For example, on July 25, 2016, a coalition composed of Dutch police, Europol and two private cybersecurity companies launched the website www.nomoreransom.org. This website provides users with advice for avoiding ransomware and provides de-encryption keys that may help users recover their data. The website's homepage boasts that: "The battle is over for these ransomware threats. If you have been infected with one of these types of ransomware click on the link under its name and it will lead you to a decryption tool." This claim is overly optimistic since ransomware attacks continue to increase at a rapid pace.

"Ran scam," which appears to be ransomware but destroys rather than encrypts the data, is becoming increasingly common. The victims get nothing in return for their ransom payment, since the files no longer exist. A survey by the cybersecurity company Symantec reported that 64% of Americans were willing to pay digital ransom demands, the highest percentage of any country in the world.

The WannaCry Ransomware Attack of 2017

In May 2017, an estimated 300,000 computers in 150 countries running an outdated Microsoft Windows version suffered a ransomware attack that demanded $300 in Bitcoin to unencrypt the victim's locked data. Microsoft had issued a patch for this malware but many computer users had not installed it. U.S. federal government employees of the National Security Agency (NSA) originally created this malware.

However, a hacker group called Shadow Brokers leaked details about this and other secret software stockpiled by the NSA to the public. Particularly vulnerable were the estimated seven percent of the world's computers using a 15-year-old Window's operating system, XP, which Microsoft stopped supporting in 2014, although it later released a patch for the XP version.

The damage would have been even far more extensive had it not been for the actions of a 22-year-old, self-taught English cybersecurity researcher, Marcus Hutchins, who noticed that the program referred to an unregistered domain name. Hutchins quickly purchased the domain as he has done many times before in other investigations.

When his newly acquired website went live, the malware attack stopped, as the cybercriminals had luckily included instructions within the software to stop spreading the ransomware if that website ever became active. This was presumably because the attackers wished to have a way to terminate the process if the cyberattack became uncontrollable.

Hutchins notes in his blog, that he felt joy when he realized that he had accidently stopped the hack, "Now you probably can't picture a grown man jumping around with the excitement of having just been ransomwared, but this was me." Ironically, Hutchins' status as a hero was short-lived. Hutchins was arrested and charged with creating the Kronos banking Trojan. Multiple stolen or fake credit cards funded his online defense account.[57] Additional ransomware attacks are inevitable, as the potential rewards for cybercrime are high, while the risk of identification and punishment are low. The Bitcoin wallets tied to the WannaCry perpetrators were collected, presumably by the perpetrators.

[D] Illegal Markets on the DarkNet

The term "dark side hacker" derives from George Lucas' film, *Star Wars*, in which the dark side of the Force seduced Darth Vader into evil actions. By extension, dark side hackers steal data for personal gain or other unethical motive. The .su domain, assigned to the former Soviet Union more than three decades ago, is home to an estimated half of all criminal websites. In such areas, cybercriminals can often act with impunity because of inadequate computer crime statutes, weak law enforcement and the refusal to extradite criminals in other nations.

Popular fiction romanticizes the DarkNet as a place of admirable freedom, where the oppressed can resist and strike back against the overreach of repressive governments and corporations. In season two of Netflix's *House of Cards*, the character Lucas Goodwin accesses the DarkNet to contact hackers and uncover information about Vice President Frank Underwood. Likewise, in USA Network's *Mr. Robot*, the main character, Elliot Alderson, uses the DarkNet to covertly contact his underground allies and simultaneously hack into the FBI's computers.

The deep web is the part of the Internet that is not accessible through standard search engines. Deep web data is largely harmless, being composed principally of such prosaic information as flight schedules, medical studies and detailed pricing information. Most U.S. universities use Blackboard or Twen to communicate with their students, which are examples of the non-criminal nature of most of the deep web.

The DarkNet is the miniscule proportion of the deep web where criminals act anonymously.[58] By using specialized software to conceal their secretive activities, criminals conduct illegal enterprises such as selling drugs or weapons, illicit gambling, trading in counterfeit identity documents, exchanging child abuse materials and even advertising hitman services. These underground criminal activities came to the public's attention in 2013 when the Federal Bureau of Investigation shut down the Silk Road, a black-market website that hosted dealers who trafficked in unlawful products and services.[59]

DarkNet markets parallel legitimate market websites which sell legal goods on the surface net in which "buyers can also provide feedback on products and services, communicate through internal messaging and take part in website forums. Forums on DarkNet marketplaces focus on topics like the quality of child pornography images, the potency of a particular poison, or the speed at which a cache of guns is mailed to its buyer."[60] In 2015, the FBI coordinated an effort with law enforcement authorities from 20 countries to charge, arrest or search seventy

Darkode members and associates from around the world. [61] The complaint charged that Darkode was:

> an online, password-protected forum in which hackers and other cyber-criminals convened to buy, sell, trade and share information, ideas and tools to facilitate unlawful intrusions on others' computers and electronic devices. Before becoming a member of Darkode, prospective members were allegedly vetted through a process in which an existing member invited a prospective member to the forum for presenting the skills or products that he or she could bring to the group. Darkode members allegedly used each other's skills and products to infect computers and electronic devices of victims around the world with malware and, thereby gain access to, and control over, those devices.[62]

BROWSE CATEGORIES	
Fraud	23382
Drugs & Chemicals	122919
Guides & Tutorials	9472
Counterfeit Items	4580
Digital Products	10786
Jewels & Gold	1030
Weapons	1906
Ammunition	262
Pistols	733
Long-Range Guns	188
Explosives	151
Hand Weapons	197
Other	375
Carded Items	2409
Services	5067
Other Listings	2242
Software & Malware	1643
Security & Hosting	460

Browse Categories: Dark Web
Source: Federal Bureau of Investigation, A Primer on DarkNet Marketplaces: What They Are and What Law Enforcement is Doing to Combat Them (November 1, 2016), Retrieved from https://www.fbi.gov/news/stories/a-primer-on-darknet-marketplaces.

§ 4.8: GLOBALIZED CYBERCRIME

[A] New Forms of Old Crimes

Cybercrime does not always originate in remote locations. Pictures posted during a lengthy vacation, for example, may identify targets for local burglars. The *BBC* reported that an Australian teenager posted a picture of a massive cache of cash that she was helping to count. Within hours, armed masked men appeared at the door and demanded the money.

Terrorism is a traditional crime that may be launched, coordinated and enabled over the Internet from distant locales. In June 2016, a citizen of Kosovo pleaded guilty to charges of providing material support to the Islamic State of Iraq and the Levant (ISIS), a designated foreign terrorist organization. He also violated the CFAA by accessing a protected computer without authorization and obtaining personally identifiable information for 1,300 U.S. service members. The Kosovar stole information pertaining to military communities and gave it to an ISIS member who posted a taunting tweet bragging that:

> we are in your emails and computer systems, watching and recording your every move, we have your names and addresses, we are in your emails and social media accounts, we are extracting confidential data and passing on your personal information to the soldiers of the khilafah, who soon with the permission of Allah will strike at your necks in your own lands![63]

The Federal Communications Commission does not believe that it has the authority to shut down terrorist-linked websites, but private Internet Service Providers often have terms of use that forbid advocating violence. In 2016, Twitter shut down 125,000 terrorist-linked websites for violating this portion of its terms of use.

[B] Cyberterrorists in Remote Locations

As the world becomes increasingly interconnected by the Internet, cybercrimes launched from remote locations become more difficult to detect, police and prosecute. Global cybercriminals steal money, information, intellectual property and state secrets while located in countries that are unlikely to cooperate with American authorities. The FBI divides cybercrimes that are serious enough for the agency to investigate into three categories:

(1) Organized crime groups that are primarily threatening the financial services sector, and are expanding the scope of their attacks;

(2) State sponsors—foreign governments that are interested in pilfering data, including intellectual property and research and development data from major manufacturers, government agencies, and defense contractors; and

(3) Terrorist groups who want to affect this country the same way they did on 9/11, when they flew planes into buildings.[64]

Law enforcement faces multifaceted ethical and legal challenges in dealing with these complex crimes. For example, on September 30, 2011, the U.S. military used a drone to kill Anwar al-Awlaki, an American citizen who had been labeled "the bin Laden of the Internet."[65] From his home base in Yemen, al-Awlaki blogged and posted speeches calling for the death of "U.S. devils" and urging armed attacks against American and British targets. This targeted killing was approved in a closed executive decision-making process, without being reviewed in open court.

Before the drone killings in Yemen occurred, the American Civil Liberties Union (ACLU) and the Center for Constitutional Rights brought a lawsuit on behalf of al-Awlaki's father, arguing that ordering the killing of a non-combatant American citizen in a foreign nation was a violation of the Due Process Clause of the U.S. Constitution and of international law. The federal court held that this targeted killing was judicially unreviewable because the father of Anwar al-Awlaki had no legal standing to file the case.[66]

Law enforcement authorities may differ about the categorization of some groups and the proper tactics to combat their activities. For example, the collective of hacktivists known as Anonymous, which engages in online sabotage against groups that it believes are undermining Internet and other freedoms, is viewed by some authorities as merely an unimportant group of loosely organized online pranksters, while others depict the collective as being a disruptive cross-national network that merits serious attention.[67]

[C] State-Sponsored Cybercrime

Former FBI Director James Comey described the U.S. as facing tangible cybersecurity "threats from criminals, terrorists, spies and malicious cyber actors. The playground is a very dangerous place right now."[68] A 2014 PWC survey states: "Nation-state actors pose a particularly pernicious threat. We are seeing increased activity from nation-state actors, which could escalate due to unrest in Syria, Iran and Russia."[69]

A new era in which state sponsored hackers interfere with foreign elections may be dawning. In 2016, the Democratic National Committee (DNC) was compromised and information undermining the political campaign of Hillary Clinton released through the WikiLeaks website. A hacker with the screen name Guccifer claims to be a Romanian individual who stole the information without help from any organization, but U.S. government investigators believe that Russian intelligence agents carried out this information theft as a form of state-sponsored espionage.

In 2014, the U.S. government charged Chinese military hackers, under the Computer Fraud and Abuse Act and the Economic Espionage Act, with breaking into the electronic records of leading U.S. technology companies such as Westinghouse Electric, SolarWorld AG, U.S. Steel, Allegheny Technologies and Alcoa Inc.

This was the first time in history that the United States has filed charges against another nation for hacking. Several officers of the Third Department of the Chinese People's Liberation Army (PLA) made the FBI's most wanted list of cybercriminals, but it is very unlikely that China will extradite them to stand trial in the United States. In July of 2016, a Chinese national who admitted to participating in a years-long conspiracy that involved Chinese military officers hacking to discover U.S. defense contractors' secrets was sentenced to 46 months in federal prison.

[D] The Cybercrime Convention

The United States became a signatory country of the Cybercrime Convention, sometimes called the Budapest Convention, in 2006. This Convention recognizes the need for a mechanism allowing law enforcement to investigate offenses and obtain evidence quickly and efficiently, while remaining aware of each nation's sovereignty and constitutional and human rights. The Cybercrime Convention does not demand "dual criminality," that the act be illegal in both nations, as a precondition to invoking mutual assistance.

The Cybercrime Convention is a modest first step toward creating harmonized computer crime statutes and international law enforcement coordination. However, such cross-border cooperation falls far short of the initiatives necessary to combat the growing menace of crimes launched from remote corners of the world. Google's general counsel complains that:

> the laws that govern evidence-gathering on the Internet were written before the Information Revolution.... These rules are due for a

> fundamental realignment in light of the rapid growth of technology that relies on the cloud [and] the very real security threats that face people and communities.[70]

The Cybercrime Convention contains no effective mechanism for enforcing cyberlaws and lacks clear guidelines for when a nation is obligated to cooperate with another. No cross-border treaty defines computer crimes or sets international standards for trans-border searches and seizures. Some observers advocate countering international cybercriminals through a process that parallels the multinational coordination that brought the "golden age of piracy" to an end in the early 1700s:

> Piracy was a product of colonialism, when maritime trade grew so fast that law enforcement couldn't keep up, and pirates briefly thrived. The way piracy was largely ended, however, was when countries started focusing less on stopping the pirates, and more on cutting off their access to land-bases where stolen goods could be sold. The Darknet is to online crime what the land-bases were to pirates, and fighting crime online will inevitably move toward the black markets found in the deeper parts of the Internet.[71]

Cybercrime enforcement is often compared to the arcade game of whack-a-mole, in which players use a mallet to attempt to drive randomly appearing moles back into their holes. As soon as the player whacks one mole, another pops up. International criminal law enforcement is often a futile task because when one nefarious website is taken down, numerous similar sites quickly pop up. Often the targeted site itself revives under a different domain name.

§ 4.9: USING CYBERCRIME ETHICS

[A] Consequentialism

Utilitarianism is the dominant perspective applied to the drafting and enforcement of cybercrime statutes. Consequentialists are pragmatic in their use of deception to combat cybercrime. The enormous social and economic costs of cybercrime justify the use of honeypots like the one that lured Aleksey Ivanov into the hands of U.S. authorities. Consequentialists advocate increased Internet surveillance, restrictions on Internet freedoms, enhanced punishments and other methods of making cybercrime less rewarding.

From this perspective, law enforcement needs new tools, both legal and technical, to monitor and to intercept the explosion of criminal activity. To consequentialists, cross-national law enforcement coordination, accompanied by harsher penalties, is necessary to cripple cybercrime, even though such methods threaten Fourth Amendment rights.

[B] Virtue & Duty Theory

Kantians and other deontological theorists argue that law enforcement agents who construct deceptive honeypot traps and "hack back" schemes to catch cybercriminals are unethical. Human beings must not be treated as merely a means to larger ends. Law enforcement itself should set a moral example. Good outcomes do not justify immoral government policies.

Kantians are likely to support educational programs to instill an intuitive sense of virtuous behavior. If the public considers intellectual property misappropriation to be morally justified, for example, legal authorities will find themselves in the same position that they faced in major U.S. cities during Prohibition. Without widespread public support for their cybercrime suppression policies, law enforcement will be ineffective.

[C] Conflict Theory

The cure for the cybercrime epidemic lies in creating a fairer society, not the use of deceptive law enforcement techniques. Conflict theorists would explain much of cybercrime as a response to blocked opportunities for legitimate pursuits. If Eastern European cybercriminals had meaningful work, they would be far less likely to resort to criminal activities. Cybercrime is an inevitable outgrowth of social dislocation and injustice in the region.

Law enforcement generally focuses on economic crimes. The criminal law must change from protecting the profits of the "owners" of intellectual property to an emphasis on protecting the weak against systemic patterns of oppression. Gendered, racist and homophobic cybercrimes should be a higher priority because this hateful behavior creates so much misery.

(1) Gendered Cybercrime

Feminists question the patriarchal assumptions behind how law enforcement defines, prioritizes and pursues cybercrime.[72] For example, women are disproportionately victims of cyberstalking, online harassment and revenge pornography, but these crimes are rarely prosecuted. Women often lack the financial resources to pursue civil remedies since they earn lower average salaries than men.

Lawmakers are finally beginning to strengthen enforcement against cybercrimes targeting women. In 2015, a California jury convicted a revenge porn operator "of extortion and identity theft for operating a website that allowed people to post thousands of explicit photographs of women and a second site that required payment to take down the images."[73]

In a deeply gendered cyberbullying case, Phoebe Prince, a 15-year-old Massachusetts high school student, committed suicide after being subject to systematic harassment from her classmates. Phoebe, a recent immigrant from Ireland, dated a senior football player, who previously had been the boyfriend of one of her tormentors. Phoebe was called "Irish slut" and "whore" on Twitter, Craigslist, Facebook and Formspring by anonymous posters. She killed herself two days before the winter cotillion dance at her school. Even after her death, her classmates left vicious messages on a Facebook page created in her memory.

A Massachusetts District Attorney charged Phoebe's harassers with violating the teenager's civil rights. The high school students were also charged with criminal harassment, disturbing a high school assembly and cyberstalking. The students accepted an agreement to plead guilty to lesser charges so it is uncertain whether they would have been convicted on the more serious charges.

The question of whether the criminal law was adequate to deal properly with this high-profile school bullying case inspired legislators in Massachusetts and New York to strengthen their anti-harassment laws so that these statutes clearly apply to cyberbullying. Weak criminal law enforcement leaves many victims of gendered cybercrime with no recourse except the tort system.

The female reproductive role was at issue in *Planned Parenthood, Inc. v. Am. Coalition of Life Activists,*[74] a case where anti-abortion activists posted Old West-style "wanted dead or alive" posters portraying doctors who performed abortions. Each time a doctor was murdered, the website displayed the victim's name with a line through it. Planned Parenthood filed an action against the anti-abortion activists who developed the website, contending that the wanted posters constituted a true threat of imminent harm.

The trial court granted a permanent injunction, which prohibited the defendants from publishing the posters or contributing materials to the pro-life website because such publication was made with intent to harm. The physicians depicted on the virtual posters won a $109 million verdict, including punitive damages, one of the largest Internet-related verdicts in history.

(2) Sexual Orientation

In *McVeigh v. Cohen,*[75] a federal court ruled that the U.S. Navy violated the plaintiff's rights under the Electronic Communications Privacy Act, Navy policy and the Fourth and Fifth Amendments by intercepting America Online emails in which McVeigh referred to his homosexuality. McVeigh, a U.S. Navy officer, demonstrated that he was likely to prevail on the merits of his claim that the Navy violated its own "Don't Ask, Don't Tell, Don't Pursue" policy when it investigated his sexual orientation. The ECPA civil violation occurred when the Navy sought information from an online service provider without a warrant.

[D] Social Contract Theory

Social contract theory, as found in the theories of Hobbes, Locke and Rawls, views society as a contract in which individuals agree to be bound by certain rules of government in return for the benefits of a just and stable social order.[76] The challenge for social contract theorists is to forge the proper balance between the rights of citizenry to security in their property and to personal dignity without unduly restricting their freedom of expression. The Trump Administration's proposals to provide law enforcement with enhanced powers may upset this delicate balance by undermining Fourth Amendment protections against unlawful electronic searches.

Apple's 2016 dispute with the FBI over whether to produce a backdoor to benefit law enforcement's investigation of the San Bernardino terrorist attack illustrates the complex balancing necessary in applying social contract theory. The FBI's position was that unlocking the iPhones of terrorists is a time-sensitive necessity that is justified by the FBI's responsibility to safeguard the public from future terrorist attacks.[77] Apple contended, in response, that any backdoor to the iPhone would inevitably fall into the hands of cybercriminals and intrusive foreign governments, undermining the privacy that Apple's customers expect from the iPhones' encryption.

If Apple were to give in to this demand, it would open the door to widespread government surveillance. Apple received more than 5,000 government requests to unlock its iPhones during the first six months of 2015. The Trump Administration is likely to seek legislation requiring Apple to cooperate with federal law enforcement in decrypting mobile devices of criminal suspects. In 2016, presidential candidate Donald Trump strongly opposed Apple's resistance. " 'Boycott Apple until they give up the information,' Trump said at a rally in South Carolina in February. He said Tim Cook, Apple's chief executive officer, 'is looking to do a big number, probably to show how liberal he is. Apple should give up.' "[78]

The core social contract principle of balancing security versus privacy rights remains unresolved because this dispute between the FBI and Apple ended when a private company assisted the government to unlock the terrorists' iPhone. This leaves a great deal of uncertainty about how the judiciary would have responded if courts were required to rule on the enforceability of the FBI's demand for decryption.

The Fourth Amendment's restriction on unreasonable searches and seizures needs to be updated to address metadata such as URLs and search histories.[79] The proper legal standards for protecting the privacy of data stored on cloud servers is likely to become an area of intense debate for the near future.

[E] Cyberlibertarianism

Libertarians charge that governments are exploiting the widespread fear of cybercrime to illegitimately expand their law enforcement powers into cyberspace. For example, cyberlibertarian Aaron Swartz was prosecuted for releasing JSTOR's highly priced collection of academic articles to the public. Swartz committed suicide while awaiting trial in 2013 on a variety of felony charges that could have subjected him to huge fines and as many as fifty years in jail.

Libertarians contend that federal prosecutors overcharged Swartz to intimidate other hackers from similar activities. Swartz had idealistic reasons for violating the Computer Fraud and Abuse Act. Like Martin Luther King Jr. and Mahatma Gandhi, cyberlibertarians believe that resistance to unjust laws is necessary to advance social justice.

CFAA Overreach? The Case of Aaron Swartz

On July 11, 2011, federal prosecutors in Boston charged Aaron Swartz, a 26-year-old, with violating the Computer Fraud and Abuse Act and the Electronic Communications Privacy Act for downloading and releasing millions of copyrighted articles on JSTOR without authorization. JSTOR, which is an abbreviation for Journal Storage, is an electronic subscription service that provides electronic access to libraries and research organizations for 1,900 journals in more than fifty disciplines.

Swartz was angered that independent scholars and impoverished students could not afford to access this costly database. In November of 2011, he was indicted in Middlesex County Superior Court on state charges of grand larceny and the violation of Massachusetts computer crime statutes. The state charges were dropped but Swartz still faced up to 35 years in prison as well as large criminal fines in federal district court.

Swartz pleaded not guilty on all counts and was released on $100,000 bail. While awaiting trial, Swartz hanged himself in his Brooklyn, New York apartment. Prosecutors often "overcharge" defendants in their indictments to pressure them to pleading guilty in return of a lesser sentence. Is it unethical for prosecutors to overcharge knowing that it intimidates criminal defendants from asserting their right to go to trial? Cyberlibertarians believe that punishing Swartz's idealistic actions at all was immoral. Jennifer Granick of Stanford's Center for Internet and Society contends:

> The CFAA is incredibly broad and covers swaths of online conduct that should not merit prison time. To point out that under the CFAA, Aaron's defense was hard, is not to say that I believe Aaron was guilty. Aaron was authorized to access JSTOR as the result of being on MIT's campus. The CFAA may protect the box from unauthorized access, but it does not regulate the means or the speed of access. If you are allowed to download, and Aaron was, then it is not a crime to download really, really fast. Even if the server owner would prefer you took your time.

Source: Jennifer Granick, *Toward Learning from Losing Aaron Swartz: Part II*, CIS: The Center for Internet and Society (January 15, 2013).

CONCLUSION

The Internet is an instrumentality for carrying out a dizzying array of information age crimes. This chapter has reviewed the major computer crime statutes: (1) the Computer Fraud and Abuse Act, (2) Electronic Communications Privacy Act and (3) the Economic Espionage Act. Congress has empowered private plaintiffs to supplement public enforcement through "crimtort" remedies. At present, there is no Internet wide treaty addressing cybercrimes or even the procedural aspects of policing Internet-reality crime.

The international community needs better mechanisms for coordinating cybercrime enforcement around the world. Relatively few cybercriminals are prosecuted, let alone convicted, because of the problems of anonymity, the paucity of investigatory resources, limited cross-national cooperation and the lack of expertise among many law enforcement units. As the Internet becomes increasingly central to all aspects of the world's economy and the human experience, demands for more effective globalized enforcement policies will inevitably increase.

CHAPTER FOUR: REVIEW QUESTIONS

4.1: What are some of the ways that the enforcement of cybercrimes is different from that of traditional crimes in the streets? Should police academies teach all police officers to understand cybercrime or should this be a specialization that is restricted to only law enforcement personnel with computer science backgrounds?

4.2: Should sentencing guidelines consider the motivations of computer hackers or be primarily based on the amount of damage caused by the hackers? Alternatively, based on the potential sales value of the information that was stolen or released to the public? What other factors might be taken into account so that the punishment fits the crime?

4.3: What are the difficulties in drafting a federal criminal law statute that punishes and deters online stalking? How should the First Amendment be applied to threatening anonymous Internet postings?

4.4: The Computer Fraud and Abuse Act, The Electronic Communications Privacy Act and now the Economic Espionage Act all permit civil actions whereby victims of computer intrusions file suit to obtain monetary damages. What purpose do these crimtorts serve? Is this a good idea? What is the potentially negative effect of subjecting defendants to both criminal and civil liability?

4.5: Ivanov, who violated the Computer Fraud & Abuse Act, was caught in a sting operation created by the FBI, where he was invited to interview for a position in a fake computer company, which was set up as a honeypot by FBI agents in Seattle. He was arrested during the "job interview." Do you think that the FBI acted ethically? What are some objections to luring cybercriminals to come to the U.S. through similar methods? What methods would you favor to combat such cybercriminals?

4.6: In 2015, a California jury convicted a revenge porn website operator "of extortion and identity theft for operating a website that allowed people to post thousands of explicit photographs of women and a second site that required payment to take down the images."[80] What would each of the five ethical perspectives say about this revenge porn conviction?

4.7: The U.S. would be more likely to receive co-operation in prosecuting cybercriminals in countries that do not follow U.S. civil liberty standards if they would agree to help these nations detect and punish dissidents. To what degree should the U.S. compromise its free speech principles to obtain international mutual assistance treaties? Is it ethical to make agreements to enforce the computer laws of dictatorial regimes? Should the U.S. help dissidents to undermine the undemocratic governments of their home countries?

4.8: Is it ethical for law enforcement agencies to "hack back" by, for example, planting viruses in the systems of those they suspect of hacking U.S. websites? What are the arguments for and against taking a more aggressive role in dealing with cybercriminals? Should U.S. authorities and private companies restrict themselves to passively fighting cybercrime by merely blocking economic espionage?

4.9: The U.S. and Israel are widely believed to have infected Iranian uranium purifying centrifuges with the STUXNET virus. This slowed down Iran's efforts to refine the raw materials that could be used in a nuclear weapon. Should the U.S. engage in this type of sabotage in foreign nations? Why or why not from each perspective?

4.10: Should harmful postings such as revenge pornography or mugshot websites be criminal offenses or should the First Amendment rights of posters protect them from prosecution? Should the owners of these websites be held responsible for the humiliation that the postings caused? Should the websites be required to take down postings at the request of the victim? Should websites be required to reveal who made the posting so that a person can be prosecuted? Why or why not from each perspective?

4.11: A top priority of the FBI and other federal law enforcement agencies is to hire more computer professionals to combat the tremendous growth of global cybercrime. The FBI currently insists that job candidates for these positions, except in exceptional circumstances, have a degree in computer science. Is this a good policy? Should they be hiring hackers who lack formal educational credentials? Should they make genuine job offers to talented foreign cybercriminals? Kevin Mitnick, who served five years in prison for hacking, now works catching other hackers. Is the policy of "set a thief to catch a thief" ethical?

4.12: Aaron Schwartz was very disillusioned by the fact that MIT played a key role in his arrest for illegally downloading JSTOR files so that he could make them available to researchers and students who could not afford to buy these academic articles. Should MIT and other top universities collaborate in prosecutions with law enforcement agencies even when there is no clear crime committed?

4.13: Do you have sympathy with cyberlibertarians or are they just destructive vandals who should be criminally prosecuted? What, if any, circumstances could turn you into a hacker or lead you to protect a hacker from law enforcement?

What circumstances, if any, would justify breaking into a government or company computer system?

4.14: Is U.S. cybercrime policy too patriarchal in not making women's issues such as revenge pornography, online stalking and Internet misogyny higher enforcement priorities? Should the law and its enforcement be changed to better reflect the concerns of women and other disadvantaged groups?

REFERENCES FOR CHAPTER FOUR

---

1 Rebecca Riffkin, *Hacking Tops List of Crimes Americans Worry About Most*, Gallup (October 27, 2014).

2 Wendy Nather, *Hollywood Cyber vs. Vegas Cyber* (December 28, 2016).

3 CloudBric, *Good or Bad, Here Are 4 New Hacker Shows That Debuted in 2015.*

4 Federal Bureau of Investigation, *What We Investigate* (2016), https://www.fbi.gov/investigate/cyber.

5 *Id.*

6 Office of Legal Education, Executive Office for United States Attorneys, Prosecuting Computer Crimes: Computer Crime and Intellectual Property Section Division, United States Division of Justice (hereinafter U.S. DEPT. OF JUSTICE, MANUAL ON PROSECUTING COMPUTER CRIMES) at 1.

7 18 U.S.C. § 1030.

8 U.S. DEPT. OF JUSTICE, MANUAL ON PROSECUTING COMPUTER CRIMES at 2.

9 *Id.*

10 JULIE E. COHEN, CONFIGURING THE NETWORKED SELF: LAW, CODE, AND THE PLAY OF EVERYDAY PRACTICE 159 (New Haven: Yale University Press, 2012).

11 *Id.* at 158.

12 U.S. DEPT. OF JUSTICE, MANUAL ON PROSECUTING COMPUTER CRIMES.

13 18 U.S.C. § 1030(e)(2)(B) (2001).

14 Computer Crime and Intellectual Property Section Criminal Division, *Prosecuting Computer Crimes* (2017) at 5.

15 *United States v. Drew*, 259 F.R.D. 449, 457 (C.D. Cal. 2009) ("[T]he latter two elements of the section 1030(a)(2)(C) crime [obtaining information from a protected computer] will always be met when an individual using a computer contacts or communicates with an Internet website."); *United States v. Trotter*, 478 F.3d 918, 921 (8th Cir. 2007) ("No additional interstate nexus is required when instrumentalities or channels of interstate commerce are regulated.").

16 Yin Wilczek, *Cybercrime: DOJ Stymied in Pursuit of Insider Cyberthreats*, BLOOMBERG BNA: CRIMINAL LAW REPORTER (October 16, 2015).

17 259 F.R.D. 449 (C.D. Cal. 2009).

18 18 U.S.C. § 2510(12).

19 *In re DoubleClick Inc. Privacy Litig.*, 154 F. Supp. 2d 497, 507 (S.D.N.Y. 2001) ("Title II . . . aims to prevent hackers from obtaining, altering or destroying certain stored electronic communications.").

20 *United States v. Moriarty*, 962 F. Supp. 217, 227 (D. Mass. 1997).

21 *In re Pharmatrak Inc.*, Privacy Litig., 329 F.3d 9, 18 (1st Cir. 2003).

22 18 U.S.C. § 2510(5)(a).

23 18 U.S.C. § 2702(c)(3).

24 U.S. DEPT. OF JUSTICE, MANUAL ON PROSECUTING COMPUTER CRIMES (2012) at 84.

25 "An interception is lawful if the interceptor is a party to the communication, or if one of the parties to the communication consents to the interception." *Id.* at 79.

26 18 U.S.C. § 2511(2)(c)–(d).

27 18 U.S.C. § 1835.

[28] Section 1832 was enacted as part of the Economic Espionage Act of 1996, Pub. L. No. 104–294, 110 Stat. 3488; *United States v. Genovese*, No. 05 CR.04 (WHP), 2005 U.S. Dist. LEXIS 11947, at *4 (S.D.N.Y. June 21, 2005). "The first offense, 'economic espionage,' arises only when the theft benefits a foreign government. This carries higher penalties than the second offense, 'theft of trade secrets,' which is more sweeping, and concerns theft benefiting any person but the true owner." Sylvia N. Albert, Jason A. Sanders & Jessica M. Mazzaro, *Twentieth Survey of White Collar Crime: Intellectual Property Crimes*, 42 AMERICAN CRIMINAL LAW REVIEW 631, 634 (2005).

[29] *Id.* at 1030(g).

[30] To bring a civil action under 18 U.S.C. § 1030(a)(5) the action "must involve one of the five factors in (a)(5)(B) [but] it need not be one of the three offenses in (a)(5)(A)." *Shamrock Foods Co. v. Gast*, 535 F. Supp. 2d 962, 964 (D. Ariz. 2008).

[31] 18 U.S.C. § 1030(e)(11).

[32] Audra A. Dial & John M. Moye, *The Computer Fraud and Abuse Act and Disloyal Employees: How Far Should the Statute Go to Protect Employers From Trade Secret Theft?* 64 HASTINGS LAW JOURNAL 1447, 1448–49 (2013).

[33] 440 F.3d 418 (7th Cir. 2006).

[34] 581 F.3d 1127 (9th Cir. 2009).

[35] U.S. DEPT. OF JUSTICE, MANUAL ON PROSECUTING COMPUTER CRIMES (2012) at 8 (interpreting recent CFAA case law on insiders charged with CFAA offenses).

[36] Alexis Kramer, *U.S. Supreme Court Won't Review Computer Fraud Cases*, BLOOMBERG BNA: TECH & TELECOMM (October 17, 2017).

[37] Jeffrey G. Weill & Robert A. Chu, *Email Theft: What Are Your Damages,* METROPOLITAN COUNSEL (December 1, 2009) (discussing *Van Alstyne v. Elec. Scriptorium, Ltd.*, 560 F.3d 199, 205 (4th Cir. 2009)).

[38] *LaRocca v. LaRocca,* 2014 WL 5040720 (E.D. La. Sept. 29, 2014).

[39] 791 F.Supp.2d 705 (N.D. Ca. 2011).

[40] *Ehling v. Monmouth-Ocean Hospital Service Corp.*, No. 2:11–cv–3305(D.N.J. Aug. 20, 2013).

[41] 18 U.S.C. § 1839(6).

[42] Fahmida Y. Rashid, *Fair Trade? The Value of Bug Bounties*, INFOWORLD (Sept. 9, 2015).

[43] Scott Helme, *Bug Bounties and Extortion*, https://scotthelme.co.uk/bug-bounties-and-extortion/ (Feb. 10, 2017).

[44] One of the earliest commentators described how the Internet raised new dilemmas for disparate fields of the law. See LANCE ROSE, NETLAW: YOUR RIGHTS IN THE ONLINE WORLD (New York, New York: McGraw-Hill, 1995).

[45] 175 F. Supp.2d 367 (D. Conn. 2001).

[46] Laurence R. Muir Jr., *Revising the CFAA: How Stronger Domestic Cybercrime Law Can Improve International Cybersecurity,* GEORGETOWN JOURNAL OF INTERNATIONAL AFFAIRS (May 8, 2015).

[47] 787 S.E.2d 814 (N.C. Sup. Ct. 2016).

[48] 565 U.S. 400 (2012).

[49] 997 N.E.2d 468 (N.Y. 2013).

[50] Benjamin Weiser, *D.E.A. Need Warrant to Track Suspect's Phone, Judge Says,* NEW YORK TIMES (July 12, 2016).

[51] Chris Strohm, *FBI, NSA Poised to Gain New Surveillance Powers Under Trump*, BLOOMBERG BNA: CRIMINAL LAW REPORTER (November 29, 2016) (quoting Oregon Democrat Congressman Ron Wyden).

[52] *Id.* ("Pompeo and Sessions want to repeal a 2015 law that prohibits the FBI and NSA from collecting bulk phone records—'metadata' such as numbers called and dates and times—on U.S. citizens who aren't suspected of wrongdoing").

[53] H.R. 3276: Child Pornography Prevention Act, Section 2C (2005–2006).

[54] "Any violation of federal child pornography law is a serious crime, and convicted offenders face severe statutory penalties. For example, a first-time offender convicted of producing child pornography under 18 U.S.C. § 2251, face fines and a statutory minimum of 15 years to 30 years maximum in prison. A first-time offender convicted of transporting child pornography in interstate or foreign commerce under 18 U.S.C.

§ 2252, faces fines and a statutory minimum of 5 years to a 20 year maximum in prison. See generally, THE UNITED STATES DEPARTMENT OF JUSTICE, CITIZEN'S GUIDE TO U.S. FEDERAL LAW ON CHILD PORNOGRAPHY (2016).

55 8 U.S.C. § 2252.

56 2012 U.S. Dist. LEXIS 105189 (W.D. Wash. July 27, 2012).

57 Shona Ghosh, *The Online Fundraiser for WannaCry 'Hero' Marcus Hutchins Had to Block $150,000 in Donations,* BUSINESS INSIDER (August 25, 2017).

58 INTERPOL, *The Threats: Cybercrime* (2016).

59 *Id.*

60 Federal Bureau of Investigation, *Primer on DarkNet Marketplaces: What They are and What Law Enforcement is Doing to Combat Them* (November 1, 2016).

61 United States Justice Department (July 15, 2015).

62 Internetcrimefighters.org, Ransomware, (June 8, 2016).

63 United States Department of Justice, *ISIL-Linked Hacker Pleads Guilty to Providing Material Support* (June 15, 2016), https://www.justice.gov/opa/pr/isil-linked-hacker-pleads-guilty-providing-material-support.

64 Federal Bureau of Investigation, *The Cyberthreat: Part 1: On the Front Lines with Shawn Henry*, (March 27, 2012).

65 Aamer Madhani, *Cleric Al-Awalki Dubbed 'Bin Laden of the Internet,'* USA TODAY (August 25, 2010).

66 Evan Perez, *Judge Dismisses Targeted-Killing Suit*, WALL STREET JOURNAL (December 8, 2010).

67 KRISTIN FINKLEA & CATHERINE A. THEOHARY, CONGRESSIONAL RESEARCH SERVICE, CYBERCRIME: CONCEPTUAL ISSUES FOR CONGRESS AND U.S. LAW ENFORCEMENT (January 15, 2001).

68 Federal Bureau of Investigation, *The FBI and the Private Sector: Closing the Gap in Cybersecurity*, Feb. 26, 2014.

69 Price, Waterhouse, & Coopers, *U.S. Cybercrime: Rising Risks, Reduced Readiness: Key Findings from the 2014 U.S. State of Cybercrime Survey* (June 2014) at 4 (quoting "Sean Joyce, a PwC principal and former FBI deputy director who frequently testified before the US House and Senate Intelligence committees.").

70 Kent Walker, *Digital Security Threats and Due Process: A New Legal Framework for the Cloud Era*, The KeyWord Blog, Google (June 22, 2017).

71 Joshua Philipp, *Darknet*, EPOCH TIMES (May 29, 2015).

72 Flavia Fascendini, *Cybercrime Legislations and Gender*, GENDERIT.ORG (July 1, 2016).

73 *People v. Bollaert*, No. SCD252338 (Cal. Super. Ct., Feb. 2, 2015) reported in Bloomberg BNA's Electronic Commerce & Law Report).

74 *Planned Parenthood Inc. v. American Coalition of Life Activists*, 290 F.3d 1058 (9th Cir. 2002).

75 983 F. Supp. 215 (D.D.C. 1996).

76 JOHN RAWLS, A THEORY OF JUSTICE (Cambridge, Massachusetts: The Belknap Press of the Harvard University Press, 1971).

77 Jessica DaSilva, *Apple, FBI iPhone Fight Reveals Fourth Amendment Flaws*, BLOOMBERG BNA: CRIMINAL LAW REPORT (February 23, 2016).

78 Chris Strohm, *FBI, NSA Poised to Gain New Surveillance Powers Under Trump*, BLOOMBERG BNA: CRIMINAL LAW REPORTER (November 29, 2016)

79 DaSilva, *Apple, FBI iPhone Fight*, *Id.*

80 *People v. Bollaert*, No. SCD252338 (Cal. Super. Ct., Feb. 2, 2015) reported in BLOOMBERG BNA'S ELECTRONIC COMMERCE & LAW REPORT).

CHAPTER FIVE

Information Privacy

> F. Scott Fitzgerald's *The Great Gatsby* has been described as "The Great American Novel," because it is the quintessential work which captures the mood of the 'Jazz Age.' The second chapter in Fitzgerald's novel describes an outsized billboard advertising optical services. The billboard sign, with its faceless blue eyes gazing out at the valley of ashes, today, would be symbolic of the loss of privacy in the electronic workplace. The omniscient eyes on Dr. Eckleberg's billboard are now locked on workers in the electronic workplace where network administrators indiscriminately copy screen shots in real time, scan data files, read email, analyze keystroke performance, and even overwrite passwords. Electronic surveillance by employers is 'the merciless electronic whip that drives the fast pace of today's workplace.'[1]
>
> —Michael L. Rustad & Sandra Paulsson

§ 5.0: THE NEW ERA OF GLOBAL PRIVACY

The Internet is a "network of networks," linking hundreds of millions of devices around the world, and, thus creating new threats to privacy. Data packets do not pass through customs when they cross national borders, nor do routers pause to consider whether local privacy rules are being breached. What does the right to privacy mean in an America where employers and commercial entities are largely free to gather data about online users? Scott McNealy, the co-founder of Sun Microsystems Inc., famously stated, "Consumer privacy is a red herring. You have zero privacy anyway. Get over it."

U.S. courts, for example, have universally rejected the claim that employees have an expectation of privacy in their email communications. This chapter examines the most significant online privacy issues, including the dilemmas involved in cross-border data protection. Policymakers are debating how to best achieve the benefits of big data while complying with radically divergent global privacy laws. European and Chinese laws approach individual privacy very differently than those of the U.S.

§ 5.1: THE FOUR PRIVACY-BASED TORTS

Privacy-based torts were not recognized in America until 1890, when Louis Brandeis and his law partner, Samuel Warren, published an influential law review article that proposed a tort action for the invasion of privacy. Warren and Brandeis argued the right to be left alone is implicit in the Bill of Rights of the U.S. Constitution. Every state now recognizes privacy-based torts, either through case law developments or statutory reforms. State laws vary, but generally fall into the four categories discussed below.

[A] Intrusion upon Seclusion

To prevail in an intrusion upon seclusion claim, plaintiffs must prove:

(1) The defendant committed an unauthorized intrusion or pried into the plaintiff's seclusion;

(2) The intrusion would be highly offensive or objectionable to a reasonable person;

(3) The matter intruded upon was private; and

(4) The intrusion caused the plaintiff anguish and suffering.

Actions such as eavesdropping, wiretapping or intercepting emails can qualify as intrusions upon seclusion. For example, Ubisoft's game, Watch Dogs 2, captured publicly available screenshots of players' moves. Many users felt that Ubisoft overstepped its legal bounds by archiving screenshots of players' Internet play, ostensibly as a measure to prevent cheating. Ironically, the game is about hackers trying to overcome omniscient government scrutiny. In *Remsburg v. Docusearch Inc.*,[2] an information broker sold the personal information of Amy Boyer to a deranged former high school acquaintance who was obsessed with her. The ex-classmate used this information to locate Boyer's work address and fatally shot her as she was leaving work. The murderer then committed suicide. Docusearch's investigator masqueraded as being affiliated with Boyer's insurer, requesting a verification of her address so she could receive a refund. Docusearch sold this information to Boyer's killer, along with her social security number that it had obtained from a credit-reporting agency.

Amy Boyer's estate filed a lawsuit against Docusearch and the individual private investigator for wrongful death, the invasion of privacy, as well as for violation of the New Hampshire Consumer Protection Act. Amy Boyer's estate argued that she had a reasonable expectation of privacy in her address and social security number, and that Docusearch's action in releasing this information was unreasonably offensive. The New Hampshire Supreme Court was asked to address the question of whether Docusearch and its private investigator were liable for the privacy tort of intrusion upon seclusion. The court held that the plaintiff had established a basis for the claim of invasion of privacy against the database provider. The tort case against Docusearch ended with an $85,000 out-of-court settlement that was paid to Amy Boyer's estate.

[B] Public Disclosure of Private Fact

To pursue an action for public disclosure of private facts, the plaintiff must plead that:

(1) Publicity was given to the disclosure of private facts;

(2) The facts were private, not public;

(3) The matter made public was such as to be highly offensive to a reasonable person; and

(4) The matter publicized was not one of legitimate public concern. "The tort of public disclosure of private facts is meant to protect against the disclosure of intimate. . . details the publicizing of which would be not merely embarrassing and painful but deeply shocking to the average person subjected to such exposure."[3]

Public disclosure of private facts is often asserted in revenge pornography cases. The injury is the disclosure of intimate information or details that would shock the conscience of the average person. The disclosure of private facts requires that the facts be true. A federal judge dismissed a public disclosure of private facts for derogatory comments posted about a Missouri woman, reasoning that because the posting consisted of outright fabrications, there was no invasion of privacy so she would need to sue on other grounds.

In *Lee v. Penthouse International Ltd.*,[4] Tommy Lee and Pamela Anderson Lee sued *Penthouse Magazine* for publishing allegedly stolen honeymoon pictures, which showed the couple in various stages of undress and engaging in sexual conduct. The photos had previously been published in the French edition of *Penthouse* as well as in the American magazine *Screw*. The *Lee* court held that the celebrity couple could not maintain their action for public disclosure of private facts because the photographs had previously appeared in the other magazines.

[C] False Light

False light is the privacy tort that "includes embellishment (the addition of false material to a story, which places someone in a false light), distortion (the arrangement of materials or photographs to give a false impression) and fictionalization (references to real people in fictitious articles or the inclusion in works of fiction of disguised characters that represent real people)."[5] False light privacy actions requires proof that;

(1) The defendant published the information widely (i.e., not to just a single person, as in defamation);

(2) The publication identifies the plaintiff;

(3) It places the plaintiff in a "false light" that would be highly offensive to a reasonable person; and

(4) The defendant was at fault in publishing the information.[6]

False light differs from defamation in that it protects a plaintiff's emotional well-being, rather than a reputational interest. One such false light case in San Francisco arose out of a chiropractor's former patient posting negative reviews about him on Yelp.com. The former patient's postings suggested that the chiropractor engaged in an insurance swindle through fraudulent "time of service" billing practices.

The chiropractor contended that his former patient's postings placed him in a false light toward the public and defamed him. He also claimed that the publicity created by the Yelp.com posting was offensive and objectionable to "a reasonable person of sensibilities and that the posting was done with malice and knowledge of its falsity, and in reckless disregard of the truth."[7] The former patient removed the posting but the chiropractor and the parties entered into a confidential settlement.

A California state court found a sufficient basis for false light privacy in a case filed by a server against her employer, the Café Lu. After being hired, the waitress was instructed by the owner to remove her clothes. Body paint was applied to her and photos were taken of her naked body. The defendants posted one of the pictures on Facebook and on the restaurant's website as "Café Lu's new waitress." The new waitress requested that the photo's immediate removal.

While she had agreed to be photographed wearing body paint as a job requirement, the ex-waitress asserted that Café Lu's owner failed to inform her that the photos of her practically naked body would be posted online. The false light privacy claim was predicated upon her portrayal on the websites as an unchaste, lewd and lascivious woman. The Café Lu argued that her claims were frivolous amounting to a "shake down suit."[8]

Most states do not recognize a false light claim because of the overlap with other defamation torts and because of the potential chilling effect on speech. Journalists argue that the false light tort impedes their ability to research and publish stories useful to the public.

[D] The Right of Publicity

Many states recognize a privacy right to protect one's name and likeness against appropriation by others, which is referred to as the right of publicity. In *Fain v. Silkening Techns.*,[9] a company used an actress's image to promote an online hair care product without her authorization. The professional actress permitted a modeling agency to use her image for advertising but later discovered that another company had appropriated her likeness to sell its products. A Florida jury returned a verdict in favor of the actress for $100,000 in damages for losses based on a violation of the model's right of publicity. The right of publicity can survive a celebrity's death. In Illinois, the estate of the late singer James Brown filed a lawsuit against a website for the unauthorized commercial use of Brown's image on its website. The case settled after an appeals court refused to grant the website's summary judgment motion.

Proving the Appropriation of Name or Likeness Claim

There have been several cases where plaintiffs have sued for right of publicity based on their likenesses appearing on the Internet. The tort of right of publicity, sometimes called the tort of commercial appropriation, protects the "inherent right of every human being to control the commercial use of his or her identity."[10] Most appropriation or right of publicity claims arise out of a defendant's use of a person's name or likeness to advertise the defendant's product, or the defendant's impersonation of the person for personal gain. The misappropriation tort is an intellectual property right in protecting the *value* of one's name rather than one's name *per se*. To prevail in an appropriation of name or likeness claim, the plaintiff must plead facts to establish:

(1) The defendant's use of the plaintiff's identity;

(2) The appropriation of plaintiff's name or likeness;

(3) Lack of consent; and

(4) Resulting injury.

§ 5.2: FEDERAL ENFORCEMENT OF PRIVACY

[A] Federal Trade Commission's Privacy Mission

The Federal Trade Commission (FTC) is the chief U.S. federal agency protecting individual privacy. The FTC primarily uses injunctive relief to enjoin unlawful behavior. When appropriate, the Commission can order that companies implement comprehensive privacy and security programs. In addition, the FTC can impose civil penalties and order restitution to consumers. The FTC has primary jurisdiction to enforce the Children's Online Privacy Protection Act, the Fair Credit Reporting Act, Telemarketing Sales Rule or other privacy regulations.

The FTC launches investigations and enforcement actions when businesses are suspected of violating Section 5 of the FTC Act, which bars unfair and deceptive acts and practices in or affecting commerce.

For example, the FTC filed suit against Snapchat for its friend-finder feature that "enabled attackers to compile a database of 4.6 million Snapchat usernames and phone numbers." When users registered, the app prompted them to, "Enter your mobile number to find your friends on Snapchat!"

Snapchat's privacy policy claimed that its app only collected the user's email, phone number and Facebook ID. Despite this representation, when iOS users entered their phone number to find friends, Snapchat collected the names and phone numbers of all the contacts in their mobile devices' address books. Snapchat informed its users that "snaps," photographs, and video messages were all completed deleted 10 seconds after they were opened and viewed.

The FTC charged that "Snapchat deceptively told its users that the sender would be notified if a recipient took a screenshot of a snap. In fact, any recipient with an Apple device that has an operating system pre-dating iOS 7 can use a simple method to evade the app's screenshot detection, and the app will not notify the sender."[11] Snapchat continued to collected and stored photographs, without notifying users or obtaining their consent, until Apple modified its operating system to provide such notice with the introduction of iOS 6.

As part of their settlement with the FTC, Snapchat agreed to hire a data protection professional for the next twenty years and immediately develop a comprehensive privacy program. The FTC action against Snapchat was part of a multi-national enforcement sweep to police the privacy policies of mobile app providers. In 2017, the FTC issued a privacy primer for app developers, which is reproduced in textbox below.

[B] FTC Software Application Designer Privacy Rules

FTC Privacy Guidelines for App Developers

Disclose Key Information Clearly and Conspicuously.

If you need to disclose information to make what you say accurate, your disclosures have to be "clear and conspicuous." What does that mean? That they're big enough and clear enough that users actually notice them and understand what they say. Generally, the law doesn't dictate a specific font or type size, but the FTC has taken action against companies that have buried important terms and conditions in long licensing agreements, in dense blocks of legal mumbo jumbo or behind vague hyperlinks. Clear and conspicuous disclosures make good business sense. Most people react negatively if they think a company is trying to pull a fast one by hiding important information. Users are more likely to continue to do business with a company that gives them the straight story up front.

Build Privacy Considerations in From the Start.

The FTC calls this "privacy by design." What does it mean? Incorporating privacy protections into your practices, limiting the information you collect, securely storing what you hold on to, and safely disposing of what you no longer need. Apply these principles in selecting the default settings for your app and make the default settings consistent with what people would expect based on the kind of app you're selling. For any collection or sharing of information that's not apparent, get users' express agreement. That way your customers aren't unwittingly disclosing information they didn't mean to share.

Be Transparent About Your Data Practices.

Even if you need to collect or share data so your app can operate, be clear to users about your practices. Explain what information your app collects from users or their devices and what you do with their data. For example, if you share information with another company, tell your users and give them information about that company's data practices.

Offer Choices That Are Easy to Find and Easy to Use.

Give your users tools that offer choices in how to use your app—like privacy settings, opt-outs or other ways for users to control how their personal information is collected and shared. It's good business to apply the "clear and conspicuous" standard to these choice mechanisms, too. Make it easy for people to find the tools you offer, design them so they're simple to use, and follow through by honoring the choices users have made.

Honor Your Privacy Promises.

"But we don't make any promises." Think again and reread your privacy policy or what you say about your privacy settings. Chances are you make assurances to users about the security standards you apply or what you do with their personal information. At minimum, app developers—like all other marketers—have to live up to those promises. The FTC has taken action against dozens of companies that claimed to safeguard the privacy or security of users' information, but didn't live up to their promises in the day-to-day operation of their business. The FTC also has taken action against businesses that made broad statements about their privacy practices, but then failed to disclose the extent to which they collected or shared information with others—like advertisers or other app developers.

Protect Children's Privacy.

If your app is designed for children under age 13 and collects personal information, you have additional requirements under the Children's Online Privacy Protection Act (COPPA) and the FTC's COPPA Rule. But COPPA compliance doesn't end there. Regardless of the kind of app you sell, if you know you're collecting personal information from children under 13—or if you know you're collecting personal information from another website or online service (including another app) that's designed for kids under 13—COPPA applies, too.

Source: Federal Trade Commission, *Marketing Your Mobile App: Get It Right from the Start* (2017).

The FTC promulgated three core principles for inclusion in all Internet-related platforms:

(1) *Privacy by Design*: Companies should build in privacy at every stage while developing their products.

(2) *Simplified Consumer Choice*: For practices not consistent with the context of a transaction or a consumer's relationship with the business, companies should provide consumers with choices at a relevant time and context.

(3) *Greater Transparency*: Companies should disclose details about their collection and use of consumers' information.

[C] Children's Online Privacy Act (COPPA)

COPPA requires that websites take reasonable measures to protect the confidentiality, security and integrity of information collected from children. Congress enacted the Children's Online Privacy Protection Act (COPPA) in 1998 to protect children's privacy on the Internet. This federal privacy statute is becoming increasingly important as more school children join social networks and play online multiplayer games such as Minecraft.

(1) COPPA Rule

The FTC's COPPA rules prohibit collecting personally identifiable information from children under the age of 13 without "verifiable parental consent." The site operator must give conspicuous notice about its information practices and give a child's parents the opportunity to deny further use or collection of information. A website may not condition a child's use of the website on disclosing personal information. Personal information is defined to include:

(1) An individual's first and last name,

(2) Home or other physical address,

(3) Email address or other online contact information,

(4) Telephone number,

(5) Social Security number,

(6) Persistent identifier such as an ID number or access code and

(7) Other information about the child collected by the operator.

On December 19, 2012, the FTC issued amended rules updating the definitions of personal information to include geolocation, screen names and audio files, thus adapting COPPA to modern social media. The FTC has developed a multi-factorial test to determine whether a given website is directed at children. The most important factors include the subject matter (visual or audio content), the age of models depicted on the site, as well as the age of the actual or intended audience and whether the site uses child-oriented animations. Under the amended COPPA Rule, websites that collect geolocation information without obtaining parental consent must immediately obtain such consent. Courts can hold operators who violate COPPA Rule liable for civil penalties of up to $16,000 per violation. Courts tailor civil penalties based upon multiple factors which include:

(1) The egregiousness of the violations,

(2) Whether the operator has previously violated any COPPA rules,

(3) The number of children involved,

(4) The amount and type of personal information collected,

(5) How the information was used,

(6) Whether it was shared with third parties and

(7) The size of the company.

If COPPA applies to the website, its operator must create a clear and conspicuous link to a notice spelling out its information practices. This notice must be displayed wherever the site collects personal information from children, whether this information is collected directly or passively via tracking devices. Social media sites such as Facebook must also comply with COPPA by not allowing members under the age of 13 to sign up.

(2) COPPA Enforcement Actions

Information industry advocates complain that COPPA enforcement is expensive and ineffective, as businesses have no reliable way of determining whether a user is a child or an adult. Children often misstate their age to evade this sign-up restriction. In May of 2011, an estimated 7.5 million Facebook users were below the minimum COPPA threshold of age 13.[12]

In May 2008, the Texas Attorney General settled the state's first COPPA action. The Texas Attorney General charged DollPalace.com, a site for cartoon dolls, with violating COPPA by unlawfully collecting personal information from children without obtaining parental consent. DollPalace.com conditioned website access on children completing a ten-page questionnaire about themselves and their friends. The Texas Attorney General found that COPPA was violated because third parties could easily circumvent the parental consent feature of the site.

In March of 2012, the FTC announced that it had settled a COPPA case with RockYou Inc., where the privacy of thirty-two million children was at stake. The FTC's complaint charged the social media site with violating COPPA rules by not spelling out its disclosure policy, not obtaining verifiable parental consent prior to data collection and not implementing reasonable security to protect children's privacy.

In December 2015, the FTC entered into a settlement with two app developers who agreed to pay $360,000 in civil penalties for violating COPPA. LAI Systems and Retro Dreamers were charged with allowing "advertisers to use persistent identifiers to serve advertising to children." Persistent identifiers tie data to a particular user or device. LAI Systems created a large number of apps directed to children "including My Cake Shop, My Pizza Shop, Hair Salon Makeover, Friday Night Makeover, Marley the Talking Dog and Animal Sounds."[13]

The gist of the complaint against LAI was that it allowed third-party advertisers to collect personal information from children in the form of persistent identifiers. The COPPA rules require that apps directed to children provide notice to or get consent from, children's parents for collecting and using the information. RetroDreamer was also charged with allowing third-party advertisers to collect children's personal information through apps like Ice Cream Drop, Sneezies and Cat Basket. The settlement prohibited the app developers from further violations of COPPA rules and required them to pay civil penalties.

The FTC charged InMobi.com, a website that helps advertisers target and motivate consumers, with violating COPPA by collecting personal information from apps that were clearly directed at children without obtaining parental consent, despite claiming that it had not done so. InMobi was also charged with misrepresentation when it claimed that its advertising software would not track consumers' locations when they opted in to the provider's standard settings. In reality, InMobi tracked consumer locations even when users did not give them permission to access their location information.

[D] Health Insurance Portability and Accountability Act

Congress enacted the Health Insurance Portability & Accountability Act of 1996 (HIPAA) to allay the increasing public concern about the threat to privacy posed by interconnected electronic medical information systems. HIPAA's goals included: (1) protecting and enhancing the rights of consumers by providing them access to their health information and controlling the inappropriate use of that information; (2) improving the quality of health care in the U.S. by restoring trust in the health care system among consumers, healthcare professionals and health care organizations; and (3) improving the efficiency and effectiveness of health care delivery by creating a national framework for health privacy protection and building on efforts by states, health systems and individual organizations.

HIPAA prohibits a person from knowingly using unique health identifiers or wrongfully obtaining "individually identifiable health information relating to individuals or disclosing individually identifiable health information to another person." HIPAA applies to health care providers that engage in certain electronic transactions, health plans and health care clearinghouses. The HIPAA Privacy Rule defines a data breach as:

> an impermissible use or disclosure under the Privacy Rule that compromises the security or privacy of the protected health information. An impermissible use or disclosure of protected health information is presumed to be a breach unless the covered entity or business associate, as applicable, demonstrates that there is a low probability that the protected health information has been compromised.[14]

HIPAA includes both a Privacy Right and a Security Rule. HIPAA's Privacy Rule consists of federal standards to protect the privacy of patients' medical records and health information. HIPAA's Security Rule requires that messages sent to patient must be secure. Covered entities must also implement policies and procedures to ensure that health care data is not improperly altered or destroyed. A covered entity must implement technical security measures that guard against unauthorized access to personal health data transmitted over electronic networks. If a security breach affects 500 or more individuals, the health provider must notify the Secretary of Health and Human Services as well as the main media outlets in the affected states or jurisdictions.

Fines for violating HIPAA range from $25,000 up to $250,000 for multiple violations of the same standard in a calendar year. The criminal penalty for egregious violations of HIPAA is up to 10 years in prison. Yet, the Internet poses a major continuing risk to the safety and security of HIPAA information. Pharmaceutical manufacturer Eli Lilly and Co. inadvertently released the email addresses of 669 medical patients who had registered at its website to receive messages regarding health-related matters, such as reminders to take certain medications. Eli Lilly and Co. settled with the states, but no individual patient received a monetary award. To date, the most common HIPAA violations in order of frequency are:

> (1) Impermissible uses and disclosures of protected health information;
>
> (2) Lack of safeguards for protected health information;
>
> (3) Lack of patient access to their protected health information;
>
> (4) Lack of administrative safeguards for electronic protected health information; and
>
> (5) Use or disclosure of more than the minimum necessary protected health information.

Health care providers that are covered by HIPAA must implement computer security measures that allow only authorized persons to access electronic protected health information. Covered entities must implement audit controls in the form of hardware, software and procedural mechanisms to record and examine access in information systems. The U.S. has relatively strong privacy protections for health information and children's online activities, but lacks the comprehensive approach of the European Union, which covers all sectors.

§ 5.3: E-MONITORING OF EMPLOYEES

A growing number of U.S. companies monitor email and Internet communications to reduce their exposure to intellectual property infringement, torts, crimes and hostile workplace claims by their employees. Sexually-charged emails, ribald screensavers or downloaded pornography may expose an employer to sexual harassment lawsuits. The *Chicago Sun-Times* newspaper, by way of example, found itself with just such a smoking gun with this sexually-charged email from a supervisor to a female employee: "I know I'm getting to be a pain [in] the butt with these ride offers. And I apologize. But I can't help myself."

In another case, an employee's sexual harassment claim was evidenced by an email message from a co-employee asking the plaintiff whether she wanted to enjoy a "horizontal good time" together. Employers have a responsibility to respond quickly when they become aware that their company systems are being misused in this way because they can be liable for enabling a hostile workplace.

American employers can lawfully intercept, search and read any and all email stored on a workplace computer because employees have no expectation of privacy in workplace electronic communications. The computer system is the employer's property and they may monitor at will. Before monitoring their employees' electronic communications, managers should consider their responses to the series of ethical quandaries raised below:

Ethical Issues on Internet Monitoring

Should you read the private email of your network users just "because you can?"

Is it okay to read employees' email as a security measure, to ensure that sensitive company information is not being disclosed?

Is it okay to read employees' email to ensure that company rules (for instance, against personal use of the email system) aren't being violated?

If you do read employees' email, should you disclose that policy to them? Before or after the fact?

Is it okay to monitor the Web sites visited by your network users? Should you routinely keep logs of visited sites? Is it negligent to *not* monitor such Internet usage, to prevent the possibility of pornography in the workplace that could create a hostile work environment?

Is it okay to place keyloggers on machines on the network to capture everything the user types? Screen capture programs so you can see everything that's displayed? Should users be informed that they're being watched in this way?

Is it okay to read the documents and look at the graphics files that are stored on users' computers or in their directories on the file server?

Source: Deb Shinder, *Ethical Issues for IT Professionals*, Computer World (August 2, 2015).

[A] Why Companies Monitor Internet Communications

Employers are increasingly facing ethical dilemmas as to whether to monitor their employees' email and Internet activities using company computers. Should employers monitor their employees? What restrictions, if any, should be placed on covert employer surveillance? Do employees have the right to notice of monitoring? The potential for widespread surveillance concerns cyberlibertarian privacy advocates, such as the Electronic Frontier Foundation, because corporate or governmental elites could secretly monitor employees in protected categories such as age, gender or race. Organizations often defend monitoring their employees on consequentialist grounds to protect valid business interests such as protecting their rights and avoiding liabilities.

(1) Why Employers Monitor

Common justifications for electronic surveillance include:

(1) Preventing the misuse of bandwidth, as well as the loss of employee efficiency when employees surf the Internet;

(2) Ensuring that the company's networking policies are being implemented;

(3) Preventing lawsuits for discrimination, harassment or other online torts;

(4) Preventing the unauthorized transfer of intellectual property and avoiding liability due to employees making illegal copies of copyrighted materials;

(5) Safeguarding company records which must be kept to comply with federal statutes;

(6) Deterring the unlawful appropriation of personal information and potential spam or viruses; and

(7) Protecting a company's intellectual property, business plans, customer lists and other potentially valuable information.

A recent study supports corporate concerns about misuse of office computer systems, finding that nearly two-thirds of the employees studied, visited non-work websites on a daily basis. Seventy-three percent of younger workers admitted to being recreational web surfers online each day.[15] Employees' downloads of unauthorized copies of copyrighted software, music and entertainment on office computers may lead to investigations by the Software Publishers Association. A company will generally not be liable if an employee releases malware or a virus outside the scope of his duties. However, the adverse publicity could potentially be very harmful to a company.

(2) Case Law on the Internet Monitoring of Workers

In the U.S., courts are unanimous in rejecting the argument that employers' interception of their employees' email intruded upon seclusion, claiming that the company has a substantial interest in preventing inappropriate and unprofessional conduct over its email system. This has left employees without meaningful remedies for abuses of email and Internet surveillance.

The court in *McLaren v. Microsoft Corp.*[16] applied a consequentialist approach in balancing the employee's privacy interests against Microsoft's business purpose. McLaren filed suit against Microsoft, charging that it invaded his privacy by breaking into his personal folders on his office computer and releasing the contents of these folders to outside investigators. The company uncovered email evidence that McLaren was engaging in systematic sexual harassment, which was used as a reason to terminate him. Microsoft argued that its search was a necessary part of an internal investigation of sexual harassment and internal theft.

The *McLaren* court did not recognize a cause of action for invasion of privacy, even though the employee had a special password and had marked his files "personal." The computer was the property of Microsoft and was only to be used in the office, so he had no reasonable expectation of privacy. The court contrasted an employee's private email folder with a search of his locker, where there would be an expectation of privacy. The court reasoned that an employee was issued a locker for the specific purpose of storing personal belongings, whereas, the office computer was provided solely for employment-related communications. With the prevalence of corporate issued laptops, which blends work and personal activities, the court's rationale suffers from legal lag.

In the absence of federal safeguards against secret monitoring of workers, a few states have enacted statutes granting limited privacy rights for workers. Delaware requires that employees receive notice before the employer may is permitted to monitor their email or Internet usage. To comply with this statute, employers can provide employees with "an electronic notice of monitoring policies or activities" each time they access their business computers.

The employer can also comply with the statute by giving a "1-time notice" to the employee in writing or in electronic form that must be acknowledged by the employee. Connecticut also requires employers to warn workers prior to implementing monitoring of electronic communications. New York courts have ruled that the state's privacy statute gives employees a right of publicity, which may be violated by an employer's electronic monitoring.

(3) The European Perspective on Workplace Monitoring

The European Court of Human Rights (ECHR) takes a diametrically opposed view of workplace monitoring of email and Internet communications. In September 2017, the ECHR delivered a judgment in favor of a Romanian worker terminated for personal use of the Internet during work hours. At his employer's request, Barbulescu, the employee, created an instant messaging account using Yahoo Messenger, for communication with customers. His employer monitored Barbulescu's communications and terminated him for using a company computer to exchange personal messages with his brother and fiancé. Barbulescu challenged his termination, filing an action with the ECHR, which agreed that the workplace monitoring violated Article 8 of the European Convention on Human Rights respecting private and family life.[17] The ECHR ruled in his favor concluding that the employer violated his privacy.

[B] Applying the Five Ethical Perspectives to Workplace Surveillance

Employers frequently review the social media postings of prospective job candidates. Hiring managers were surveyed and more than a third found to base their rejection of candidates on red flags uncovered from a review of the candidate's social media profile and postings.[18] Discovery of photos deemed obscene are the most common deal-breakers statistically followed by posted information about them soliciting drugs and alcohol. Negative postings about previous employers, poorly written posts reflecting weak communication skills, and blasphemous remarks about race, gender and sexual orientation were also important discoveries. Employers often screened out applicants for misrepresentations about their job qualifications and competencies uncovered on in online postings.

A growing number of employers demand that job candidates reveal their private social media accounts as a background check for the final stage of the hiring process. Those candidates that refuse to grant the surprise demand are simply not hired. Employers may not legally inquire about sexual orientation, race or other protected statuses. However, by examining social media postings, employers can unethically consider such information, without prospect of being held accountable. The following section applies five perspectives to the ethics and law of workplace monitoring.

(1) Consequentialism

Companies often apply a cost/benefit analysis to determine whether they will monitor their workers' communications. Utilitarian reasons for monitoring include cost reduction and protecting third party trade secret held by the employer. Monitoring reduces the risk that the employer will be sued for their employees' misuse of its system.

Loss of social cohesion and morale in workplace are the principal costs of online surveillance. One study concluded that excessive surveillance weakens morale, leads to greater employee turnover and due to increased stress, increased in health care costs.[19] In response, employees may simply sidestep the rules, looking things up such as scores of games from their own mobile device rather than on their office computer.[20]

(2) Virtue and Duty

A virtue perspective focuses on the motives of employers in monitoring their workers. An employer who spies on employees' Internet usage because of curiosity, for revenge or for some other unworthy motives violates Kant's categorical imperative. In *Restuccia v. Burk Technology,*[21] the company's President dishonestly informed his employee that he would not monitor their electronic communications but secretly read them. In so doing, he learned his employees referred to him with disparaging nicknames. Restuccia's emails discussed the president's extra-marital affair with a subordinate. During a performance review, the president warned Restuccia that he was spending too much time using the email system for personal reasons. Shortly after this meeting, the president terminated Restuccia and several other co-employees on the pretext that there were overusing the company's computers.

This type of surreptitious monitoring is unethical from a virtue perspective because the company president was using surveillance for his own personal benefit, not to advance the company's interests. The *Restuccia* case is a rare example of a plaintiff's victory, perhaps because of the company president's questionable ethics in lying about whether he would monitor and concealing his true reasons for terminating the employees. This was a limited victory, however, as the court merely denied summary judgment. Like most civil cases, this lawsuit settled confidentially instead of going to trial.

(3) Conflict Theory

The conflict perspective focuses on the power differentials between employers and employees, especially when gender and age discrimination are involved. In *Garrity v. John Hancock Mutual Life Insurance Co.*,[22] two middle-aged female employees of the insurance company were terminated after forwarding sexually explicit emails from Internet joke websites. One of their co-employees complained to management after receiving a forwarded email from the plaintiffs, and John Hancock promptly investigated the email folders of everyone involved.

John Hancock contended that the search of the employees' computers constituted a legitimate business interest in protecting and preventing workplace harassment under Title VII of the 1964 Civil Rights Act and its Massachusetts counterpart. Both statutes require an employer to affirmatively investigate and take remedial action following any complaints of workplace harassment. The court concluded that the employees violated the insurer's Internet policy that prohibited "messages that are defamatory, abusive, obscene, profane, sexually oriented, threatening or racially offensive," which justified firing them.

The terminated women filed suit contending that Hancock's email policy was dense and extremely difficult to locate on Hancock's intranet system. The reminders sent by the employer, they argued, did not accurately communicate the email policy. The ex-employees disputed the insurer's characterization of the emails in question as sexually explicit and in violation of the insurer's computer usage policy.

The court found the risqué jokes to be sexually explicit within the meaning of Hancock's email policy. The *Garrity* court dismissed the plaintiff's privacy-based actions because the employees had no reasonable expectation of privacy in their emails. The court ruled that whether the company had a formal email policy or not was not of any importance. The interest of the insurer in taking affirmative steps against harassment outweighed the plaintiff's privacy interest.

The *Garrity* case illustrates the complexities of social context in resolving ethical dilemmas. Courts often ignore significant sociological variables such as age, gender and social class in determining legal outcomes. This termination could be interpreted as a pretext to replace aging employees with younger and lower paid workers. After all, it is not unusual for co-employees to share jokes on office computers. Intersectionality is a concept used in conflict theory to explain that multiple sources of bias, such as race, class, gender, sexual orientation or handicapped status, often overlap as causes of discrimination. From the conflict perspective, courts should pay more attention to the social inequities that exist in the workplace as reflections of the larger society.

(4) Social Contractualist Approaches

Lockean social contract theory weighs the worker's right to privacy against the employer's legitimate concern that its property is being misused. Empirical evidence show reveals that the "enemy within" is far more likely to harm American corporations than outside hackers.[23] Employers must appropriately balance their worker's privacy interests against their interest in protecting a company from excessive liability when employees' misuse company computers.

In *United States v. Ziegler*,[24] the Ninth Circuit weighed a worker's reasonable expectation of privacy against an employer's monitoring of his office computer. In *Ziegler*, Frontline, an electronic payments entity, had given their employees notice that it had the right to monitor their electronic communications. The IT department contacted the FBI with a tip that a current employee was accessing child-pornography websites from a workplace computer. Frontline's IT administrator checked the sites Ziegler had visited and told the FBI that that these illicit sites depicted "very, very young girls in various stages of undress." A review of the employee's search engine cache disclosed that he had searched for "things like 'preteen girls' and 'underage girls.' " It was definitely child pornography accessed by the employee.

A federal grand jury handed down a three-count indictment, charging the employee with the receipt of child pornography. He appealed his federal criminal conviction, arguing for the suppression of evidence, because it was discovered during an unreasonable governmental search and seizure that violated the Fourth Amendment of the U.S. Constitution. The Ninth Circuit held that Ziegler had a reasonable expectation of privacy and the FBI should have complied with the Fourth Amendment's constraints on warrantless searches and seizures, but the court still found the search itself was not unreasonable because the company's highest-ranked company executive had consented to the search of Ziegler's office and computer.

In upholding Ziegler's conviction, the court distinguished between the search of personal luggage and of an office computer owned by the company. The court held that Frontline retained the ability to consent to the FBI search because the computer and the office space belonged to the company. The employee forfeits certain rights in return for employment.

(5) Libertarianism

A traditional libertarian would likely support a company's decision to monitor its workers and fire them at will. A private corporation has the right to set its own policies without government interference or second-guessing by the courts. Workers have the right to seek alternative employment if they disagree with their employer's Internet policy. The company's primary responsibility is to make profits for its stockholders. Employees have only the rights that they have voluntarily established in their employment contracts. Cyberlibertarians, in contrast, oppose surveillance of any kind, not just government spying.

The U.S. courts' consequentialist rulings are also largely in accord with a libertarian, property-based approach that gives maximum discretion to employers. The law of email and Internet monitoring universally favors employers by adopting a narrow property rights theory approach over the privacy rights of the employees. Employers own the computer system used in the workplace and may search it for any reason because employees have no reasonable expectation of privacy.[25]

The European Union's employment laws, in sharp contrast with those of the U.S., favor consultation with trade union representatives serving on the corporate board. The Europeans object to America's "peculiar attachment to the notion of 'employment-at-will.' "[26] The U.S. approach to the electronic surveillance of employees may be traced back to the Lockean view that employers enjoy sovereignty through property rights. The next section compares and contrasts the European Union's recognition of the "right to be forgotten" with the U.S. rejection of such a concept on First Amendment grounds.

§ 5.4: GLOBAL PRIVACY LAW & ETHICS[27]

[A] EU/US Data Privacy Safe Harbor 1.0

The European Commission approved the EU Directive on the Protection of Individuals with Regard to the Processing of Personal Data and on the Free Movement of Such Data, in 1995. The Data Protection Directive harmonizes privacy protection laws among the EU Member States to ensure that contradictory national privacy laws among the twenty-eight Member States. Each European Union member had to enact national statutes implementing the directive.

Article 25 of the Data Protection Directive prohibits the transfer of personal information across national borders, unless the receiving country had an adequate level of privacy protection. The European Commission concluded that the United States lacks privacy standards outside of few industries and therefore European personal data could not be transferred to the United States. To avert this potential financial disaster, the United States Commerce Department and the European Commission agreed to Safe Harbor 1.0 in 2000.

The Safe Harbor Principles required companies to agree that they would follow EU privacy norms such as giving consumers' notice and control of how their data would be used. The uneasy compromise behind Safe Harbor 1.0 papered over a deep ethical dispute over data protection. Legal developments in Europe are enlarging the gulf between European and U.S. law, requiring continuing efforts to keep the channels of electronic exchange open between these two huge trading partners.

In May 2017, for example, France's *Commission Nationale de l'Informatique et des Libertés*, a regulatory agency, fined Facebook €150,000 for violating France's data protection laws. The regulators explained in an emailed statement that the penalty had been levied because "Facebook proceeded to a massive compilation of personal data of internet users in order to display targeted advertising .... Facebook collected data on browsing activity of internet users on third-party websites without their knowledge."[28]

[B] The Google Spain Case

The most significant gulf between EU and U.S. privacy law lies in the European Union's recognition of "the right to be forgotten." The Court of Justice of the European Union (CJEU) recognized a right to be forgotten and ruled in 2014 that Google was subject to the requirements of the EU's Data Protection Directive. In *Google Spain SL, Google Inc. v. Agencia Española de Protección de Datos*

(*Google Spain v. AEPD*), the CJEU required Google and other search engines to delink information at the data subject's request if the search results "appear to be inadequate, irrelevant or no longer relevant or excessive in the light of the time that had elapsed." The court rejected Google's argument that removal requests were the duty of the website publisher not the search engine. The CJEU reasoned that Google, as the preeminent search engine, was far more likely to interfere with a consumer's right to privacy than a website publisher. Google does not actually erase postings, but delinks them, making them more difficult to locate.

[C] CJEU's Striking Down of the Safe Harbor

In October 2016, the CJEU invalidated the data protection Safe Harbor agreement between U.S. Commerce Department and the European Commission in *Schrems v. Data Protection Commissioner* (Case C–362/14). The Electronic Privacy Information Center (EPIC) summarizes the *Schrems* case:

> Max Schrems, an Austrian citizen, has been a Facebook user since 2008. As is the case with other subscribers residing in the EU, some or all of the data provided by Mr. Schrems to Facebook is transferred from Facebook's Irish subsidiary to servers located in the United States, where it is kept. Mr. Schrems lodged a complaint with the Irish data protection authority (the Data Protection Commissioner), taking the view that, in the light of the revelations made in 2013 by Edward Snowden concerning the activities of the United States intelligence services (in particular the National Security Agency 'the NSA'), the law and practices of the United States offer no real protection against surveillance by the United States of the data transferred to that country.[29]

The Irish data protection authority rejected the complaint, but the CJEU disagreed, invalidating Safe Harbor 1.0.

[D] Safe Harbor 2.0

On February 29, 2016, the European Commission published the *EU-U.S. Privacy Shield*, which is a revised framework for enabling cross-data flow from the EU to the U.S. (Safe Harbor 2.0). This new safe harbor was possible because U.S. authorities assured European authorities that they would not conduct mass surveillance of European citizens. Under Safe Harbor 2.0, the U.S. Department of Commerce will administer a self-certification program where U.S. companies will register their promise to comply with EU data protection principles. While Safe Harbor 1.0 agreement lacked a meaningful enforcement mechanism, Safe

Harbor 2.0 assesses significant fines against non-compliant U.S. companies. Before using the Privacy Shield Arbitration Panel, the individual must exhaust any other remedies through the company or the U.S. Commerce Department. The textbox below explains the terms of Safe Harbor 2.0.

How Does the Privacy Shield Work?

To transfer personal data from the EU to the U.S. different tools are available such as contractual clauses, binding corporate rules and the Privacy Shield. If the Privacy Shield is used, U.S. companies must first register compliance to this framework with the U.S. Department of Commerce. The obligation applying to companies under the Privacy Shield are contained in the "Privacy Principles." This Department is responsible for managing and administering the Privacy Shield and ensuring that companies live up to their commitments. In order to be able to certify, companies must have a privacy policy in line with the Privacy Principles. They must renew their "membership" to the Privacy Shield on an annual basis. If they do not, they can no longer receive and use personal data from the EU under that framework. If you want to know if a company in the U.S. is part of the Privacy Shield, you can check the Privacy Shield List on the website of the Department of Commerce (https://www.privacyshield.gov/welcome). This list will give you details of all the companies taking part in the Privacy Shield, the kind of personal data they use, and the kind of services they offer. You can also find a list of companies that are no longer part of the Privacy Shield. This means they are no longer allowed to receive your personal data under the Privacy Shield. In addition, these companies may only keep your personal data if they commit to the Department of Commerce that they will continue to apply the Privacy Principles.

The Privacy Shield provides you with a number of rights and companies are obliged to protect your personal data in line with the "Privacy Principles."

Your Right to Be Informed

A Privacy Shield company must inform you about:

(1) The types of personal data it processes;

(2) The reasons why it processes your personal data;

(3) If it intends to transfer your personal data on to another company and the reasons why;

(4) Your right to ask the company to access your personal data;

(5) Your right to choose whether you allow a company to use your personal data in a "materially different" way or to disclose it to another company (also known as the right to "opt-out");

(6) When the data are sensitive, (that is, data that reveal, for example, your ethnic origin or the state of your health) the Privacy Shield company has to inform you about the fact that it may only use or disclose such data if you allow this (also known as the right to "opt-in");

(7) How to contact the company if you have a complaint about the use of your personal data;

(8) The independent dispute resolution body, either in the EU or the U.S., where you can bring your case;

(9) The government agency in the U.S. that is responsible to investigate and enforce the company's obligations under the framework;

(10) The possibility that it may have to respond to lawful requests from U.S. public authorities to disclose information about you.

Source: European Commission, Guide to the EU/U.S. Privacy Shield (2017).

[E] General Data Protection Regulation

On January 1, 2012, the European Commission published a General Data Protection Regulation (GDPR), which will displace the Data Protection Directive in May 2018. This unified regulation will give all European Union citizens a statutory right to be forgotten. The GDPR's scope "applies to all companies processing the personal data of European consumers, regardless of the physical location of the company.[30] The GDPR extends:

> to the processing of personal data of data subjects in the EU by a controller or processor not established in the EU, where the activities relate to: offering goods or services to EU citizens (irrespective of whether payment is required) and the monitoring of behaviour that takes place within the EU. Non-EU businesses processing the data of EU citizens will also have to appoint a representative in the EU.[31]

The GDPR gives all European citizens more control over the personal data including:

Easier access to your own data: individuals will have more information on how their data is processed and this information should be available in a clear and understandable way;

A right to data portability: it will be easier to transfer your personal data between service providers;

A clarified "right to be forgotten": when you no longer want your data to be processed, and if there are no legitimate grounds for retaining it, the data will be deleted;

The right to know when your data has been hacked: For example, companies and organizations must notify the national supervisory authority of serious data breaches as soon as possible so that users can respond appropriately.[32]

The GDPR exacerbates the tension with U.S. law, which neither a right to be forgotten or has implemented a national data breach notification requirement. Additionally, many EU businesses complain that keeping up with changing privacy law requirements subjects them to excessive regulatory difficulties. U.S. companies have new legal obligations to protect data as it travels globally on the Internet. The European Union's Universal Declaration of Human Rights (UDHR) protects against interference with an individual's privacy, honor and reputation.

[F] National Privacy Enforcement Against U.S. Companies

EU enforcement actions have already forced several social media websites to revise their privacy policies that excessively infringed upon consumer rights. In August of 2012, the German Federation of Consumer Groups charged Facebook "with giving away customer data via its new app center without notifying users."[33] In 2012, a Berlin court ruled that Facebook violates German data protection laws by targeting emails from current members' accounts through its Friend Finder feature. The German court also ruled that the intellectual property rights of pictures and other content posted on Facebook "should remain with users."[34]

A Northern Ireland man filed suit in a Belfast High Court, contending that salacious photographs of his daughter, which she had posted on Facebook, placed her in "danger of attracting pedophiles," resulting in her receiving suggestive messages and requests from men for additional pictures.[35] A Dusseldorf, Germany court ruled that Facebook's "Like" button violated German data protection law because it detects whether a user has visited a page and forwards the user's data without properly informing him or her of the data transfer.[36] This type of privacy is not legally protected in the U.S. Hamburg Germany's Commissioner for Data Protection and Freedom of Information has reopened an investigation of Facebook's privacy policies relevant to tagging photos and deleting personally identifiable data.[37]

The Federal Trade Commission (FTC) is responsible for policing Safe Harbor 2.0. In September 2017, the FTC entered into settlements with three companies falsely claiming that they were certified to take part in the Privacy Shield when they had not completed their applications.[38] These FTC enforcement actions send a message of deterrence to companies that they must not misrepresent whether they comply with the Privacy Shield. The Trump Administration's "America First" stance has led European privacy scholars to contend that Safe Harbor 2.0 as unstable, resting on a bed of sand. The European Parliament's head of data protection argued that a Trump executive order could even invalidate the Privacy Shield.[39]

§ 5.5: THE RIGHT TO BE FORGOTTEN

[A] Google as a Privacy Gatekeeper

This next section will apply the five ethical perspectives on the right to be forgotten and will consider the ethical dilemmas surrounding specific takedown requests. Search engines contend that implementing EU's right to be forgotten is burdensome and costly. In less than three months in the spring of 2016, Google received more than 600,000 requests to be forgotten online. Consider what ethical concerns Google would have in responding to the following actual takedown requests. Thinking about how you would decide these cases would help to clarify what combinations of ethical principles you hold and which you tend to feel are meritless:

> A French priest convicted for possession of child sexual abuse imagery asked Google to remove articles reporting on his sentence and banishment from the church.
>
> A high-ranking Hungarian public official asked Google to remove recent articles discussing a decades-old criminal conviction.
>
> A German rape victim asked Google to remove a link to a newspaper article about the crime.

Subsidiary questions revolve around what factors Google should use in determining whether to comply with a takedown request. How should the right of expression be taken into account in responding to a removal request? Does it matter whether the person making the request is a public official, a celebrity or someone who has voluntarily injected himself into a public policy debate? Should criminals have a right to a fresh start after they have served their sentence? Should the desire of a victim of a humiliating crime to have her name delisted have priority over the public's right to know about the potential danger posed by the criminal?

[B] Five Perspectives Applied to the Right to Be Forgotten

(1) Consequentialism

The social benefit of allowing the public to have information about a person's past bad behavior is preventing future victimization. When a criminal defendant's conviction is difficult to remove from the Internet, it is a digital tattoo that may deter some wrongdoers because of the stigma of perpetually being associated with a crime, long after they have served the sentence. Reading a newspaper story about a rape may alert potential victims about the prevalence of this crime and encourage them to take precautions. In the case of the French priest, the man may transfer to another parish or join another denomination, so the public would benefit from a warning that he is a sexual predator.

The cost of refusing to delink the story is to reduce the possibility that the criminal may undergo rehabilitation and receive a fresh start after serving their sentence. The rehabilitation rationale is less persuasive for the Hungarian public official who sought to remove references to stories about his criminal conviction. The public benefits from knowing about his past conviction for corruption has a continuing relevance.

U.S. law often subordinates an individual's privacy rights against the First Amendment because free expression is a fundamental right and encouraging robust political and social debate is integral to the American legal system. The standard of fault in U.S. defamation cases, for example, is far higher for public officials than private persons. The U.S. Supreme Court reasoned:

> Those among the hierarchy of government employees who have, or appear to the public to have, substantial responsibility for or control over the conduct of "governmental affairs" and where that position "has such apparent importance that the public has an independent interest in the qualifications and performance of the person who holds it, beyond the general public interest in the qualifications and performance of all government employees.[40]

Similarly, in U.S. law, unlike that of Europe, the public's right to know about a criminal past trumps the right of the criminal to a fresh start. Europe does not allow mugshot websites and police records are not publicly available, unless the public interest is at stake as in domestic terrorism. In European continental countries, there are no "national databases of arrests, at least none that are accessible to anyone other than the police."[41] Criminal records are held by each country and arrest records are not shared or circulated beyond the police.

(2) Virtue and Duty

Each of the featured takedown cases (priest, public official and rape victim) involves immoral as well as criminal activities. The key difference is that in the first two cases, it is the criminal seeking concealment of his identity, whereas in the third case, it is the victim. The request of the innocent prey in a rape case should weigh heavily, whereas the perpetrators' requests are more likely be denied unless there is clear evidence of repentance that is sincere enough to earn them another chance.

Moral grounds exist for offering rehabilitation to people who have served their sentences, but forgiveness should certainly not be presumed. Immanuel Kant argues for the importance of retributive justice levied against criminals so that they receive their just desserts. More liberal views of morality may extend the doctrine of repentance to permit past sinful behavior to be forgotten.[42] Unethical website creators are merchants of misery that earn millions of dollars from lucrative revenge porn and mugshot websites. The victims of these harmful postings should have the right to have them taken down since there is no valid public interest in allowing this type of invasion of privacy. Increasingly, employees, property owners and other gatekeepers use Google and other digital searches to evaluate fitness, morality, and character.[43]

(3) Conflict Theory

Google has provided an insufficient social context to evaluate the proper treatment of the three takedown requests should operate under a conflict theory. The public official, who breached his fiduciary duty by engaging in corruption, is the least likely requester to find sympathy from this perspective because this is a crime of the powerful against the public interest. The sexual assault victim, by contrast, is not only a victim of rape but may be victimized a second time by being blamed for acting or dressing too provocatively.

The victim of an armed robbery does not face the shame and possible social condemnation experienced by the rape victim. The right to be forgotten can be a valuable defense against social media postings and newspaper reports that can reinforce insidious stereotypes. The poor, the poorly educated and minorities are often stigmatized on social media, sometimes by their own foolish postings that they would like to retract.

The Internet has created a permanent and pervasive treasure trove of digital fingerprints beyond any scale created by prior information technologies such as television, radio or the telephone. Palm County Florida posts the mugshot pictures and charges for everyone booked into the county jail. Many other counties create online websites of mugshots. Joe Arpaio, Maricopa County, Arizona's former sheriff "held a contest in which visitors voted on a mug shot of the day."[44]

For profit websites assemble mugshots and charge huge fees for taking them down from their site.[45] A *Naked Truth* episode explained how private companies are preying upon "tens of millions of Americans, especially minorities that no one has been able to stop."[46] These for-profit websites cause incorrect and dismissed records to permanently stigmatize as they go viral and are not corrected.[47] Mugshot websites charge fees for accessing public criminal records such as DUI/DWI offenses and misdemeanors including contact information, address history, relatives and business associates and personally identifiable financial information.

Internet users increasingly live their private lives in public through the self-immolation of their own privacy. Blogging, photo sharing, texting, instant messaging and other postings on social media sites obliterate the division between the public and the private spheres. Facebook is where a less educated person can share with friends but this also means sharing how inept he is in managing privacy settings. The Miami police have shared pictures of Hurricane looters on Facebook with captions. The Houston Police Department shared a video of a young black man looting while the city was under siege from flooding. Another user commented: "It's about survival, how are they going to make it through a hurricane without a 60 inch LCD TV to keep them warm and safe?"

Vulnerable populations require increased protection against harms resulting from the permanent digital memory of social media sites. The misfortunes of the poor are often blamed on their membership in the "culture of poverty," a set of stereotypes that increase the likelihood of criminal convictions. Media images of women receiving welfare may depict them as "lazy, disinterested in education and promiscuous."[48] Impoverished women are commonly demeaned as Welfare Queens, Bag Ladies or Trailer Park Trash. "People here say, 'She's on welfare' the way they would say, 'she kills baby seals.' "[49]

Conflict perspective advocates contend that having a right of erasure helps disadvantaged groups by giving them a reputational fresh-start improving their opportunities for future employment and education. *Black Lives Matter* advocates argue that lower class African-American males are particularly likely to be arrested for minor misdeeds or for "walking while being black." Mugshot websites will then publish their pictures, even if the charges are dropped. Such websites prey on the stigmatized by demanding payment to take down these damaging images.

(4) Social Contractualism

The U.S. refuses to recognize a right to be forgotten because it clashes with the First Amendment. U.S. websites have no legal duty to take down postings of third parties under Section 230 of the Communications Decency Act. Websites are shielded from liability for third party postings even if these constitute ongoing torts or crimes.

Article 17(3) of the European Data Protection Regulation recognizes that the data subject's right of erasure must be balanced against the right of expression. At present, the U.S. and the EU have radically different approaches to fundamental rights. Websites that post revenge porn or mugshots violate EU law not U.S. law. EU citizens have a clear right to delink objectionable content so long as there is no countervailing reason to continue posting potentially humiliating information. Criminal mugshot websites are illegal throughout Europe. In Germany, for example, once individuals have served their criminal sentence, they have a right to a fresh start. An exception is made where the ex-convict would pose a public danger. The UK frequently releases mugshots of foreign nationals accused of terrorism. The public's right to security than can trump privacy.

(5) Libertarianism

Libertarians reject the right to be forgotten and any governmentally mandated erasure of public record information. The free press and freedom of information is a basic human right that is also vital to a market-based economy. Rewriting history to accommodate privacy is an unacceptable governmental overreach that creates bureaucratic gatekeepers who screen out information that is important for the public to access. The history of governmental censorship to consolidate their power is a shameful record of abuse. In China, Nazi Germany and the Soviet Union, dictators rewrote history with disastrous consequences. A slippery slope is created where regulatory bodies are increasingly tempted to erase information that may be embarrassing to some influential groups. The Libertarian

Party agrees that the U.S.'s market-based approach is superior to the alternative of accepting control of expression by a rigid government bureaucracy.

A libertarian would argue that the European Union is unjustly imposing crippling costs on search engines like Google and Bing, which will hamper their ability to develop new technologies. The right of erasure is the functional equivalent of a tax imposed on the world's leading information moguls because of the sheer cost of responding to demands to erase postings. As the Supreme Court's founding Chief Justice John Marshall famously stated, "The power to tax involves the power to destroy." Regulators should be careful not to weigh down the most dynamic sector of the international economy with a raft of onerous regulations.

These same libertarian arguments could be made to oppose nearly every regulation constraining business. Google and other big stakeholders employ their organizational and economic power to lobby Congress against adopting any restrictions on their activities. Libertarians are concerned that laws and court rulings that appear on the surface to protect the public interest hamper startups without the resources to protect their interests. Google has ample resources to administer and process the enormous number of delinking requests but less well-known providers may find themselves bankrupted by the expense of responding to takedown requests, which is a massive unfunded government mandate.

§ 5.6: ETHICAL ISSUES WITH THE "GIRLS AROUND ME" APPLICATION

[A] Geolocation Technology & Privacy

Now consider another privacy dilemma. How do the five ethical perspectives apply to "Girls Around Me," a geolocation app that could enable stalking, harassment and other gender-based civil wrongs. The company that created Girls Around Me claimed that its app never had the technical capacity to single out any specific female victim. Critics of the app, however, recognize more sinister abuses of this app:

> The Girls Around Me app correlated geolocation data with personal identifiers publicly available on Facebook to perform an unusual function: by clicking on the Girls Around Me icon (a James Bond film-like silhouette against the backdrop of a radar screen), the user was presented with a map showing photographs and personal details of young women located nearby, including their names, ages, marital status, dates of birth and interests.[50]

This controversial application was created in a policy vacuum, as there is no federal or state statute that prohibits this use of geolocation, but "Girls Around Me" raises ethical quandaries. The first step in any ethics analysis is to identify the most important moral issues arising out of new technology. For example, in the release of the Girls Around Me application, one of the central issues is the complete lack of any safeguards to prevent the application from being misused to stalk women.

A person downloading this application possesses total information control regarding the women around him, whereas the targeted women have no information about the person using the application. The women may not even realize that they have made their personal information public. One technology expert observed:

> The settings determining how visible your Facebook and Foursquare data are complicated, and tend to be meaningless to people who don't really understand issues about privacy," I explained. "Most privacy settings on social networks default to share everything with everyone, and since most people never change those. . . well, they end up getting sucked up into apps like this.[51]

By using the Girls Around Me application to link to other social media sites, the predatory user could gather extensive information about those who carelessly overshare personal information and images online:

> I know where she is. I know what she looks like, both clothed and mostly disrobed. I know her full name, her parents' full names, and her brother's full name. I know what she likes to drink. I know where she went to school. I know what she likes and dislikes. All I need to do now is go down to the Independent, ask her if she remembers me from Stoneham High, ask her how her brother Mike is doing, buy her a frosty margarita, and start waxing eloquently about that beautiful summer I spent in Roma.[52]

Is the creation of this application immoral or is it a morally neutral technology that can be useful in connecting young people? Do the persons located through geolocation and whose personal information is linked up with the application have rights to protect their personal privacy? Do users waive their personal privacy by voluntarily providing their personal information and agreeing to the website's terms of use?

Should a regulatory agency such as the Federal Trade Commission shut down similar applications or evaluate them on an *ad hoc* case-by-case basis? Should the free market prevail by forbidding government interference with the voluntary activities of others? Alternatively, it is possible to stretch the common law privacy torts such as intrusion upon seclusion to constrain abuses. One of our computer science-trained students observed that plenty of his "American tech brothers would make an application like this." Just because it is technically possible to create such an application, should software developers be designing an application that may be an instrumentality of stalkers, rapists and other cybercriminals to do enormous harm.

Journalists have noted that the shadowy Russian company that created the application does not have any contact information. What can be said of the ethical conduct of the untraceable software engineers that developed the application? Is it acceptable for an application designer to disclaim responsibility from its product and not address privacy and safety issues? The next stage in such an ethics exercise is to systematically apply the five ethical theories to explore the morality of the Girls Around Me application, its users, its developers and its marketers.

[B] Applying Ethics to Geolocation Technologies

(1) Consequentialism

U.S. consequentialists eschew the European approach, viewing America as a society of "privacy pragmatists,"[53] who weigh privacy risks against consumer and business interests to arrive at the greatest good for the greatest number.

Declaring privacy to be a legally protected, fundamental right seems inefficient and unrealistic, arguing that costs of the European approach outweigh the benefits:

> Europe's strict privacy rules threaten to reduce the potential revenue from online advertising, which will reduce the quantity and quality of content produced for European consumers. Compliance costs for these regulations can be high as well.[54]

One larger societal benefit is that the application makes it more efficient to locate possible mates. The sign-up is voluntary, suggesting that the application produces happiness for those utilizing it. The government should only intervene if there is strong evidence that the women gave up their privacy in joining a social network like Facebook without knowing what they had agreed to or have seriously underestimated the dangers that might arise from using the app.

The potential costs include the app's intrusiveness and the likelihood of misuse by sexual predators or cybercriminals. The principle of the "greatest happiness for the greatest number" is almost impossible to apply in the absence of systematic data about the real-world use of this application.

A consequentialist might collect empirical evidence to establish the ratio of happy outcomes versus unhappy ones. If the costs of misuse were small compared to the number of people who had enjoyable encounters, the app would produce "the greatest good for the greatest number," even though a few victims might suffer substantially.

While the utilitarian cost/benefit analysis seems simple on its face, it may be difficult to determine costs and benefits of the Girls Around Me application even after extensive empirical study. Unanticipated negative consequences may emerge such as enabling new types of crimes or torts. The misuse of the application makes some users happier but the victims unhappier at the same time. Maximizing happiness is easier said than empirically verified.

(2) Virtue and Duty

An ethicist evaluating this app from virtue or moral rights perspectives might object because it empower those with devious intentions to harm others. In Kant's words, "humans have an infinite worth or dignity—that is, humans are 'ends-in-themselves'—and this sets them above all merely conditionally valuable things in the world." Software developers must forgo their own economic interests and make moral decisions based on whether this app furthers respect for humanity.

This violates Kant's imperative to treat humanity as an end in itself. Virtue theorists would question this commercialization of locating prospective dating partners. Truly virtuous software designers would not rely upon highly sexist imagery to produce applications because it objectifies women and inevitably enables stalkers.

Christianity, Judaism, Islam, and other leading world religions would likewise object to the sale of an application to "hook up" with young women to enable sexual indiscretions. Girls Around Me illustrates the eternal truth of the Biblical warning that "the love of money is the root of all evils." The Holy Qur'an instructs its believers to "let those who cannot marry keep chaste, until Allah makes them free." These religious admonitions are unlikely to constrain either designers or users of this morally ambiguous app. The aggregation and release of personal information of the users of Girls Around Me without concern for the impact on vulnerable teens would require a revision of the application.

(3) Conflict Perspective

An ethicist analyzing the controversial software application from a conflict perspective would focus on its disparate negative impact on women. This tool reinforces demeaning gender roles where males are the aggressors and women are passive recipients of male attention. The application reinforces a sexualized view of young women via stylized holograms of female strippers:

> The splash screen elicited laughter all around. It's such a bitmap paean to the tackiest and most self-parodying of baller "culture"; it might as well be an app Tom Haverford slapped together in *Parks And Recreation.* But it does, at a glance, sum up what Girls Around Me is all about: a radar overlaid on top of a Google Map, out of which throbs numerous holographic women posing like pole dancers in a perpetual state of undress.[55]

Women who log into Facebook will not likely review the terms of use and might be unaware of how third party application developers can exploit their publicly available personal information. After connecting to Facebook, the Girls Around Me app asks for access to everything, requiring people to share their basic information, profile information, photos, information people share with them and email address.

(4) Social Contractualism

Apple's decision to remove the Girls Around Me from its app store soon after journalists informed the company of the potential for abuse reflects a Rawlsian version of the social contractualist position. Rawls' theory asks what social contract people would choose if they were operating under a "veil of ignorance," in which they did not know what body or social status they would be assigned at birth. Under this veil of ignorance: "No one knows his place in society, his class position or social status; nor does he know his fortune in the distribution of natural assets and abilities, his intelligence and strength and the like."[56]

Contractualism proved to be the death knell of Girls Around Me. This app violated Apple's terms of use and its API. Users potentially risked having their youthful escapades exposed at some future date. In a sexual harassment case, for example, a defense attorney might deploy this evidence in an unjustified way. Under social contract theory, the Girls Around Me application is problematic because it violates fundamental rights by enabling stalking. The app's advertising was misleading because it advertised the application as free, when, in fact, it required users to remit payment after only a few searches.

(5) Libertarianism

Proponents of the libertarian perspective contend that there should be little or no regulation of such applications, so that willing consumers can freely access desirable technological advances. The ultimate success or failure of the application will depend on how well it does in the marketplace. If consumers find the application creepy and intrusive, the application will not fare well and will vanish without costly government enforcement.

The reasoning goes that that these women voluntarily provided their personal information and agreed to share it. If females refuse to allow their data to be accessed by this app, it has no future. These women may not initially understand the full ramifications of their agreement, but it is paternalistic and demeaning to the intelligence of women for government to protect them from their personal decisions.

Under this perspective, the software developer can conceal his identity and deny all responsibility. If users are uncomfortable with this policy, they do not have to use the application. Apple, as a private corporation, has the right to not carry the app, but no one should have the right to tell other companies and private users what to do. Users need to take responsibility for their actions and understand online contracts before clicking "I agree," rather than complaining when their carelessness creates bad outcomes. Libertarians contend that Internet users can best protect their own privacy using pseudonyms and not using personal profile pictures (e.g. photos related to hobbies or cartoon renditions of themselves, such as those generated by Bitmoji).

CONCLUSION

This chapter examines the most significant online privacy issues including the problem of trans-border data protection, where the legal norms are in flux. In the late 1900s and early twentieth-century, privacy-based torts, along with remedies for misuse of novel technologies such as "instantaneous photographs," were being born. In the new millennium, American society is once again undergoing a technological revolution of great consequence.

The development of new technologies for harvesting personal information creates the potential for widespread invasions of privacy. Privacy advocates, such as the Electronic Frontier Foundation warn about the potential for widespread surveillance and the emergence of a new form of Jeremy Bentham's Panopticon, where anyone and everyone can be watched without being able to tell when they are being monitored. In the global Internet age, personally identifiable data does not stop at national borders and may be exported to dozens of countries at the click of the mouse.

Unlike the U.S., the right of privacy is a comprehensive, fundamental and constitutional right throughout the European Union. Tackling the fundamental ethical conflicts between the U.S. and Europe over how to balance the right of free expression against the right to privacy is necessary to enable a smooth data flow between the two continents. As we will see in later chapters, solutions to fundamental ethical disputes may involve not only normative changes but also changes in the operation of the Internet, such as alterations that could make secrecy and anonymity more available or more difficult to achieve.

CHAPTER FIVE: REVIEW QUESTIONS

5.1: In the United States, privacy is not a fundamental right nor is there comprehensive privacy protection like the General Data Protection Regulation in Europe. The law of privacy in the United States is a patchwork of legislation, regulation and market-based solutions. The federal Privacy Act of 1974 does not apply to data collection information outside the federal government. U.S. privacy is sectorial with statutes, such as HIPAA governing health care providers. What are some of the reasons why the U.S. has not developed privacy as a fundamental right? Why do Europeans seem to value privacy more than Americans do? What practical problems do information-based companies face in transferring data from Europe to the United States?

5.2: The right to be forgotten is not well developed outside of California, which recognizes a right to be forgotten for juveniles. California's 2015 Eraser Law gives those under age 18 the right to "remove or request and obtain removal of content or information" that they posted on an operator's website, application or online service. The minor must be a registered user of the website to exercise this right. Several U.S. states allow juvenile offenders to expunge a court conviction from their record but California is the only state where anyone has a right to take down or erase online postings. Expungement applies only to juvenile offenders, but a few courts have expanded this right to young adult offenders. Do you believe that all states should recognize a right of expungement for minors? For everyone? Why or why not?

5.3: Many people have an embarrassing photograph, blog comment, tweet, speeding ticket or some other digital mistake that they would rather forget. Is the Internet a "cruel historian?" Do you think that young people should have a right to ask a search engine to delink or delete an embarrassing party picture of them? Should a picture of a young fraternity member, arrested for disorderly conduct follow him throughout his entire life? Should fraternity members who were secretly photographed singing a racist song have a right to have the video taken down? What would a virtue theorist say about having a fresh start and a right to remove objectionable posts? What would a libertarian or a consequentialist say in response?

5.4: What are some of the practical problems of implementing a right to be forgotten? How should your right to be forgotten be reconciled with the First Amendment of the U.S. Constitution? By giving data a right to be forgotten, are we rewriting history? What is the downside of recognizing a right to be forgotten?

5.5: The human brain's default state is to forget information. Twenty minutes after you read the end of this chapter exercise, you will remember only about 58% of the information. A month later, only about 1/5th of what you wrote or thought about when answering this question will remain in your memory. Viktor Mayer Schönberger, an Oxford University professor says that the Internet creates digital tattoos that stigmatize us. More prearraignment mugshots are being posted and these records are a permanent digital record. Mugshot lookup sites charge fees for accessing these arrest records. Revenge porn websites and other merchants of misery like Mugshots.com are in effect, permanent digital Scarlett Letters, which you are forced to display on a digital scaffold. Should they be legal?

5.6: The Streisand Effect is the phenomenon whereby an attempt to hide, remove or censor a piece of information has the unintended consequence of publicizing the information more widely. John Oliver, the host of *Last Week Tonight with John Oliver*, explained that singer Barbara Streisand attempted to remove pictures of her Pacific Coast home from a collection of 12,000 California Coastline pictures. At the time, the image of her house had been downloaded only six times. After publicity about her lawsuit to remove these pictures, there were 420,000 downloads. Should celebrities like Barbara Streisand have a right to delete information from the Internet? What about someone running for office like Donald Trump or Hillary Clinton whom have had flagrant lies posted about them on websites? Could the Streisand effect prove beneficial to someone running for the U.S. Presidency?

5.7: A very important factor to consider when discussing the right to be forgotten is how far the right can be extended. What do you do when you want to have things removed and someone posts a report on your removal? Can you then also remove the information about the removal? A European citizen has called for a website for posters who wish to report on removals. If these reports undermine the right to be forgotten, should they be allowed?

5.8: Obesity, tattoos, and bizarre clothes all feature as fodder for snarky comments on a website called "The People of Walmart." The site's content makes a mockery of the appearance and presentation of the low-status people who tend to shop at Walmart. Should the Walmart shoppers depicted on The People of Walmart have a right to remove pictures that humiliate them? Suppose one of the pictures on the website was an elderly grandmother with dementia? Should there ever be a right to remove a photograph taken of shoppers in a public place?

5.9: Revenge porn sites feature nude and sexually explicit photos of people, mostly of women posted by their ex-lovers. Several different websites host these images. Many sites include identifying details, such as the person's full name, employer, and hometown, as well as links to the person's Facebook or other personal webpages. Although some revenge porn sites have been shut down, new sites pop up all the time. California recently convicted a revenge pornographer of posting a picture of his ex-girlfriend in compromising sexual positions. However, courts have not imposed a duty on these websites to take down postings by third parties. These websites are partially financed by demanding payments from those who want their pictures removed. Do you think that the victims of revenge porn should have a right to take down intimate pictures secretly taken by their ex-boyfriend or significant others?

5.10: In the United States, liberty trumps "personality, honor and human dignity," which take priority in many other countries. Should Congress or the U.S. Supreme Court join Europe in recognizing privacy as a comprehensive right? What do you think accounts for the United States' delay in adopting privacy as a fundamental right? To combat the recent wave of terrorist attacks across Europe, should Europeans enact legislation that reduces privacy to combat terrorism? Should hate groups that encourage, but do not employ violence, be censored?

5.11: The Girls Around Me app uses geolocation technology showing photographs and personal details of young women located nearby, including their names, ages, marital status, dates of birth and interests. Do you think that the U.S. should allow this use of geolocation technology? If the application is not illegal, do you think it is unethical? Is this a case where the media has unnecessarily drummed up fear? Explain your reasoning.

5.12: In right to be forgotten cases, a fair balance must be struck between the right of reputational reset for data subjects and the right of free expression, both of which varies significantly between countries. With hundreds of countries connected to the Internet, it is unclear whose community standards apply. The same information posted on the Internet may be protected in the United States, for example, while considered offensive by non-Western countries that value personal honor over expression. A Muslim woman might be held in contempt for appearing on a website that shows her unveiled face. A Hindu might be humiliated if she were unwittingly featured in a hamburger chain's online advertisement. What factors should Google, Bing and other search engines use in deciding whether to take down content? What will prevent a race to the bottom towards adopting the norms of the most restrictive legal system?

5.13: In a 2013 case, a college student got expelled one semester short of graduation because of Facebook posts that the college found "disturbing." The student claimed that one of the postings in question was a joke and that the other occurred after his account had been hacked. He does not know how the college obtained access to his private Facebook account, which he claims is a violation of his Fourth Amendment rights against "unreasonable search and seizure." He wants to be readmitted and to be paid damages. When should a college be allowed to expel a student for off-campus activities? Should it matter whether the college is public or private? Should it matter whether the behavior was public or private? The lawsuit is still posted on the Internet. Should the plaintiff have the right to be forgotten? Would it be unethical or a violation of tort law to use his actual name in this book?

5.14: In a real lawsuit with parallels to the case above, a female student was expelled from a college where she was studying for a degree in elementary education. A picture of her in a revealing costume during a Halloween party with the caption "sexy pirate" was posted on Facebook and reposted elsewhere. The college's justification for expelling her was that no one with knowledge of this picture would hire the student as an elementary school teacher. Was the college's action unethical? Should the college be forced to readmit her? Is this a clear case for the right to be forgotten? If the U.S. adopted a limited right to be forgotten what decision rules should be used to determine whether someone can take advantage of that right?

5.15: President Donald Trump argues that the U.S. permits itself to be pushed around by other countries and needs to be led by a tougher negotiator. Is the potential willingness to weaken U.S. free expression rights to accommodate the laws of the European Union evidence that he is correct?

REFERENCES FOR CHAPTER FIVE

---

1 Michael L. Rustad & Sandra R. Paulsson, *Monitoring Employee Email and Internet Usage: Avoiding the Omniscient Electronic Sweatshop*, 7 UNIVERSITY OF PENNSYLVANIA JOURNAL OF LABOR AND EMPLOYMENT LAW 829 (2005).

2 149 N.H. 148, 151–53 (2003).

3 *Chisholm v. Foothill Capital Corp.*, 3 F. Supp.2d 925, 940–41 (N.D. Ill. 1998).

4 No. CV96–7069, 1997 WL 33384309 (C. D. Cal. Mar. 19, 1997).

5 Reporters' Committee for Freedom of the Press, *False Light*, https://www.rcfp.org/first-amendment-handbook/false-light-misappropriation-right-publicity.

6 Electronic Frontier Foundation, Digital Media Law, *False Light*, http://www.dmlp.org/legal-guide/false-light.

7 Complaint in *Biegel v. Norberg*, No. 08–472522 (Super. Ct. S.F., July 25, 2008).

8 *Mendoza v. Double Lu Inc. v. D/B/A Café Lu & Nguyen*, 30–2011–00521440–CU–DF–CJC (Superior Court, Orange County California, February 25, 2013).

9 *Fain v. Silkening Techns.*, 2012 WL 7004385 (Fla. Cir. Ct., Sept. 24, 2012).

10 J. THOMAS MCCARTHY, THE RIGHTS OF PUBLICITY AND PRIVACY, § 1.2, 1–8 (New York: Thomson/Reuters, 1992).

11 *Id.*

12 Tony Bradley, *Kids Under 13 Are Already Allowed on Facebook*, PC WORLD (May 21, 2011) ("However, a recent Consumer Reports survey indicates that as many as 7.5 million Facebook users are under 13, and two-thirds of those kids are under 10. Either they, or their parents, simply lied about their age to set up the account").

13 Federal Trade Commission, *Two App Developers Settle FTC Charges They Violated Children's Online Privacy Protection Act: Companies' Apps Shared Kids' Information with Ad Networks; Will Pay $360K in Civil Penalties* (December 17, 2005).

14 HHS.gov, Health Information Privacy, Breach Notification Rule (2016).

15 Cheryl Connor, *Wasting Time at Work: The Epidemic Continues*, FORBES (July 31, 2015) (citing empirical study by Harris on how workers waste time at work).

16 *McLaren v. Microsoft Corp.*, 1999 WL 339015 (Tex. App., May 28, 1999).

17 *Barbulescu v. Romania,* Application No. 61496/08, (Grand Chamber, European Court of Human Rights).

18 Thomas H. Koenig & Michael L. Rustad, *Digital Scarlet Letters: Social Media Stigmatization of the Poor and What Can Be Done*, 93 NEBRASKA LAW REVIEW 592, 600 (2015).

19 Jay P. Kesan, *Cyber-Working or Cyber-Shirking?: A First Principles Examination of Electronic Privacy in the Workplace*, 54 FLORIDA LAW REVIEW 289, 319–320 (2002).

20 Corey A. Ciocchetti, *The Eavesdropping Employer: A Twenty-First Century Framework for Employee Monitoring*, 48 AMERICAN BUSINESS LAW JOURNAL, 285 (2011).

21 *Restuccia v. Burk Technology, Inc.*, 1996 WL 1329386 (Mass. Super. Aug. 13, 1996).

22 *Garrity v. John Hancock Mutual Life Ins. Co.*, 2002 WL 974676 (D. Mass. 2002.).

23 Jay P. Kesan, *Cyber-Working or Cyber-Shirking?: A First Principles Examination of Electronic Privacy in the Workplace*, 54 FLORIDA LAW REVIEW 289, 319–320 (2002).

24 474 F.3d 1184 (9th Cir. 2007).

25 Michael L. Rustad & Sandra R. Paulsson, *Monitoring Employee Email and Internet Usage: Avoiding the Omniscient Electronic Sweatshop*, 7 UNIVERSITY OF PENNSYLVANIA JOURNAL OF LABOR AND EMPLOYMENT LAW 829, 833 (2005).

26 *Id.* at 848.

27 This section draws upon Michael L. Rustad & Sanna Kulveska, 28 *Reconceptualizing the Right to Be Forgotten*, 28 HARVARD JOURNAL OF LAW AND TECHNOLOGY 349 (2015).

28 Mark Scott, *Facebook Gets Slap on the Wrist from 2 European Privacy Regulators*, N.Y. Times (May 16, 2017).

29 Electronic Privacy Information Center (EPIC), *Max Schrems v. Irish Data Protection Commissioner* (Safe Harbor) (2015).

30 EUGDPR.ORG, *Key Changes: An Overview of the Key Changes Under GDPR and How They Differ From the Previous Directive*, http://www.eugdpr.org/key-changes.html.

31 *Id.*

32 European Commission, *Agreement on Commission's EU Data Protection Reform Will Boost Digital Single Market* (Dec. 15, 2015).

[33] Reuters News Service, *German Consumer Group Sets Facebook Privacy Ultimatum*, (Aug. 27, 2012).

[34] Loek Essers, *Facebook Must Comply with German Data Protection Law, Court Rules*, PC WORLD (Feb. 18, 2014).

[35] Emil Protalinski, *Daughter Posts Sexually Explicit Photos, Dad Sues Facebook*, ZDNET.COM (Sept. 7, 2011).

[36] Jabeen, Bhatti, *Facebook's "Like" Button on Company Websites Isn't Legally Justified, German Court Rules*, Bloomberg BNA: Computer Technology Law Report (March 9, 2016).

[37] Reuters, *German Consumer Group Sets Facebook Privacy Ultimatum*, REUTERS NEWS SERVICE (Aug. 27, 2012).

[38] Jimmy H. Koo, *FTC Takes First EU-U.S. Privacy Shield Enforcement Action*, BLOOMBERG BNA: PRIVACY & DATA SECURITY REPORT (Sept. 9, 2017).

[39] Natasha Lomas, *Trump Order Strips Privacy Rights from Non-U.S. Citizens Could Nix EU-US Data Flows*, TECHCRUNCH.COM (Jan. 26, 2017).

[40] *Rosenblatt v. Baer*, 383 U.S. 75, 87 (1966).

[41] James B. Jacobs, *Expungement of Criminal Records in Spain* (January 21, 2015).

[42] Peter Koritansky, *Two Theories of Retributive Punishment: Immanuel Kant and Thomas Aquinas*, 22 HISTORY OF PHILOSOPHY QUARTERLY, 319 (October 2005).

[43] Sarah Esther Lageson, *Digital Punishment's Tangled Web*, CONTEXTS (Winter 2016).

[44] Tim Stelloh, *Innocent Until Your Mugshot Is on the Internet*, THE NEW YORK TIMES (June 3, 2017).

[45] *Id.*

[46] Fusion.tv, *The Naked Truth: In 'Mugged' We Show You Who's Getting Rich Off Mugshots and Who's Paying the Price (*September 15, 2017).

[47] Sarah Esther Lageson, *Digital Punishment's Tangled Web*, CONTEXTS (Winter 2016).

[48] Heather E. Bullock, Karen Fraser Wyche, & Wendy R. Williams, *Media Images of the Poor*, 47 JOURNAL OF SOCIAL. ISSUES 229 (2001).

[49] Page, Lucas-Stannard, *I'm a Welfare Mom*, EVERYDAY FEMINISM (September 2012).

[50] *In re Smartphone Geolocation Data Application*, 977 F.Supp.2d 129 (E.D. N.Y. 2013).

[51] John Brownlee, *This Creepy App Isn't Just Stalking Women Without Their Knowledge, It's a Wake-Up Call About Facebook Privacy*, CULT OF MAC (March 30, 2012).

[52] *Id.*

[53] Castro, Daniel, *Benefits and Limitations of Industry Self-Regulation for Online Behavioral Advertising*, THE INFORMATION TECHNOLOGY & INNOVATION FOUNDATION (2011) at 11.

[54] *Id.* at 8.

[55] Richard Volkman, *Being a Good. Computer Professional: The Advantages of Virtue Ethics* in *Computing*, PROCEEDINGS OF ETHICS & COMPUTERS (Tokyo, Japan: Meiji University 2007) at 1.

[56] JOHN RAWLS, A THEORY OF JUSTICE (Cambridge, Massachusetts: Harvard University Press, 1971) at 18.

CHAPTER SIX

Computer Contracts

§ 6.0: INTRODUCTION TO COMPUTER CONTRACT LAW

Did you ever read the terms of use (ToU) to join your favorite website, which you accepted by clicking "I agree?" If not, you may be surprised to find that you have agreed to replace your Seventh Amendment right to a trial with a hearing before an arbiter who is located a continent away. You may have also agreed to cap your potential damages at far less than the cost of filing a claim, depriving every consumer of any meaningful remedy. One-sided clauses like these are overwhelmingly enforced by U.S. courts.

In July of 2017, Photobucket, an image and video-hosting website, announced that its previously free service would now cost $400 per year.[1] Photobucket's unilateral modification of its ToU provoked outrage because consumers could no longer access their stored images without paying a subscription fee. Consumers complain that their content is being held hostage but Photobucket is likely to prevail with its argument that it may modify contractual terms at any time without notice. Should U.S. courts refuse to enforce contracts of adhesion, which are agreements completely dictated by the stronger party?

One-sided ToU can pose difficult legal, cultural and ethical issues. For example, Chinese Uber drivers operating in New York City, who spoke very little English, were originally provided with a ToU written in Chinese with a Chinese language interface.[2] This agreement was modified in an April 2015, including an Addendum that was only available in English. The drivers filed a class action alleging that they were owed compensation under Uber's New York City 2015 Guarantee Program, in which Uber promised New York drivers a minimum of $5,000 to $7,000 per month. Uber defended against these claims with a motion to dismiss the lawsuit on the grounds that the drivers had agreed to mandatory arbitration, when they accepted the Addendum.

The drivers contended that they did not knowingly agree to arbitration because they could not read the English-only revision to the ToU. The *Uber* court ruled in favor of the ride-matching service, finding its revised ToU was enforceable and ordering the drivers to submit to arbitration. The court reasoned that "the fact that it is not worth the expense involved in proving a statutory remedy does not constitute the elimination of the right to pursue that remedy."[3]

This recent Uber case encompasses many of the compelling computer contract issues that remain unresolved. How should law apply traditional contracting principles to the online environment? Should courts permit providers like Uber to coerce less educated, non-English speaking drivers into agreeing to mandatory arbitration, despite knowing that the cost of pursuing the claim exceeds any possible recovery? It may be legal to use contract law to eliminate any realistic remedy, but is it ethical? While there is a well-established duty to read contracts, should there be a legal or moral duty to make a contract readable?

Increasingly, disputes such as the Uber case will be tried in jurisdictions with mandatory consumer protection rules not recognized by U.S. courts. European and Chinese courts refuse to enforce one-sided terms commonly found in U.S. style agreements. What should U.S. companies do to tailor their contracts to comply with radically different legal systems? This chapter will present the background information needed to resolve the legal issues and ethical concerns raised by information age contracts.

§ 6.1: THE PRINCIPAL COMPUTER CONTRACTS

Computer professionals encounter four common types of information technology contracts: (1) Sales, (2) Leases, (3) Licenses and (4) Cloud Computing Contracts (Software-as-a-Service). Consumers often say that they purchased a software application, however this is not legally correct. Mass market software is licensed, not sold. The buyer would have title to the software and the right to make unlimited copies if it were sold. Chart One below describes the parties and subject of the four most common contracting methods.

CHART ONE: COMMON CONTRACTING FORMS

Type of Contract & Source of Law	Parties to the Contract	Subject of Contracts
Uniform Commercial Code (UCC) Article 2—Sales of Goods	Seller and Buyer (sales of contracts) Example: Dell sells laptops to	Title passes from seller to buyer and buyer takes possession of tangible good or movable

	customers and passes title to these goods.	property, such as computer hardware.
Uniform Commercial Code (UCC) Article 2A—Leases	Lessor and Lessee Example: Dell leases laptops to customers.	In a true lease, the computer lessor gives possession and right to use a computer system to the lessee for a fixed term in return for renting the property.
The Uniform Computer Information Transactions Act (UCITA) as enacted in Maryland and Virginia. Principles of the Law of Software Contracts	Licensor and Licensee Example: Dell users must accept the terms and conditions of the licensing agreement before they can install its operating system.	Software publishers make copies of their product available to customers through Software license agreements.
Cloud Computing or Software as a Service (SaaS) (common law services contracts)	Cloud Provider and Customer enter into a contract for services, software-as-a-service, platform-as-a-service and infrastructure-as-a-service (i.e. Amazon AWS, IBM Cloud & Microsoft Azure)	Cloud computing is delivering software for services over the Internet through on-demand network access. This services model allows the user to access a shared pool of configurable computing resources.

[A] UCC Article 2 Sales of Goods & Computer Systems

A contract for the sale of goods is one in which the seller agrees to transfer goods that conform to the contract in exchange for a predetermined price. Article 2 of the Uniform Commercial Code (UCC) governs contracts for the sale of physical goods such as hardware. An owner of an Apple iPod claiming that there were hair-line cracks on her iPod when she opened the box has a UCC Article 2 cause of action because the screen is classified as goods. Since the birth of the software industry, courts have routinely applied UCC Article 2 to sales where hardware and software are bundled and sold as a turnkey computer system.

Courts began to stretch UCC Article 2 to computer systems in the mid-1980s. In contracts involving both hardware and software, courts decide whether the predominant purpose is the hardware or the software aspect. If the hardware predominates, they apply UCC Article 2 to the entire computer system. If a court finds that software or services predominate, they turn to non-UCC law. Some courts are willing to stretch UCC Article 2 to a computer contract that is predominately about software.

In *Toshiba America HD DVD Marketing and Sales Practices Litigation*,[4] the court applied UCC Article 2 to determine whether Toshiba made an express warranty in selling their HD DVD Player. Toshiba's DVD players functioned well, but were largely useless because no more films would be distributed in this obsolete format. Despite knowing that this equipment would have little value in the coming Blu-Ray era, Toshiba advertised its player as "For Today, Tomorrow, and Beyond." The consumers who purchased this outmoded player filed a class action lawsuit, contending that Toshiba's advertising slogan misled them. The federal court ruled that Toshiba did not breach any express warranties by its failure to disclose that its technology had no future. The court reasoned that the consumer's had no UCC Article 2 cause of action because Toshiba's devices played DVD movies as advertised.

In *In re Carrier IQ, Inc.*,[5] a California district court extended UCC Article 2 to the software incorporated into smartphones. The consumers claimed that Carrier IQ violated an implied warranty of merchantability by designing software that surreptitiously collected and transferred sensitive personal data from consumer's mobile devices to Carrier IQ and other third parties. The consumers argued that the software it incorporated into smart devices was merely a network diagnostic tool for mobile phone providers and did not violate merchantability. Carrier IQ further contended that the data collecting software did nothing to impair the cell phone's functionality. The *Carrier IQ* court broke with an earlier court that rejected a merchantability claim in an iPhone case, merely because the "Siri" feature did not work.

The earlier court reasoned that these iPhones were fit for their ordinary purpose of transmitting calls, instant messages and accessing the Internet. Regardless, the *Carrier IQ* court recognized the possibility of a merchantability claim and allowed the case to go forward. In 2016, the Carrier IQ case settled for $9 million dollars.

[B] Leases of Computer Systems

Customers frequently lease computer systems to avoid buying equipment that will quickly become obsolete. Tax advantages also encourage leasing rather than purchasing equipment. The Internal Revenue Code permits computer lessees to deduct the full cost of the computer system as if it was a newly purchased asset. The full value of a computer system, for example, could be deducted in the first year of the lease.

A synthetic lease is a financing method by which a company structures the ownership of an asset so that—for financial accounting purposes—a special-purpose entity owns the asset and leases it to the operating company. Leases of equipment permit a computer company to save on taxes by classifying the computer as a cost rather than an asset on its balance sheet.

Computer lease agreements are between two parties: (1) the lessor, who owns the computer system and delivers possession, but not title, for the term of the lease and (2) the lessee, who is a customer leasing the computer system for a fixed amount of time. The customer uses the computer system for a lease period and at the end of such period returns the system to the lessor if it has any remaining economic value. In the new millennium, computer leases are giving way to the sale of computer systems and the licensing of software.

[C] Software License Agreements

(1) The Evolution of Contract Law for the Information Age

In August 1981, IBM became the first computer company to separate its software from its computer systems when it decided to sell applications as separately priced products for its personal computers. A little more than a decade later, software applications produced more revenue than hardware purchases. The software and software-services market continues to expand at a rate many times that of hardware. A software license is a legal agreement that gives the licensor control over the software code after delivery by specifying conditions governing the use or redistribution of the software.

A licensor of software, digital data or other information gives the licensee permission to use its content but its use is subject to restrictions. With a sale of goods, the seller conveys the buyer all rights as well as title. A seller of hardware such as an iPod, high definition television, or snowmobile cannot specify that the consumer may only use the device in certain locations, but a licensor of software can control the permitted locations, duration of use, number of users, geographic scope and allowable uses of the software.

(2) Proprietary Software Agreements

Source code is original work created by a software developer in a programming language such as Python, C++, or SQL. Programmers use these languages to create source code readable by humans. Compilers convert source code into object code, which is machine language that computers can process. Proprietary software is only distributed in object form. Closed source licensing is comparable to a consumer purchasing an automobile but being prohibited from looking under the hood to see how the engine works. Proprietary software makers do not give their customers access to source code because they worry that their customers may develop competitive or modified products.

(3) Open Source Software Agreements

"Open source" gets its name from the distribution model in which source code accompanies the software module. Free software gives users the freedom to run, copy, distribute, study, change and improve the software. Apple Corporation's Public License, Intel's Open Source License, The University of California's BSD License, Sun Microsystems' Common Development and the General Public License (GPL) are examples of open source software licenses.

Under open source licenses, the licensee is guaranteed access to the source code, giving them an opportunity to look under the hood so they "can easily understand and change those instructions."[6] With free and open source software, there is a complete freedom to tweak and improve the code and share it with other users. "Property in open source is configured fundamentally around the right to distribute, not the right to exclude."[7]

Copyleft, which is a twist on the word copyright, gives licensees the right to freely distribute copies and modified versions of a work with the stipulation that they must give other users the same rights. Open source software is distributed with a mandatory term that requires the licensee or any other downstream user to distribute derivative products under the same terms. More precisely, open source refers to four kinds of freedom, for the users of the software:

(1) The freedom to run the program, for any purpose (freedom 0);

(2) The freedom to study how the program works, and adapt it to your needs (freedom 1), access to the source code is a precondition for this;

(3) The freedom to redistribute copies so you can help your neighbor (freedom 2); and

(4) The freedom to improve the program, and release your improvements (and modified versions in general) to the public, so that the whole community benefits (freedom 3) access to the source code is a precondition for this.

The most popular open source license agreement is GNU/GPL Version 3, which requires the licensor to distribute the software's source code ("human readable code") to encourage collaboration and sharing by future users. The General Public License version 3 (GPL/V3) requires licensees to return modifications to the public under the same terms. The GPL permits end users to copy and distribute licensed software so long as they include a notice that the product is distributed in source code and allows modifications and improvements for all distributed works.

The GPL license also prohibits licensors from including restrictions on other software modules included in an application. Free and open source software is controlled by those who create it, whereas proprietary software reflects an older model, where the software publishers impose total control over source code. Open source programmers have developed a long list of products that includes Apache, the Linux operating system and Sendmail.[8]

(4) Open Source/Closed Source Hybrids

The once clear dichotomy between open and proprietary software licensing is evolving into hybrid forms that combine features of both approaches. Established companies such as HP, Oracle, and IBM are adapting Linux and other open software to run on their proprietary systems.[9] An estimated 78% of all U.S. companies incorporate open source software licensed code in their products. The rate of usage doubled between 2010 and 2015.[10] Former Microsoft CEO Steve Ballmer once denounced open source providers "as a cancer that attaches itself in an intellectual property sense to everything it touches.[11] By 2016, Ballmer had reversed his position, acknowledging that open source makes Microsoft a "ton of money."[12] In 2017, Microsoft open sourced the Git Virtual File System that enabled efficient management of files.

[D] Cloud Computing Contracts

The term, "cloud," is an imperfect metaphor used to describe remote storage of software applications, tools and data accessed via the Internet. Despite the metaphor, cloud computing always has a physical location. The National Institute of Standards and Technology (NIST) defines cloud computing as a "model for enabling convenient, on-demand network access to a shared pool of configurable computing resources (e.g., networks, applications and services) that can be rapidly provisioned and released with minimal management effort or service provider interaction."[13] Nearly every consumer uses cloud computing whether they are posting to social media site or saving data on Google Drive.

Cloud computing is an attractive alternative to the expense of developing and maintaining an IT department, which requires substantial investments in real estate, capital equipment, and long-term maintenance.[14] By the end of 2018, nearly eighty percent of all data is predicted to be processed by cloud data centers. Neither Congress nor state legislatures have enacted statutes to address the questionable practices of some cloud computing providers, who offer "service credits" as opposed to meaningful remedies for interruptions of service. Cloud providers typically disclaim all warranties and eliminate remedies such as the recovery of consequential damages stemming from lost or missing data, excessive data and losses due to inadequate security.

Service level agreements (SLA) spell out terms such as specifications for privacy, responsiveness, resource efficiency, metrics for measuring usage, interoperability and remedies in the event of a service interruption. The most important negotiating point in SLAs is to clarify response and resolution procedures if service is interrupted.

Customers also express dissatisfaction with SLA security provisions.[15] SLAs often reassign the risk of service interruption, security breaches and other lapses in service to customers. Lawyers negotiating SLAs need to tailor their choice of law, choice of forum, performance standards, and security provisions tailored to their business objectives. Many new issues arise out of the multi-tenant cloud computing model, where multiple companies access the same data storage facilities. Chart Two depicts the key clauses in SLAs that need to be taken into account.

CHART TWO: KEY ISSUES ADDRESSED BY SERVICE LEVEL AGREEMENTS

Business Level Objectives: An organization must define *why* it will use cloud services before it can define exactly what services it will use. This part may be more organizational politics than technical issues: Some groups may get funding cuts or lose control of their infrastructure.
Responsibilities of Both Parties: It is important to define the balance of responsibilities between the provider and consumer. For example, the provider

will be responsible for the Software-as-a-Service aspects, but the consumer may be mostly responsible for his Virtual Machine (VM) that contains licensed software and works with sensitive data.
Business Continuity/Disaster Recovery: The consumer should ensure the provider maintains adequate disaster protection for its own interruptions. Two issues come to mind: first, while users may store valuable data on the cloud as backup, the cloud provider needs their own backup facility. And second, cloud providers may choose to offer cloud bursting services (switchover when in-house data centers are unable to handle processing loads).
Redundancy: Consider how redundant your provider's systems are. Redundancy means that the provider has duplicate copies of various data, equipment, systems, or the like, to be used in the event that part of the cloud fails, or cannot be accessed.
Maintenance: The cloud computing provider generally offers maintenance, but consumers should know when providers will do maintenance tasks: Will services be unavailable during that time? Will services be available, but with much lower throughput? Will the consumer have a chance to test their applications against the updated versions?
Data Location: There are regulations whereby particular types of data can only be stored in certain physical locations. Providers can respond to those requirements with a guarantee that a consumer's data will be stored in these locations only and that the consumer will have an ability to audit that situation.
Data Seizure: If law enforcement seizes a provider's equipment to capture the data and applications belonging to a particular consumer, that seizure is likely to affect other consumers that use the same provider. Consider a third party to provide additional backup.
Provider Failure: Make contingency plans that take into account the financial health of the provider.
Jurisdiction: Understand the local laws that apply to your provider, as well as the laws that apply to you.
Brokers and Resellers: If your provider is a broker or reseller of cloud services, you need to understand the policies of your provider and the actual provider.
Source: IBM.com, *Review and Summary of Cloud Service Level Agreements* (2017).

Apple announced it would establish "its first data center in China to speed up services such as iCloud for local users and abide by laws that require global companies to store information within the country."[16] Apple's new data center will give the Chinese government greater "control over the collection and movement of Chinese users' data, and can also grant the government unprecedented access to foreign companies' technology."[17] Is it ethical for Apple to enter into a joint venture to assist China's government in monitoring its citizens' Internet communications?

Google Cloud Services recently stopped "one of the most controversial advertising formats: ads inside Gmail that scan users' email contents."[18] The decision did not come from a regulatory or statutory requirement but from Google's desire "to sign up more corporate customers."[19] Neither Congress nor regulators have weighed in on whether Apple or Google's decisions violate U.S. law.

Cloud computing also creates new legal dilemmas such as how electronic storage is defined, a key issue of the Stored Communications Act. [20] What should constitute electronic storage where there is a synchronization of copies across servers located in many countries? Cloud computing disrupts traditional licensing laws and challenges territorially-based jurisdiction.

§ 6.2: CONSUMER CONTRACTS IN CYBERSPACE

In contrast to contracts negotiated between sophisticated parties, the Internet has spurred the development of countless business-to-consumer "agreements" where the provider dictates one-sided terms. A federal judge explains these information-age contracts:

> All of us who have signed up for an online service recently will recall the experience. After entering the service provider's website, we were presented with a 'sign up' or 'create account' button prominently displayed on the screen. Next to the button—less prominent, no doubt—was the ubiquitous advisory that, by signing up, we would be accepting the provider's terms of service (ToS). Perhaps there was a separate check box prompting us to indicate our agreement to those terms. Regardless, eager to begin using the service and realizing that the provider's contractual terms are non-negotiable, most of us signed up without bothering to click the accompanying link to reveal the contractual terms. Those who did undoubtedly found numerous pages of legalese. The intrepid few who actually read all the terms almost

> certainly learned that one of them requires users to relinquish their right to have a jury resolve any dispute with the provider. Moreover, that clause bars class actions.[21]

These mass market, consumer license agreements raise both ethical and legal issues. Increasingly, U.S. licensors, social media providers and other websites create terms of use where the consumer manifests assent by clicking on a hyperlink. In contrast, browsewrap terms of use assert that a user manifests assent or agreement to contractual terms by merely accessing or browsing a website or other content. Few consumers realize that when they access a website, they may be subject to a ToU even though they did not click "yes" in agreement, read the agreement or were even aware of the contract's existence.

Internet-related consumer contracts impose terms such as mandatory arbitration, prohibitions against joining class actions, caps on damages and often dictating the dominant party's choice of law and forum. In 2014, General Mills, the producer of numerous popular consumer products such as Cheerios, Yoplait Yogurt, Häagen-Dazs Ice Cream, Progresso Soups and Gold Medal Flour, altered the terms on its website, adding a clause that required all disputes related to the purchase or use of any of its products be resolved through mandatory arbitration.

Consumers, under this one-sided provision, waived their right to file suit in court simply by downloading coupons from company-sponsored contests. After a public outcry, General Mills terminated this questionable, although legal, practice and no longer requires its consumers to submit to mandatory arbitration. A company such as General Mills may be forced to change practices that the user community perceives to be unfair or unethical.

[A] Airbnb's Contracting Practices & Social Justice

Even when they result in the possibility of removing racial discrimination claims from the court system, U.S. courts have not been receptive to striking down browsewrap agreements. The district court for the District of Columbia upheld Airbnb's terms of service agreement in *Selden v. Airbnb, Inc.*[22] In that case, Gregory Selden, an African-American, signed up with Airbnb's residential rental service just prior to booking a weekend getaway to Philadelphia. Selden submitted the required user profile, including his photograph and contacted a possible Airbnb "host":

> The host allegedly responded that the residence was not available. Smelling a rat, Selden created a second account under a pseudonym, with a photograph of a white person in the user profile, and contacted

> the same host about the same accommodation. This time, Selden claims, the host was very happy to rent the residence. Selden filed suit against Airbnb for race discrimination on behalf of himself and fellow African-American travelers who have reported similar treatment on Airbnb. Likening Airbnb to a hotel and its hosts to rental agents or hotel employees, Selden sought to hold the company responsible under federal civil rights laws for the discriminatory conduct of those who offer accommodations on its website.[23]

Airbnb filed a motion to dismiss and requested a court order to compel arbitration of Selden's racial discrimination claims. Selden argued the arbitration clause did not apply, as the sign-up process did not place him on adequate notice that he was agreeing to Airbnb's Terms of Service, including the mandatory arbitration clause. He also contended that even if the arbitration clause was enforceable, it did not apply to discrimination causes of action and was unconscionable. The court enforced Airbnb's arbitration clause, reasoning mutual arbitration provisions are enforceable as long as the user had notice of them when signing up for the service.

Selden first created his Airbnb account in March 2015, using an iPhone mobile device. Airbnb's mobile sign-up screen presented him with three options in descending order: "Sign up with Facebook," "Sign up with Google," and "Sign up with Email." Below the "Sign up with Email" button was a text that read: "By signing up, I agree to Airbnb's Terms of Service, Privacy Policy, Guest Refund Policy, and Host Guarantee Terms." The diagram below depicts what Selden saw when he clicked "Sign Up with Facebook" at the top of the page, creating his Airbnb profile.

iPhone 5

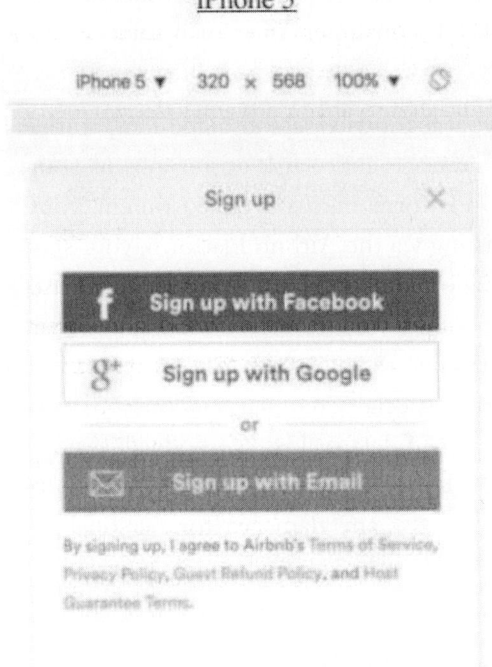

Source: *Selden v. Airbnb, Inc.*, 2016 WL 6476934, S.D. N.Y. Nov. 1, 2016) at *9 (Appendix).

The federal district court found that the above Airbnb mobile sign-up screen adequately placed Selden on notice of Airbnb's Terms of Service. The court ruled that Selden assented to those terms by clicking the sign-up box and using the service. The court found that any reasonable observant user would have known that they were manifesting assent when signing up for the service. The court ruled that any doubts about the scope of arbitration should be resolved in favor of arbitration even in federal racial discrimination claims. The court also rejected Selden's argument that the agreement was unconscionable, noting that both parties were subject to arbitration and that Airbnb paid the arbitrator's fees unless the claim was frivolous.

The *Selden* court validated arbitration even though the costs of filing, travel expenses, lost time and the plaintiff's disadvantage in this forum made it likely that the consumer would not pursue their rights. In February 2017, the D.C. Circuit ruled that the district court's decision ordering arbitration and the decision to stay litigation was not be appealed.

The *Selden* court's willingness to compel arbitration for a federal racial discrimination claim demonstrates how entrenched consumer arbitration is in the U.S. legal landscape. In contrast, Airbnb could not compel EU consumers to waive mandatory rights, such as the right to go to before a court in their country of residence. Airbnb's terms of use imposes arbitration for U.S. but not EU consumers. The Airbnb ToU exempts EU consumers from many of its limitations such as in the following clause:

> Unless you reside in the EU, you acknowledge and agree that, to the maximum extent permitted by law, the entire risk arising out of your access to and use of the Airbnb Platform and Collective Content, your publishing or booking of any Listing via the Airbnb Platform, your stay at any Accommodation, participation in any Experience or Event or use of any other Host Service or any other interaction you have with other Members whether in person or online remains with you. . . . [Airnbnb will] not be liable for any incidental, special, exemplary or consequential damages, including lost profits, loss of data or loss of goodwill, service interruption, computer damage or system failure or the cost of substitute products or services, or for any damages for personal or bodily injury or emotional distress.

The Airbnb terms of use that exempt EU consumers from caps on damages reflects the growing gulf between U.S. and European consumer law. EU consumer law generally prohibits disclaimers, limitations and one-sided choice of law and forum clauses, whereas U.S. law gives providers a wide discretion in limiting their liability.

[B] The Legal Reception of Wrap Contracts

When most students consider software licensing, they think of the ToU they agree to before obtaining website content or downloading software. Every Internet user has entered into a substantial number of clickwrap agreements whereby contractual assent is premised upon clicking "I accept" buttons to access online content or services. Unlike traditional contract law, in electronic contracting, there is no paper record or pen and pencil signature. Users may not be aware that they are entering into legally enforceable contracts when registering for Facebook, Twitter or even simply visiting a website.[24]

The nonnegotiable terms buried in mass market computer contracts deprive the user of important legal rights. Facebook, for example, calls its agreement, "Statement of Rights and Responsibilities."[25] Facebook requires its users agree to a choice of law clause that requires disputes to be adjudicated under the rules of Facebook's home base, Santa Clara County, California. Consumers also agree to indemnify Facebook if the social media website is sued because the user has posted something that infringes on a third party's content or results in other litigation. The earliest computer-related standard form contract to evolve was the shrinkwrap licenses invented by the software industry of the 1980s. The three major forms of mass market licenses are shrinkwraps, clickwraps and browsewraps as illustrated in Chart Three below.

CHART THREE: A TYPOLOGY OF MASS MARKET LICENSES

Type of Wrap Contracts	How Assent is Manifested	Enforceability Issues
Shrinkwrap	By opening this sealed disk package, the customer agrees to be bound.	If the user has the ability to manifest assent and an opportunity to review the terms, the shrinkwrap is enforced.
Clickwrap	By clicking on an icon or radio button link the user is bound.	Links to clickwrap agreements are sometimes inconspicuously located below the fold of a web page.
Browsewrap	By merely browsing a website or accessing a website without actively manifesting assent, the consumer is bound.	Consumers may be bound even though they neither read the terms of use nor affirmatively manifested assent to its provisions.

(1) Shrinkwrap Licenses

Shrinkwrap contracts are license agreements or other terms and conditions, which can only be read and accepted by the consumer after breaking open the shrinkwrap, the plastic or cellophane tightly wrapped around the software package. In the 1980s and 1990s, software publishers marketed their retail software packages sealed in shrinkwrap. The consumer's assent occurred when the user opened the plastic wrap surrounding the software box, as indicated by imprinted text such as:

> "Opening the Envelope containing the diskette will constitute your agreement to the license which is contained on the outside of the envelope."

Courts upheld these agreements even though the form contract could not be viewed until after the box was opened. The following text box is an example of a shrinkwrap license agreement that was in wide currency in the 1980s and 1990s.

Shrinkwrap License Agreement: The Box-Top License

Printed on the package of each copy of the program would be a copy of the box-top license. The box-top license typically contained five terms relevant to this action:

(1) The box-top license provides that the customer has not purchased the software itself, but has merely obtained a personal, non-transferable license to use the program.

(2) The box-top license, in detail and at some length, disclaims all express and implied warranties except for a warranty that the disks contained in the box are free from defects.

(3) The box-top license provides that the sole remedy available to a purchaser of the program is to return a defective disk for replacement; the license excludes any liability for damages, direct or consequential, caused by use of the program.

(4) The box-top license contains an integration clause, which provides that the box-top license is the final and complete expression of the terms of the parties' agreement.

(5) The box-top license states: "Opening this package indicates your acceptance of these terms and conditions. If you do not agree with them, you should promptly return the package unopened to the person from whom you purchased it within fifteen days from date of purchase and your money will be refunded to you by that person."

Source: *Step-Saver Data Systems, Inc. v. Wyse Technology*, 939 F.2d 91 (3d Cir. 1991).

Scott Adams lampooned shrinkwrap licenses, such as those in *Step-Saver*, in a cartoon where Dilbert is talking to Dogbert:

> Dilbert says: "I didn't read all of the shrinkwrap license agreement on my new software until after I opened it. He continues in the next panel: "Apparently I agreed to spend the rest of my life as a towel boy in Bill Gates' new mansion." Dogbert says, "Call your lawyer." In the next panel, Dilbert says, "Too late. He opened the software yesterday. Now he's Bill's laundry boy." In another dated April 7, 1997, Dilbert reads: "Software License: By opening this package, You agree. . . ." In the next panel, the license terms continue: "[Y]ou will not make copies or export to despotic nations. You will submit to strip searches in your home. . . . In the next panel, Dilbert opens the package. An employee of the software company is putting on a rubber glove and says, "Frankly, both of us would have been happier if you had just walked away."[26]

(a) ProCD as a Game-Changer

Prior to the mid-1990s, every U.S. court refused to enforce shrinkwrap agreements. This changed with the 1997 decision of *ProCD v. Zeidenberg*.[27] In that case, ProCD compiled a computer database called "Select Phone" that consisted of more than 3,000 telephone directories and sought to protect its investment in the database by requiring licensees to enter into a licensing agreement limiting use and containing restrictions. Matthew Zeidenberg purchased a copy of ProCD's Select Phone in Madison, Wisconsin.

Zeidenberg formed a company to resell access to the software on a website, which violated the ProCD license agreement. ProCD filed a copyright infringement lawsuit seeking an injunction against Zeidenberg's continuing breach of its license agreement. The federal district refused to enforce ProCD's license agreements reasoning that the software company's terms did not appear on the outside of the package and therefore a customer could not be bound by terms that could not be reviewed at the time of purchase.[28]

On appeal, the Seventh Circuit disagreed, ruling that ProCD's license agreements were enforceable contracts and not unconscionable. The Seventh Circuit noted that the exchange of money frequently precedes the communication of contractual terms in modern commerce. The court reasoned that by including the license with the software box, ProCD proposed a contract that the buyer could accept by using the software after having an opportunity to read the license. "Notice on the outside, terms on the inside, and a right to return the software for a refund if the terms are unacceptable (a right that the license expressly extends), may be a means of doing business valuable to buyers and sellers alike."[29]

"In a rolling contract, a purchaser orders goods and pays for them before seeing most of the terms," which are sent later or modified by posting changed terms on a website.[30] The Seventh Circuit adopted a consequentialist approach in upholding this novel contracting as an efficient form of private business practice. If the Seventh Circuit had not enforced ProCD's shrinkwrap agreement, the entire software industry would have been in jeopardy, as a single end-user could resell an unlimited number of copies of the software, destroying any opportunity for the software publisher to make a profit.

(b) Hill v. Gateway

In *Hill v. Gateway 2000*,[31] a companion case to ProCD, a consumer picked up the telephone, spoke with a Gateway customer representative and ordered a Gateway personal computer with his credit card. Gateway shipped a computer that had Gateway's standard terms packed in the box containing the computer equipment. The shrinkwrap agreement mandated arbitration and bound the consumer if they did not return the computer after only five days.

In this case, the court enforced Gateway's shrinkwrap agreement, even though it was included in a sealed software box, giving the licensee no opportunity to review the terms prior to payment. The Seventh Circuit upheld the entire agreement, including the arbitration clause, finding that the inaction of Hill constituted a manifestation of assent. The court validated delayed contract formation; the consumer pays for the product and receives the terms in the packaging of the product when the shipper sends it at a later point.

The appeals court found Hill to be the offeree and Gateway the offeror who had the power to dictate the manner of acceptance. The court enforced a shrinkwrap agreement even though it was included in a sealed software box giving the licensees no opportunity to review the terms prior to payment. The Seventh Circuit said that the "terms inside Gateway's box stand or fall together." The *Hill* court determined there was acceptance by silence and Gateway's standard terms were binding. Consumer advocates charge that rolling contracts are comparable to the bait and switch practices prohibited by the FTC.[32]

(c) Klocek v. Gateway

In *Klocek v. Gateway 2000*,[33] a Kansas district court refused enforcement of Gateway's Standard Terms and Conditions. As in *Hill*, Gateway included a copy of its Standard Terms in the box that contained the computer battery power cables and instruction manuals. Gateway provided the consumer with the following notice:

> NOTE TO THE CUSTOMER:
>
> This document contains Gateway 2000's Standard Terms and Conditions. By keeping your Gateway 2000 computer system beyond five (5) days after the date of delivery, you accept these Terms and Conditions.[34]

Klocek filed an individual and class action for breach of warranties and another claim that Gateway had falsely promised technical support. Gateway contended that Klocek accepted the arbitration clause by retaining the computer more than five days, which was acceptance by inaction. Gateway also sent Klocek and all other current customers a copy of its quarterly magazine, which contained notice of a change in its arbitration policy.

The *Klocek* court refused to order arbitration, concluding that Gateway's Standard Terms and Conditions had not been accepted by the consumers rejecting *ProCD* and *Hill's* rolling contract theory of enforcement. Gateway contended that Klocek demonstrated acceptance of the arbitration clause by retaining the computer more than five days after delivery. The court refused to find that Klocek had accepted the terms by silence. However, in the cases decided since *Klocek*, the vast majority of U.S. courts have enforced rolling contracts.

(2) Clickwrap Licensing

A clickwrap agreement "collects all of the terms of the agreement in a single dialog box and then requires the user to affirmatively accept the agreement before proceeding, makes every term equally visible."[35] The typical "click through" website agreement requires end users to click on an "I agree" button that creates a contract where the user agrees to submit to all the terms and conditions set forth by the licensor. Generally, the user must indicate acceptance of the clickwrap agreement to proceed with the installation. U.S. courts will enforce clickwrap agreements so long as the user has an opportunity to review the terms and manifest assent, even though users overwhelmingly fail to read the terms before clicking the "I agree" button.

In *Nguyen v. Barnes & Noble Inc.*,[36] the Ninth Circuit court refused to enforce the online bookseller's terms of use on its website where hyperlinks to the agreement were featured on every website page. The consumer contended that Barnes & Noble had engaged in deceptive trade practices when it cancelled orders from a deeply discounted liquidation sale of its Touchpad device. When Nguyen filed suit, Barnes & Noble argued that he was subject to an arbitration agreement in its terms of use.

The Ninth Circuit ruled that Barnes & Noble's terms of use agreement was not enforceable, since it failed to offer users reasonable notice of the terms. The court observed the terms of use were not binding, as "consumers cannot be expected to ferret out hyperlinks to terms and conditions to which they have no reason to suspect they will be bound." Clickwrap agreements need to be situated on a website to ensure that users understand that they are entering into a contract.

(3) Browsewrap

A "browsewrap" agreement is a standard form agreement, where website terms and conditions of use are posted on the website. Browsewrap terms, on the other hand, do not require the user to manifest assent but contract formation is based on using the site. Indeed, "in a pure—form browsewrap agreement, 'the website will contain a notice that—by merely using the services of, obtaining information from, or initiating applications within the website—the user is agreeing to and is bound by the site's terms of service.' "[37]

The theory behind contract formation for a browsewrap agreement is that a legally binding contract is formed simply by a website visitor's use of the website or browsing the website. In a "browsewrap," website terms of use are typically posted as a hyperlink at the bottom of the screen. The user can continue to use the website or its services without visiting the agreement page and be completely unaware of the agreement. Browsewrap agreements tacitly assume that browsing beyond the homepage constitutes mutual assent.[38]

U.S. courts are much less likely to enforce browsewrap because there is no proof that the user manifested assent to the posted terms.[39] In 2016, the Second Circuit ruled that Amazon.com Inc.'s terms of use were inconspicuous because the publisher situated it amidst a confusing jungle of hyperlinks and text.[40] In *Nicosia v. Amazon.com*, Dean Nicosia purchased a weight loss product containing sibutramine, a controlled substance that had been removed from the market in October 2010, on Amazon's website.

The federal district court granted Amazon's motion to dismiss because a mandatory arbitration clause and class action waiver governed all claims. The court described Amazon's 2012 Conditions of Use agreement as a hybrid between a clickwrap and a browsewrap agreement. "While the Conditions of Use are only available by navigating through a hyperlink, like a browsewrap agreement, a purchaser using Amazon's website could only place his or her order after viewing a conspicuous hyperlink to the current Conditions of Use and agreeing to make his purchase subject to those conditions."[41] It is increasingly common for providers to develop hybrid contracting forms that combine browsewrap and clickwrap given that U.S. courts are more likely to strike down browsewraps.

The Second Circuit reversed the lower court, finding that there was nothing in the "Place your order" button alone suggesting that additional terms apply. The presentation of terms was not next to the "Place your order" button. The message "By placing your order, you agree to Amazon.com's. . . conditions of use" was not bold, capitalized or conspicuous in light of the whole webpage. The checkout screen did not give Nicosia or any other user notice that they were waiving their right to file a legal action by agreeing to submit to mandatory arbitration.

§ 6.3: FTC'S POLICING OF WRAP CONTRACTS

[A] What Defines a Consumer and What Does the FTC Protect?

A consumer is defined as an individual (not a business entity) entering into a contract for personal, household or family purposes. Congress enacted mandatory consumer statutes to protect consumers in diverse fields such as credit repair, distance contracts and email offers. The FTC states that it "pursues vigorous and effective law enforcement; and advances consumers' interests by sharing its expertise with federal and state legislatures and U.S. and international government agencies."

[B] FTC & U.S. Consumer Law

(1) Unfair and Deceptive Trade Practices

Consumer transactions are the advertisement or offer for the sale, lease or licensing of goods or intangible products, including software or website content. The FTC Act, originally passed in 1914, prohibits unfair or deceptive acts or practices, and is being applied to unethical practices on the Internet. The FTC has determined that a representation, omission or practice is deceptive if it is likely to mislead consumers and affect consumers' behavior or decisions about the product or service. The FTC administers many Internet-related laws governing consumer contracts, including the Children's Online Privacy Protection Act, the Safe Web Act and the Controlling the Assault of Non-Solicited Pornography and Marketing Act of 2003.

The FTC targets websites that do not live up to the Commission's required privacy policies. The FTC's Division of Advertising Practices enforces laws against "unfair, misleading or false advertising." The FTC considers three factors in determining whether a practice is unfair: (1) Does the practice injure consumers? (2) Does the practice violate public policy?; (3) Is the practice unethical? The Commission may "prosecute any inquiry necessary to its duties in any part of the United States." The FTC's chief remedies are civil penalties and injunctive relief.

In 2012, the FTC entered into a settlement with one of the largest U.S. consumer reporting agencies, Equifax Information Services LLC, to settle charges that it improperly sold lists of consumers who were late on their mortgage payments. The FTC required Equifax and companies that purchased this information to pay a fine of nearly $1.6 million to resolve charges that these violated the FTC Act and the Fair Credit Reporting Act (FCRA).

Such settlements are part of the FTC's ongoing efforts to protect consumers in financial distress and to protect consumer privacy. Equifax will pay $393,000 to resolve allegations that its inadequate procedures led to the sale of lists of consumer information to firms that should not have received them. According to the FTC, Equifax sold more than 17,000 prescreened lists of consumers to companies including Direct Lending Source, Inc., which subsequently resold some lists to third parties, who used their data to pitch loan modification and debt relief services to people in financial distress.

Equifax's September 2017 breach compromised the data of greater than half of the U.S. population. Equifax's terms of service contains both a mandatory arbitration clause and a class action waiver, which will make it cost-prohibitive for individual consumers to file legal actions against the consumer reporting agency.[42] The FTC is likely to be the only means that consumers can seek recourse against Equifax for their negligence in enabling the theft of their personal information.[43]

[C] The FTC's Enforcement Action Against Snapchat

Snapchat reserves the right to change its ToU and its services at any time at its sole discretion, without any notice or warning. Snapchat marketed its application as a service for sending "disappearing" photo and video messages, declaring that the message sender "control[s] how long your friends can view your message."[44] Before sending a snap, the application requires the sender to designate a period—with the default set to a maximum of 10 seconds—which the recipient will be allowed to view the snap. Snapchat represented that when sending a message through its application, the message would disappear forever after the user-set time period expired. Snapchat's "frequently asked questions" page on its website promised that it would permanently destroy photographs:

> **Is there any way to view an image after the time has expired?** No, snaps disappear after the timer runs out. . . ." Despite this assurance, Federal Trade Commission investigators concluded that, "several methods exist by which a recipient can use tools outside the application to save both photo and video messages, allowing the recipient to access and view the photos or videos indefinitely.

The FTC charged Snapchat with knowingly breaching its promise to destroy images after a few seconds. A security consultant had warned Snapchat a year earlier that it would be easy for a software developer to write a program that would download and save the images a user receives. In fact, such tools for saving Snapchat photographs were being sold on Apple's iTunes Store.

The FTC took issue with Snapchat's promise that users would be notified if a recipient of a photo or video took a screenshot of this content. In fact, recipients could easily bypass Snapchat's screenshot detection mechanism. Snapchat falsely claimed it would not collect geolocation data without the user's consent. The FTC further found Snapchat's Friend Finder interface and privacy policy to be deceptive and unfair. In December 2014, the FTC entered into a settlement agreement with Snapchat which prohibits:

> Snapchat from misrepresenting the extent to which it maintains the privacy, security or confidentiality of users' information. In addition, the company will be required to implement a comprehensive privacy program that will be monitored by an independent privacy professional for the next 20 years.[45]

On January 1, 2014, hackers released 4.6 million Snapchat usernames and redacted telephone numbers. "The data was posted on a website called SnapchatDB.info, which has since been suspended. The hackers censored the last two digits of the phone numbers" but offered to disclose the uncensored database "under certain circumstances."[46] Shortly after this cyberattack, Snapchat issued an apology to its customers and released an update that decoupled their users' usernames from their phone numbers.

Snapchat's users never filed an individual or class action lawsuit to obtain compensation for disclosure of their personal data, as Snapchat's terms of service effectively shielded the company from any liability for their security flaw. Snapchat's ToS imposes mandatory arbitration, requiring consumers to waive their right to litigate and agree to appear before an arbitrator in Los Angeles. Snapchat's ToS states that "[o]ther than class procedures and remedies discussed below, the arbitrator has the authority to grant any remedy that would otherwise be available in court."

Contrary to its assertion about the arbitrator's power to order equivalent remedies, Snapchat uses the ToS to eliminate every category of damages and, in any event, does not permit the arbiter to award more than a hundred dollars. The basic $250 claim filing fee with JAMS—Snapchat's designated arbitral provider—in a consumer case is two and a half times the total possible recovery.

In addition, Snapchat users may not initiate or join class actions against the provider, even though the potential recovery is a minuscule fraction of the cost of filing consumer arbitration. An out-of-state consumer attempting to arbitrate a claim would also need to incur the cost of journeying to Los Angeles, California for an arbitral hearing, where the provider chose the rules of arbitration and had extensive experience on selecting arbitrators likely to rule in their favor. Consequently, Snapchat was never sued for negligent security due to their aggressive use of contract law to disclaim and limit liability.

[D] The FTC's Settlement with Jerk.com

An act is unfair, according to the FTC's guidelines, if the injury "is substantial and not outweighed by other benefits and not reasonably avoidable." On April 7, 2014, for example, the FTC filed a complaint against Jerk.com, a website that invited users to "post a jerk," with a pattern of "deceptive representation."[47] The FTC alleged that Jerk.com improperly harvested personal information from Facebook to create between 73.4 and 81.6 million profiles. Users then voted on whether the person was a "Jerk" or "not a Jerk."

Any user could create additional profiles that included another's personal information, such as the "subject's age, address, mobile phone number, email address, occupation, school, employer, home phone number, work phone number, license plate number, Twitter, MySpace, LinkedIn and eBay account information."

Jerk.com encouraged users to post degrading comments underneath profiles. The profiles also contained personally identifiable information, such as work and home addresses. A "Jerk" rating could have a negative viral effect when viewed by strangers, acquaintances, friends, family members, employers and potential employers. The FTC contended that Jerk profiles often featured photographs of children, culled from other social media, without either the child or the parents' knowledge or consent.

The social media site often led viewers to believe that acquaintances had made the profiles and authored the offensive posts. In reality, Jerk.com generated most these insulting profiles internally in order to profit from those who wished to have the undesirable reviews taken down. Jerk.com earned revenue "by selling 'memberships' for $30, by charging a $25 customer service fee to contact the website and by placing third-party advertisements on Jerk."

"Numerous consumers believed that purchasing a Jerk membership would permit them to alter or delete their Jerk profile and dispute false information on their profile." The FTC's Director of the Bureau of Consumer Protection stated: "In today's interconnected world, people are especially concerned about their reputation online, and this deceptive scheme was a brazen attempt to exploit those concerns." Jerk.com's response to the FTC investigation was to denounce it as "clearly a fishing expedition," however the court denied their petition to quash the civil investigative demand.

Prior to the FTC's complaint, users had engaged in self-help to no avail. After getting the $25 along with the contact form, Jerk.com's responses would inform the victims that the website had no ability to take down "unwanted profiles because 'it's not possible to remove things from the Internet.' " For $90 per year, however, the website offered to "redirect" searches away from the objectionable profiles. Even those victims who retained attorneys were unsuccessful in removing the unwanted content. A Minnesota lawyer specializing in these cases stated that Jerk.com had violated copyright law through the unpermitted copying of profiles from Facebook and violated the tort of privacy.

The Jerk.com operators, however, "demonstrated a willingness to spend time and money fighting these matters, and generally victims don't have the money required for their legal battles." Those who suffered from Jerk.com's invasion of privacy, misappropriation of their right of publicity and other intellectual property rights, found themselves without meaningful warranties or remedies.

Jerk.com made access to their website subject to a browsewrap agreement that stated, "By using Jerk.com, you agree to be bound by the terms and conditions of this Agreement." Jerk.com formed its agreement as a rolling contract: "The Terms are subject to change by Jerk LLC, at any time, without notice, effective upon posting of a link to same on our website."

Jerk.com also capped all liability at zero dollars, disclaiming every conceivable category of damages. Jerk's ToU eliminated all incidental, consequential or indirect damages and all liability for its acts and omissions. Jerk LLC offered its services "on an 'as is' basis and grants no warranties of any kind, express, implied, statutory," and held its users accountable to the limits of the law.

Because Jerk.com's ToU precluded users from filing lawsuits against the website and its creator and owner, John Fanning, the FTC was the only realistic enforcement agency. The FTC sought a remedial order to change Jerk.com's business practices as opposed to a class action, which would have compensated the victims directly for losses arising out of the fraudulent website. According to the FTC's 2014 complaint:

> Jerk.com profiles often appeared in search engine results when consumers searched for an individual's name. Upon viewing their photos on Jerk.com, many believed that someone they knew had created their Jerk.com profile. Jerk reinforced this view by representing that

users created all the content on Jerk. Nevertheless, in reality, the defendants created the vast majority of the profiles by misusing personal information they improperly obtained through Facebook. They registered numerous websites with Facebook and then allegedly used Facebook's application programming interfaces to download the names and photos of millions of Facebook users, which they in turn used to create nearly all the Jerk.com profiles.

The FTC's vote to issue the administrative complaint against Jerk.com was 4–0. The First Circuit, in *Fanning v. Federal Trade Commission*,[48] vacated and remanded part of the FTC's remedial order against Jerk.com as overbroad, stripping part of the decision of its legal force. However, the court upheld the FTC's findings that Jerk.com violated Section 5 of the FTC Act and conducted unfair and deceptive trade practices by misrepresenting the source of its online profiles, the benefits of membership and its premium takedown service. As of mid-2017, Jerk.com was shut down and its domain name was available for public sale. The Jerk.com is currently for sale for $183,000.

§ 6.4: SOFTWARE DEVELOPMENT CONTRACTS

[A] What Computer Professionals Need to Know About SDAs

A software development agreement (SDA) is a contract between a developer and a customer to develop new software or adapt old software to new tasks. Software developers tailor a product to the specific needs of a single customer, while the SDA establishes the contracting rules for the project. A typical SDA will spell out the specifications for deliverable software such as training, maintenance, updates and services. The customer must not only pay for the entire development costs of the software, but often must also give the developer the projected profits of the software as well.

Due to the confidential nature of the information provided by customers in most cases, computer professionals developing the software often sign non-disclosure agreements (NDAs). A non-compete agreement (NCC) requires only one party (most often an employee) to agree not to engage in a competitive enterprise for a specified time. An NDA, in contrast, is a broader agreement between the commissioning party and the developer to mutually protect confidential and proprietary information.

Typically, the SDA begins with a statement of work, which is a written description of the specified project's details and services. Lawyers for both the software developer and commissioning party review and refine the terms, often through many rounds of negotiated changes. In this agreement, the parties will clearly define the software specifications, change orders documentation, deliverables, development costs, improvements and systems completion.

A more complex SDA divides the project into discrete phases called milestones, where each payment is contingent upon satisfactory completion of a specified portion of the project. SDAs spell out the explicit terms in the contract; however, the success of the project is ultimately based upon the parties' relationship of trust, good faith and fair dealing, which are all implied terms in any successful software project.[49] The customer frequently agrees to give the developer additional "error correction" time to attempt a redesign or fix.

The software project manager is responsible for establishing workable milestones, timetables and managing changes to specifications during the development cycle. To streamline this process, the software developer will typically involve the client in the design of the software or computer system to avoid requests from the client changing specifications, which often result in delays and additional expenses. A typical SDA will also address factors, such as whether the developer may employ subcontractors to develop modules or perform other functions.

If the developer is unable to produce a system in conformity with the specifications, the customer can terminate the contract. In the software industry, the typical metrics might include subroutines, units, integration, virus protection, error handling and recovery.[50] Attorneys drafting SDAs will work closely with software engineers and project managers to determine what software the commissioning party seeks and whether the milestones are realistic and clearly defined.

[B] Lessons from Failed SDAs

(1) Obama Care's Healthcare.gov Failed Website

Software development projects are complex and often fail due to cost overruns or the inability of the developer to comply with agreed upon specifications. Healthcare.gov is perhaps the best known failed software project. The U.S. Government Accountability Office (GAO) found that the failures of Health.gov, where people were trying to register for health care under the Affordable Care Act, resulted in significant cost increases, schedule slips and delayed system functionality. From September 2011 to February 2014, the expense of the website increased from $56 million to more than $209 million, primarily due to an excessive number of changes in the specifications and too many oversight gaps.

Late in the development process, the government identified major performance issues with the developer, but took only limited steps to hold the contractor accountable. Less than 1% of those who attempted to sign up for Obama Care were successful. In January 2014, the U.S. government fired the first developer and awarded a new contract to another firm for $91 million to continue website development. The federal government wasted an estimated $2 billion as well as the loss in public confidence in the website.

(2) State of Indiana's Failed Software Project

State of Indiana v. IBM[51] is an example of a lengthy and expensive lawsuit that arose out of a failed software development project. In 2004, Indiana's new governor, Mitch Daniels, announced that his state's welfare system was "broken" and "plagued by high error rates, fraud, wasted dollars and poor conditions for its employees, and very poor service to its clients."

In 2006, the state of Indiana and IBM entered into a 10-year and $1.3 billion Master Services Agreement (MSA) to update the state's welfare system. The SDA required the establishment of call centers and remote electronic access for welfare applications. A paperless documentation system would reduce fraud. Indiana would benefit from the cost-savings in hiring fewer caseworkers if welfare applicants could apply online.

The IBM/Indiana MSA was extremely complex, containing more than 160 pages and extensive attachments, which included ten exhibits, twenty-four schedules and ten appendices. The parties agreed to a ten-year MSA, but Indiana terminated the agreement less than three years into the SDA, declaring that IBM was in breach. In its twelve-county pilot implementation, Indiana documented several problems early on, such as call center miscues, the delayed processing of applications and multiple problems with processing applications for the redetermination of welfare benefits.

Both parties filed suit against each other for breach of contract. Indiana charged that IBM's product was slow, incorrectly imaged key documents, missed scheduling benchmarks and failed to satisfy Indiana's policy objectives. IBM defended against these claims, charging that Indiana had created delays by continually changing specifications. IBM also invoked a commercial impracticability defense based upon the large number of new claims for welfare that flooded the system in the wake of the 2008 economic meltdown.

The Indiana Supreme Court found that IBM had materially breached its contract with the state. IBM, however, had negotiated millions of dollars in early termination fees that the state had to pay. The Indiana Supreme Court upheld the lower courts' awarding of $40 million in assignment fees and $9,510,795 in equipment fees to IBM. The trial court's award of $2,570,621 in early termination damage payments and $10,632,333 in prejudgment interest to IBM was reversed and the case was remanded to determine both parties' damages.

This case illustrates the need for careful negotiation by attorneys to protect their clients if the contract is terminated and to clearly specify rights and remedies in the event of breach. Computer companies must be realistic as to what projects they can successfully complete and deliver, while also protecting themselves in the negotiation stage against foreseeable hazards, such as unclear benchmark specifications and excessive change orders.

CHART FOUR: A CHECKLIST OF LEGAL AND ETHICAL ISSUES FOR SOFTWARE DEVELOPERS

(1) Should software companies be liable for software failures?

(2) What is the definition of negligence with respect to software development?

(3) Do existing laws account for the unique characteristics of software engineering?

(4) What ethical responsibilities do software engineers have to users?

(5) How should the terms appropriate use and appropriate care be defined in software liability law?

(6) What influence have corporations had in the development of existing law?

(7) Is software a tangible product? Tangibility is an important concept in products liability law. In 1991, the dicta of a 9th Circuit Court of Appeals opinion (actually dealing with a book about mushrooms) hinted that software could be considered a tangible product in certain circumstances.

(8) What is the concept of information liability? Should software companies be liable for information generated by their software?

(9) Would increased liability stifle the quick release of new software?

(10) What would be the economic ramifications of an increased level of liability?

(11) Would such a change discourage the development of software for medical and other high-risk fields?

(12) Is a computer program a product or a service?

(13) If an expert system using artificial intelligence gives bad advice, should the programmers be held liable?

(14) Should programmers be considered professionals and thus subject to malpractice suits?

(15) What risks should users naturally assume when using software?

Source: Adapted from Ravi Belani, et. al, *Liability Law and Software Development*, Stanford University (2017).

§ 6.5: GLOBAL CONSUMER RIGHTS

[A] European Rejection of Unfair Wrap Contracts

(1) The Unfair Contract Terms Directive

A U.S. company must comply with mandatory EU consumer law if it targets EU consumers. U.S. companies are subject to fines and regulatory actions if they fail to localize their consumer contracts to comply with EU Community Legislation such as the 1993 *Unfair Contracts Term Directive* (UCTD). Contract provisions may not waive Eurozone-wide consumer rights and remedies.

The European Commission observed: "In consumer contracts, sellers and suppliers possess a considerable advantage by defining the terms in advance that are not individually negotiated."[52] For this reason, the UCTD requires each Member State to enact national legislation that satisfies the Commission's minimum standards of consumer fairness. The Directive defines a contract as unfair when it causes "a significant imbalance in the parties' rights and obligations" that harms the consumer. Contractual provisions determined to be even slightly unfair under the Directive are unenforceable in the European Union. For example, the UCTD requires that contract terms be drafted in plain and intelligible language. The UCTD construes any ambiguity in a consumer contract in favor of the weaker party.

(2) Test for Unfair Contract Terms

The EU court, consumer administrative agency or other authority will deploy the UCTD to strike down oppressive terms in consumer contracts such as an unfair ToU. EU courts and consumer authorities apply a two-part test to determine whether a given contract is legally permissible. First, the consumer contract cannot be significantly imbalanced to the detriment of the consumer. Second, any imbalanced term must not be "contrary to good faith."

An Annex to the UCTD is composed of a non-exclusive list of terms considered suspect. This Annex invalidates many common terms in U.S.-style contracts such as (1) disclaimers of warranties, (2) limitations of liability, (3) mandatory arbitration clauses, (4) unilateral modifications to contract terms and (5) acceptance of a license agreement by performance. Since the UCTD sets only minimum standards, Member States have the discretion to turn the gray list of suspect terms into a black list of forbidden terms to further enhance protection against U.S.-style one-sided, imposed contracts.

[B] Rewriting U.S. ToS for Europe

In March 2017, the European Commission ordered Google, Facebook and Twitter to revise their standard terms of service (ToS) for European consumers to comply with the UCTD.[53] The EU Commission characterized these companies' contracting practices as fraudulent and threatened them with potential fines unless revised terms were initiated. The Brussels Regulation on Jurisdiction and the Enforcement of Judgments gives EU consumers a non-disclaimable right to file suit in their home court, whereas these companies require consumers to litigate in the provider's home court. The Rome I Regulation gives EU consumers the right to litigate under their home country's consumer law, while most U.S. terms specify the law, location and venue for filing a complaint.

U.S. courts allow companies to use ToS to exclude warranties and limit their liability. When U.S. companies are targeting consumers in the twenty-eight EU countries, they are committing fraud and engaging in unfair practices by attempting to exclude their liability through contract law. The Commission strikes down clauses where social networks attempt to unilaterally change terms and conditions without notice. Below is an EU Press Release on the EU Commission's contention that these three Internet giants must revise their contracting practices.

EU Consumer Authorities Ask Social Media Companies to Comply with Consumer Rules

Brussels, 17 March 2017

EU consumer authorities sent a letter to Facebook, Twitter and Google+ last November asking them to address two areas of concern. On Thursday 16 March, EU consumer authorities and the European Commission met with these companies to hear and discuss their proposed solutions. The companies in question will finalize detailed measures on how to comply with the EU regulatory framework within one month. The Commission and the consumer authorities will review the final proposals. If they are not satisfactory, the consumer authorities could ultimately resort to enforcement action. U.S. companies have agreed to propose changes focusing on two areas:

- Unfair terms and conditions, and
- Addressing fraud and scams that mislead consumers when using the social networks.

Clarification of Terms or Removal of Illegal Terms

Social media platforms' terms of service should be brought into conformity with European consumer law. Indeed, the Unfair Contract Terms Directive requires that standard terms, which create a significant imbalance in parties' rights and obligations, to the detriment of the consumer (Article 3), are deemed unfair—and therefore invalid. The Directive also requires that terms be drafted in plain and intelligible language (Article 5) so that consumers are informed in a clear and understandable manner about their rights. This means in practice that, amongst other things:

- Social media networks cannot deprive consumers of their right to go to court in their Member State of residence;
- Social media networks cannot require consumers to waive mandatory rights, such as their right to withdraw from an on-line purchase;
- Terms of service cannot limit or totally exclude the liability of social media networks in connection with the performance of the service;
- Sponsored content cannot be hidden, but should be identifiable as such;
- Social media networks cannot unilaterally change terms and conditions without clearly informing consumers about the

change and without given them the opportunity to cancel the contract, with adequate notice;

- Terms of service cannot confer unlimited and discretionary power to social media operators on the removal of content;
- Termination of a contract by the social media operator should be governed by clear rules and not decided unilaterally without a reason.

Source: Adapted from European Commission: Press Release Database, March 17, 2017.

The European Commission's decision demonstrates the necessity of modifying computer contracts to comply with EU consumer law. This regulatory action has implications for every computer professional marketing data services, applications or software licenses in the EU marketplace. In addition to EU Commission enforcement, U.S. companies face a significant risk of lawsuits in EU national courts for unfair contracting practices.

(1) AOL France and The Union Federale des Consommateurs

European courts are not inclined to enforce ToU that disclaim all warranties and provide no meaningful remedy for service interruptions. French courts, for example, take a proactive role in policing consumer ToU. *The Union Federale des Consommateurs v. AOL France* court refused to enforce AOL's standard term contract that disclaimed all liability for service interruptions.[54]

The French court struck down thirty-six clauses in AOL France's standard terms of use agreement. The online provider was required to remove the unfair clauses from their ToU within one month and to notify its French customers of the resulting changes to its terms of use. The court imposed a fine of €30,000 for each day that AOL failed to comply.

The list of invalidated terms includes many of the standard terms incorporated in U.S. wrap contracts. On September 15, 2005, the *Cour d'Appel* of Versailles affirmed the decision of the lower court on all counts, finding AOL France's ToU to be unfair. There is little doubt that U.S. courts would enforce the same clauses struck down by the French court in the AOL France case, but courts and consumer agencies in other European countries are likely to adopt the French courts' skeptical attitude toward U.S.-style ToU.

A French court of appeals recently ruled that a European Facebook user is not bound by the social network's forum selection provision that requires disputes to be brought exclusively in a state or federal court located in Santa Clara County, California. Facebook's ToU, the French court found, violated the French implementation of the Unfair Contract Terms Directive, which requires, among other things, that any choice-of-forum clause be highly visible. The court also found that such a restrictive clause is only valid between businesses, not in business-to-consumer transactions.

(2) Dell & the British Office of Fair Trading

In another example of EU's mandatory consumer rights, the British Office of Fair Trading (OFT) investigated Dell's consumer license agreements. Ultimately, the OFT required Dell to revise its consumer license agreements by eliminating several of its prohibited clauses to comply with the United Kingdom's mandatory consumer rules. Dell settled the case by agreeing to modify its standard licensing agreements by eliminating its clauses excluding its liability for software failure. The United Kingdom's National Consumer Council examined twenty-five consumer-software license agreements, concluding that the typical U.S.-style end user license agreement is misleading and eliminates important consumer rights.

[C] China's Consumer Protection in Computer Contracts[55]

Mass market license agreements that are enforceable in the United States are typically unenforceable in China. China's 2014 Contract Law of the People's Republic of China (PRC Law) prohibits business operators from including "format contracts, notices or announcements" to reduce their liability or impose greater burden on the consumer. The PRC Law defines standard terms as "contract provisions which were prepared in advance by a party for repeated use, and which were not negotiated with the other party in the course of concluding the contract."

The PRC's 2014 Law on the Protection of Consumer Rights and Interests states, "[b]usiness operators shall guarantee the quality, function, usage and term of validity, which the commodities or services they supply should possess under normal operation or acceptance, except that consumers are aware of the defects before they buy the commodities or receive the services." PRC Law enables customers to recover damages, despite the provider's inclusion of an assumption of risk clause.[56] Under the Chinese statute governing contracts, a "buyer's assumption of the risk of damage or loss of the subject matter" has no legal effect on whether a buyer can hold a seller liable for "non-conforming performance."

The PRC Law on the Protection of Consumer Rights and Interests, gives consumers the right to "fair transactions," which prohibits the often buried or inconspicuous anti-consumer terms in standard-form contracts that are common in U.S. online agreements. *Guo Li v. Microsoft Corp.*, decided by Judge Jiangyin in Beijing Intermediate People's Court in 2011, provides evidence that U.S.-style licensing agreements will likely be invalidated by Chinese courts.[57]

In *Guo Li*, a Chinese customer filed suit against Microsoft, challenging several clauses in their standard licensing agreement, which disclaimed warranties and limited the software publisher's liability. The Microsoft terms were typical of ToU in the United States but ruled unfair and unenforceable by the Chinese court. The *Guo Li* case is a template for which U.S. computer contracts will be enforceable and which contracts are presumptively unenforceable.

In the post-*Guo Li* period, Chinese consumer associations will probably challenge, and likely overturn, other one-sided provisions that, in effect, strip customers of any meaningful remedy. American companies targeting the Chinese marketplace must comply with PRC mandatory consumer law or risk large fines. Online companies with global ambitions need to draft localized terms of use. The lesson of the *Guo Li* case is that U.S. companies will need to revise their standard ToS in China, just as they must in the EU.

While China polices ToU to protect consumers, it closely monitors and suppresses Internet communications critical of government policy. The Chinese government has blocked public access to Facebook, Twitter and other social media sites in order to censor content threatening to the regime. Many Chinese consumers, however, bypass content controls to these sites by using Virtual Private Networks, proxies or Tor. The PRC is currently taking steps to more effectively block these foreign social media in China. In August 2017, for example, the PRC sought to shut down virtual private networks used by Chinese to bypass the nation's censored Internet.[58]

The PRC currently is developing a "Social Credit System" that scores each citizen on criteria such as financial stability, criminal record and social media behavior. *The Economist* criticizes the Chinese government's ranking of its citizens according to the pro-social content of their social media messages as a "digital dictatorship."

> It says the idea is to harness digitally stored information to chivvy everyone into behaving more honestly, whether fly-by-night companies or tax- and fine-dodging individuals. That sounds fair enough. But the government also talks about this as a tool of "social management": i.e.,

> controlling individuals' behaviour. . . any fear that bad scores might result in sanctions, such as being denied a bank loan or permission to buy a railway ticket, even for political reasons. They have reason to worry. The government decreed this year that the system should record such vaguely defined sins as "assembling to disrupt social order."[59]

Contract law operates in an increasingly flattened global economy. Rapidly expanding social media sites in both nations, will likely result in expensive and time-consuming legal conflicts, unless providers in both countries localize their terms for a globalized social media world. Chinese social media terms of use contain government mandated restrictions on free speech, which are unenforceable in Western legal systems. Similarly, there are numerous American-style limitations of liability and warranty disclaimer clauses in social media agreements that contravene Chinese consumer law.

§ 6.6: FIVE ETHICAL PERSPECTIVES APPLIED TO COMPUTER CONTRACTS

Nancy Kim coined the term "wrap contract" to describe Internet-related contracting forms such as terms of use, browsewrap, clickwrap or shrinkwrap. She defines wrap contract as "a blanket term to refer to a unilaterally imposed set of terms which the drafter purports to be legally binding and which are presented to the non-drafting party in a nontraditional form."[60] Wrap contracts take the form of a traditional contract but operate in a "coercive contracting environment."[61]

Wrap licenses are seldom read before being entered into by millions of online consumers around the world. Nevertheless, consumers have a love/hate relationship with these mass market license agreements:

> On the one hand, consumers admit that they have no interest in reading form contracts, enjoy the convenience and efficiency of form contracting, and routinely accept forms "dressed up" as deals without stopping to read or question their content. On the other hand, consumers are often frustrated with the effectively nonnegotiable nature of these contracts and complain that they lack the requisite time or understanding to read or negotiate companies' impenetrable purchase terms.[62]

The following sections apply the five major ethical perspectives to the issue of mass market computer contracts as a guide to examining questionable online contracting practices.

[A] Consequentialism

Consequentialists might justify these unbalanced terms using a cost/benefit analysis. The ethicists who oppose mass market licenses do not suggest an alternative contracting form that will be equally cost-efficient. These contracts do not present even the possibility that the terms are negotiable. In some software contracts, the licensee does not even learn about the terms until after payment. Despite this disadvantage to the licensee, this form of contracting has created a thriving industry whose benefits have massively outweighed its costs. In their defense, "these adhesive contracts have the potential to reduce transaction costs by eliminating the need to negotiate the many details of a contract for each instance a product is sold or a service is used."[63] Licensing enables the software publisher to add social and economic value by being able to slice and dice pricing based upon a complex array of variables. Differential pricing is a social benefit to groups with fewer economic resources such as non-profits or students, enabling them to pay less than wealthy corporations. This form of price discrimination benefits society by strengthening U.S. scholarship and critical thinking.

[B] Virtue & Duty

The Association for Computing Machinery (ACM) Code of Ethics and Professional Conduct explicitly makes contract performance an ethical mandate:

> Honoring one's commitments is a matter of integrity and honesty. For the computer professionals this includes ensuring that system elements perform as intended. In addition, when one contracts for work with another party, one has an obligation to keep that party properly informed about progress toward completing that work. A computing professional has a responsibility to request a change in any assignment that he or she feels cannot be completed as defined. . . The computing professional's ethical judgment should be the final guide in deciding whether to proceed. Regardless of the decision, one must accept the responsibility for the consequences.[64]

Virtue ethicists would encourage fairer contract terms that do not systematically favor the stronger party. The warranties offered in mass market transactions are in effect, anti-warranties, which require the user to waive all rights to a remedy if the software or computer contract fails. All duties, including contractual duties, should derive from Kant's categorical imperative, which treats human consumers fairly and with dignity. U.S.-style online contracts lull users into a false sense of complacency:

> There is no right to deceive the consumer by labeling consumer arbitration as "dispute resolution" when the cost of arbitration makes this remedy illusory. Social media providers, service providers, and software developers must always be truthful in their contracting practices. Providers are bound to fulfill their legally enforceable promises "because he is moved to his duty to do so, and acts ethically."[65]

In the Kantian worldview, Jerk.com's entire business model is immoral as it is based upon lies and treating consumers deceptively. From a virtue perspective, the FTC is providing an invaluable public service by exposing and eliminating this callous, profit-seeking scheme, which created misery for substantial numbers of people. "Ultimately, it comes down to some pretty simple ideas: be honest, responsible, respectful of privacy, and treat both customers and vendors as we would like to be treated. Cloud computing can only reach its full potential if a real, lasting trust is established between providers and customers through a well-defined system of ethics."[66]

[C] Conflict Theory: Contracts to Limit Consumer Rights

The *Airbnb* opinion validates the use of contract law to eliminate federal remedies for racial discrimination. Conflict theorists contend that big business is abusing the public interest by using contract law to create a liability-free zone by eliminating consumer rights and remedies. Boilerplate contracts ensnare "consumers into an insidious peonage through the 'tricks and traps of fine print.' "[67] Mass market contracts are frequently difficult to read, making it easier to divest consumers of all meaningful rights:

> Sometimes longer than a Shakespeare play but far less readable, boilerplate contracts are indecipherable to most humans. The opportunity to negotiate does not exist. Comparison-shopping for better terms is improbable if not impossible. . . . We should think of boilerplate contracts as "contract asbestos." They may "facilitate" commerce by maximizing corporate efficiencies, entitlements and immunities; but as with asbestos, they are toxic to consumers. We are exposed to often invisible, rights-denying terms that may harm us years after the initial agreement.[68]

A consumer rights organization argues that one-sided contracts are frequently calculated to trick the ordinary consumer.[69] The stronger party uses contract law to eliminate warranties and remedies, creating a liability-free zone.[70] The empirical reality is that everyday consumers do not know the terms of use:

> In short, consumers do not read long documents. They do not, therefore, consent in the sense of understanding that to which they are consenting. Moreover, no one can honestly say that consumers ought to read long documents of this kind.[71]

The use of unbalanced ToU is becoming increasingly aggressive. A growing number of companies are including non-disparagement clauses where the user agrees not to post negative reviews of a company's products or services. "These 'gag' clauses are designed to muzzle consumers—even when the facts are true—from expressing their dissatisfaction with a product or service."[72] Mandatory arbitration agreements are essentially an anti-remedy for social media users, since the cost of arbitration will usually far exceed the monetary amount that is at stake, and with class action waivers, there is no aggregation of claims.

According to classical Marxist theory, under industrial capitalism, the means of production are solidly in the hands of the bourgeoisie. The information age economy has the potential of allowing larger proportions of the population to control the means of intellectual capital production.[73] The larger battle is over this opportunity to build an "open, diverse, liberal equilibrium."[74] Greater control of the means of production by Internet users could potentially lead to a more participatory and egalitarian society.

[D] Social Contractualism

(1) More Balanced Terms of Use

Social contractualists emphasize finding a balance between the usefulness of mass market licenses and protecting fundamental consumer rights. Social contractualist judges are far more likely than consequentialists to sacrifice the efficiency of browsewrap terms of use to require clearly warning users about the implications of surrendering their personal information. A careful evaluation is necessary to achieve the best balance between the benefits of encouraging a robust social media industry and protection of the public's fundamental rights. Sophisticated government intervention is required to protect the greater good from an exploitive minority of Internet fraudsters, such as email scammers or the owners of websites like Jerk.com.

John Rawls' ethical principle of the veil of ignorance would not permit software licensors, content providers or social media websites to systematically strip away rights and remedies, particularly when the victims tend to be the already disadvantaged. Software licensees, social media consumers and other users with a higher educational level are more likely to understand how to protect their rights without help from the court system. Social media terms of use and privacy policies may be incomprehensible to those with less than a high school education.

A healthy legal system expands to counter new forms of oppression. U.S. companies are being required to redraft their terms of service to eliminate unfair clauses such as choice of law, choice of forum, rolling contract provisions and exclusions of liability when doing business globally.[75] This balanced approach protects fundamental human rights without denying Internet content providers their right to make a profit by producing highly valued services.

(2) Net Neutrality & Social Contract Theory

Net neutrality is the core principle that Internet service providers and governments should treat all data on the Internet equally and not engage in price discrimination or arbitrage. In the United States, the Federal Communications Commission (FCC) has jurisdiction over interstate and foreign communications by wire and radio. The FCC's role in net neutrality arises out of "specific statutory mandates in the Communications Act and the Telecommunications Act of 1996 including provisions that direct the Commission to promote Internet investment and to protect and promote voice, video and audio communications services."[76] The FCC adopted three basic principles to promote net neutrality as displayed in Chart Four. President Trump's new FCC Commissioners are likely to reverse course, allowing libertarian-style tiered pricing at the discretion of the service provider.

CHART FOUR: FCC'S THREE PRINCIPLES OF NET NEUTRALITY

Transparency. Fixed and mobile broadband providers must disclose the network management practices, performance characteristics and terms and conditions of their broadband services;
No Blocking. Fixed broadband providers may not block lawful content, applications, services, or non-harmful devices; mobile broadband providers may not block lawful websites, or block applications that compete with their voice or video telephone services; and
No Unreasonable Discrimination. Fixed broadband providers may not unreasonably discriminate in transmitting lawful network traffic.

Neutrality regulations prevent broadband providers from blocking or slowing Internet traffic based upon the customer's relative wealth or financial condition. The FCC noted that, as early as 2005, a broadband provider that was a subsidiary of a telephone company paid $15,000 to settle a Commission investigation into whether it had blocked Internet ports used for competitive VoIP applications. In 2008, the Commission found that Comcast disrupted certain peer-to-peer (P2P) uploads of its subscribers, without a reasonable network management justification and without disclosing its actions.[77] AT&T, a major DSL provider, blocked Pearl Jam after its lead singer, Eddie Vedder, criticized President George W. Bush's foreign policy.[78] If the Trump Administration's FCC reverses net neutrality regulations, those businesses whose content is de-prioritzed are likely to file lawsuits asserting that a free and open Internet is a fundamental right.

[E] Libertarian Perspective

(1) Traditional Libertarian View

Consumers are developing market-based solutions to challenge one-sided contract provisions. For example, "viral class actions," organized through social media are emerging to allow victims to protect their fundamental rights:

> The term "viral" or "virtual" class action is often used in reference to *John True et al. v. American Honda Motor Co., Inc.*, No. 5:07–cv–287–VAP–OP (C.D. Cal.), in which Honda settled a class action lawsuit that provided Civic hybrid drivers the option to get either a discount off the purchase of a new Honda or a cash payout if they could prove that they complained about the mileage problem to Honda. One class member, who thought that the class settlement was unfair, opted out of the settlement and went "viral." She filed a small claims court action and turned to social media to encourage other class members to do the same. She set up DontSettleWithHonda.org, opened a Twitter account, and posted a video on YouTube to share information about what is now called a "small-claims flash mob" case establishing a new precedent for righting the wrongs toward the public and opening the floodgates for small claims lawsuits.[79]

Social network ToU often contain pre-dispute mandatory arbitration clauses that funnel disputes away from the traditional, public litigation model and into private tribunals where cases are decided in confidential hearings convened by private judges who are often paid by the provider. A libertarian attorney testifying before Congress on behalf of the United States Chamber of Commerce attributed the rise of predispute mandatory arbitration clauses to market forces and contended that "[b]anning or otherwise limiting the use of arbitration clauses would ignore these market dynamics, and likely force consumers to pay more for products or services."[80]

Libertarian individualism assumes that human beings have a right to pursue self-interest "without interference from others or the imposition of alternative conceptions of the good by others."[81] It is not the business of government or other third parties to determine whether users were foolish to accept clickwrap agreements, or too irresponsible to bother to look for browsewrap terms. A website can save substantial legal fees and costs by employing mandatory arbitration clauses, which incentivizes investors to produce better products and to protect consumers from the slow, costly and often overly-emotional jury system.

According to traditional libertarians, consumers have the responsibility to read ToU, and have the freedom to not use the service if they are unwilling to accept the terms. It is paternalistic to believe that the poor need protection from the wiles of online service providers. If websites do not satisfy their customers, the free market will replace them with companies that do a better job. Government do-gooders will impose onerous, one-size-fits-all restraints on dynamic capitalism.

(2) Cyberlibertarian View

The distinction between the definition of freedom used by traditional libertarians and cyberlibertarians, is seen clearly in comparing their views on those Internet ToU that specify mandatory arbitration for consumer disputes. Cyberlibertarians have little faith in the court system, but also tend to denounce the expensive and secretive rent-a-judge proceedings that characterize the arbitration system. They favor defending consumers by hacking to release information that exposes corporate abuses of power. Traditional libertarians, on the other hand, see such behavior as undermining important property rights.

Information, the cyberlibertarians believe, should be liberated and used for the common good. The Electronic Frontier Foundation described America's proprietary model as being like prohibiting an automobile purchaser from looking under the hood to see how the engine works. "Open software projects invite computer programmers from around the world to view software code and make changes and improvements to it."[82]

Open source software is distributed with a mandatory term that requires the licensee or any other downstream users to distribute derivative products under the same terms. The GNU/GPL Version 3, like its predecessors, requires the licensor to distribute the software's source code ("human readable code") to encourage collaboration and sharing by future users. Conversely, "field of use" is a restriction placed on how software may be used.

Open source software licenses have libertarian roots. Richard Stallman, the founding father of the open source movement, is a long-time advocate of users' freedoms to use and distribute software. Stallman began the free software movement in response to his frustration in not having access to the code computer for the MIT's Artificial Intelligence Lab's printer:

> Stallman decided to solve a problem with the lab's centralized printer: paper jams. With access to the printer's software source code, Stallman modified the printer software so that it would notify all lab members when the printer jammed. When the lab received a new Xerox printer, Stallman tried to improve it in the same manner. However, Xerox would not release the printer's source code. Stallman's encounter with this proprietary software model marked the beginning of his vision of the free software movement. For Stallman, sharing source code was, and is, a moral obligation.[83]

The Apache web server, Linux operating system and Eclipse development program are all widely adopted open source products. These open source projects keep the generative benefits of openness alive and well. The intellectual property rights in open source licenses are, "configured fundamentally around the right to distribute not the right to exclude."[84]

§ 6.7: ELECTRONIC REPOSSESSION & UNDISCLOSED DISABLING CODE

[A] Deactivating Software

Traditionally, when buyers breached their duty to pay for a product, the seller exercised self-help by enlisting people like Ron, Amy, Bobby and their team of muscular repossession agents, as portrayed in the TV series *Lizard Lick Towing,* to physically repossess the property. Today, if the seller does not pay licensing fees or interest payments in a timely fashion, they may disable the product using remote software rather than employing human agents.

Electronic repossession of automobiles using GPS-based kill switches, or starter-interrupt devices, shifts the balance of power away from the consumer towards the subprime auto dealer. By using these devices, the dealer no longer needs to employ people to locate the non-paying customer's vehicle and physically take possession of it.

The term "disabling code" encompasses all software instructions designed to prevent a computer from producing intended results or to cause a computer to produce unintended results. States are wrestling with the ethical issues raised by the installation of undisclosed disabling code into consumer products. The customer may not know that their automobile will not start because of a remote repossession. The disabling device may also damage the licensee's computer system, resulting in business losses. The user's contracts with third parties may be breached because of the disabling device.

From the licensor's point of view, such a termination approach is very useful, particularly in demonstration licenses, where the program is loaned for a month or so to a potential client on a trial basis: "If you like it, pay us the license fee; if you don't like it, send it back." However, the use of undisclosed deactivation software in some situations is ethically, and perhaps legally, questionable. The licensee may have a valid reason for withholding payment. The disabling device may also cause damage by malfunctioning.

[B] The ALI's Limitations on Electronic Repossession

The American Law Institute (ALI) "has concluded that remote repossession by undisclosed disabling code is a controversial and unethical practice." The ALI's Principles, which are drafted and endorsed by leading legal scholars, take a hard stance against remote deactivation of consumer devices. For business-to-business computer contracts, this deactivating software may only be included if it is conspicuously disclosed in the licensing agreement. Such disabling software may not be used in a mass market contract, where there is a standard form contract that is not negotiated.

Customers should require software vendors to warrant that their product does not contain any computer code designed to disrupt, disable or harm in any manner the operation of the customer's software or hardware, unless there is an explicit agreement to the contrary. A software vendor that delivers a product with a secret disabling device may be found to have violated the covenant of good faith and fair dealing or to be responsible for a tort of trespass to chattels or conversion (as discussed in Chapter Three) for interfering with the customer's computer system. Business licensees have generally been successful in challenging disabling software. In contrast, consumers generally lack the legal resources to mount effective challenges to these devices.

[C] Model Contractual Language About Disabling Devices

The prudent customer should require its licensor to warrant that it will not use disabling devices that may result in consequential damages like business interruption. In their contracts with providers, customers concerned with electronic repossession should negotiate for a clause like the following in order to ensure that the licensor does not incorporate harmful code into its products:

> No Disabling Code Warranty: The Licensor warrants that it will not cause any unplanned interruption of the operations of, or accessibility to, customer's IT Environment. Licensor warrants that it will not install any device including "viruses," "lockups," "time bombs," "key locks," or harmful code in its software. Licensor warrants that it will not install code that will: (1) cause any unplanned interruption of the operations of Customer's computer system; (2) alter, destroy, or inhibit the use of Customer's computer system; or (3) block access to, or prevent the use/accessibility of the licensed software. In the event of breach of this clause, Licensor will promptly remove the Disabling Device and restore the software at no cost to the customer. Any expenses arising out of the use of a disabling device will be reimbursed by the Licensor.

§ 6.8: ELECTRONIC REPOSSESSION & LEASES OF GOODS

[A] Electronic Repossession of Automobiles

The ALI's prohibition against disabling software in consumer products is violated when an automobile dealer disables software remotely in a consumer transaction. *The New York Times* reported that automobile dealers are engaging in ethically questionable electronic repossessions of consumer vehicles:

> The thermometer showed a 103.5-degree fever, and her 10-year-old's asthma was flaring up. Mary Bolender, who lives in Las Vegas, needed to get her daughter to an emergency room, but her 2005 Chrysler van would not start. The cause was not a mechanical problem—it was her lender. Ms. Bolender was three days behind on her monthly car payment. Her lender, C.A.G. Acceptance of Mesa, Ariz., remotely activated a device in her car's dashboard that prevented her car from starting. Before she could get back on the road, she had to pay more than $389, money she did not have that morning in March.[85]

[B] Legal Cases on Failure to Disclose Disabling Software

The vendor's failure to disclose the existence of such a device can create serious legal problems for the licensor. In *Frank & Sons v. Information Solutions, Inc.*,[86] Information Solutions (ISI) included what the court called a "drop-dead device." This device locked the software at a pre-set expiration date. Franks stated that the software did not live up to its expectation and refused to make full payment. Franks sought an injunction against the locking of his software. In granting a preliminary injunction, the court expressed its reservations about electronic disablement of software applications without notice:

> Public policy favors the non-enforcement of abhorrent contracts. Here, without the knowledge of Plaintiff, Defendants have included a surprise in their product which chills the functioning of any business whose operation is a slave to a computer. If the Plaintiff had known of this device at the time it entered into the contract with the Defendant then the result would be different. Here it would be unconscionable for the Court to give credence to this economic duress.

In *Clayton X-Ray v. Professional Systems Corp.*,[87] PSC used a software lock to shut down the system when Clayton fell behind in its payments. PSG had not given Clayton any notice about the lock. The jury awarded $10,000 in punitive damages against PSG:

> PSC had no legal right or any colorable legal right to lock up Clayton's computer system . . . . The effect of the lockup was to prevent Clayton's access to the records of its business. Only by the fortuity of being able to enlist the aid of a former employer . . . . PSC's stratagem did not accomplish the intended paralysis of Clayton's business. This evidence made a submissible case for punitive damages.[88]

The failure to disclose the existence of such a device could, arguably, be a criminal offense under federal and state computer crime legislation that prohibits "unauthorized entry." Suppose the remotely repossessed device in *Clayton X-Ray* was critical to a medical procedure and that a patient died as the result of the machine shutting down. The software company might face liability for wrongful death and even criminal charges for manslaughter.

§ 6.9: FIVE ETHICAL PERSPECTIVES ON ELECTRONIC REPOSSESSION

[A] Consequentialism

Consequentialists would reject the emotionality of the New York Times article in favor of an objective cost/benefit analysis. The ability of subprime lenders to remotely gain control of the vehicles through GPS-based kill switches or starter-interrupt devices can benefit the greater good by incentivizing dealers to make loans to customers with poor credit scores. Because the dealer does not face the expense and uncertainty of needing to locate the auto and regain control through physical repossession, they will be more willing to entrust vehicles to economically unstable consumers. People with poor credit might be shut out of the car market or charged far higher interest rates if the seller had no easy way to retrieve the vehicle in the event the buyer defaults.

Market forces may produce a good outcome in this situation but new laws or government regulations may make them more efficient. For example, consumers might be provided with a statutory grace period before disablement so that they do not suffer severely when a payment is slightly delayed or erroneously not recorded. Unexpected disablement of an auto can leave drivers stranded in hazardous locations or cost them their job, which reduces the greater good without creating any real benefit.

[B] Virtue or Moral Duty

When car sellers force desperately poor consumers to accept predatory automobile loan terms, they are not behaving as virtuous members of the community. Legal Services of Southern Piedmont summarized several legal and ethical issues raised by electronic repossession:

> Privacy and consumer advocates have raised concerns about drivers stranded far from home, the safety of escapees from domestic violence, cars suddenly disabled in moving traffic, and conflicts with state laws and contractual provisions controlling repossession and when a default is deemed to have occurred. Many times, a lender may jump the gun and mistakenly repossess prior to default or after waiving its right to default by habitually accepting late and partial payments from the borrower.[89]

Predatory lenders have too much leverage over their customers without the enactment of legal safeguards against extortionate lending practices. The ease of electronic repossession allows unethical dealers to extort payments from desperate people in emergency situations.

[C] Conflict Theory

Conflict theorists would point to electronic repossession as another tool that strengthens the power of predatory lenders over the disadvantaged. Minorities and women are particularly vulnerable to repossession, due to their often-lower salaries and enhanced family responsibilities. Discrimination against minorities may also result from the assumptions used in assessing credit scores, trapping the poor in exploitative leasing agreements. The handicapped, the elderly, people with young children, the unemployed and those making minimum wage are the most in need of reliable transportation and the most likely to be targeted by electronic repossession.

This is especially true in the U.S., where mass transit alternatives are often severely inadequate. People may lose their jobs when they cannot get to work. Electronic repossession reinforces popular attitudes about the undeserving poor and their imputed "characterological deficiencies and moral failings (e.g. substance abuse, crime, sexual availability)."[90]

[D] Social Contractualism

Social contractualists balance a contract provider's rights against consumer protection. The European Commission assumes that consumer contracts are inherently unbalanced and therefore enacts mandatory rules forbidding mandatory arbitration, anti-class action waivers, warranty disclaimers and caps on damages. The European Commission would forbid electronic possession as violating the Unfair Contracts Terms Directive. Rawlsians would argue that government financed legal services should be available to challenge electronic repossession clauses. A more balanced U.S. law might give consumers a legal right to a warning period, or even a court hearing, before allowing immobilization of their vehicle.

[E] Libertarianism

Libertarians contend that placing limitations on electronic repossession could dry up credit for the poor. The installation of a kill switch makes it cheaper for lenders to enforce security agreements. If auto lending and leasing becomes more profitable because of these shut off devices, more providers will enter the market, thus giving consumers increased options and negotiating power. In any case, contracts are voluntary and people should not enter them unless they are prepared to live up to the terms. The free market of willing buyers and willing sellers, not intrusive government regulators, does the best job of providing consumers with better choices. Entrepreneurs such as Uber or ride sharing services may find ways to tap this market if auto lenders become too greedy.

CONCLUSION

This chapter introduced the ethics and law of computer contracts, emphasizing mass market contracts, such as shrinkwrap, clickwrap and browsewrap agreements. Prior technological advances—the automobile, the telegraph and the telephone, for example—have brought dramatic improvements for society, but have also created new legal dilemmas. U.S. contract law lags behind these rapidly evolving social media networks, which are taking advantage of this failure by aggressively foreclosing consumer rights, compromising privacy and divesting users of their intellectual property rights.

The development of cloud computing creates new contracting issues, such as whether reasonable security is an implied norm for off-site storage. New legal and ethical rules must deal with corporate responsibility for such information age problems as setting requirements for data and software accuracy and resource efficiency, developing metrics for measuring and improving usage, and establishing standards of privacy, security, interoperability and responsibility for software failures. Attorneys for entities with an Internet presence will need increasingly to take a global perspective when drafting, negotiating and enforcing computer contracts.

CHAPTER SIX: REVIEW EXERCISES

6.1: On April 2, 2014, General Mills changed its terms of use to include the following clause: These terms are a binding legal agreement (Agreement) between you and General Mills. In exchange for the benefits, discounts, content, features, services, or other offerings that you receive or have access to by using our websites, joining our sites as a member, joining our online community, subscribing to our email newsletters, downloading or printing a digital coupon, entering a sweepstakes or contest, redeeming a promotional offer, or otherwise participating in any other General Mills offering, you are agreeing to these terms.[91] These terms included, in bold, capital letters, a mandatory arbitration clause that extended to any consumer dispute with General Mills.

In the face of strong of consumer resistance, General Mills reversed this new policy that would have blocked lawsuits against the company by anyone who had downloaded a General Mills coupon, redeemed one of their promotional offers, or even "liked" the food manufacturer on its Facebook site. Yet, many social media websites have quietly inserted even stronger forced arbitration clauses. Do you think it is ethical to include such provisions in consumer license agreements and terms of use? Do you think courts should enforce these provisions? Please explain.

6.2: Cloud computing providers are often criticized for using contract law to disclaim all warranties and meaningful remedies for harms such as loss of data. Under what, if any, situations should cloud providers be held responsible if an outside hacker interrupts service or misappropriates data? What if an insider misappropriates data? Who should decide how much security should be sufficient to protect the company from being sued? How should lawsuit penalties be calibrated? Under what situations would the loss of data be a criminal matter?

6.3: Instagram's revised ToU prohibits users from joining a class action lawsuit "unless they mail a written 'opt-out' statement to Facebook's headquarters in Menlo Park within 30 days of joining Instagram." On the surface, this seems like users have a choice about whether to agree to arbitration. A more cynical reading, however, suggests that the user had only thirty days to opt out of arbitration after the revised terms first applied—a period that has long since expired. Should the FTC mount a regulatory action against online companies that employ misleading terms of use or is it the consumer's responsibility to read carefully? Less than one in a thousand users read these agreements. What are the ethical implications of this fact?

6.4: Instagram's arbitration clause, which went into effect in 2013, mandates the American Arbitration Association (AAA) as the arbitral provider. Under the AAA, consumers must essentially waive their Seventh Amendment right to a jury trial, the right to an appeal or ability to compel discovery. They can choose, however, to have their issue judged in small claims court. Should social media providers have the power to foreclose the right to a jury trial? The ToU also forbids joining claims into a class action. Class actions are often the only meaningful way to pursue a small dollar claim, such as for claims of inadequate privacy protections. Should courts uphold these "agreements" even though very few people understand the implications of such clauses?

6.5: One true measure of a fundamentally fair process is whether consumers have an opportunity to read a comprehensible agreement. In reality, consumers "rarely read or understand" pre-dispute mandatory arbitration agreements. Your assignment is to read Instagram's terms of use found at https://help.instagram.com/478745558852511. Do a Goggle search using the terms Instagram and "terms of use" if the above link is not working. After you have reviewed Instagram's terms of use, please answer the following questions:

(1) Did you find Instagram's legalese to be understandable?

(2) Does the terms of use explain how arbitration works?

(3) Does the arbitration clause disclose what rights you will lose by arbitrating?

(4) Does the arbitration clause explain the cost of arbitrating a claim?

6.6: An educational technology website named italki helps foreign language learners connect with online teachers and native-speaking language partners. However, this social media website specifies that consumers must conduct any arbitration in Hong Kong:

> For any claim arising between you and italki (excluding claims for injunctive or other equitable relief) where the total amount of the award sought is less than HKD 50,000, the party requesting relief may elect to resolve the dispute in a cost-effective manner through binding non-appearance-based arbitration. A party electing arbitration must initiate such arbitration through an established alternative dispute resolution (ADR) provider mutually agreed upon by the parties.

If it is unfair to require U.S. users to travel to Hong Kong to arbitrate this agreement under that region's legal regime, is it equally unfair to require a user in Hong Kong to travel to California to arbitrate a claim? In the European Union, consumers have the right to pursue a claim in their home court. Is it unduly burdensome for the social media provider to be prepared to arbitrate in diverse jurisdictions around the world?

6.7: Life360, a social media website, gives users a warning that its ToU contains an arbitration clause in the first few paragraphs: "PLEASE READ THIS AGREEMENT CAREFULLY TO ENSURE THAT YOU UNDERSTAND EACH PROVISION. THIS AGREEMENT CONTAINS A MANDATORY ARBITRATION OF DISPUTES PROVISION THAT REQUIRES THE USE OF ARBITRATION ON AN INDIVIDUAL BASIS TO RESOLVE DISPUTES, RATHER THAN JURY TRIALS OR CLASS ACTIONS."[92]

Should making the mandatory arbitration agreement more visible lead a court to uphold it? How would each perspective handle this question?

6.8: Christian Mingle, a Christian dating website, requires users to defend, indemnify and hold the social networking site the website and officers harmless "for any losses, costs, liabilities or expenses relating to or arising out of any third-party claim" based upon a user's postings. Christian Mingle makes it clear that the site is not liable to its users for damages:

> TO THE MAXIMUM EXTENT PERMITTED BY APPLICABLE LAW, IN NO EVENT WILL WE BE LIABLE TO YOU OR TO ANY OTHER PERSON FOR ANY INCIDENTAL, CONSEQUENTIAL, OR INDIRECT DAMAGES (INCLUDING, BUT NOT LIMITED TO, DAMAGES FOR LOSS OF DATA, LOSS OF PROGRAMS, COST OF PROCUREMENT OF SUBSTITUTE SERVICES OR SERVICE INTERRUPTIONS) ARISING OUT OF THE USE OF OR INABILITY TO USE THE SERVICE, EVEN IF WE OR OUR AGENTS OR REPRESENTATIVES KNOW OR HAVE BEEN ADVISED OF THE POSSIBILITY OF SUCH DAMAGES.

Christian Mingle's website requires the user to waive its recovery of damages for every conceivable form of injury. How would a consequentialist, a libertarian and a Kantian view the above clause? What, if any, responsibility should Christian Mingle have to investigate their clients to ensure that you are not matched up with a thief, rapist or another person who might harm you?

6.9: Snapchat requires its users to indemnify the social media company for any losses due to how a user uses its services, including being responsible for Snapchat's attorney's fees. An indemnity clause is a contractual transfer of risk between the social networking site and its users. Snapchat eliminates the possibility of users recovering for any injuries caused by postings on its service but requires users to indemnify (reimburse) the provider if the user causes losses to the company. Should Snapchat be able to reject any responsibility for postings that are defaming or humiliating? Under what circumstances should Snapchat be liable for any third party postings?

6.10: Snapchat's liability for what they do to users "shall in no event exceed $1.00."[93] Snapchat requires its members to arbitrate claims before JAMS, the second largest arbitral provider in the United States. JAMS' filing fee alone is 200 times the total possible recovery of $1. How would each perspective view the $1 cap on damages, given the cost of filing and pursuing claims through arbitration?

6.11: In 2015, a group of hackers broke into Ashley Madison's online website for persons seeking illicit affairs. The hackers released personal information about the private sex lives of hundreds of thousands of users. The victims of this security breached suffered substantial harms such ass divorces and job losses. Ashley Madison requires users to submit to arbitration simply because a user has clicked "yes" to the terms of service. Should a court dismiss the class actions and impose arbitration? Why or why not? Is it ethical for a website like Ashley Madison to shunt its users to a private dispute resolution system where users have no right of discovery or to an appeal?

6.12: The Ashley Madison hack disclosed that many of the female listings were false, allegedly made by the website to entice male subscribers to purchase gifts from Ashley to win the favor of these nonexistent "women." As many as 70,000 of the "engagers" were, in fact, bots with fake female profiles that would chat with curious men on the site in exchange for a fee. Can Ashley disclaim responsibility for this deceptive use of bots because their terms of use state that they take no responsibility to ensure that all their listings are real? Under which, if any, of the ethical theories is this a valid defense? Who would most strongly oppose this argument?

6.13: Conflict theorists would denounce one-sided terms of use as capitalist exploitation, especially for the poorly educated. Does it make sense to require websites to have terms that can be read at a ninth grade level, the comprehension level of the average American? If not, should the required writing level be higher or lower? Should people with advanced legal education be held to a higher standard than persons who are not high school graduates?

6.14: Sally buys two iPads on Apple's website. Because Apple was running a promotion she got them each for $100. Thereafter, she received an email confirming the transaction. The next day, however, Apple informs Sally that it had cancelled her order because of high demand and that the company would not honor the sale. The Terms of Use, which were underlined and appeared at the bottom of the screen during checkout next to "Privacy" and "Copyright," permitted sales to be cancelled at the discretion of the seller. Should a court uphold this agreement? Why or why not?

6.15: Suppose you are working for a social media giant that asks you for assistance in presenting Terms of Use for their website. The provider will draw more eyeballs and make bigger profits if users do not set their privacy preferences in order to restrict viewing. Your manager makes it clear that bonuses and promotions will be based on company profitability. How could users be encouraged to not use the privacy settings? What are the ethics of doing this? Under what circumstances could you file a lawsuit if you were fired for failing to perform your work in a way that risks harm to the provider's customers?

6.16: Pokémon GO's terms of service agreement premises contract formation on the following clause:

> By using our Services, you are agreeing to these Terms, our Trainer Guidelines, and our Privacy Policy. If you are the parent or legal guardian of a child under the age of 13 (the "Parent"), you are agreeing to these Terms on behalf of yourself and your children who are authorized to use the Services pursuant to these Terms and in our Privacy Policy. If you don't agree to these Terms, our Trainer Guidelines, and our Privacy Policy, do not use the Services.

Mass market contracts fall into shrinkwrap, clickwrap or browsewrap agreements. How would you classify Pokémon GO's ToS agreement? What suggestions would you make to increase the likelihood that a court will enforce this boilerplate? Should the company have any responsibility if a child is severely injured because the game distracted her?

6.17: Software-as-a-Service (SaaS) is a model of software storage and access over the Internet. Should cloud providers be able to disclaim responsibility for securing consumer data or should there be a non-disclaimable duty to reasonable security?

REFERENCES FOR CHAPTER SIX

1 Natt Garun, *What Is This, 2002?* THE VERGE.COM (July 4, 2017).

2 *Kai Peng v. Uber Techs., Inc.*, 237 F. Supp. 3d 36 (E.D.N.Y. Feb. 23, 2017).

3 *Id.* at 42.

4 2009 WL 2940081 (D.N.J. 2009).

5 78 F.Supp.3d 1051 (D. Calif 2015).

6 Brief of Amicus Curiae Electronic Frontier Foundation, *KSR Int'l Co. v. Teleflex Inc.*, 2004 U.S. Briefs 1350 (Aug. 22, 2006).

7 STEPHEN WEBER, THE SUCCESS OF SOURCE CODE 1 (2004).

8 Jay P. Kesan & Rajiv C. Shah, *Deconstructing Code*, 6 YALE JOURNAL OF LAW AND TECHNOLOGY 277, 350 (2003–2004) (retelling the story of the open source software movement and its accomplishments).

9 *Open-Source Software, Going Hybrid*, THE ECONOMIST (July 25, 2002).

10 Steven J. Vaughan-Nichols, *It's an Open-Source World: 78 Percent of Companies Run Open-Source Software,* ZDNET (April 16, 2015).

11 Liam Tung, *Ballmer: I May Have Called Linux a Cancer But Now I Love It*, ZDNET (March 11, 2016).

12 *Id.*

13 Peter Mell & Timothy Grance, National Institute of Standards, U.S. Dept. of Commerce, Special Publication No. 800–145, *The NIST Definition of Cloud Computing* (September 2011) at 2.

14 Up-to-the Cloud, *Business Drivers for Cloud* (2015).

15 Gartner Research Report, *Cloud Contracts Need Security Levels to Better Manage Risk* (March 13, 2013).

16 *Apple to Build First China Data Center to Comply With Law,* ELECTRONIC COMMERCE & LAW REPORT (July 17, 2017).

17 *Id.*

18 Mark Bergen, *Google Will Stop Reading Your Emails for Gmail Ads*, ELECTRONIC COMMERCE & LAW REPORT (June 28, 2017).

19 *Id.*

20 Nearly thirty years ago, the Stored Communications Privacy Act was enacted to fill a gap in the then relatively new ECPA. *See* Russell S. Burnside, *The Electronic Communications Privacy Act of 1986: The Challenge of*

Applying Ambiguous Statutory Language to Intricate Telecommunication Technologies, 13 RUTGERS COMPUTER & TECHNOLOGY L. J. 451, 516–17 (1987) (lamenting "the 1986 Act's circumscription of legal protections for electronic communications, E-Mail, and remote computer services.).

[21] *Selden v. Airbnb, Inc.*, 2016 WL 6476934 at *1 (D.D.C., Nov. 1, 2016).

[22] 2016 WL 6476934 (D.D.C., Nov. 1, 2016).

[23] *Id.*

[24] NANCY S. KIM, WRAP CONTRACTS: FOUNDATIONS AND RAMIFICATIONS (New York, New York: Oxford University Press, 2013) at 1 ("When I ask my law or business school students whether they have entered into any contracts in the past week, few raise their hands [although they] have checked their online banking account, or downloaded software or music, or posted to their Facebook or Twitter accounts. . .").

[25] Facebook, *Terms of Use*, http://www.facebook.com/terms.php?ref=pf.

[26] Stewart Macaulay, *Relational Contracts Floating on a Sea of Custom? Thoughts About the Ideas of Ian Macneil & Lisa Bernstein*, 94 NORTHWESTERN LAW. REVIEW 1, 777 n. 17 (1999).

[27] 86 F.3d 1447, 1447 (7th Cir. 1996).

[28] 86 F.3d at 1450.

[29] *Id.* at 1453.

[30] Robert A. Hillman, *Rolling Contracts*, 71 FORDHAM L. REV. 743, 743 (2002).

[31] *Hill v. Gateway 2000, Inc.*, 105 F.3d 1147, 1149 (7th Cir. 1997) (applying *ProCD* to the sale of a boxed computer and noting, "[p]laintiffs ask us to limit *ProCD* to software, but where's the sense in that? *ProCD* is about the law of contract, not the law of software.").

[32] Jean Bracer, *Delayed Disclosure in Consumer E-Commerce as an Unfair and Deceptive Practice*, 46 WAYNE LAW. REVIEW 1805, 1852–53 (2000) (stating that "[h]olding back terms can be seen either as involving a deceptive representation or a deceptive omission" and FTC policy presumes this practice will mislead consumers).

[33] 104 F. Supp.2d 1332 (D. Kan. 2000).

[34] *Id.* at 1334–1335.

[35] *Liberty Syndicates at Lloyd's v. Walnut Advisory Corp.*, Slip Copy, No. 09–1343, 2011 WL 5825777 (D. N.J. Nov. 16, 2011).

[36] 763 F.3d 1171 (9th Cir. 2014).

[37] *Fteja v. Facebook, Inc.*, 841 F.Supp.2d 829, 837 (S.D.N.Y.2012).

[38] Woodrow Hartzog, *Website Design as Contract*, 60 AMERICAN UNIVERSITY LAW REVIEW 1635, 1642 (2011).

[39] *Id.*

[40] *Nicosia v. Amazon.com, Inc.*, 834 F.3d 220 (2d Cir. 2016).

[41] *Id.* at *7.

[42] Brian Fung, *Equifax Finally Responds to Swirling Concerns Over Consumers' Legal Rights*, THE WASHINGTON POST (September 8, 2017).

[43] On September 8, 2017, Equifax issued a statement that the arbitration clause and anti-class action waiver did not apply to this data breach. A former state attorney general cautions that Equifax's statement that it will not enforce the arbitration clause should not engender complacency: "Just because someone in the marketing department wrote that the terms of service don't apply to the cybersecurity incident means nothing compared to the contractual obligations of the terms of use." *Id.* (quoting Joel Winston, former New Jersey Deputy Attorney General).

[44] Federal Trade Commission, *In the Matter of Snapchat, Inc., a Corporation*, Docket No. C–4501 (Dec. 23, 2014).

[45] Federal Trade Commission, *FTC Approves Final Order Settling Charges Against Snapchat* (December 31, 2014).

[46] Sophie Curtis, *Snapchat Leaks 4.6m Users' Details*, THE TELEGRAPH (January 2, 2014).

[47] *In the Matter of Jerk, LLC*, a limited liability company, also d/b/a JERK.COM, and John Fanning, individually and as a member of Jerk, LLC, Docket No. 9361 (FTC complaint filed May 2, 2014) at 4.

[48] *Fanning v. Federal Trade Commission*, 821 F.3d 164 (1st Cir. 2016).

[49] Stewart Macaulay, *Relational Contracts Floating on a Sea of Custom? Thoughts About the Ideas of Ian Macneil & Lisa Bernstein*, 94 NORTHWESTERN LAW REVIEW 1 (1999).

[50] MICHAEL L. RUSTAD, SOFTWARE LICENSING, CLOUD COMPUTING AGREEMENTS, OPEN SOURCE, AND INTERNET TERMS OF USE: A PRACTICAL APPROACH TO INFORMATION AGE CONTRACTS IN A GLOBAL SETTING (New York, New York: LexisNexis IP Law & Strategy Series, 2016–2017 ed.) at § 7.18[1] at 776.

[51] 4 N.E.3d 696 (Ind. 2016).

[52] European Commission, Unfair Contract Terms, EUROPEAN COMMUNICATIONS, http://ec.europa.eu/consumers/cons_int/safe_shop/unf_cont_terms/index_en.htm.

[53] Kelly Fiveash (UK), *Law & Disorder—Google, Facebook, Twitter Must Amend ToS for EU Users or Face Fines: Trio Given One Month to Clean Up Fraud, Scams, and Make Other Fixes*, ARSTECHNICA.COM (March 17, 2017).

[54] R.G. N 02/03156 (tgin020604), Tribunal de Grande Instance [T.G.I.] [ordinary court of original jurisdiction] Nanterre, 1e ch., June 2, 2004 (Fr.).

[55] This section draws upon Michael L. Rustad, Wenzhuo Liu, and Thomas H. Koenig, *Destined to Collide? Social Media Contracts in the United States and China*, 37 UNIVERSITY OF PENNSYLVANIA JOURNAL OF INTERNATIONAL LAW 647 (2015).

[56] Contract Law of the People's Republic of China (adopted at the Second Session of the Ninth National People's Cong. March 15, 1999, effective on October 1, 1999), art. 149 (1999) (China).

[57] The discussion of Guo Li Su v. Microsoft (郭力诉微软格式合同无效案) (*Guo Li v. Microsoft*), (Beijing Interm. People's Ct. June 20, 2011), Pku.cn is drawn from Michael L. Rustad, Wenzhuo Liu, and Thomas H. Koenig, *Destined to Collide? Social Media Contracts in the United States and China*, 37 UNIVERSITY OF PENNSYLVANIA JOURNAL OF INTERNATIONAL LAW 647, 712–715 (2015) (discussing *Guo Li v. Microsoft*).

[58] James Palmer, *China Is Trying to Deal a Death Blow to the Free Internet*, BUSINESS INSIDER (August 27, 2017).

[59] *Big Data and Government, China's Digital Dictatorship: Worrying Experiments with a New Form of Social Control*, THE ECONOMIST (December 17, 2016).

[60] NANCY S. KIM, WRAP CONTRACTS: FOUNDATIONS AND RAMIFICATIONS (New York, New York: Oxford University Press, 2013) at 2.

[61] *Id.* at 1–3.

[62] Amy J. Schmitz, *Pizza-Box Contracts: True Tales of Consumer Contracting Culture*, 45 WAKE FOREST LAW REVIEW 863, 864–65 (2010) (arguing that consumers bear some responsibility for acquiescing to the stronger party "run[ning] roughshod over their rights").

[63] *What Are Standard Form Contracts?* FAIR CONTRACTS.ORG (2016).

[64] Association of Computing Machinery (ACM), Code of Ethics & Professional Conduct (Adopted by the ACM Council, October 16, 1992) at § 2.6, "Honor contracts, agreements, and assigned responsibilities." (This Code and the supplemental Guidelines were developed by the Task Force for the Revision of the ACM Code of Ethics and Professional Conduct: Ronald E. Anderson, Chair, Gerald Engel, Donald Gotterbarn, Grace C. Hertlein, Alex Hoffman, Bruce Jawer, Deborah G. Johnson, Doris K. Lidtke, Joyce Currie Little, Dianne Martin, Donn B. Parker, Judith A. Perrolle, and Richard S. Rosenberg. The Task Force was organized by ACM/SIGCAS and funding was provided by the ACM SIG Discretionary Fund. This Code and the supplemental Guidelines were adopted by the ACM Council on October 16, 1992).

[65] *Id.* at 385.

[66] Seth Payne, *The Ethics of Cloud Computing*, DATA CENTER KNOWLEDGE (November 24, 2014).

[67] Theresa Amato, *How Boilerplate Contracts Strip Our Rights*, THE NATION (January 8, 2014).

[68] *Id.*

[69] *What Are Standard Form Contracts?* FAIR CONTRACTS.ORG (2016).

[70] Ralph Nader & Theresa Amato, *The Strip Mining of Contract Rights*, HARVARD LAW RECORD (April 3, 2015).

[71] Stewart Macaulay, *Relational Contracts Floating on a Sea of Custom? Thoughts About the Ideas of Ian Macneil & Lisa Bernstein*, 94 NORTHWESTERN LAW REVIEW 1, 777 n. 17 (1999) (quoting Ian Macneil).

[72] *Senate Passes Bill Banning Non-Disparagement Clauses*, TECHDIRT.COM (December 15, 2015).

[73] James Boyle noted that for the "past twenty years we have been told that we are shifting from the industrial to the information society." JAMES, BOYLE, SHAMANS, SOFTWARE, AND SPLEENS: LAW AND THE CONSTRUCTION OF THE INFORMATION (Cambridge, Massachusetts: Harvard University Press, 1996) at ix.

[74] "No benevolent historical force will inexorably lead this technological-economic moment to develop toward an open, diverse, liberal equilibrium." *Id.* at 22.

[75] Kelly Fiveash (UK), *Law & Disorder: Google, Facebook, Twitter Must Amend ToS for EU Users or Face Fines: Trio Given One Month to Clean Up Fraud, Scams, and Make Other Fixes*, ARSTECHNICA.COM (March 17, 2017).

[76] Federal Communications Commission, Report and Order (December 23, 2010).

[77] *Id.*

[78] *See generally,* DAWN NUNZIATO, VIRTUAL FREEDOM: NEUTRALITY AND FREE SPEECH IN THE INTERNET AGE (Stanford, California: Stanford University Press, 2009).

[79] *Id.*

[80] *Arbitration: Is It Fair When Forced?: Hearing Before the United States Senate Committee on the Judiciary*, (statement of Victor E. Schwartz, Partner, Shook Hardy & Bacon, LLP, on behalf of the U.S. Chamber of Commerce and the U.S. Chamber Institute for Legal Reform).

[81] MICHAEL J. TREBILCOCK, THE LIMITS OF FREEDOM OF CONTRACT (Cambridge, Massachusetts: Cambridge University Press, 1993) at 8.

[82] *Jacobsen v. Katzer*, 535 F.3d 1378, 1378–1379 (9th Cir. 2008).

[83] John Tsai, *Review 2008: For Better or Worse: Introducing the GNU General Public License Version 3, Annual Review 2008*, 23 BERKELEY TECHNOLOGY LAW JOURNAL 547, 549 (2008).

[84] STEPHEN WEBER, THE SUCCESS OF SOURCE CODE (Cambridge, Massachusetts: Harvard University Press, 2004) at 1.

[85] Michael Corkery & Jessica Silver-Greenberg, *Miss a Payment? Good Luck Moving That Car*, THE NEW YORK TIMES (September 24, 2014).

[86] *Frank & Sons v. Information Solutions, Inc.*, 1988 WL 1107405 (N.D. Okla. 1988).

[87] 812 S.W.2d 565 (Mo. App. 1991).

[88] *Id.* at 567.

[89] Legal Services of Southern Piedmont, *Repossession Without the Repo Man* (2016).

[90] Heather E. Bullock, Karen Fraser Wyche, & Wendy R. Williams, *Media Images of the Poor*, 47 JOURNAL OF SOCIAL ISSUES 229, 230 (2001).

[91] General Mills' Arbitration Clause, http://www.indisputably.org/?p=5564.

[92] italki, *Terms of Service*, https://www.italki.com/tos.

[93] Snapchat, *Terms of Use*, http://genius.com/Snapchat-terms-of-use-annotated.

CHAPTER SEVEN

Patents, Copyrights & Computers

§ 7.0: OVERVIEW OF INTELLECTUAL PROPERTY: THE POWERS OF IMAGINATION

Intellectual property (IP) is the commodification of creations of the mind, which represents a significant portion of the monetary value of most computer companies.[1] Microsoft, Oracle, Salesforce.com, Symantec and many other high technology companies earn much of their revenue through software licenses, whose terms are enforced by copyrights, patents, and trademarks. Chapter Seven focuses on the ethical and legal issues arising from the two wholly federal branches of intellectual property law; patents and copyrights. Chapter Eight will examine trademarks and trade secrets and how these branches of IP law protect computer technologies.

A patent for an invention is a grant of an intellectual property right to the inventor from the government that excludes others from making, using or selling the invention without permission throughout the United States for a limited term. Patents serve the public interest by endowing their owners with a temporary monopoly in return for fully describing and disclosing inventions. As the U.S. Supreme Court observed:

> Patents endow their holders with certain superpowers, but only for a limited time. In crafting the patent laws, Congress struck a balance between fostering innovation and ensuring public access to discoveries. While a patent lasts, the patentee possesses exclusive rights to the patented article—rights he may sell or license for royalty payments if he so chooses. . . . But a patent typically expires 20 years from the day the application for it was filed. When the patent expires, the patentee's prerogatives expire too, and the right to make or use the article, free from all restriction, passes to the public.[2]

Similarly, copyright law gives owners the right to a "legal monopoly" for the copyright term. Courts have generated a distinct body of copyright law to accommodate modern technologies. Creators are granted exclusive rights over their literary and artistic works, a category which has been expanded to include software, databases, photographs and countless other digital works. Peer-to-peer file sharing, the licensing of content, the Digital Millennium Copyright Act and social media content have revolutionized U.S. copyright doctrine.

Computer companies with global aspirations must comply with international copyright law, which includes different national rules for moral rights, database protection, fair use and other IP concepts. Who owns the copyright when an employee develops software? How different does software need to be as not to infringe on third party's applications? How does the Internet change the concept of fair use? How do service providers obtain immunity from claims of copyright infringement for materials posted by third parties? How can copyright owners exercise their right to take down infringing content? What rights and remedies do copyright owners have if they prove infringement? These are just a few of the many Internet-related copyright issues examined in this chapter.

[A] A Hidden Figure in Patent Law: Fred Jones

To set the stage for an understanding of patent law, a brief recounting of the life of an early African-American inventor, Frederick McKinley Jones (1893–1961), will be presented. Few Americans know the story of Fred Jones or his impact on daily life as his story is largely hidden from history. Jones was a grade school dropout who was raised by a Catholic priest after his mother's early death. Despite his humble beginnings, Jones revolutionized the refrigeration, transportation and film industries with his many inventions.

Jones worked as a master mechanic and engineer on James J. Hill's bonanza farm in Northwestern Minnesota in the early twentieth century. Hill, known as the "Empire Builder," was the fabulously wealthy chief executive officer of The Great Northern Railway, which was one of America's most important railroad systems. One of the authors of this book, Michael L. Rustad, grew up on a farm outside of Humboldt, Minnesota that had been carved out of what had once been part of Hill's 50,000 acre farm.

James J. Hill's northwest Minnesota estate was extremely atypical, being the largest wheat-growing farm in the United States. Its 24-room house featured internal elevators, dumbwaiters, brass fixtures and French doors. The Hill farm's two massive grain elevators were the largest silos in the world at the time. James

J. Hill built a barn large enough to house two-hundred horses and four hundred head of cattle.[3]

Hill appointed his youngest son, Walter, to manage the massive estate. Walter had no experience with farming and a reputation as a dissolute playboy. Local farmers speculated that Walter's father had set him up in this remote corner of Minnesota to keep him far from the immoral temptations available in Minneapolis. Walter Hill left this farm the night his father died in 1916, never to return. Despite Walter's disinterest in agriculture, his farm was a success, due in large part to the contributions of Jones, who was hired by Hill in 1912 as the estate's head mechanic.

Jones was responsible for servicing and repairing the tractors, combines, swathers, augers, harrows, grain dryers and other farm machinery on the Hill estate, but he did far more. Jones made countless improvements in the farm's agricultural implements and machinery. The Minnesota Historical Society credits Jones with the pioneering designs for a variety of significant innovations, including the first refrigerated truck, the portable x-ray machine, an air conditioning unit for military field hospitals, a self-starting gas engine and major advances in motion picture and box office technology.[4] Jones was posthumously awarded the National Medal of Technology in 1991, the first Black inventor ever granted this honor.[5]

Fred Jones received no financial benefits from his earliest inventions since he knew little about the patent system and did not file claims. His condenser microphone "was eventually patented and manufactured by another party."[6] A similar situation occurred when Jones developed a portable X-ray machine at the request of a local doctor. This significant innovation was later patented by a German inventor.

In addition to his work on the farm, Jones helped the local theatre owner develop a technique for synchronizing pictures and sound. Hearing that Jones had improved the quality of the films he was showing in the small town of Hallock, Minnesota, a Minneapolis entrepreneur, Joseph A. Numero, hired Jones as an engineer in his movie equipment company. With Numero's sponsorship and financial support, Jones prepared and filed patent applications with the United States Patent Office (USPTO).

The USPTO awarded Jones his first patent in 1939, which was an automatic ticket-dispensing machine for movie theaters. Jones eventually received sixty-one patents and became quite prosperous. Without Joseph Numero's financial and legal help throughout lengthy and costly patent prosecution, it would have been unlikely that Fred Jones would ever have sought patent protection.

After Numero's golfing partner complained that a truckload of freshly butchered chickens had spoiled while being transported, Jones invented the first mobile refrigeration units, which revolutionized the handling of perishable foodstuffs. Jones' refrigeration patents formed the basis for U.S. Thermo King, a highly successful corporation founded by Numero in 1937. Joseph Numero appointed Fred Jones as chief engineer and, later, as Vice President of the company.

The Thermo King Corporation, now a subsidiary of Ingersoll Rand, is a leader in the production of temperature control systems for trucks, trailers, shipboard containers and railway cars. In 2007, the company held a special dedication ceremony for The Frederick McKinley Jones Research and Development Center, named after this instrumental figure whose electronic innovations forever changed everyday life. "Thermo King's $7.1 million-dollar investment in the company's quality and reliability testing capabilities, which includes facility updates and new equipment, is a tribute to Fred's dedication in creating innovative, reliable products."[7]

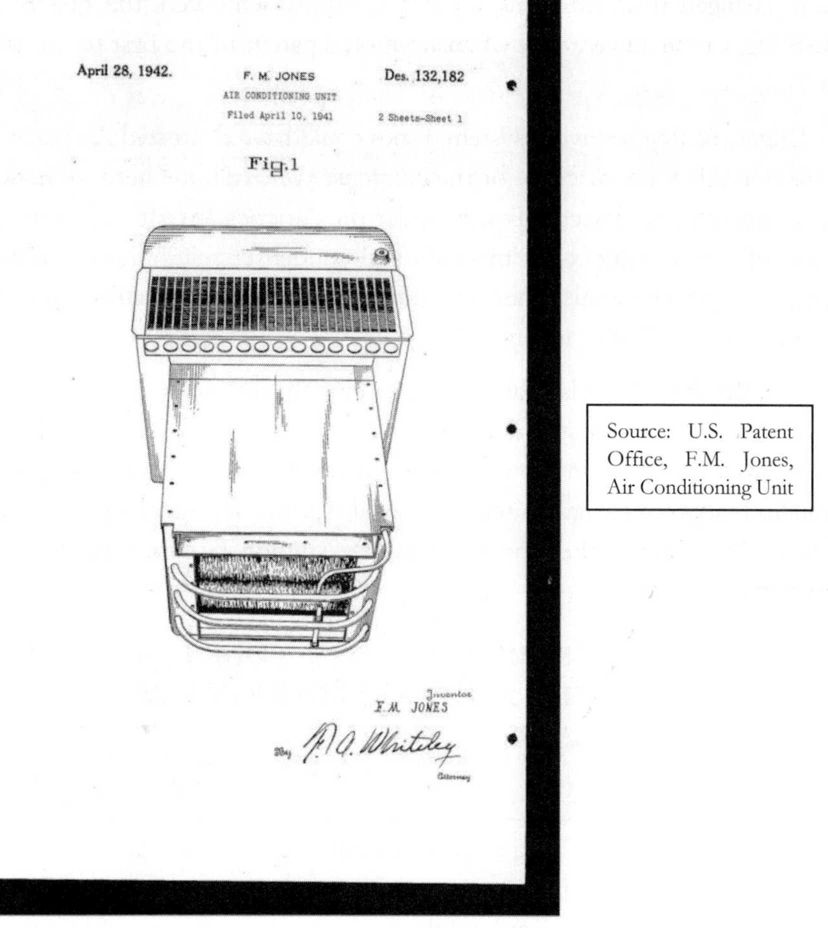

Source: U.S. Patent Office, F.M. Jones, Air Conditioning Unit

[B] Jones' Assignment of His Patents

The inequities of the Jim Crow era made it difficult for Jones to secure patent protection on his own. Fred Jones and Joseph Numero originally had an unequal relationship because of the asymmetries of wealth, power, legal resources and race between the two men.[8] Jones took the best deal he could get, assigning his first patents to Numero in exchange for a modest salary and housing. Still, most people would concede that, in the end, the patent system furthered social justice by allowing this brilliant inventor to eventually become a wealthy man, while society benefited by encouraging this genius to continually develop useful inventions.

Patent law vested Fred Jones and Joseph Numero with temporary monopolies to make, use and sell their joint inventions. After their patents expired, the others could freely copy Jones' inventions. Keep this story in mind as you read further about patent law. For example, an Obama era U.S. patent law reform changed from awarding a patent to those who were the first to invent something, to the current rule of awarding the patent to the first to file with the USPTO.

Under the first to invent system, Jones could have contested the patents filed for his portable x-ray machine or the condenser microphone because he was the first to invent these devices. Today, under the America Invent Act's reform, the makers of the portable x-ray machine and condenser microphone would have priority over Jones because they were the first to file patent claims, even though they were not the first to invent.

The remainder of this chapter will examine the intersection of ethics and law for information age patent and copyright law, while trademarks and trade secrets will be covered in detail in Chapter Eight. Chart One compares the four branches of intellectual property law in terms of what is protected, the length of the term of protection and whether there are any registration requirements involved in obtaining protection.

CHART ONE: SUMMARY OF THE FOUR BRANCHES OF INTELLECTUAL PROPERTY LAW

Branch of Intellectual Property Law	*How Protection is Obtained*	*Registration Requirements, Length of Term*
Patents (federal law) protect software, business methods and computer innovations by securing a monopoly for a limited period in return for later disclosure.	To qualify for patent protection, a claim describing the invention must be novel, non-obvious and useful. Example: Utility patent covering Jones' refrigeration units or his condenser microphones.	Patents are registered in the United States Patent Office, giving owners 20 years from the date on which the application was filed in the United States.
Copyrights (federal law) protects works of authorship including software as literary works and protection for object and source code.	Copyright is protected automatically upon creation of an "original works of authorship." Copyright registration gives the owner the right to pursue statutory damages for infringement.	Copyright protection is automatic once content is fixed in a tangible form for the first time. Copyrights last for 70 years after the author's death.

Computer companies create distinctive trademarks (state and federal law) that help consumers identify their software, products and services.	The owners of trademarks acquire rights through use but register their marks in order to access the federal courts and seek statutory remedies for infringement. Example: Apple, Amazon, Microsoft and IBM register hundreds of trademarks with the USPTO.	Registered trademarks give the owner indefinite protection, unless abandoned. The initial trademark term is ten years. A trademark owner may file for renewal terms perpetually.
Trade Secrets (state law) protect commercially valuable secret information, such as customer lists, business models, formulas, business methods and computer code.	Nearly anything can be protected as a trade secret so long as it has a potential or actual economic value and the company uses reasonable means to keep the information secret. Example: Trade Secrets can protect source code and other information that is potentially valuable.	Trade secrets law is the only branch of IP without a provision for registration. After the enactment of the 2016 Defend Trade Secrets Act (DTSA), trade secret owners have a federal cause of action for trade secret misappropriation.

(1) Patent Law & Modern Information Technologies

The U.S. Constitution grants Congress the power "to promote the progress of science and useful arts, by securing for limited times to. . . inventors the exclusive right to their respective . . . discoveries." Congress enacted the Patent Act of 1793, which today is embodied in the Patent Act of 1952. Patent protection is available for the invention of "any new and useful process, machine, manufacture, or composition of matter, or any new and useful improvement."[9] Laws of nature, abstract ideas and physical phenomena are not patentable.

Congress revised U.S. patent law significantly in 2011 when it enacted the America Invents Act (AIA). The AIA aligned U.S. law with the rest of the world in recognizing patents on a first-inventor-to-file (FITF) basis and removing the previous the first-to-invent (FI) system. Under the FI system, applicants got a patent "after disclosing the invention as long as a patent was filed within one year of the disclosure." Under the AIA, the FITF is determined by the race to the United States Patent and Trademark Office.

The FI patent system had created problems for multinational companies, which must file patents in numerous countries that have different procedures and substantive law standards. The first-to-invent system had led to extensive litigation over who invented valuable products such as the telephone, which multiple competing inventors worked upon during the same time period.

Patent examiners "identify the boundaries of the protection sought by the applicant and to understand how the claims relate to and define what the applicant has indicated is the invention."[10] Patent applicants can pay an additional fee to have the USPTO review their patent application on an expedited basis. Small business entities and independent inventors receive a 50 percent discount on the $4800 payment that is required to use this fast track option. This reform is a response to widespread industry grievances about the protracted patent approval process.

During the 1980s, IP lawyers turned to trade secrets and the law of copyright because they assumed that software was not patentable. Today, software patents are well established, especially utility patents for software such as compilers, application programs and protection for a "process or method performed by a computer game."[11] To qualify for patent protection, software must be novel, non-obvious and have utility. Software patents have been granted for such diverse Internet related activities as hyperlinking, audio software, file formats and search engines. A software patent application must clearly describe what the computer does when it performs the steps dictated by the code.

Hardly a week goes by without a multi-million-dollar award in a patent infringement lawsuit. In December of 2016, a Delaware jury awarded $2.54 billion to Merck in a patent dispute over a rival's infringement of its hepatitis C treatment patent. In August 31, 2017, a Texas jury handed down a $10 million patent infringement verdict against Nintendo. The jury found that "Nintendo Wii™ products when used with certain Wii™ and Mario Kart™ video games infringed the single asserted claim of the patent at issue," awarding $10 million for reasonable royalties lost.[12]

In February 2015, IBM filed suit against Priceline as well as Kayak and OpenTable for refusing to purchase a patent license. Attorneys for IBM describe the contested patents as "a system of showing applications and ads that relied more on user computers, reducing load on Prodigy servers."[13] Software patents are controversial, in large part, because of computer professionals' distrust of them.[14]

(2) Business Method Patents

Business method patents cover a wide variety of applications pertaining to such topics as incentive programs, operations research, electronic shopping, reservations, shipping, transportation and business processing as shown in the text box above. Business method patents were thought to be unpatentable as an abstract idea until *State Street Bank & Trust Co. v. Signature Financial Group.*[15] The business method patent in dispute was Signature's method of calculating the value of a customer's share of multiple mutual funds. The USPTO granted Signature Financial Group, Inc. U.S. Patent 5,193,056 entitled "Data Processing System for Hub and Spoke Financial Services Configuration." State Street sued, contending that this business method for computing interest in mutual funds was purely mathematical, did not provide a tangible result, and, therefore, was not patentable.

The federal district court found Signature's patent invalid. The Federal Circuit reversed, upholding the validity of Signature's business method patent, because it was useful, concrete and produced a tangible result. The appeals court reasoned that patent laws protect any new method, including those that are computer-aided. Critics charge that this decision creates a vast expansion of software patents as any computer program can be displayed as a set of mathematical expressions. Tens of thousands of business method patent applications have been filed since *State Street* opened the floodgates. In the immediate aftermath of the July 1998 decision, there was a 45% increase in the number of computer-related patents issued during the patent office's fiscal year ending on September 30, 1998.[16]

In 2000, "Amazon.com was granted a patent on its affiliates program, which allows owners of other Websites to refer customers to Amazon.com in exchange for a fee." Amazon.com's 1-Click patent was for a "method, and system for placing a purchase order via a communications network." This software permitted customers to make online purchases with a single click, using a pre-defined address and credit card number.

A federal court granted Amazon.com an injunction enjoining Barnes & Noble from using a single-click Express Checkout on their online store. Barnes & Noble settled the patent dispute by agreeing to license the 1-Click patent. Richard Stallman, President of the Free Software Foundation, published a letter calling for a boycott of Amazon.com, saying the Barnes & Noble lawsuit was "an attack against the World Wide Web and against E-Commerce in general."

Jeff Bezos, Chairman and CEO of Amazon.com, published an open letter in response, calling for patent law reforms. Bezos proposed to abbreviate the life of the patent term to three to five years for software and business method patents. The rationale for an abbreviated patent term is that most software or business methods will have a short shelf life. On September 11, 2017, Amazon's 1-Click patent expired, which saves money for every company that has been licensing this invention. Apple, Facebook, American Express and other member of the World Wide Web Consortium are currently designing industry standards for the era of freely available 1-click shopping.[17]

Yahoo! filed a patent infringement lawsuit against Facebook, alleging that the social media giant had infringed ten different Yahoo! patents such as "personalized advertising, customized portal pages and news feeds, recommendations to connect with other suggested users (and screen out spammers), social music and messaging applications, and authorizing some users (but not others) to see different sections of your content." Facebook counterclaimed that Yahoo! had breached ten Facebook patents, enabling such features as photo-sharing and content personalization. The two companies settled their lawsuits by agreeing to cross-license their technologies.

(3) How Copyright Law Protects Software

The 1976 Copyright Act generally gives the copyright owner the exclusive right to reproduce the work, to prepare derivative works, to distribute copies or phonorecords of the copyrighted work, to perform the copyrighted work publicly and to display the copyrighted work publicly. Copyright law protects the form of expression rather than the subject matter of the writing. For example, a description of a machine could be copyrighted, but this would only prevent others from copying the description; it would not prevent others from writing a description of their own or from making and using the machine. Copyrights are registered by the Copyright Office of the Library of Congress.

The U.S. Code defines "computer program" and "software" to mean "a set of statements or instructions to be used directly or indirectly in a computer in order to bring about a certain result."[18] Computer programs can qualify as original "works of authorship," classified as literary works so long as the code is fixed in a tangible medium.[19] Computer software is protectable whether it is in object code (the binary code—a series of zeros and ones—that computers can read) or in source code, which human programmers can read.

The overlapping protection of copyright, trademark and patent law has allowed computer companies like Google to claim multiple types of protection for their IP simultaneously. Google asks that users recognize their copyrights and trademarks with the following prescribed notices:

© 2018 Google Inc. All rights reserved. Google and the Google Logo are registered trademarks of Google Inc.

© 2018 Google Inc. All rights reserved. [Insert Trademark] is a trademark of Google Inc.

When using a Google product screenshot or data

We ask that you put the following tagline beneath any image featuring a Google product screenshot or data:

> © 2018 Google Inc., used with permission. Google and the Google logo are registered trademarks of Google Inc.

The expansion of the subject matter within both patent law and copyright law has lessened the traditional divide between industrial product design, traditionally covered by design patent law and the protection of artistic works under copyright law. Google claims copyright protection for the layout of its search engine page interface as it appears on a computer screen. Additionally, Google obtained a design patent that protects the same subject matter (with the exclusion of the words and numbers that are shown in broken line format).[20]

[C] Trademarks and Trade Secrets

(1) Trademarks

A trademark is a word, symbol, or design that distinguishes the source of goods or services of one party from another. Trademark rights prevent others from using confusingly similar marks, but do not prevent them from selling the same goods or services under a clearly different mark. Google's trademark is ranked as the most valuable in the world, with an estimated worth of $44 billion. Google has also registered hundreds of other trademarks in the U.S. Trademark Office. Presenting the first eleven from an alphabetical listing below, illustrates the broad subject matter covered by the company's trademarks:

- AdSense for Content™ program
- AdWords™ advertising service
- Android Market™ media store
- Android Pay™ payment service
- Androidify™ mobile app
- Android™ platform

- □ Ara™ software and mobile device
- □ Art, Copy & Code™ marketing project
- □ BigTable™ data storage system
- □ Blink™ software
- □ Blogger™ web publishing service

(2) Trade Secrets of Computer Companies

Roger Milgrim, the leading trade secrets scholar, contends that computer software is the "single most important 'product' eligible for trade secret protection."[21] Trade secrets protect the intangible assets of information companies such as their source code, customer lists, design plans, patent applications and other proprietary information. Internal security, such as confidentiality procedures that require a firm's employees, independent contractors and anyone else with access to enter into nondisclosure agreements, are necessary to preserve valuable secrets.

To qualify as a trade secret, the information must: (1) be not generally known to the public; (2) confer some potential or actual economic benefit on its owner specifically because it is not publicly known; and (3) the owner must implement reasonable efforts to maintain secrecy such as the encryption of software or other computer security. Trademarks and trade secrets will be discussed in depth in Chapter Eight.

§ 7.1: PHILOSOPHICAL ROOTS OF IP PROTECTION

[A] Social Contract Theory

Intellectual property is a field where there are "important philosophical arguments about what content can be owned, protected and enforced."[22] Social contract theorists describe IP as "a contract between society and innovators. Society recognizes that innovation is socially beneficial and that the knowledge underlying innovation is intangible."[23] The U.S. Supreme Court recounted how Thomas Jefferson's work on the first U.S. patent board sought to strike the proper balance between patent rights and the public interest:

> Jefferson rejected a natural-rights theory in intellectual property rights and clearly recognized the social and economic rationale of the patent system. The patent monopoly was not designed to secure to the inventor

> his natural right in his discoveries. Rather, it was a reward, an inducement, to bring forth new knowledge. The grant of an exclusive right to an invention was the creation of society—at odds with the inherent free nature of disclosed ideas—and was not to be freely given. Only inventions and discoveries which furthered human knowledge, and were new and useful, justified the special inducement of a limited private monopoly. Jefferson did not believe in granting patents for small details, obvious improvements, or frivolous devices.[24]

The social contract is that inventors, like Fred Jones, will disclose their inventions in exchange for the right to exploit their utility patent for a twenty-year period, which usually begins from the date on which the application for the patent was filed in the United States. Design patents filed on or after May 13, 2015 have a term of 15 years from issuance. However, design patents filed prior to May 13, 2015 have a term of 14 years from issuance.

(1) The Lockean Social Contract

John Locke, America's "intellectual founding father," believed that people have inalienable natural rights to life, liberty and property.[25] Legal scholars have found support for the philosophy of intellectual property in two of Locke's arguments from his 1689 essay, the *Second Treatise of Government*:

> (1) God gave the World to "the Industrious and Rational, not to the Fancy or Covetousness of the Quarrelsom and Contentious." It is thus fitting that the former acquire, through their labour, title to that which they labor upon. . . . [and]
>
> (2) Most of the value of things useful to men derives not from the value of the raw materials from which they are made, but from the labour expended on them. It is thus not "so Strange" that, when determining whether ownership should be assigned to the worker or the community, the individual Property of labour should be able to overbalance the Community of Land.

Locke's "labor desert" theory defends private property rights based upon the principle that the creator's labor becomes part of the product. He would hold that a creative genius like Fred Jones earned his inalienable right to reap profits from his skillful work as an imaginative inventor. Jones and Numero each have the right to appropriate profits from Jones' inventions, since both contributed expertise and arduous work to the process of obtaining and enforcing patent claims.

Abraham Lincoln shared Locke's logic, warning that in the absence of a robust patent system, any man might "instantly use what another man had invented, so that the inventor had no special advantage from his invention." Lincoln noted that the U.S. "patent system changed this, secured to the inventor for a limited time exclusive use of his inventions, and thereby added the fuel of interest to the fire of genius in the discovery and production of new and useful things."[26] In the information age, this Lockean logic extends to the granting of intellectual property rights. Without sufficient financial remuneration, innovators might not perfect new inventions and society would lose out.

(2) The Rawlsian Version of Social Contract Theory

John Rawls' egalitarian version of the social contract theory requires that IP owners' rights also take into account a fair distribution of wealth and power.[27] A Rawlsian would oppose the societal inequalities reflected in the unbalanced contract that Fred Jones entered into with his business partner, when Joseph Numero named himself as co-inventor of inventions solely developed by Jones. But Rawlsians also view the intellectual property system as providing a valuable incentive:

> It is hard to think how Rawls' Difference Principle would work except through incentive mechanisms like we have now, including intellectual property. Under the Difference Principle, if an individual does something to make humans better off, particularly those in the worst-off classes, then we give that individual a little more than everyone else. If the individual were Samson and he kept the roof from falling instead of bringing it down, the Difference Principle would say it's fine to reward him (particularly if the roof was that of a homeless shelter, not Saks Fifth Avenue).[28]

The major problem with the patent system, from a Rawlsian perspective, is that it is complex and costly to navigate. Obtaining a patent presents practical difficulties for the individual tinkerer, like Fred Jones, who lacks the financial resources to hire patent prosecutors. It is not surprising that Jones was willing to assign his early patents to Numero for a modest sum. Without the backing of a sophisticated business organization like Numero's firm, a poorly educated inventor like Fred Jones would be forced to watch while others profited from his creativity.

[B] Consequentialism: Today's Dominant IP Justification

The consequentialist approach to intellectual property is predicated on the assumption that creators need economic incentives to invest in research and development. The proper term of protection should be based on the greatest possible social benefit, rather than an abstract respect for the property rights of the innovator. "Adopting systems of protection like copyright, patent and trade secret yields an optimal amount of intellectual works being produced, and a corresponding optimal amount of social utility. Coupled with the theoretical claim that society ought to maximize social utility, we arrive at a simple yet powerful argument for the protection of intellectual property rights."[29]

Before the development of trade secrets law, some profit maximizing inventors expended great efforts to keep their creations secret therefore harming society. For example, around the time that Locke was writing in England, the Chamberlen family invented the obstetric forceps, which made breach and other difficult births much safer. The Chamberlens concealed the nature of this invention through elaborate ruses because their reputation for having sole possession of a uniquely successful birthing technique brought prosperity to their midwifery business.

The Chamberlen family's secrecy reflects "ego utilitarianism," where private advantage subordinates the public benefit. The inventors gained wealth and prestige at the cost of a substantial number of childbirth fatalities because this life-saving device was unavailable to anyone except the Chamberlens' patients.[30] The patent system is designed to realign incentives so that society can benefit by rewarding the Chamberlens and other imaginative inventors for relinquishing control after a limited period.

Other viable solutions for benefiting from inventions besides intellectual property law exist. During Europe's Middle Ages, for example, craft guilds, such as masons and apothecaries, kept production secrets from the public. Those who belonged to craft guilds restricted knowledge of their techniques and inventions to the insiders. A lengthy period of underpaid apprenticeship—generally receiving only room and board—was required to be admitted to full guild membership.

By obtaining years of cheap labor from the apprentices, guild members profited. Apprentices benefited because they received training and could prosper when they achieved the status of master artisan.[31] Guilds created "haves" who learned the hidden technologies of their given craft and "have nots" who were kept from knowing the organization's secrets. The guild method of protecting intellectual property imposes more societal costs than the patent system because inventions are likely to be concealed for far longer periods.

Pharmaceutical inventions are the most cited example of the necessity of patent protection to spur innovations. The development of blockbuster drugs often requires hundreds of millions of dollars of investment in research, development and testing. The Tufts Center for the Study of Drug Development estimates that each new drug costs $2.6 billion. Critics claim that the true cost of developing new drugs is closer to $150 million, but either amount is an enormous amount of money.[32] Many medical products and drugs are never marketed because of the pharmaceutical company's failure to clear the hurdle of FDA mandated testing. Technology companies cannot survive multi-million-dollar product failures unless they can reap substantial profits on successfully marketed products.

The up-front investment in fields such as pharmaceuticals and biotechnology is so expensive that medical innovations are not viable without the limited monopoly granted by patent protection. Software patents, however, are more controversial as new software algorithms often do not involve years of research and extensive investments before being released to the marketplace. Critics argue that the short shelf life of software innovations makes a twenty-year patent term excessive.

Nevertheless, for all the stories about computer software and hardware giants being founded by twenty-something college dropouts working in their parent's garage, significant capital and legal expertise, generally provided at high cost by venture capitalists, is necessary to produce the great majority of lucrative computer inventions. One Microsoft engineer, with sixteen years of experience, estimated that Windows 8 cost $18.75 billion to develop.[33] Microsoft needs to recoup this enormous sum through large profits that would not exist without an enforceable IP granting system. Microsoft hires talented in-house lawyers, patent prosecutors and marketers to establish and defend its intellectual property.

Venture capitalists and companies require large incentives to fund the risky research and development necessary to develop diverse patent portfolios. One story, famous in Silicon Valley, tells of a software start-up founder, who, upon learning that his financiers were appropriating the entire value of his company, exclaimed ruefully, "I always knew that venture capital was a game, but I thought it was a game like chess, not like the *Game of Thrones.*"

Consequentialist logic endorses carving out some exceptions to copyright law, such as permitting reverse engineering to enable "interoperability." Reverse engineering is the process of examining a product in depth and then re-producing it based on the extracted information. A person may legally reverse engineer software by extracting its non-protected elements to improve its functionality. The Electronic Frontier Foundation describes reverse engineering as a long-established practice by persons who tinker with inventions to make improvements.

[C] The Libertarian Perspective of Intellectual Property

Libertarians contend that the market-based approach to IP worked appropriately that when Joseph Numero hired the African-American inventor Jones as an engineer, promoted him to chief engineer and eventually partnered with him at Thermo King. Libertarians would argue that Jones was free to make a contract with his employer and the government has no business interfering in Jones' market-based decisions. As Jones proved himself in the company, he was rewarded with promotions, finally becoming a co-principal. Jones' freedom to find another job gave him leverage in dealing with Numero.

Government overreach, libertarians contend, is responsible for most downsides of the patent system. Excessive patent litigation stifles innovation by diverting resources from product development into legal conflicts. Mozilla, producer of the Firefox browser, is critical of excessively wide-ranging software patents. The company's general counsel blogged:

> The threat posed by the growing pervasiveness of. . . overbroad and vague software patents is the shroud of [fear, uncertainty, and doubt] they cast over emerging and innovative technologies. It can feel impossible to know whether you are infringing someone else's software patent, which can slow or frustrate innovation. . . It is sadly ironic that much of the increasing cost of software patent issues are being borne by innovators themselves, the very individuals the patent system was supposed to incentivize.[34]

Ted Ullyot, an attorney for Facebook, acknowledges the valuable role played by IP law in the information industry but notes that "the widespread perception among Silicon Valley technologists today is that IP laws are often more of an impediment to progress and innovation than an enabler."[35]

Libertarians praise the Internet for its ability to liberate the free market from the giant corporations that attempt to use government power to obtain quasi-monopoly profits. Canada and Mexico, for example, allow more competition than the U.S. in pharmaceutical sales, resulting in lower prices for consumers. In the

United States, it is illegal to buy cheaper patented prescription drugs from other nations. However, U.S. officials have not been enforcing this unpopular law for purchases of less than three month's supply because punishing the poor and elderly for buying life-saving drugs at affordable prices has the potential to create a political firestorm. "E-pharmacies thrive despite the illegality of these foreign suppliers selling prescription drugs to American customers."[36]

[D] The Virtue and Duty Approach

Virtue theorists view intellectual property laws as ethical to the extent that they advance essential moral values, rather than maximize profits. For Immanuel Kant, intellectual property was not just an economic right to exploit but also a moral right, which was personal to its creator. Kant observed that intellectual property was "an inalienable property right but ironically could be transferred in commission and licensed to a publisher."[37]

During Kant's day, publishers frequently reprinted books without the author's permission.[38] Kant condemned copyright infringement as a violation of moral duty in a 1785 essay:

> If the idea of book publishing as such . . . were to be elaborated with the requisite elegance of Roman juridical scholarship, then actions against reprinters could very well be brought before the courts without it being necessary to apply beforehand for a new law to be promulgated in this respect.[39]

Virtue and duty ethicists would find that those who unilaterally misappropriated Jones' inventions, Martin Luther's writings or Immanuel Kant's books were morally wrong since these actions were treating these creators as a means to gain personal advantage as opposed to respecting "that person's dignity by allowing each the freedom to choose for himself or herself."[40]

[E] The Conflict Perspective Approach

The substantial number of inventors and authors who "create independently of the commercial rewards they may expect to receive" challenges the consequentialist justification for IP protection.[41] Lone software developers are often more driven by the love of creating a superior algorithm than the opportunity to become wealthy. Tim Berners-Lee, the inventor of the World Wide Web, allowed people to freely use this revolutionary development because his desire to have the system widely adopted was more important to him than collecting royalties. Berners-Lee explained, "Had the technology been proprietary, and in my total control, it would probably not have taken off. You can't propose that something be a universal space and at the same time keep control of it."[42]

Conflict theorists argue that most innovations build on a long chain of inventors. It is unjust that someone with legal expertise grabs the credit and the profits from what is really a creation with many contributors. Thomas Edison, for example, was only one of many people who could credibly claim to have invented the light bulb.[43] His brilliant former employee and later rival, Nicolas Tesla, died in poverty.

All patents must balance antitrust concerns against market dominance. Too much patent protection will undermine competitiveness and divert resources from research and innovation to litigation expenses. Congress' continuous expansion of the term of copyright casts doubt on the consequentialist rationale for IP law, according to conflict theorists.

Congress has amended the U.S. Copyright Act many times over the last two centuries, significantly expanding the term of copyright. The first copyright statute specified a fourteen-year term, until, in 1831, Congress doubled the copyright term to 28 years. The term expanded again in 1978, when Congress stretched the copyright term from 56 years to life of the author plus 20 years.

Walt Disney, the creator of Mickey Mouse, died in 1966. In 1998, with only five years left on the copyright protecting the Mickey Mouse character, Congress enacted the *Sonny Bono Copyright Term Extension Act of 1998*. The federal copyright statute expanded the terms of:

> copyrights for works created on or after January 1, 1978, to "life of the author plus 70 years," and extended copyrights for corporate works to 95 years from the year of first publication, or 120 years from the year of creation, whichever expires first. That pushed Mickey's copyright protection out to 2023.[44]

Without this Mickey Mouse bailout, the famous Disney character would have gone into the public domain in 2004. It is absurd, a conflict ethicist might argue, to suggest that this retroactive expansion will create increased incentives for creators such as Walt Disney or George Gershwin who have been dead for many decades. It is even a greater absurdity to extend the term of copyright for software by treating it as a literary work since the shelf life of software is often only a year or two. By the time copyrighted software enters the public sphere, 70 years after the death of the coder/author, the product is very unlikely to be of any public benefit.

Even social contract theorists express skepticism about retroactively extending the length of copyright protection:

> Under social contract theory, increasing the rewards to an existing innovation represents a violation of the contract. The innovator and society entered a contract at the time of the publication of the copyright-protected work; later changes to this contract break this agreement. Amendments also fail to provide incentives to innovate: how does extending the term of protection now encourage innovation occurring 50 years ago? For supporters of labour-deserve theory, term extension is less problematic. Innovators still deserve to benefit from the fruits of their labour and to receive a "just reward." If these fruits are still culturally and economically relevant, why shouldn't innovators continue to benefit from their efforts?[45]

§ 7.2: COMPUTER-RELATED PATENTS

[A] Patents in Early America

The idea of patents was controversial in early America, with some colonial inventors like Benjamin Franklin arguing that useful ideas should be virtuously shared for the benefit of the public. Franklin refused to patent the Franklin stove, writing:

> Gov'r. Thomas was so pleas'd with the construction of this stove . . . that he offered to give me a patent for the sole vending of them for a term of years; but I declin'd it from a principle which has ever weighed with me on such occasions. That, as we enjoy great advantages from the inventions of others, we should be glad of an opportunity to serve others by any invention of ours; and this we should do freely and generously.[46]

President George Washington's first Inaugural Address, in contrast, advocated for the establishment of laws that would provide "effectual encouragement as well to the introduction of new and useful inventions from abroad as to the exertions of skill and genius in producing them at home."[47]

[B] What Is Protectable by Patent Law?

The United States is a signatory to several multilateral treaties administered by the World Intellectual Property Organization (WIPO). WIPO, which was formed by a Convention signed at Stockholm on July 14, 1967, is an agency of the

United Nation dedicated to the rights of IP owners worldwide. WIPO describes a patent as a:

> document, issued, upon application, by a government office (or a regional office acting for several countries), which describes an invention and creates a legal situation in which the patented invention can normally only be exploited (manufactured, used, sold, imported) with the authorization of the owner of the patent. "Invention" means a solution to a specific problem in the field of technology. An invention may relate to a product or a process. The protection conferred by the patent is limited in time (generally 20 years).

[C] The Patent Examination Process

The United States Patent and Trademark Office, located in Alexandria, Virginia, is the federal agency that issues U.S. patents. There are two kinds of patent applications, provisional and regular. A provisional application is typically the first step towards getting a patent. It is typically filed 12-months before the "regular" application, giving the inventor a year-long grace period before the invention is made public. Once the "regular" application is filed, the invention is made publicly available and the patent term begins.

Under U.S. patent law, utility patent applications consist of a brief abstract of the invention, background about the invention, descriptions or drawings, a detailed explanation of how to make/use the invention, and one or more claims. A patent application is required to contain drawings, if drawings are necessary to understand the subject matter to be patented. The drawings must show every feature of the invention as specified in the claims.

(1) The Elements of a Patent

Patent prosecution encompasses the interactions between lawyers and patent agents and U.S Patent Office employees, who are called patent examiners. A claimed invention is what is given legal protection. Claims are the part of the application that determines the boundaries of the invention. They must demonstrate novelty, non-obviousness and utility.

(a) Novelty

Novelty means that a patent claim was not anticipated by technology disclosed in any prior patent or its equivalent. No novelty exists if the claimed invention was previously described in a printed publication or was available for public use before the filing of the claim. Novelty also requires that the patent claim include an inventive step that is different from the prior art. Companies threatened with patent infringement lawsuits will often defend against these lawsuits by demonstrating prior art such as "technical papers, scientific articles and even patent application that show technology already exists," thus invalidating the claim.[48]

Patent applications must not only describe in full and exact terms the claim but also satisfy enablement, which means the claim must "enable" a person of ordinary skill in the relevant art or science to make and use the invention. An application is be rejected if it is described without being enabling, such as a chemical formula with no disclosed or apparent method of making. A patent application is also likely to be rejected if it enables without providing an adequate description, such as a method of making a material without any specific formulation.

(b) Non-Obviousness

The non-obviousness requirement is the most difficult obstacle to overcome. The test for non-obviousness, is whether the subject matter of the patent, as a whole, would have been obvious at the time of invention to "a person having ordinary skill in the art."[49] "To invalidate a patent claim based on obviousness, a challenger must demonstrate by clear and convincing evidence that a skilled artisan would have been motivated to combine the teachings of the prior art references to achieve the claimed invention, and that the skilled artisan would have had a reasonable expectation of success in doing so."

The non-obvious requirement ensures that one cannot patent an invention after it has been accessible in the public domain. The statutory bar rule forbids issuing a patent for an invention that has previously been described in any printed publication in the U.S. or foreign country before the applicant invented it. Without this requirement, the ability to patent something found in nature, or something already publicly available, might be plausible.

(c) Utility

A claimed invention must have a utility that is specific, substantial and credible. This means that the invention must satisfy some practical use, which is not against public policy. For example, nuclear fusion occurs at temperatures in the tens of millions of degrees. In the late 1980s, two scientists claimed that they could create nuclear fusion at cold temperatures. The problem with the process was that no other scientist could replicate it. The USPTO would not grant a patent for the cold fusion process as it lacked utility because the patent applicant could not show how cold fusion achieved a useful result.[50]

(2) The Two Types of Computer-Related Patents

CHART TWO: COMPUTER INDUSTRY PATENTS

Patent Type	Description
Utility Patents (*Examples:* MRI scanner; telecommunication networking systems; software systems; satellite technologies)	Issued for the invention of a new and useful process, machine, manufacture, or composition of matter, or a new and useful improvement thereof, it generally permits its owner to exclude others from making, using, or selling the invention for a period of up to twenty years from the date of the patent application filing, subject to the payment of maintenance fees.
Design Patents: (i.e. iPhone face's configuration)	Issued for a new, original and ornamental design embodied in or applied to an article of manufacture, it permits its owner to exclude others from making, using, or selling the design. After May 13, 2015, design patents are granted for a term of fifteen years. Design patents are not subject to the payment of maintenance fees.

Chart Two above depicts the two most common types of patents: utility and design. A third type, plant patents, currently play no role in computer technologies. In the future, it is possible that advances in biotechnology will lead to computer-designed asexual plants that would make this category relevant. Ninety percent of the patent applications are for utility patents, which are sometimes referred to as "patents for inventions." Design patents are commonly used to protect the look of a computer monitor such as an Apple or Acer monitor. Computer technology disputes are disproportionately about utility patents, but design patent conflicts sometimes arise as in the litigation between Samsung and Apple over design features of the iPhone.

(a) Utility Patents

Utility patents are those granted to inventors who discover a new and useful process or a new and useful improvement to an existing patent. The U.S. Supreme Court in *Diamond v. Chakrabarty*[51] upheld a patent for genetically modified bacterium, observing that Congress had intended patentable subject matter to "include *anything under the sun* that is made by man." Utility patents are issued for four general types of inventions/discoveries: (1) machines, (2) human made products, (3) compositions of matter and (4) processes. Internet-related patents are typically utility patents, subcategorized as process patents, if they qualify as new and useful.

The television show, *Silicon Valley*, depicts the inventor of a valuable compression program who is naïve about the importance of filing a software patent that covers the technique:

> At the meeting, the Pied Piper people, prompted by admiring questions from the audience, quickly fill every white board with details of Pied Piper's clever compression technology. Finally one of the Pied Piper people catches on that the purpose of the meeting was not at all for Branscomb Ventures to invest in Pied Piper, but instead for people at the meeting to learn as much as possible about how Pied Piper's compression algorithm works. Surely, every intellectual property practitioner who was watching this episode of *Silicon Valley* shouted at the television, as I did, "file a patent application before you go to that meeting!" In a subsequent episode, a startup company called Endframe shows off its compression technology in the live streaming of a daredevil event sponsored by "Homicide energy drink". It turns out that Endframe is Branscomb's "compression play" and that Endframe's people were among the audience during the previously mentioned meeting. Had Pied Piper filed a patent application before going to the Branscomb Ventures meeting, its position with Endframe would be so much stronger.[52]

Internet utility patent disputes can result in awards of hundreds of millions of dollars to patent owners. In *Smartflash LLC v. Apple, Inc.,*[53] the Texas-based plaintiff was a holder of several U.S. patents, three of which were integral to storing and providing access to data through electronic payment systems. Smartflash asserted that the defendant, Apple Inc., infringed those patents through their iTunes software. The jury determined that the three patents were valid, and that the iPhone, iPod touch, and iPad devices that used certain functionality in the App Store and the iTunes store infringed the asserted claims.[54] It awarded the plaintiff $532,900,000 in damages. A 2012 study concluded that smartphones accounted for more than 250,000 patents;[55] sixteen percent of all active U.S. patents.[56] From 2006 to 2012, the USPTO granted 163,970 utility patents related to smartphones.[57]

(b) Design Patents

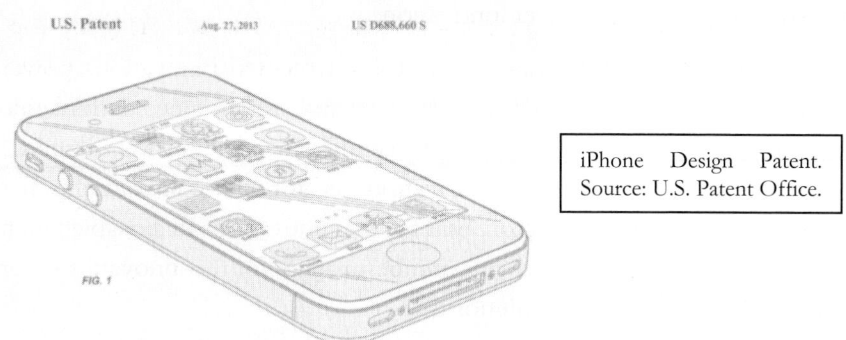

iPhone Design Patent. Source: U.S. Patent Office.

Utility patents protect the way an article is used and works, in contrast to design patents, which protect an article's appearance.[58] Design patents may be granted to anyone who invents a new, original and ornamental design for an article of manufacture. The USPTO considers computer-generated icons, including full screen images and type fonts, to be patentable.

Design patents are granted to those who invent a new, original and ornamental design for an article of manufacture. The design must be purely aesthetic and have no functional benefit. Design patents have a fourteen-year term, compared to the 20-year term for utility patents. Apple computers, iPads, or smart phones are all protectable by design patents for the exterior appearance of the objects. Manufactured products may possess both functional and ornamental characteristics, hence, the same object may be protected by both design and utility patents.[59] The USPTO requires that design patents not offend any race, religion, sex, ethnic group, or nationality.[60]

[D] Computer Industry Patent Issues

(1) Software Patents

Patent portfolios are increasingly valuable assets for technology companies. Defensive patents are secured not with an eye toward future royalties, but to prevent others from suing owners over their products and processes. Google purchased Motorola Mobility for $12.5 billion, principally to acquire its patent portfolio. An Apple-Microsoft-Oracle-Nokia consortium purchased Nortel's patent portfolio for $4.5 billion. Microsoft bought Novell's patent portfolio for $450 million and some of AOL's patents for $1 billion.

(2) Software Patent Litigation

The USPTO Director noted that patent protection is not given for mere lines of code that do not qualify as processes and apparatuses. Patents are not granted for abstract ideas but to protect innovation:

> Because many breathtaking software-implemented innovations power our modern world, at levels of efficiency and performance unthinkable even just a few years ago, patent protection is every bit as well-deserved for software-implemented innovation as for the innovations that enabled man to fly, and before that for the innovations that enabled man to light the dark with electricity, and before that for the innovations that enabled the industrial revolution.[61]

Software patents are particularly vulnerable to challenge because of their abstract nature and their lack of clear boundaries. Most of the high-profile cases against software moguls are for patent infringement. Eolas successfully sued Microsoft for $521 million for the "browser plugin patent" in 1998. British Telecommunications claimed it owned the patent for web hyperlinks and sued Prodigy for patent infringement in 1989. The Eolas case was stayed on appeal and the parties entered into a confidential settlement in 2007.

(3) Combating Patent Trolls

Critics of Internet-related patents contend that innovations would develop more rapidly without the type of patent protection that dampens competition. Companies like Facebook need a robust portfolio of software patents to stave off lawsuits by Patent Assertion Entities (PAE), pejoratively referred to as "patent trolls." PAEs are accused of acquiring patents just to extort productive companies through the threat of costly litigation:

> Founded in 2000, Intellectual Ventures (IV) has earned a special brand of hatred in the business world as the ultimate patent troll. It doesn't delay your flight like United, buffer your movie stream like Comcast, or shellac your shrimp with oil like BP. Rather, it hoards ideas. Over the past 14 years, IV has bought tens of thousands of patents and hired teams of scientists and lawyers to brainstorm and file for thousands

more. It then wields this intellectual-property portfolio—the world's largest—like a weapon. Companies can either pay up or face a lawsuit.[62]

A 2013 White House Report charged that these Patent Assertion Entities "focus on aggressive litigation, pursuing such practices as: threatening to sue thousands of companies at once without specific evidence of infringement against any of them; creating shell companies that make it difficult for defendants to know who is suing them; and asserting that their patents cover inventions not imagined at the time they were granted." On June 4, 2013, the White House introduced legislation to counter PAEs. Former President Barack Obama spoke about the problem of patent litigation at a Google+ hangout, saying that patent trolls 'don't actually produce anything themselves' and instead develop a business model 'to essentially leverage and hijack somebody else's idea and see if they can extort some money out of them.' "

The America Invents Act deters patent trolling by eliminating the practice of suing unrelated defendants in the same lawsuit unless the entities have coordinated their actions or there are common questions of fact. IP owners are calling for further measures against what they claim are extortionate tactics by non-practicing entities. The Business Software Alliance declares the patent troll's business is a form of litigation abuse because these patent owners have no economic purpose in obtaining patent protection other than holding up companies who build actual software products. Non-practicing entities are not always trolls. The label can also apply to universities and research institutes that have patent portfolios but do not themselves use the patents in inventions. Such entities are not the intended target of the AIA limitations on litigation.

(4) Patents & the Internet of Things

America's information-based economy increasingly rests on an infrastructure of software patents. Patents protect useful software processes in such fields as data analysis, computer graphics processing, multiplex and digital communications, cryptography, audio signal processing, image analysis, information security and electronic funds transfer. The rapid growth of semi and fully autonomous vehicle technology makes the auto industry increasingly dependent on patented software code. Modern high-end automobiles include over 100 million lines of code, which control ignition, anti-lock braking systems, assisted steering, parking systems and other features.[63]

The Internet of Things (IoT) is referred to as the "next industrial revolution." Researchers "project that there will be 34 billion devices connected to the internet by 2020, up from 10 billion in 2015," which will require $6 trillion to be invested in IoT solutions.[64] From agriculture to defense, retail to healthcare, everything is going to be impacted by the growing ability of businesses, governments, and consumers to connect to, and control their environments. A wide variety of Internet-connected devices will soon be coming to market:

> "Smart mirrors" will allow consumers to try on clothes digitally online, enhancing their shopping experience and reducing returns to the retailer.
>
> Assembly line sensors will detect tiny drops in efficiency that indicate that critical equipment is wearing out and schedule down-time maintenance in response.
>
> Agricultural equipment guided by GPS and IoT technology will soon plant, fertilize, and harvest vast croplands like a giant Roomba while the "driver" reads a magazine.
>
> Active people will share lifestyle data from their fitness trackers in order to help their doctors make better health care decisions (and capture discounts on health insurance premiums).[65]

(5) The Uncertain Borderline Between Patent and Copyright Law

The United States Supreme Court decided that two-dimensional designs appearing on the surface of cheerleading uniforms were entitled to copyright protection in the 2017 case of *Star Athletica L.L.C. v. Varsity Brands Inc.*[66] Varsity Brands filed a copyright lawsuit against Star Athletica, contending that its cheerleading uniforms infringed their copyrighted designs.

The Court held that an artistic feature of a useful article's design is eligible for copyright protection only if the artistic feature (1) can be perceived as a two- or three-dimensional work of art separate from the useful article (referred to as the separate identification requirement) and (2) would qualify as a protectable pictorial, graphic or sculptural work—either on its own or fixed in some other tangible medium of expression—if it were imagined separately from the useful article into which it is incorporated.[67] Prior to *Athletica*, the conventional wisdom was that apparel was outside the sphere of Copyright Act protection, which does not give protection to "useful items." Prior to *Athletica*, it was thought that ornamental features of useful articles was the province of patent law. Stretching copyright protection to ornamental design of useful articles gives owners a far long term of protection than for design patents.

§ 7.3: COPYRIGHT LAW FOR THE INTERNET

1882 Photograph of Irish playwright Oscar Wilde; *Burrow-Giles Lithographic Co. v. Sarony*, 111 U.S. 53 (1884) (the first copyrighted photograph); Public Domain Photograph

[A] Overview of Copyright Law

Copyright is the branch of intellectual property law that protects creative works such as books, drawings, videos and other forms of communication. "Copyright law protects the owner of rights in artistic works against those who 'copy,' that is to say those who take and use the form in which the original work was expressed by the author."[68] Federal enforcement protects IP rights to original works of authorship, including literary, dramatic, musical, artistic productions and even software. "Works covered by copyright range from books, music, paintings, sculpture and films, to computer programs, databases, advertisements, maps and technical drawings."[69]

Since the U.S. entered the Berne Convention in 1988, an author's copyright protection is automatic, beginning as soon as a work is created. For works first published on or after March 1, 1989, use of the copyright notice is optional. Before 1978, statutory copyright was generally secured by the act of publishing a work with a notice of copyright physically on the work. If a work remained unpublished, statutory copyright could be secured by the act of registration. If a work was published without a copyright notice, the work could enter the public domain and it would not have copyright protection.

Any work that was in the public domain on or before January 1, 1978, continues in the public domain. Originality requires independent creation by the author, accompanied by a minimal spark of creativity. An author may use a device such as a camera to create copyrighted works like the Oscar Wilde portrait shown above, which was the first time that copyright was recognized for a photograph in 1884. The U.S. Supreme Court ruled that it was within the constitutional power of Congress to extend copyright protection to photographs that qualified as a representation of an author's original intellectual conceptions.

[B] Software Copyright's Sphere of Application

Contemporary copyright protection extends to diverse, computer-related works of authorship, including clip-art, video games, thumbnails of copyrighted images, MP3s, DVDs and photographs. Software copyrights are a bundle of rights that include reproduction, adaptation, distribution, public performance and public display. The functionality of a website, protocol, or programming language does not qualify for copyright or trademark protection. In practice, it is difficult to separate functionality from expression.

Until the second half of the 1970s, software was largely protected by trade secrets because of uncertainty about whether code was copyrightable. The federal government's Commission on New Technological Uses of Copyright (CONTU) released a 1978 report urging Congress to further expand copyright protection for software. The Computer Act of 1980 amended the U.S. Copyright Act of 1976 to include "computer programs" within the sphere of application as "literary works" if they met the criteria of qualifying as an original work of authorship fixed in any tangible medium of expression.[70]

Courts determine whether certain portions of computer programs are protectable as "expression" or are outside the sphere of copyright law, being abstract ideas. Courts consider not only direct copying of computer code but also weigh the "structure, sequence, and organization" of a program. Copying the "look and feel" of a computer program's interface can also constitute copyright infringement.

(1) Originality

To prevail on a claim of copyright infringement, an owner must demonstrate that it owns a valid copyright and that someone copied protectable elements of the work without authorization. Copyright protection does not extend to ideas, program logic, algorithms, systems, methods, concepts or layouts. For software program creators, copyright is automatic, so long as there is a minimum spark of originality and the fixation requirements are satisfied. "For original computer programs . . . copyright automatically inheres in the work at the moment it is created without regard to whether it is registered."[71]

(2) Fixation

Copyright protects "original works of authorship fixed in any tangible medium of expression, now known or later developed, from which they can be perceived, reproduced, or otherwise communicated, either directly or with the aid of a machine or device." Owners secure a copyright automatically, only when the material is fixed in a copy, whether it be a manuscript, a script, a videotape, or another material object where a work can be read or visually perceived.

The U.S. Copyright Office states that fixation is rarely a problem for a copyright applicant. "Most works are fixed by their very nature, such as an article printed on paper, a song recorded in a digital audio file, a sculpture rendered in bronze, a screenplay saved in a data file, or an audiovisual work captured on film. Nevertheless, some works of authorship may not satisfy the fixation requirement, such as an improvisational speech, sketch, dance, or other performance that is not recorded in a tangible medium of expression." A computer program inscribed on a silicon chip satisfies the fixation requirement. Courts have held that a computer program is fixed when it exists in the RAM of a computer even though it will disappear when the computer is powered off.

(3) Derivative Works

Derivative works include translations, musical arrangements, motion picture versions of literary material or plays, art reproductions, abridgments and condensations of preexisting works. To be copyrightable, a derivative work must add original authorship to the incorporated work. Book editions that consist of editorial revisions, annotations and elaborations are examples of derivative works.

Courts have not provided clear guidance as to what constitutes a derivative work for computer programs. Software programs may qualify as derivative works if the author adapts existing software. A proprietary software licensor prohibits customers from developing derivative works without the licensor's permission, while open source licensors gives their customers the right to create derivative works that build upon the original code. Websites may also be protectable as derivative works.

The author of a copyrighted work has the exclusive right to prepare or authorize derivative works, sometimes called adaptation rights. For example, Jack Torne recently wrote the play "Harry Potter and the Cursed Child," which is an authorized derivative work where he collaborated with J.K. Rowling, author of the Harry Potter series. The Harry Potter stories have been translated from English into derivative works in at least sixty-eight other languages.

The movie "Frozen," released on November 2014, was a derivative work adapted from "The Snow Queen," originally published by Hans Christian Andersen in 1844. Disney was free to create a derivative of "The Snow Queen" as the work entered the public domain after its copyright expired.

[C] The Rights of Copyright Owners

Every Internet user has accessed copyrighted images or content on the Internet. YouTube alone claims more than a billion views daily "with more than 24 hours of new video uploaded to the site every minute."[72] Visitors upload 300 hours of content per minute.[73] James Rustad, singer-songwriter and psychiatrist from Burlington, Vermont, has dozens of videos on his YouTube channel. James' music and his website (www.jamesrustad.com) are protected by copyright, in large part, because it is easy to obtain protection.

James Rustad registered his first song, "Prozac Baby," with the U.S. Copyright Office, when he was only sixteen. Copyright not only protects James' musical works (e.g., his parodies), but also his articles published on a political website and the academic PowerPoint presentations he posts online for the psychiatry residents and medical students who work under his supervision. His article on "Risk Factors for Alcohol Relapse Following Orthotropic Liver Transplantation: A Systematic Review," which is published in *Psychosomatics*, the official journal of the Academy of Psychosomatic Medicine, is protected by a copyright held by Elsevier Inc., a leading medical research publisher.

"Prozac Baby" is not only an original work, but also a product of James' own mind. Prior to January 1, 1978, James would only have had common law copyright protection unless "Prozac Baby" had been registered in the U.S. Copyright Office. After January 1, 1978, registration is not a requirement for copyright protection. Copyright protection attached as soon as James created an original work of authorship and rendered it into a tangible form through fixation. When James registered "Prozac Baby" with the U.S. Copyright Office, he gained the right to bring a federal lawsuit against potential infringers, including persons who might copy, transmit or distribute his music without permission.

The 1976 Copyright Act defines publication as "distribution of copies or phonorecords of a work to the public by sale or other transfer of ownership, or by rental, lease, or lending." It also includes an offering to distribute copies or phonorecords to a group of persons for purposes of further distribution, public performance or public display. The owners of registered copyrights will qualify for statutory damages and attorney's fees in a copyright infringement case, so long as the registration occurs within three months after publication. Statutory damages are valuable because they do not require the copyright owner to establish the actual dollar amount lost by the infringement. These damages range between $750 per work for innocent infringement up to $150,000 per work for willful infringement.

Congress has bestowed upon those who register their copyrighted works before or within five years after first publication of the work, a presumption of validity in judicial proceedings. James' certificate of copyright registration is treated as evidence of the validity of the copyright.

U.S. copyright owners may not file infringement actions in federal court unless they have completed a registration. Registration makes it possible to obtain statutory damages and attorney's fees and makes it easier to enforce rights against foreign infringers. Registration also makes it easier to license copyrighted content and collect royalties. James holds the exclusive right to use or to authorize others to use his music, videos, journal articles and other copyrighted works. For example, James can authorize or prohibit downloading. He has the right to prevent other musicians from publicly performing his music in public, broadcasting it or translating it into other languages.

[D] The Advantages of Copyright Registration

Copyright owners register their copyrighted works with the U.S. Copyright Office at the Library of Congress. To register a work, the copyright owner submits a completed application form and submits a nonreturnable copy or copies of the work to be registered along with a fee. An application for copyright registration contains three essential elements: a completed application form, a nonrefundable filing fee and a nonreturnable deposit of the work—that is, a copy or copies. "Because computer programs are literary works, registration as a 'Literary Work' (Form TX) is usually appropriate."[74]

To register a software program, an author must: (1) file a copyright application, (2) pay a fee of $35 for a single work, single author and (3) deposit copies of the code with the U.S. Copyright Office. Forms to register copyrights are available at: www.copyright.gov. For computer software, the U.S. Copyright Office requires:

> For published or unpublished computer programs, send one copy of identifying portions of the program (first 25 and last 25 pages of source code) reproduced in a form visually perceptible without the aid of a machine or device, either on paper or in microform, together with the equivalent unit containing the copyright notice, if any. Online registration is ideal for computer programs not embodied in a CD-ROM. The source code may be uploaded electronically, preferably in PDF format. For a program less than 50 pages in length, send a visually perceptible copy of the entire source code.

For computer programs containing trade secrets, the author must include a cover letter stating that the claim contains trade secret material, along with the page containing the copyright notice, if any. The following textbox provides instructions on how to apply for a copyright for software.

How to Register a Computer Program and Its Screen Displays

An application for copyright registration contains three essential elements: (1) a completed application form, (2) a nonrefundable filing fee and (3) a nonreturnable deposit—that is, a copy or copies of the work being registered and "deposited" with the Copyright Office.

A single registration may be made for a computer program and its screen displays. When answering the "Type of work being registered" in eCO, choose the type most appropriate to the predominant authorship. Because computer programs are literary works, registration as a "Literary Work" is usually appropriate. However, if pictorial or graphic authorship predominates, registration as a "Work of the Visual Arts" may be made. Similarly, if motion picture authorship or audiovisual material predominates, registration as a "Motion picture/audiovisual work" may be made.

The registration will extend to any copyrightable screens generated by the program, regardless of whether identifying material for the screens is deposited.

Option 1: Answer "computer program" to the "Author Created" question. In this case, deposit the source code as described above. Depositing identifying material for screens is optional.

Option 2: Answer "computer program, including text of screen displays," or "computer program including audiovisual material" or "computer program including artwork on screen displays" in the "Other" portion of the "Author Created" question. In this case, you must deposit identifying material for the screen displays in addition to the required source code. Identifying material for the screen displays should consist of images or printouts clearly revealing the screens. If using online registration, images of the screens may be uploaded electronically to the electronic Copyright Office.

For works that are predominantly audiovisual, such as video games, ½-inch VHS videotapes, CD-ROMs, or DVDs, an upload of the audiovisual material to eCO (provided the file is not too large to upload) is acceptable. Note, too, that if the screens are reproduced in an accompanying manual, the manual will suffice as identifying material. The identifying material will be examined for copyrightability. When the screens are essentially not copyrightable (e.g., *de minimis* menu screens, blank forms, or the like), the application should not refer to screens. The description of authorship on the application should not refer to elements such as "menu screens," "structure, sequence and organization," "layout," "format," or the like.

Note: Registration of html or other formatting code for a website does not automatically cover any visible or audible copyrightable elements that are generated by the code. To register those portions of an online work, the entire copyrightable content must be deposited. It is possible to register the computer program together with the online work, but the deposit requirements for both the program and the online work must be fulfilled. See Circular 66, *Copyright Registration for Online Works*, for important information on the required deposit and how to complete the application when registering online works.

Source: U.S. Copyright Office, Copyright Registration for Computer Programs.

Copyright registration is simple and inexpensive, with only three easy requirements to satisfy: (1) a completed application form, (2) a nonrefundable filing fee and (3) a nonreturnable deposit. The copyright applicant must provide the U.S. Copyright Office with two copies of published works and one copy of works that have not yet been published. Copyright registration is not required but it is beneficial to include a copyright notice with or on any work—i.e., the letter c in a circle: ©, or the word "Copyright" and the first year of publication of a work (e.g., Copyright 2018 Thomas H. Koenig & Michael L. Rustad.)

If someone were to copy a pre-publication draft of this book before Westlaw registers a copyright, the copyright owner could not seek statutory damages or attorneys' fees. Registration also allows copyright owners to order the U.S. Customs Service to seize publications of copyright infringing copies. The textbox below summarizes the advantages of copyright registration:

The Advantages of U.S. Copyright Registration

Copyright Registration: In general, copyright registration is a legal formality intended to make a public record of the basic facts of a particular copyright. However, registration is not a condition of copyright protection. Even though registration is not a requirement for protection, the copyright law provides several inducements or advantages to encourage copyright owners to make registration. Among these advantages are the following:

Registration establishes a public record of the copyright claim.

Before an infringement suit may be filed in court, registration is necessary for works of U.S. origin.

If made before or within five years of publication, registration will establish prima facie evidence in court of the validity of the copyright and of the facts stated in the certificate.

If registration is made within three months after publication of the work or prior to an infringement of the work, statutory damages and attorney's fees will be available to the copyright owner in court actions. Otherwise, only an award of actual damages and profits is available to the copyright owner.

Registration allows the owner of the copyright to record the registration with the U.S. Customs Service for protection against the importation of infringing copies. For additional information, go to the U.S. Customs and Border Protection website at www.cbp.gov/. Registration may be made at any time within the life of the copyright.

Unlike the law before 1978, when a work has been registered in unpublished form, it is not necessary to make another registration when the work becomes published, although the copyright owner may register the published edition, if desired.

Source: U.S. Copyright Office, Copyright Basics (2017).

[E] Works Made for Hire

In general, the creator of a copyrightable work is the rights holder. The "work for hire" doctrine, however, is an exception to this general rule; it applies where a person creates, but is not the owner, of a copyrightable work. Once it has been established that a work made for hire was created, the hiring party is considered the author of the work. The doctrine considers an employer the copyright owner for works prepared by its employee within the scope of employment, even if the employer does nothing more than hire the employee who creates the work. Programmers who are employees of a software company will be writing code, subject to the work made for hire doctrine.

The employer owns copyrighted computer programs, computer applications and digital data produced by the employee within his or her scope of duties. The U.S. Copyright Office defines "work made for hire" as:

> (1) a work prepared by an employee within the scope of his or her employment;" or (2) "a work specially ordered or commissioned for use as a contribution to a collective work, as a part of a motion picture or other audiovisual work, as a translation, as a supplementary work, as a compilation, as an instructional text, as a test, as answer material for a

test, or as an atlas, if the parties expressly agree in a written instrument signed by them that the works shall be considered a work made for hire.[75]

§ 7.4: INTERNET-RELATED COPYRIGHT LAW

[A] Types of Copyright Infringement

U.S. copyright law recognizes three principal kinds of copyright infringement: (1) primary copyright infringement, (2) contributory copyright infringement and (3) vicarious copyright infringement as depicted below. Primary or direct infringement is copying by the primary wrongdoer without authorization, and this involves direct infringement of exclusive rights granted to the copyright holder, such as the right to reproduce, distribute, display or perform the protected work, or to grant permission for the making of derivative works. The peer-to-peer (P2P) sharing of online information such as videos, software and music has jump-started the law of secondary copyright infringement. Chart Three examines the three types of infringement addressed in the *Napster* case.

CHART THREE: TYPES OF COPYRIGHT INFRINGEMENT

Type of Infringement	*Test for Infringement*
Direct Infringement	Anyone who violates any of the exclusive rights of the copyright owner is an infringer and culpability is based upon strict liability. Common computer-related defendants include individuals, governments, organizations, and entities.
Contributory Infringement	(1) Did the defendant have actual or constructive knowledge of the copyright infringement by the primary wrongdoer(s)? (2) Did the defendant materially contribute to the copyright infringement by the wrongdoer? Common computer-related defendants include Online Service Providers, Device Manufacturers, and Peer-to-Peer Software Makers.

Vicarious Infringement	(1) Did the defendant have the right and ability to supervise the primary wrongdoer? (2) Did the defendant have a direct financial interest in the infringement by the primary wrongdoer? Common computer-related defendants include Online Service Providers and Device Manufacturers.

[B] The Digital Millennium Copyright Act

On October 12, 1998, Congress passed the Digital Millennium Copyright Act (DMCA), which is now part of the U.S. Copyright Act. Section 512 of the DMCA gives websites a safe harbor from secondary copyright infringement if they respond quickly to takedown requests for infringing third party postings. Each month, copyright owners request 75 million takedowns under the DMCA.

In the ordinary course of their operations, service providers must engage in all kinds of acts that expose them to potential copyright infringement liability. For example, service providers must make innumerable electronic copies simply to transmit information over the Internet. Certain electronic copies are made to speed up the delivery of information to users. Other electronic copies are made in order to host World Wide Web sites.[76]

The Online Copyright Infringement Liability Limitation Act (OCILLA) created limitations on liability for network service providers who fulfill specific safe-harbor exemptions. OCILLA developed a mechanism of takedown notices for infringing content on websites. In response, the service provider must remove the infringing material from its website. Upon receipt of a counter-notice objecting to the takedown, the service provider must replace the subscriber's material on the website.

The OCILLA seeks to limit the liability of ISPs for copyright infringement by their subscribers. The notice, takedown, put back and immunity sections of the DMCA are prime examples of how the Internet has reshaped copyright law. The takedown and put back rules of the DMCA arose out of the Internet's role as the world's largest copyright infringement machine.

The OCILLA protects online service providers (OSPs) who satisfy certain safe harbor requirements from having to pay monetary damages for direct, vicarious and contributory infringement.[77] To qualify for protection under any of the DMCA Section 512 safe harbors, a party must meet a set of threshold criteria. First, the party must in fact be a service provider, defined, in part, as an OSP.

Second, the network access provider also must adopt, reasonably implement and inform subscribers of, policies that provide for termination of accounts of recidivist copyright infringers.[78] Section 512 of the DMCA gives websites like YouTube a safe harbor for secondary copyright infringement so long as they comply with the statutory requirements, such as registering a copyright agent to respond to takedown down requests from copyright owners.

[C] Anti-Circumvention Provisions

The DMCA makes it a criminal offense for a person to produce or traffic in technologies intended to circumvent Digital Rights Management (DRM), which controls access to copyrighted works, whether or not there is actual infringement of a copyright. Software "that circumvents 'digital walls' in violation of the DMCA . . . is like a skeleton key that can open a locked door, a combination that can open a safe, a device that can neutralize the security device attached to a store's products, or a digital crowbar."[79] Protection technologies that limit the number of copies that infringers can make of music files, videos, or software are examples of DRM.[80]

In *Riot Games v. Argote*,[81] a California court awarded Riot Games $10 million for copyright infringement against a game-cheating bot maker whose product circumvented Riot's technological measures for controlling access to games such as Leaguesharp and League of Legends. Riot used anti-circumvention protection to prevent players from hacking, running automated software programs, cheating, or using unlicensed copies of Riot's games.

Riot charged the German defendants and their Peruvian shell company with selling game-breaking software that bypassed Riot's access controls. The court ordered the defendants to halt their sales of game-breaking software and to destroy all copies of their illegal software. The defendants were also prohibited from reverse engineering or decompiling Riot's games in the future. The latest DRM systems use forensic watermarking to augment traditional controls. This process conceals identifying marks in the software to make it easy to prove that the software had been copied in violation of the rights of its owner.

[D] Direct Copyright Infringement

Section 501(a) of the Copyright Act defines direct infringers as: "[a]nyone who violates any of the exclusive rights of the copyright owner."[82] To prevail in a direct infringement case, a plaintiff must satisfy two requirements: (1) it must show ownership of the allegedly infringed material and (2) it must demonstrate that defendants committed an act of "copying" this material.[83] A plaintiff must prove copying in fact by direct proof of the defendant's copying or proof that he or she had access. In *Napster*, the Ninth Circuit ruled that the P2P software provider's users directly infringed the copyrights owned by music and video makers.[84]

In a direct infringement case, the copyright holder must prove that the defendant had access to the plaintiff's work and copied it without authorization. A prevailing plaintiff in a copyright infringement case must choose between actual or statutory damages.[85] A defendant in a copyright infringement suit cannot use an "innocent infringer" defense to mitigate actual or statutory damages when the copyright owner attached a proper copyright notice.[86]

[E] Secondary Infringement

Secondary infringement is the enablement or inducement of copyright infringement by others and is akin to aiding and abetting a crime. Active steps to induce direct copyright infringement include advertisements directed to users of a P2P system that has been taken down for copyright violations. For example, Grokster's solicitations to former Napster users were used to prove secondary liability.

The first peer-to-peer service to impose copyright infringement liability was the Napster case. A federal district court found Napster liable for both contributory and vicarious liability because Napster's "Music Share" software enabled peer-to-peer exchanges of infringed copyrighted works. Because the user's equipment, and not Napster's, actually reproduced and distributed the MP3 file copies of the copyrighted works, Napster was not directly liable but instead liable for secondary infringement. The district court issued a preliminary injunction against Napster in July 2000. The Ninth Circuit affirmed that decision in 2001.

The appeals court found that Napster met the requirements for both contributory infringement and vicarious liability. As to contributory infringement, the Ninth Circuit found that Napster had actual knowledge of infringing activity being made possible by its software. The Ninth Circuit ruled that the software and services Napster provided materially contributed to its users' copyright infringement. As to vicarious liability, the panel found that Napster was benefiting from the infringement. The P2P network had both the right and ability to supervise the infringing conduct by blocking their users' access to Napster.[87]

[F] Fair Use in Cyberspace

Fair use, as codified in 17 U.S.C. § 107, is a statutory defense to copyright infringement designed to strike a balance between authors' exclusive rights and the public interest in having access to protected works for criticism, comment, news reporting, teaching, scholarship and research. Section 107 presents the four statutory factors courts must consider in determining if a particular use is fair or infringing:

> (1) The purpose and character of the use, including whether such use is of a commercial nature or is for nonprofit educational purposes;
>
> (2) The nature of the copyrighted work;
>
> (3) The amount and substantiality of the portion used in relation to the copyrighted work as a whole; and
>
> (4) The effect of the use upon the potential market for, or value of, the copyrighted work.[88]

The U.S. Copyright Office acknowledges that the line between fair use and infringement is often a difficult one to draw. No definitive rule determines how much of the content can be used without permission. Fair use protects teachers when they use a small portion of a work to illustrate a point in a lecture or in a book like this one. Fair use also protects quotations of excerpts in a scholarly work or a book review. Similarly, the First Amendment gives commentators the right to parody or poke fun at copyrighted works, which is also considered fair use.

In *Lenz v. Universal Music Corp.*,[89] a California district court ruled that a copyright owner had to consider the fair use doctrine when formulating a good faith belief about a takedown notice under the DMCA. Universal acted in bad faith in issuing a takedown notice for a 29-second video of an 18-month-old child dancing to Prince's song, "Let's Go Crazy," that had been uploaded to YouTube:

> Stephanie Lenz videotaped her young children dancing in her family's kitchen. The song "Let's Go Crazy" by the artist professionally known as Prince ("Prince") played in the background. The video is twenty-nine seconds in length. "Let's Go Crazy" can be heard for approximately twenty seconds albeit with difficulty given the poor sound quality of the video. The audible portion of the song includes the lyrics, "C'mon baby let's get nuts" and the song's distinctive guitar solo. Lenz is heard asking her son: "What do you think of the music?" Lenz titled the video "Let's Go Crazy # 1" and uploaded it to YouTube.com, a popular Internet

video hosting site, for the alleged purpose of sharing her son's dancing with friends and family.[90]

Universal sent a takedown notice to YouTube's designated address for receiving DMCA notices, "copyright@youtube.com," and demanded that YouTube remove Lenz's video from the site because it infringed its copyright. YouTube removed the video the next day and notified Lenz that they had taken down the dancing baby video because of Universal's charge that it infringed its copyright. YouTube's email also advised Lenz of the DMCA's counter-notification procedures.

YouTube also warned her that any repeated incidents of copyright infringement could result in them deleting her account. Lenz sent YouTube a DMCA counter-notification that their baby video constituted fair use of Prince's "Let's Go Crazy" and thus did not infringe Universal's copyrights. "Lenz demanded that the video be re-posted. YouTube re-posted the video on its website about six weeks later. As of the date of this order, the "Let's Go Crazy # 1" video has been viewed on YouTube more than 593,000 times."[91]

The *Lenz* court found that the dancing baby video was protected by fair use and that Universal's takedown notice was issued in bad faith. The court's ruling provided a deterrent message to copyright owners that they cannot mechanically file DMCA takedown notices without considering fair use. In the post-*Lenz* period, content creators who abuse the takedown notice system by filing meritless claims of infringement will be liable for damages.[92] Copyright owners have a legal duty to consider fair use before sending a DMCA takedown notice. Harvard Law Professor Larry Lessig satirizes the unpredictability of court decisions in fair use cases by labeling this doctrine as the fundamental "right to hire a lawyer."

§ 7.5: IS "LOOK AND FEEL" PROTECTABLE

The term look and feel refers to the graphical user interfaces, which encompass colors, shapes, layout and typefaces (the "look"), as well as the behavior of dynamic elements such as buttons, boxes and menus (the "feel").[93] Today, courts sometimes refer to this concept as the "total concept and feel," the "overall impression," or the "total feel."[94] By the mid-1980s, it was settled that the literal elements of a computer software program were copyrightable. It remained unclear whether copyright protection extended to the "look and feel" of a program, including its interfaces, menus, subroutines and methods of operation.

Perhaps the broadest interpretation of the look and feel doctrine is in *Data East USA, Inc. v. EPYX, Inc.*,[95] where access was only available to the plaintiff's arcade version of the video game KARATE CHAMP. The court found that the British developer of a home computer version had studied the arcade version so completely that it could program a competing game that duplicated its functions. However, on appeal, the Ninth Circuit held that the lower court had gone too far. The court reasoned that the substantial similarity between the two games was inherent in the nature of karate and was required by the constraints of the computer. Copyright protection is never granted for an idea, only for expression. Because the similarities related solely to the unprotected elements, the court granted summary judgment to the defendant.

The modern revisiting of the "look and feel" controversy is over Application programming interfaces (APIs). An API can be broadly defined as software specifications that enable programs to communicate with each other. The Electronic Frontier Foundation explains: "So when you read an article online, and click on the icon to share that article via Twitter, for example, you are using a Twitter API that the site's developer got directly from Twitter."[96] Oracle's predecessor company wrote these and other API packages in the Java programming language.

In *Oracle America Inc. v. Google, Inc.*,[97] the court applied the "look and feel" doctrine to thirty-seven packages of source code. Oracle's APIs are in widespread use by software developers. "Many software developers use the Java language, as well as Oracle's API packages, to write applications (commonly referred to as 'apps') for desktop and laptop computers, tablets, smartphones, and other devices."[98] A programmer who wishes to incorporate the functions of one or more of Oracle's API packages into a program that he or she is creating, could do so by using a short bit of "declaring code," which would command the computer to execute one of the specific prewritten programs. The code that the identified program used to carry out its function is called the implementing code.

The program packages were copyrighted by Oracle, which licensed them to users.[99] In May of 2012, the jury found that Google did not infringe on Oracle's patents and the trial judge ruled that the structure of the Java APIs used by Google was not copyrightable. In 2014, the Federal Circuit partially reversed the district court, ruling in Oracle's favor on the copyrightability issue. In 2016, a district court ruled in favor of Google, holding that its use of Oracle's API was protected by fair use. The appeals court reversed the district court, holding that the "structure, sequence and organization" of an API is copyrightable. It also ruled in favor of Oracle regarding the small amount of literal copying, holding that it was insignificant.

§ 7.6: ETHICAL DEBATES OVER PEER-TO-PEER COPYING

[A] Peer-to-Peer Copyright Infringement

With the invention of photocopying in the late 1930s, it was suddenly possible to quickly and cheaply duplicate a text. Today's technologies make it even easier to copy texts without permission. The ease of misappropriation has made the protection of intellectual property an important legal and ethical issue. Is it immoral to reproduce texts without the author's permission? The field of IP law provides mechanisms of enforcement against unauthorized copying, but has had limited success in addressing situations in which young people do not consider unauthorized copying immoral.

The Internet has spawned a copyright infringement ecosystem with "one-click hosters" or "cyberlockers" such as Rapidshare, Megaupload and Hotfile. Peer-to-peer file sharing programs, such as UTorrent, Bit Torrent and Vuze, allow their members to share all types of digital media with ease.[100] In many countries, people buy legal software and distribute it on peer-to-peer networks for no charge. For example, in much of Eastern Europe private citizens often use bootlegged versions of software applications.

[B] P2P Infringement: The Grokster Case

In *Metro-Goldwyn-Mayer Studios, Inc. v. Grokster, Ltd.*,[101] the plaintiffs filed a contributory infringement lawsuit against the developers of a P2P file-sharing program. Grokster and other P2P file-sharing defendants contended that their users employed the program for many legal exchanges, including authorized digital recordings, digital files of public domain books and authorized software files. The Court held the Grokster defendants liable for contributory infringement despite the fact that their software was capable of substantial non-infringing uses. The Court reasoned this P2P network was secondarily liable for third party infringement because it induced these illegal downloads and made no substantial effort to implement filtering.

In holding the file-sharing defendants liable, Justice David Souter imported an "inducement theory," reasoning that the defendants actively sought out former Napster users and did not develop controls to reduce P2P infringement. The inducement rule holds that "one who distributes a device with the object of promoting its use to infringe copyright, as shown by clear expression or other affirmative steps taken to foster infringement, is liable for the resulting acts of infringement by third parties."

§ 7.7: INTERNATIONAL IP LEGAL & ETHICAL ISSUES

[A] Global Patent Law Developments

Apple's iPhone success is in large part due to its design patents. Apple has filed a lawsuit, alleging that Samsung copied software found in its smartphone patents. In August of 2012, a federal jury found that numerous Samsung smartphones infringed and diluted Apple's patents and trade dresses in various combinations and awarded the innovative iPhone maker over $1 billion in damages. Trade dress is a trademarked distinctive design, packaging or other visual feature that will be discussed in Chapter Eight.

Apple contended that "Samsung copied 'rubber banding,' a term used to describe the way smartphone images pull away from the edge and bounce back when a user scrolls over with a finger." The federal jury found that Samsung willfully infringed Apple's patents for its "tap to zoom" and "finger sliding" commands. Samsung appealed this verdict to the U.S. Court of Appeals for the Federal Circuit.

The Federal Circuit affirmed the district courts, finding that Samsung had infringed on Apple's design and utility patents, while also reversing the jury's finding that Samsung infringed the iPhone's trade dress. Samsung argued on appeal that the district court erred in not excluding the functional elements of Apple's design patents in considering the alleged infringement. However, the appeals court rejected the argument and found the district court reasoning was proper.

In a related action, the U.S. International Trade Commission "ruled that Apple violated a Samsung patent covering technology used to send information over wireless networks." The ruling does not affect iPhone 5 or fourth generation iPads but it does mean that older Apple Inc., products may not be imported. The patent at issue is a "method for encoding/decoding a transport format combination indicator ('TFCI') in a CDMA mobile communication system."

[B] Global Issues in Copyright Law

Copyright law, like the other branches of intellectual property, is limited by the principle of territoriality.[102] In general, intellectual property rights are left to each nation to enforce, but increasingly international IP is harmonized through trade-related and other treaties. A copyright infringement claim may not be brought in U.S. courts for conduct committed entirely outside the territorial boundaries of the United States.[103] With the growth of the Internet, disputes between litigants in different countries are commonplace.[104]

(1) Moral Rights, Ethics & the Law

Under both U.S. and European Union law, an owner of copyrighted content has rights to publish, reproduce, distribute and perform works. European authors, in contrast to American content creators, have extensive moral rights. Under the moral right of attribution, an author has the right to be credited as the creator of a work even if the copyright has been transferred to another.

Manipulating an electronic or digitalized photograph could violate the artist's moral right not to have the work distorted, mutilated, or modified.[105]A French court ruled that the moral rights of movie director John Huston's estate were violated when Ted Turner colorized *The Asphalt Jungle*. The court concluded that the deceased director had deliberately chosen to film in black and white as an aesthetic choice. If this case had been filed in the U.S., it would have been dismissed because moral rights in the U.S. are only protected in the specific area of visual arts.

By joining the Berne Convention for the Protection of Literary and Artistic Works in 1988, the United States agreed to recognize moral rights within a very limited realm. The U.S.'s Visual Artists Rights Act of 1990 (VARA) protects the author's expectation that a visual work will not be revised, altered, or distorted. VARA has little application to the Internet because it only protects works of visual art that have attained the status of "recognized stature." VARA is the only example of moral rights recognized under U.S. Copyright Acts.

(2) Database Protection: Europe vs. U.S.

Special legislation has been enacted for computer technologies since the mid-1980s because of the uniqueness of software. In 1984, for example, Congress created a specialized statute to protect semiconductor chip mask works, which granted inventors a ten-year term of protection with copyright-like rights and remedies. These special-purpose statutes are called *sui generis* because they target a single technology, unlike copyright or patent statutes, which are general-purpose statutes applying to a broad range of diverse technologies. The Database Directive created a new *sui generis* right for database producers, valid for 15 years, protecting their investment of time, money and effort.

Similarly, the European Commission enacted the Database Directive in 1996, a specialized statute protecting collections of works, data, or other material for a fifteen-year term. The 1996 Directive requires member states to provide ways to protect the "substantial investment in obtaining, verification or presentation of the contents to prevent extraction and/or re-utilization of the whole, or a substantial part" of a database.[106] The Database Directive recognizes an exception for data used in either teaching or scientific research.[107]

Unlike copyright law's requirement that a work be original, this Directive provides protection for those compiling data that lacks originality, such as telephone or business directories, stock market quotations, sounds, images, numbers, facts, meteorological data, bibliographic data, photographs, DNA sequences, tissue banks and other compilations. Most collections of data that are arranged in a systematic way qualify for database protection, but not for copyright.

The United States has rejected Europe's work effort approach to *sui generis* protection for databases. In 1991, the U.S. Supreme Court held in *Feist Publications, Inc., v. Rural Telephone Service Co.*,[108] that compiling information alone does not satisfy the originality requirement for copyright protection. Databases must contain a "minimal degree of creativity" to be copyrightable in the U.S.[109] Rural filed suit for copyright infringement because Feist had copied entire volumes of its white page telephone listings.

The Court rejected Rural's "sweat of the brow" argument, finding that there was no infringement since Rural's compilation of phone numbers lacked minimal originality. Representatives of the Information Industry Association (IIA), the Information Technology Association of America (ITAA), the National Research Council (NRC) and other database producers regularly lobby Congress to adopt European-style database protection for non-original compilations.

(3) Cross-Border Copyright Litigation

In the first copyright dispute originating on Twitter in Germany, a Bielefeld, German court ruled that a tweet was not protectable under copyright law because it was not sufficiently original. A postcard company used a tweet commercially that had been tweeted.[110] The German regional court ruled that the following tweet lacked the linguistic creativity to qualify for copyright protection: "When exactly did sex, drugs & rock n' roll become lactose intolerance, Veganism and Helene Fischer?"[111]

Germany's Federal Court of Justice applied German civil law in making a father liable for his children's illegal downloading of Rhianna's album "Loud" on a peer-to-peer sharing service.[112] In 2016, YouTube entered into an agreement with the German Society for Musical Performing and Mechanical Reproduction Rights, which is Germany's state-sanctioned royalty collection group, which gives 70,000 musicians and songwriters' payment when their songs are played on YouTube.[113]

§ 7.8: THE ETHICS OF IP PROTECTION

[A] Consequentialism's Incentive Theory of Patents

Consequentialist theories of patents and copyright hold that we should have the laws that will produce the most beneficial results for society. "Each increase in the duration or strength of patents... stimulates an increase in inventive activity."[114] Social benefit is calculated by the value of the IP that is produced, "while administrative costs and larger deadweight losses associated with the higher prices of intellectual products that would have been created even in the absence of the enhanced incentive" are the negatives that may result from excessively lengthy patent terms.

Utilitarian scholars attempt to determine the optimal term for patent law, which will spur inventive activity while also allowing the patent to expire in a timely fashion. In *Sony Corp. v. Universal City Studios, Inc.*, the U.S. Supreme Court stated that copyright "is intended to motivate the creative activity of authors and inventors by the provision of a special reward, and to allow the public access to the products of their genius after the limited period of exclusive control has expired."[115] The Court's utilitarian view of copyright law is illustrated by its statement that "*encouragement of individual effort by personal gain* is the best way to advance public welfare through the talents of authors and inventors."[116]

The World Intellectual Property Organization (WIPO) also reasons that protecting copyrighted works spur economic growth by creating incentives for making new works:

> Copyright and related rights protection is an essential component in fostering human creativity and innovation. Giving authors, artists and creators incentives in the form of recognition and fair economic reward increases their activity and output and can also enhance the results. . . . This, in turn, helps to increase access and it enhances the enjoyment of culture, knowledge and entertainment the world over and also stimulates economic and social development.

The movie industry often uses consequentialist arguments to call for greater IP protection, asserting that America's media dominance is based on its "ability to pour into film enormous resources."[117]

[B] Virtue and Duty Theory

Virtue and duty ethicists would find much to admire in the European development of moral rights. The E.U.'s "moral rights" does not refer to the morality associated "with the religious right, but rather to the ability of authors to control the eventual fate of their works."[118] In the U.S, once a creative work is sold, the author surrenders all rights to the creation.

In contrast, the Berne Convention for the Protection of Literary and Artistic Works gives authors the "the right to claim authorship of the work and to object to any distortion, mutilation, or other modification . . . which would be prejudicial to his honor or reputation."[119] A virtue theorist would find that the author-centered moral rights law followed in Europe elevates the person, whereas in the U.S., the work-centered approach focuses too much on the economic benefits of the work.

[C] Conflict Theory & Copyright Law

Conflict theorists view the relentless expansion of copyright law as an example of how corporate publishers, filmmakers and software publishers are privatizing the cultural commons. In his 2004 book, *Free Culture*, Lawrence Lessig argued that excessive copyright robs people of their freedom to create, their freedom to build, and ultimately their freedom to imagine.[120] Yochai Benkler concludes that we should not let "yesterday's winners dictate the terms of tomorrow's economic competition." Web users must be vigilant to protect their right to freely communicate without mediation from big business and big government.

A conflict perspective would criticize the expansion of copyright law because it advances the interests of big media producers at the expense of the public domain. Is it necessary to favor Disney's IP in Mickey Mouse and other cartoon characters over those who might create more stimulating entertainment and cultural critiques by employing these cultural icons? Taking control of the means of production away from corporate elites can potentially lead to a more participatory and egalitarian society with a more robust common culture.

[D] Social Contractualism

Intellectual property law must strike the correct balance in the social contract between incentives for innovators and the rights of the public to have access to useful content. Social contract theorists contend that illegal copying threatens national competitiveness and the innovation that drives it.

The fast-growing information industries are essential for continuing American prosperity. Strict copyright laws may protect the interests of companies selling intellectual property products, but they must be fashioned in ways that give the public easy access to information through strong fair use rights.[121] The posthumous lengthening of Walt Disney's copyright protection period suggests that the balance may have swung too far toward corporate rights.

[E] Libertarian Views of Copyright Law & Patents

Lawrence Lessig describes the cyberlibertarian perspective of Internet governance as a space that cannot and should not be governed. "In its essence, cyberspace is a space of no control."[122] Cyberlibertarians vehemently oppose software patents, which are tollbooths on the Internet that block the free flow of information. Libertarians argue that these laws illustrate what Milton Friedman labelled "the tyranny of the status quo," where the established interests use their political power to thwart the free market under the guise of protecting individual rights.

Traditional libertarians have a long history of resistance to expansive intellectual property rights, stretching back to the 1800s. Benjamin Tucker, a nineteenth century editor of *Liberty*, for example, viewed intellectual property as another intrusive form of economic regulation. "Tucker agreed . . . that 'patent laws endeavor to add an artificial reward' to discovery that would 'retard, if not put a stop to, further inventions,' rather than incentivizing them."[123] The Internet's potential to increase individual freedom and creativity is threatened by overly invasive government regulation.

Some tech companies are offering bounties to uncover "patent killing evidence" through crowdsourcing invalidating the claims of patent trolls. Cloudfare, for example, offered $50,000 public bounties for any examples of prior art such as journal articles that would weaken Blackbird Technologies' patent claims. Cloudfare's bounty offer uncovered 200 sources of prior art that were useful in defending against claims that it infringed Blackbird's patent of "a system that monitors how data is transmitted back and forth across the Internet." Here, the libertarian approach of using self-help rather than government regulation is effectively countering overly aggressive claims of non-practicing entities.

CONCLUSION

Intellectual property has grown enormously in importance since Fred Jones applied for his first patent in the 1940s. Patents now protect innovations including the hardware and software that comprises the Internet's infrastructure. Business methods protection has been controversial since their inception. High-profile litigation and policy struggles over these and other issues will inevitably increase as the information age radically extends the importance of intellectual property. Multi-million-dollar litigation over Internet-related patent disputes is no longer unusual. The median cost of litigating a patent lawsuit is $1 to $3 million and it can run into the tens of millions of dollars where the amount at stake is great.

Copyrighted works are illegally transmitted and distributed as never before. Myxer.com, for example, is a cloud service allowing users to upload sound files and create ringtones, which they can then download and sent to their users' phones. Copyright law is territorial while the Internet is cross-border by its very nature. Each advance in digital interconnectivity brings new types of intellectual property concerns and novel ways to infringe property rights on a worldwide basis. However, U.S. intellectual property law is evolving to protect the rights of owners against infringing acts that originate in other countries such as IP agreements contained in international treaties.

CHAPTER SEVEN: REVIEW QUESTIONS

7.1: The Electronic Frontier Foundation notes that there is a company called Lodsys, which has a portfolio of software patents even though it neither makes nor sells products. Instead, it targets small app developers, claiming that their use of in-app purchasing technology (usually provided by Apple or Google) infringes Lodsys' patents. "It's impossible to know how many app developers Lodsys has actually threatened, but we do know that it has sued at least 11." What are the legal and ethical issues involved in obtaining patent claims with the sole purpose of charging licensing fees as opposed to incorporating patent claims in inventions? Are there legitimate reasons why a company would obtain patent protection if it is not incorporating patents into products or services?

7.2: A patent troll is the owner of a patent that does not use its intellectual property to produce products, but rather to file suit against alleged infringers. What steps should Congress take (if any) to address patent trolls?

7.3: Does it make sense to have juries composed of untrained citizens or even judges who have no technological education decide complex patent litigation? Should there be specialized courts to deal with technologically complex issues?

7.4: MyHealthInc. is the owner of U.S. Patent No. 6,612,985, which is entitled "Method and System for Monitoring and Treating a Patient." My Health also holds a trademark in the term "My Health." My Health claims that it is "the only person or entity entitled to use. . . 'My Health' in commerce."[124] Do you think the USPTO should grant this patent claim? Should the trademark office give My Health the exclusive rights to use the trademark of the same name? Please explain.

7.5: What are some of the factors courts consider in determining whether a work is a work for hire? Do you think that it is ethical for companies to require programmers to assign their copyrights to the company?

7.6: What are some of the differences between copyright law in the United States and Europe? How does the fact that American copyright law is work-centered while European law is author-centered impact software companies? Should this difference matter to a lawyer drafting a consulting agreement with a European website designer or computer programmer?

7.7: Should the look and feel of APIs be protected by copyright? What are the advantages and disadvantages of recognizing the Copyrightability of APIs? If copyright protection is given for APIs, how will this legal evolution affect the development of the seamless Internet and Internet innovation in general?

7.8: Do you think that the U.S. should recognize moral rights, such as the right of authors to prevent the distortion, mutilation or other modifications of their work that might harm their reputation?

7.9: In *Turner Entertainment Co. v. Huston*,[125] a 1995 case decided in a French regional court, the heirs of John Huston objected to Ted Turner's colorization of a 1950 film shot in black and white by Huston. The French court ruled that the Turner Company's colorization violated the creative activities of Huston and fined Ted Turner 400,000 French francs. The court also demanded that French broadcasters be forbidden from showing the colorized version of Huston's black and white film, "Asphalt Jungle." Do you agree with the French court? Why or why not?

7.10: Kant's categorical imperative provides: "Act only according to that maxim whereby you can at the same time will that it should become universal law." How would Immanuel Kant's deontological system of ethics evaluate peer-to-peer illegal sharing of copyrighted content?

7.11: What reforms, if any, do you think should be made to address the excessive litigation problem arising out of software patents? Are lawyers getting rich at the expense of the public's interest in inventors marketing new products, resulting in impeded technological progress?

7.12: Do you agree with cyber-libertarians who argue that IP is simply protectionist economic privilege? Why or why not?

7.13: Explain the different ethical theories that have made intellectual property a legal and cultural battleground. Give three or four examples of how conflict theory sheds light on IP developments.

7.14: Women victimized by revenge pornography have attempted to use copyright law to gain control over their explicit images that have been posted on the Internet. Before filing litigation to force a website to take down their salacious pictures, the victim must file with the copyright office by submitting a copy of the images they wish to control. What purpose does this requirement serve? Does it victimize the women twice by allowing a copyright official to look at the pictures? Should this requirement be modified and, if so, in what way?

7.15: The heirs of famous French author Victor Hugo, sued to block a sequel to *Les Misérables* in which the original ending of the book had been radically changed. They argued that the alternative version violated the moral rights of Victor Hugo by corrupting his original vision. Should the current owners of Hugo's copyrighted work be allowed to change it in any way they want? What if these changes harm the reputation and are counter to the identity of an author like Victor Hugo?

7.16: What should "fair use" look like in the Information Age? An author was sued for producing a version of "Gone with the Wind," entitled "The Wind Done Gone," which described the events and characters from the famous novel from the slaves' perspective. Should this be a violation of copyright and moral rights or should this be permitted as a parody?

7.17: Why do so many people who would never steal physical property believe that it is right to steal intellectual property through illegal copying? Are artists being unfairly deprived of the financial awards they should have earned? How should the laws against online piracy be modified and enforced? Should software that facilitates copying be banned through criminal law? Are lawsuits against illegal downloaders and other copyright violators ever justified? Does the United States need a Pirate Party along the lines of Sweden's political party that advocates for Internet freedom as a human right?

7.18: Girl Talk is an electronic artist who specializes in mash-up and digital sampling. His track "Shut the Club Down" samples "Girlfriend" by Avril Lavigne, who consequently sues Girl Talk. Do you think Lavigne should prevail in this lawsuit? What possible defenses can Girl Talk assert?

7.19: Adobe Illustrator allows users to "create logos, icons, drawings, typography, and complex illustrations for any medium." It essentially functions like a canvas on a computer. Should the drawings made with Adobe Illustrator qualify for the protections afforded by VARA? Explain.

7.20: Comedian Louis C.K. has a joke about Boston that goes as follows, "It's not an accent, it is a whole city of people saying most words wrong." Would Louis C.K. be able to seek copyright protection for this or any of his other jokes? Explain.

7.21: A law firm challenged the copyright of the Civil Rights anthem, "We Shall Overcome." What would a conflict theorist say about copyrighting a song that had its roots in slavery? "The song's roots run deep. Slaves sang, 'I'll overcome' in the fields; striking workers sang, 'We will overcome' on the picket lines. It was an African-American spiritual. So how did the version we know today get copyrighted at all?"[126] How should the court rule on whether this song should be copyrightable? What interests are at stake in this lawsuit?

7.22: In September 2015, a federal court considered the copyright claim for "Happy Birthday," held by Warner/Chappell. "Happy Birthday" had the same melody and similar words as the "Good Morning" song, which was written in 1893 by two sisters. The chart below illustrates the similarities:

Parallel lyrics of "Happy Birthday" and "Good Morning"

Happy Birthday Song	Good Morning Song
Happy Birthday to You	Good Morning to You
Happy Birthday to You	Good Morning to You
Happy Birthday Dear [Name]	Good Morning Dear Children
Happy Birthday to You	Good Morning to All

Publication of "Happy Birthday" occurred first in 1911 and it was mentioned at the time that the two songs shared the same tune. Do you think that the Happy Birthday song deserves copyright protection based on these facts?

REFERENCES FOR CHAPTER SEVEN

[1] Bern Carsten Stahl, *Social Issues in Computer Ethics*, Chapter 6 in LUCIANO FLORIDI (ED.), THE CAMBRIDGE HANDBOOK OF INFORMATION AND COMPUTER ETHICS, New York, New York: Cambridge University Press 2010) at 102.

[2] *Kimble v. Marvel Entertainment*, 135 S.Ct. 2401, 2406–07 (2015).

[3] Janine Rustad, *The House that Hill Built*, Minnesota State Historical Society Essay Contest (1972).

[4] VIRGINIA OTT & GLORIA BORDET SWANSON, MAN WITH A MILLION IDEAS: FRED JONES, GENIUS/INVENTOR (Minneapolis, Minnesota: Lerner Publishers Group, 1976).

[5] *Jones, Frederick McKinley* (1893–1961), BlackPast.org.

[6] Frederick McKinley Jones, Science and Technology, ENCYCLOPEDIA OF WORLD BIOGRAPHY, Enclopedia.com.

[7] Thermo King Press Release, *Thermo King Dedicates $7.1 Million R&D Center Investment to Frederick McKinley Jones* (July 30, 2007).

[8] "Jones was an African American born in Kentucky in 1893, in a country still simmering from the Civil War and all that it entailed; a country with entrenched ideas about where a black man ought and ought not go. Racism would impact the life of Frederick Jones but did not define him." *Frederick McKinley Jones,* Minnesota Hall of Fame, Minnesota Science & Technology (2016).

[9] 35 U.S.C. § 101 (Whoever invents or discovers any new and useful process, machine, manufacture, or composition of matter, or any new and useful improvement thereof, may obtain a patent therefor, subject to the conditions and requirements of this title).

[10] MPEP, 2106 Patent Subject Matter Eligibility [R-6]–2100 Patentability (2012).

[11] *See e.g., Altari Games Corp. v. Suffolk Software Company of America, Inc.*, 975 F.2d 832 (Fed. Cir. 1992).

[12] Joe Jennings, *Jury Verdict of Patent Infringement in Favor of iLife Against Nintendo Awarding $10 Million in Damages*, KnobbeMartens (September 13, 2017).

[13] Joe Mullin, *IBM Sues Priceline Over Patents, Because Prodigy Was Cool,* ARSTECHNICA.COM (Feb. 11, 2015).

[14] JAMES BESSEN AND MICHAEL MEURER, PATENT FAILURE: HOW JUDGES, BUREAUCRATS, AND LAWYERS PUT INNOVATORS AT RISK 23 (2008).

[15] 149 F.3d 1368 (Fed. Cir. 1998).

[16] John T. Aquino, *Patently Permissive: USPTO Filings Up After Ruling Expands Protection for Business and Net Software*, A.B.A. J., May 1999, at 30.

[17] Shareen Pathak, *End of an Era: Amazon's 1-Click Buying Patent Finally Expires*, DIGIDAY (September 13, 2017).

[18] 17 U.S.C. § 101.

[19] 17 U.S.C. § 106.

[20] Andrew Beckerman-Rodau, *The Problem with Intellectual Property Expansion*, 13 YALE JOURNAL OF LAW & TECHNOLOGY 35 (2010) at 81.

[21] ROGER MILGRIM, MILGRIM ON TRADE SECRETS (New, York, New York: LEXIS/NEXIS, 2005) at 1.05[5][b].

[22] *Bernd Carsten Stahl, Social Issues in Computer Ethics*, Chapter 6 in THE CAMBRIDGE HANDBOOK OF INFORMATION AND COMPUTER ETHICS (New York, New York: Cambridge University Press, 2010) at 101.

[23] Jones, Frederick McKinley (1893–1961), BlackPast.org.

[24] *Graham v. John Deere*, 86 S.Ct. 684, 690 (1966).

[25] *The Original American Mind*, Founders *and Philosophers of Freedom* (2016).

[26] Gene Quinn, Celebrating *Presidents Who Advocated for the U.S. Patent System*, IPWATCHDOG (February 11, 2013).

[27] Scott A. Allen, *'Justifying' the Public Interest in Patent Litigation*, 88 INDIANA LAW JOURNAL 1047, 1069 (2013) (discussing Rob Merges view of Rawl's theory of intellectual property rights).

[28] Justin Hughes, *Reply to Rob Merges, More on Rawls and Intellectual Property*, PRAWS BLAWGS (January 30, 2013).

[29] Intellectual Property, 3.2: *The Utilitarian Incentives-Based Argument for Intellectual Property*, STANFORD ENCYCLOPEDIA OF PHILOSOPHY (2011).

[30] Catherine Patterson, *The Chamberlen Family Secret*, Engines of Our Ingenuity (episode 2018).

[31] *Apprenticeship*, Encyclopedia.com.

[32] *A Billion Here, A Billion There: The Cost Of Making A Drug Revisited*, LIFESCI VC (November 21, 2014).

[33] John L. Miller, How *Much Does Microsoft Spend on Developing a New Operating System Like the Windows?* QUORA (January 31, 2010).

[34] *Innovation, Disruption and Intellectual Property: A View from Silicon Valley (Interview with Ted Ullyot, Facebook Attorney*, MARQUETTE LAWYER 33,35 (Summer 2017).

[35] *Id.*

[36] *Buying Prescription Drugs from Canada: Legal or Illegal?* ElderLaw Answers.

[37] Riccardo Pozzo, *Immanuel Kant on Intellectual Property* (2006) at 11.

[38] MARIA CHIARA PIEVATOLO, FREEDOM, OWNERSHIP, AND COPYRIGHT: WHY DOES KANT REJECT THE CONCEPT OF INTELLECTUAL PROPERTY? (July 2, 2010).

[39] *Id.*

[40] Claire Andre and Manuel Velasquez, *Rights Stuff*, Markkula Center for Applied Ethics.

[41] *Bernd Carsten Stahl, Social Issues in Computer Ethics*, Chapter 6 in THE CAMBRIDGE HANDBOOK OF INFORMATION AND COMPUTER ETHICS (New York, New York: Cambridge University Press, 2010) at 106.

[42] World Wide Web Foundation, *History of the Web.*

[43] Scott Berkum, THE MYTHS OF INNOVATION, O'Reilly Media, Sebastopol, California (2010).

[44] Steve Schlackman, *How Mickey Mouse Keeps Changing Copyright Law*, ART LAW JOURNAL (Feb. 15, 2014).

[45] Jeremy (no last name listed), *Katonomics 1: An Economic Perspective on IP: The Social Contract Theory of IP*, The IP Kat (November 7, 2011). http://ipkitten.blogspot.com/2011/11/katanomics-1-economic-perspective-on-ip.html.

[46] BENJAMIN FRANKLIN, AUTOBIOGRAPHY OF BENJAMIN FRANKLIN (Amazon Digital Services, Kindle Edition, 2016).

[47] Gene Quinn, Celebrating *Presidents Who Advocated for the U.S. Patent System*, IPWATCHDOG (February 11, 2013).

[48] Ayanna Alexander, *Is It Time to Offer Bounties for Patent Killing Evidence?* BLOOMBERG BNA: INTERNET LAW RESOURCE CENTER (July 19, 2017).

[49] The USPTO guidelines for determining obviousness state:

> Any obviousness rejection should include, either explicitly or implicitly in view of the prior art applied, an indication of the level of ordinary skill. A finding as to the level of ordinary skill may be used as a partial basis for a resolution of the issue of obviousness. The person of ordinary skill in the art is a hypothetical person who is presumed to have known the relevant art at the time of the invention. Factors that may be considered in determining the level of ordinary skill in the art may include: (1) "type of problems encountered in the art;" (2) "prior art solutions to those problems;" (3) "rapidity with which innovations are made;" (4) "sophistication of the technology; and" (5) "educational level of active workers in the field."

United States Patent & Trademark Office, *Examination Guidelines for Determining Obviousness* (2017).

[50] J. THOMAS MCCARTHY, MCCARTHY'S DESK ENCYCLOPEDIA OF INTELLECTUAL PROPERTY (New York, New York: Bloomberg BNA Books, 3rd ed. 2004) at 651.

[51] 447 U.S. 303 (1980).

[52] Oppedahl Blog, *Intellectual Property in 'Silicon Valley'* (June 19, 2015).

[53] 2015 WL 1907983 (E.D. Tex., Feb. 25, 2015).

[54] *Smartflash LLC v. Apple LLC*, 6 Tex. J.V.R.A. 8:C1, 2015 WL 1907983 (E.D. Tex. Feb. 25, 2015) (Verdict and Settlement Summary).

[55] "Modern products and services incorporate numerous technology components. The evolution of mobile devices provides an example. Based on our research, we believe there are more than 250,000 active patents relevant to today's smartphones, a significant increase compared to our estimate of approximately 70,000 patents that were active and relevant to mobile phones in 2000. This growth can be attributed to the expanded set of features and functionality incorporated in today's smartphones, including touchscreens, internet access, streaming video, media playback, application store readiness and other web-based services, and WiFi connectivity options." Disruptive Competition Project, *One in Six Patents Pertain to the Smartphone* (Oct. 17, 2012).

[56] Daniel O'Connor, *One in Six Active U.S. Patents Pertain to the Smartphone*, DISRUPTIVE COMPETITION PROJECT (October 17, 2012).

[57] Joel R. Reidenberg, *Patents and Small Participants in the Smartphone Industry*, World Intellectual Property Organization Study (Jan. 15, 2015) (Fordham Law School: Center on Law and Information Policy).

[58] 35 U.S.C. § 171.

[59] *Id.*

[60] 35 U.S.C. § 171 and 37 CFR § 1.3.

[61] David Kappos, Under Secretary of Commerce for IP & Director of the USPTO, *An Examination of Software Patents*, Keynote Address: Center for American Progress (November 12, 2012).

[62] Ashley Vance, *Silicon Valley's Most Hated Patent Troll Stops Suing and Starts Making*, Bloomberg (September 4, 2014).

[63] David Gelles, Hiroko Tabuchi and Matthew Dolan, *Complex Software Becomes the Weak Spot Under the Hood*, http://www.nytimes.com/2015/09/27/business/complex-car-software-becomes-the-weak-spot-under-the-hood.html (Sep. 26, 2015).

[64] BI Intelligence, *The Master Key to Understanding the IoT Revolution* (July 7, 2016).

[65] BI Intelligence, *This Exclusive Report Reveals the ABC's of IoT* (June 15, 2016).

[66] 137 S. Ct. 1002 (2017).

[67] *Id.* at 1007.

[68] World Intellectual Property Organization, *Fields of Intellectual Property Protection, Chapter 2 in World Intellectual Property Organization Handbook, Policy and Use* (2008) at 40.

[69] *Id.*

[70] 17 U.S.C. § 101.

[71] *Montgomery v. Noga*, 168 F.2d 1282, 1286 (11th Cir. 1999).

[72] *Viacom International Inc. v. YouTube, Inc.*, 940 F.Supp.2d 110 (S.D. N.Y. 2013).

[73] YouTube, *Statistics*, http://expandedramblings.com/index.php/youtube-statistics/.

[74] U.S. COPYRIGHT OFFICE, COPYRIGHT REGISTRATIONS FOR COMPUTER PROGRAMS (2015) (https://www.copyright.gov/forms/formtx.pdf).

[75] U.S. COPYRIGHT OFFICE, FORM TX.

[76] S. Rep. No. 105–190, at 8 (1998).

[77] *Hendrickson v. eBay, Inc.*, 165 F. Supp. 2d 1082 (C.D. Cal. 2001).

[78] 17 U.S.C. § 512(i)(1)(A).

[79] *Universal City Studios v. Corley*, 273 F.3d 429, 453 n. 27 (2d Cir. 2001).

[80] Bern Carsten Stahl, *Social Issues in Computer Ethics*, Chapter 6 in LUCIANO FLORIDI (ED.), THE CAMBRIDGE HANDBOOK OF INFORMATION AND COMPUTER ETHICS (New York, New York: Cambridge University Press 2010) at 105.

[81] No. 16–cv–5871 (C.D. Cal. March 3, 2017).

[82] 17 U.S.C. § 501(a).

[83] *Perfect 10, Inc. v. Amazon.com, Inc.*, 508 F.3d 1146, 1159 (9th Cir. 2007).

[84] *A & M Records v. Napster*, 239 F.3d 1004, 1013–14 (9th Cir. 2001).

[85] 17 U.S.C. § 504(a)(1)(2) (noting that copyright owner has the option of seeking actual or statutory damages).

[86] 17 U.S.C. § 401(d).

[87] *A&M Records, Inc. v. Napster, Inc.*, 239 F.3d 1004 (9th Cir. 2001).

[88] 17 U.S.C. § 107.

[89] 572 F. Supp.2d 1150 (N.D. Cal., 2008).

[90] *Id.* at 1151–1152.

[91] *Id.* at 1152.

[92] 17 U.S.C. § 512(g).

[93] David Bender & Craig Nethercott, *Lotus v. Borland At the United States Supreme Court*, 430 PRACTICAL LAW INSTITUTE 7, n. 1 (1996).

[94] *Blue Nile Inc. v. Ice.com Inc.,* 478 F.Supp.2d 1240, 1241–42 (W.D.Wash.2007).

[95] 750 F.3d 1339 (Fed. Cir. 2014).

[96] *Id.*

[97] 750 F.3d 1339, 1346 (Fed. Cir. 2014).

[98] *Id.* at 1346.

[99] *Id.* at 1350.

[100] *United States v. C.R.,* 792 F. Supp.2d 343, 352 (S.D. N.Y. 2011).

[101] 545 U.S. 913 (2005).

[102] *Suba Films, Ltd. v. MGM-Pathe Communications Co.*, 24 F.3d 1088 (9th Cir. 1994) (stating that it was indisputable that the United States' Copyright Laws do not apply outside the country's territorial borders).

[103] The leading case is *Suba Films, Ltd. v. MGM-Pathe Communications Co.*, 24 F.3d 1088 (9th Cir. 1994).

[104] PAUL GOLDSTEIN, CASES AND MATERIAL ON INTERNATIONAL INTELLECTUAL PROPERTY (New York: Foundation Press, 2000) at 18.

[105] CATHERINE COLSTON & JONATHAN GALLOWAY, MODERN INTELLECTUAL PROPERTY 450 (2010).

[106] *Id.*

[107] *Id.* at art. 9.

[108] 499 U.S. 340 (1991).

[109] *Id.* at 345.

[110] *Id.*

[111] Jabeen Bhatti, *Tweet Not Original Enough for German Copyright Protection*, BLOOMBERG BNA: INTERNET LAW RESOURCE CENTER (March 8, 2017).

[112] Jabeen Bhatti, *Copyrights: In Germany, Parents Can Be Liable for Kids Who Steal Music*, BLOOMBERG BNA: INTERNET LAW RESOURCE CENTER (April 12, 2017).

[113] Stefan Nicola, *YouTube Gets Unblocked in Germany After Truce with Rights Group*, BLOOMBERG BNA: INTERNET LAW RESOURCE CENTER (November 19, 2016).

[114] William Fisher, Harvard University Law School, *Theories of Intellectual Property* (2017) (discussing William Nordhaus' incentive theory of the term of patent protection).

[115] 464 U.S. 417, 429 (1984).

[116] *Golan v. Holder*, 565 U.S. 302 (2012).

[117] The Copyright Term Extension Act of 1995: Hearing on S. 483 Before the Senate Judiciary Comm., 104th Cong. 40–41 (1995) (statement of Jack Valenti, President and Chief Executive Officer, Motion Picture Association of America).

[118] Betsy Rosenblatt, *Moral Rights Basics*, Harvard University: Berkman Center (March 1998).

[119] Berne Convention for the Protection of Literary and Artistic Works, revised at Paris July 24, 1971, 828 U.N.T.S. 221 (Article 6bis (1)).

[120] Berne Convention for the Protection of Literary and Artistic Works, revised at Paris July 24, 1971, 828 U.N.T.S. 221 (Article 6bis (1)), *Id.*

[121] Computer Professionals for Social Responsibility, Intellectual Property (2016).

[122] LAWRENCE LESSIG, CODE AND OTHER LAWS OF CYBERSPACE (Cambridge, Massachusetts: Harvard University Press, 1999) at 24.

[123] David D'Amato, *Libertarian Views of Intellectual Property: Rothbard, Tucker, Spooner, and Rand* (May 28, 2014).

[124] Electronic Frontier Foundation, *Stupid Patent and Trademark of the Month* (May 31, 2016).

[125] *Turner Entertainment Co. v. Huston*, CA Versailles, civ. ch., December 19, 1994, translated in Entertainment Law Reporter, Mar. 1995, at 3.

[126] Elizabeth Blair, *Who Owns 'We Shall Overcome'? All of Us, A Lawsuit Claims*, NPR, All Things Considered (April 16, 2016).

CHAPTER EIGHT

Trademarks & Trade Secrets

§ 8.0: OVERVIEW OF THE LAW

[A] Introduction to Digital Trademarks

A trademark is a word, name, symbol, or device that is used in commerce to indicate the source of products and to distinguish them from the goods of others in the marketplace. Trademark law aims to ensure that, whether in Portland, Maine, or Portland, Oregon, a traveler coming upon a fast-food restaurant with the familiar golden arches will get the same food offered in all other McDonald's restaurants. Strong trademarks help companies create a solid identity, build consumer trust and distinguish their products. Trademark rights prevent others from using a confusingly similar mark, but do not prevent others from making or selling similar goods or services under a clearly different mark.

Distinctive trademarks are core assets for information technology companies. Five out of eight of the world's most valuable brands are owned by information technology companies. Apple's brand is the number one ranked trademark in the world, worth $170 billion, followed by Google at $101.8 billion and Microsoft in third place at $87 billion. Consumers purchasing an Apple iPhone are often willing to pay a premium because they know that they can expect a degree of quality consistent with the Apple brand. Apple is a trade name, meaning that it is a designation used by a company to distinguish itself from others in the same field.

A servicemark is the same as a trademark except that it identifies and distinguishes the source of a service rather than a product. E*Trade, for example, is a service mark for a particular company's online investing. Dropbox, Microsoft OneDrive or Google Documents also render services rather than sell goods. Amazon.com has a service mark that protects its Amazon Web Services. Oracle Services is a service mark owned by the Oracle Corporation.

The terms "trademark" and "mark" are commonly used to refer to both trademarks and servicemarks. The term "trademark" also extends to trade dress, which has come to include not only a product's packaging, but also the item's total image and overall appearance. Courts protect trademarks against imitation or unauthorized use, not because they represent creative or inventive leaps of the mind, but because they signify a sole source of a product and a certain level of consistency and quality to consumers. Apple Inc.'s various apple-shaped logos and the "Intel Inside" logo and sound are well-known computer-related trademarks, recognized worldwide.

Trademarks were prefigured by the use of distinctive marks made on Minoan pottery as early as 3500 B.C. The earliest English law reflecting a form of trademark was a Thirteenth Century regulation addressing bakers who stamped a distinctive mark on their bread. The guild houses of Brussels, Belgium incorporated marks as early as the Sixteenth Century. In the United States, the trademark Stetson® for hats and caps was introduced into commerce in 1866. Pillsbury® was first used in commerce in 1873 to identify the company's flour.

The growth of machine-made merchandise during the late nineteenth century and early twentieth century transformed trademark law, as mass-production allowed the creation of nationwide brands. In the last quarter of the twentieth century, courts began to expand what could be trademarked. Coca Cola®'s bottle shape was registered as a three-dimensional mark in 1977. In 1987, Owens-Corning obtained a trademark for the color pink when used in insulation. In 1991, Clarke's Osewez® was granted a trademark on a fragrance for use on their sewing thread and embroidery yarn.

U.S. courts scramble to keep pace with new types of trademark conflicts created by the digital age. Unique Internet trademark issues include: (1) domain names; (2) linking; (3) framing; (4) metatags; (5) pop-up windows; and (6) cybersquatting.[1] The misuse of a domain name that dilutes a famous mark is actionable under the federal dilution act. Commercial use of an Internet domain name may infringe or dilute another's trademark making the domain liable for trademark infringement. It is now settled law, however, that the use of a competitor's trademarks in keywords metatags does not constitute trademark infringement.

In the first trademark masquerading case, Tony LaRussa, a former Major League baseball manager, filed a complaint against Twitter for trademark infringement, false designation of origin, trademark dilution, cybersquatting, misappropriation of name, misappropriation of likeness, invasion of privacy and intentional misrepresentation. LaRussa's complaint alleged that an unknown

Twitter user opened an account under the name, "Tony La Russa." "The Twitter page consisted of unauthorized photos and written statements which included, 'lost 2 out of 3, but we made it out of Chicago without one drunk driving incident or dead pitcher.' "[2] Twitter voluntarily removed the account and LaRussa then withdrew his complaint about the La Russa Twitter account.

[B] Trade Secrets in the Digital Age

Broadly speaking, trade secrets protect "any confidential business information which provides an enterprise a competitive edge."[3] Trade secrets include industrial and commercial secrets as well as confidential information such as business plans or designs for new products. To qualify as a trade secret, some element must be unknown to the public.[4] Trade secrets are not registered, unlike copyrights, patents and trademarks. The only requirement for trade secret protection is that the owner implement reasonable security. The unauthorized use of such information by persons other than the holder is a misappropriation of trade secrets and considered a tort.

The World Intellectual Property Organization describes the broad scope of trade secrets:

> The subject matter of trade secrets is usually defined in broad terms and includes sales methods, distribution methods, consumer profiles, advertising strategies, lists of suppliers and clients, and manufacturing processes. While a final determination of what information constitutes a trade secret will depend on the circumstances of each individual case, clearly unfair practices in respect of secret information include industrial or commercial espionage, breach of contract and breach of confidence.[5]

Tesla Motors Inc. filed a trade secret misappropriation action against "the former director of its Autopilot program, accusing him of taking confidential information about the company's driver-assist system and trying to recruit at least a dozen former colleagues to a new startup."[6] In April 2017, Tesla settled the suit with its ex-employee, enjoining him from recruiting Tesla employees to Aurora Innovation, his new company, for a five year period. Tesla stated that the settlement "establishes a process to allow Tesla to recover all of the proprietary information that was taken from the company" and subjects Aurora's computer to future audits to determine whether it is using Tesla's confidential information.[7]

Information technologies have made it more difficult to protect trade secrets from hackers, disloyal employees and corporate spies as portable devices become omnipresent. Flash drives, mobile phones, and email are becoming the chief instrumentalities for stealing digital assets. Cybercriminals exploit security flaws in computer systems "to break into employees' portable devices and leapfrog into employers' networks—stealing secrets while leaving nary a trace."[8]

[C] Overlapping IP Protection

If copyright is the law of authorship and patent is the law of invention, trademark is the law of consumer marketing. Just as copyright overlaps patents, it also overlaps trademarks. When the Walt Disney Company gets a court order stopping the publication of unauthorized cartoons featuring Mickey Mouse, it is not only because Mickey Mouse is a trademark, indicating Disney as its source, but also because Disney owns the copyright of the Mickey Mouse image.[9]

Most of the value of information technology companies is vested in their intangibles; trademarks, patented processes, copyrighted content and their trade secrets. Computer companies are not unique in being deeply invested in protecting their IP. Multiple branches of IP law protect many consumer products, as shown in the example of Coca Cola that is depicted in Chart One below.

CHART ONE: HOW COCA COLA USES ALL FOUR IP BRANCHES

Branch of Intellectual Property Law	How Coca Cola Uses Each Branch
Patents	Design Patents for shape of bottle and vending machines; Utility patents for the formulation of its artificial sweeteners and drink dispensers.
Copyright	Protects advertising and promotional material.
Trade Secrets	Closely guarded formula for Coca Cola's recipe.
Trademarks	Trademark law protects slogans such as: "Taste the Feeling" as well as the contour shape of the bottle.

Coca Cola received the first design patent for a glass container when the patent office granted it protection for the "Contour" or "Hobble skirt" bottle's unique shape. The unique bottle design represents an ingredient in Coca-Cola, the Cocoa Bean Pod, which has a similar bulging middle. "In 1916, Coca-Cola debuted the patented bottle which would help distinguish it from competitors."[10]

Courts allowed the registration of the bottle's design as a three-dimensional mark in 1977.

Coca Cola holds patents for artificial sweeteners, drink dispensers, vending machines and countless other innovations.[11] Coca-Cola has patented technologies, including the Lumense's nano sensing that enables the bottler to detect contaminants in CO_2 gas for their carbonated beverages.[12] Coca Cola also claims a copyright of its website and its contents, including reviews, photographs, texts, videos, software, applications, games and audio files.

Trade secret protection lasts indefinitely, so long as the company can preserve its secrecy. The formula for Coca Cola, perhaps the best-known example of a trade secret, has been closely guarded in a vault since the company's founding in 1892.[13] Revealing a trade secret destroys its value and the right to legal protection is lost forever. Trade secrets are neither patentable nor subject to copyright, because these forms of intellectual property mandate public disclosure. Software companies will attempt to keep their proprietary source code concealed as a trade secret in situations where copyright protection is unavailable or undesirable.

[D] Overlapping IP Protection

Several branches of IP law similarly protect software, the chief asset of many information technology companies. Chapter Seven explained that software is copyrightable as a literary work, whether in source code or object code. During the 1980s, the patentability of software inventions was an unsettled question. Today, software patents protect long-distance communications networks, video and data communications, as well as Internet-related business methods.

The major technology companies control vast software patent portfolios that represent important company assets. For example, IBM inventors received 6,180 patents in 2011.[14] In 2014, IBM became the first company to earn more than 7,000 patents in a single year.[15] The next section examines how computer companies use trademark law to protect their products and services, while avoiding infringing the intellectual property rights of others.

§ 8.1: TRADEMARKS AS SOURCE IDENTIFIERS

[A] Defining Trademarks

Traditional or conventional trademarks are unique identifiers that employ words, logos, pictures, symbols, or a combination of these elements. Trademarks must be sufficiently distinctive to be protectable. Microsoft Windows' distinctive icon is an example of a trademarked picture or symbol. IBM uses trademarked letters to distinguish its products. Nike trademarked the phrase, "Just Do It."

The U.K. Intellectual Property Office "approved Amazon.com's trademarked slogans: "No Lines. No Checkout. (No, Seriously.)" and "No Queue. No Checkout. (No, Seriously)."[16] These trademarks are valuable corporate assets through which an online business can attract and retain customer loyalty. Amazon.com has a trademark clause in its license agreements listing its trade name as well as all Amazon.com related trademarks, including Amazon, Amazon.com, Amazon.com & Design, Amazon.com Anywhere, Amazon.com Auctions, Amazon.com Books, Amazon.com Outlet and scores of other marks.[17]

Mobile application names and icons are a new frontier for determining the contours of trademark law. European countries are more hesitant than the U.S. to approve motion, position, sound, color, smell, touch or texture marks. In May 2017, for example, the Chancellor of the High Court of Justice in London ruled that the dark and light purple colors on Glaxo Group Ltd.'s asthma inhaler were too imprecise to qualify for trademark protection in the European Union.[18] Even the United States has limits on what can be a source indicator. The USPTO has no taste marks currently registered, but the Trademark Trial and Appeal Board recently heard an appeal of the examining attorney's refusal to register the flavor orange for quick dissolve pharmaceutical tablets.

[B] The Strength of a Trademark

Courts evaluate whether a mark is sufficiently distinctive to warrant trademark protection based on a hierarchy of classifications. Trademark strength assessment is based on two factors: (1) "conceptual strength," or "placement of the mark on the spectrum of marks," which encapsulates the question of inherent distinctiveness; and (2) "commercial strength" or "the marketplace recognition value of the mark."[19] Fanciful or "coined" marks are the strongest marks, followed by arbitrary, suggestive, and descriptive.

A "fanciful" mark is a combination of letters or other symbols signifying nothing other than the product or service that which the mark represents. Google is a fanciful mark since before the search engine was launched, the word had no meaning. It originated as a play on the word "googol," which is 1 followed by one hundred zeroes. Apple is an arbitrary mark, since the term had no previous connection to computers. Suggestive marks require imagination and creativity, such as Microsoft's trademarked name that is suggestive because it makes consumers think of software for microcomputers.

Descriptive and generic marks reside at the bottom of the distinctiveness hierarchy. Descriptive marks, which describe the goods or services being sold, will receive protection only upon a showing they have acquired secondary meaning.[20] A descriptive mark that a trademark owner could not register initially may achieve trademark status and become subject to registration at some time in the future. "Windows," for windowing software, for example, has achieved trademark recognition. Perhaps the most famous descriptive mark that acquired secondary meaning is International Business Machines (IBM) for computers and business machines. A California district court concluded that the term "sex.com" was generic.[21] Even though it was not protectable as a mark, the domain name sold for $13 million in 2010.

Because the strength of a trademark for purposes of the likelihood-of-confusion analysis depends on the interplay between conceptual and commercial strength, the existence of inherent distinctiveness is not the end of the inquiry. "Context is critical to a distinctiveness analysis. . . [and the level of distinctiveness of a mark] can be determined only by reference to the goods or services that [the mark] identifies."[22] For example, the mark "Super-encrypted software" connotes computer security.

[C] What Cannot Be Registered as a Trademark?

The U.S. Congress created a federal system for the registration, protection and regulation of trademarks when it enacted the Lanham Act of 1946.[23] The Lanham Act has historically barred registration of marks that consist of or comprise immoral or scandalous matter, or matter which may disparage persons, institutions, beliefs, or national symbols, or bring them into contempt or disrepute ("the disparagement provision"). The Lanham Act has not traditionally permitted the registration of a mark that "comprises immoral, deceptive, or scandalous matter; or matter which may disparage or falsely suggest a connection with persons, living or dead, institutions, beliefs, or national symbols, or bring them into contempt, or disrepute."[24]

A disparaging mark " 'dishonors by comparison with what is inferior, slights, deprecates, degrades, or affects or injures by unjust comparison.' "[25] In 2014, the Trademark Trial and Appeal Board (TTAB) of the United States Patent and Trademark Office (USPTO) cancelled the Washington Redskins' trademarks, reasoning that the term "Redskins" disparages a "substantial composite of Native Americans." The Washington Redskins have continued to use the trademark for their team and merchandise, but they no longer have a right to defend their marks in federal court.

STOP THE ISLAMISATION OF AMERICA is an example of a disparaging mark that has been denied federal trademark registration as has Koran wine, Jesus juice, Buddha beachwear and wife-beater t-shirts. "The most publicized "disparaging" mark controversy in recent years is the cancellation of the Redskin football team's trademark registration because it considers the name and logo disparaging to Native Americans."[26]

The Federal Circuit developed a two-part test to determine whether a mark is disparaging:

> (1) what is the likely meaning of the matter in question, taking into account not only dictionary definitions, but also the relationship of the matter to the other elements in the mark, the nature of the goods or services, and the manner in which the mark is used in the marketplace in connection with the goods or services; and
>
> (2) if that meaning is found to refer to identifiable persons, institutions, beliefs or national symbols, whether that meaning may be disparaging to a substantial composite of the referenced group.[27]

(1) "THE SLANTS" Trademark Application

The U.S. Supreme Court recently ruled that the name of the Asian-American dance rock band, "THE SLANTS" was not disparaging, striking down the disparagement clause of the Lanham Act because it violated the First Amendment's Free Speech Clause. The case began in 2010 when Simon Tam, the "front man" for the band, sought to register the mark THE SLANTS for "Entertainment, namely, live performances by a musical band."

Tam chose this "moniker in order to reclaim the term and drain its denigrating force as a derogatory term for Asian persons."[28] THE SLANTS "draws inspiration for its lyrics from childhood slurs and mocking nursery rhymes" and has given its albums names such as "The Yellow Album," "Slanted Eyes," and "Slanted Hearts."[29] A large number of bands have registered names intended to be disparaging:

> The Slits, the Queers, Queen, Pansy Division, N.W.A. (Niggaz Wit Attitudes), and the Hillbilly Hellcats—there's that word again—are just a few examples. Other bands, looking to push the envelope both musically and culturally, have chosen names such as the Sex Pistols, the Dead Kennedys, the Butthole Surfers, Rapeman, Snatch and the Poontangs, Pussy Galore, Dying Fetus, and many, many more. Band names are also chosen to convey information about the music the group

> plays. It should come as no surprise that the Queers are not a Lawrence Welk cover band, the Revolting Cocks are not a string quartet, Dying Fetus does not play jazz standards, and Gay Witch Abortion would never open for Paul Anka. People who showed up to watch a band called Anal Cunt—yes it's real, but now defunct—knew they were probably not getting a cover of 'Careless Whisper.'[30]

(2) The Federal Circuit Court's Initial Decision

Simon Tam claimed that he had used THE SLANTS mark since 2006 in his appeal. The USPTO examining attorney again found the mark THE SLANTS disparaging and refused to register it for a second time. The initial panel of the Federal Circuit affirmed the examining attorney's refusal to register the mark, finding "it is abundantly clear from the record not only that THE SLANTS . . . would have the likely meaning of people of Asian descent but also that such meaning has been so perceived and has prompted significant responses by prospective attendees or hosts of the band's performances."[31] The Federal Circuit summarized the TTAB's reasons for finding the mark to be disparaging:

> To support this conclusion, the Board pointed to the band's website, which displayed the mark next to "a depiction of an Asian woman, utilizing rising sun imagery and using a stylized dragon image," and to a statement by Mr. Tam that he selected the mark in order to "own" the stereotype it represents. . . . The Board also found that the mark is disparaging to a substantial component of people of Asian descent because "[t]he dictionary definitions, reference works, and all other evidence unanimously categorize the word 'slant,' when meaning a person of Asian descent, as disparaging," and because there was record evidence of individuals and groups in the Asian community objecting to Mr. Tam's use of the word "slant." The Board therefore disqualified the mark for registration under § 2(a).[32]

(3) The Federal Circuit's En Banc Reversal of the TTAB

Next, Tam appealed to the full Federal Circuit Court, which, by a 9–3 vote, held that the disparagement clause of the Lanham Act violates the First Amendment's Free Speech clause.[33] The majority reasoned that the disparagement clause results in viewpoint-based discrimination. Thus, the court ruled that the disparagement clause is subject to the higher strict scrutiny standard of review, which it could not satisfy.[34] The majority also rejected the Government's argument that registered trademarks constitute government speech and that federal trademark registration is a private action rather than a form of governmental subsidy.[35]

(4) The Court's Invalidation of the Disparagement Clause

The U.S. Supreme Court accepted Tam's petition for certiorari on the issue of whether the disparagement clause "is facially invalid under the Free Speech Clause of the First Amendment." In June 2017, in a unanimous decision, the United States Supreme Court ruled that the government may not refuse to register potentially offensive names in the Trademark Office. Justice Alito, writing for the Court, ruled that the disparagement clause violates the Free Speech Clause of the First Amendment reasoning that:

> The clause reaches any trademark that disparages *any person, group, or institution.* It applies to trademarks like the following: "Down with racists," "Down with sexists," "Down with homophobes."... The clause is far too broad in other ways as well. The clause protects every person living or dead as well as every institution. Is it conceivable that commerce would be disrupted by a trademark saying: "James Buchanan was a disastrous president" or "Slavery is an evil institution"?[36]

The Court rejected the argument that trademarks are "commercial speech" or government speech, both of which afford a speaker less First Amendment protection. Justice Kennedy's concurring opinion was that the disparagement clause constituted viewpoint discrimination—the term the Supreme Court uses to classify government laws, rules or decisions that favor or disfavor one or more opinions about a contested public issue. After *Tam*, Trademark Examiners may no longer refuse or cancel a trademark on because it may "disparage . . . or bring into contemp[t] or disrepute" any "persons, living or dead." In addition to the disparagement clause Section 2 of the Lanham Act prohibits the registration of any mark that is:

> scandalous; immoral; deceptive; falsely suggestive of a connection with persons, institutions or religions; likely to cause confusion with an existing mark; descriptive; misdescriptive; functional; a geographic indication for wine or spirits other than the place of origin of the goods; government insignia; a living person's name, portrait or signature without written consent; or a surname.[37]

After *Tam*, trademark applicants are likely to challenge refusals based on many of the other categories as viewpoint discrimination under the First Amendment. An amicus brief filed by IP law professors contended that many of the broad list of bars to registration served a number of policies that went "well beyond protecting consumers from deception in the marketplace."[38] These grounds "cannot be justified on the basis that they further the Lanham Act's purpose in preventing consumers from being deceived". . . nor do they protect the markholder's investment in his mark."[39] In contrast, "bars for marks that are descriptive, misdescriptive, merely a surname, and functional limit the monopolization of words and designs that competitors may desire to use in commerce."[40]

[D] The Genericide of Trademarks

Genericide is the process by which a once strong trademark loses its distinctiveness and becomes a common noun. For example, B.F. Goodrich held the Zipper trademark, which was registered in 1925, "for overshoes with fasteners." As the fastener was incorporated into additional articles, other companies used the Zipper name as well. When B.F. Goodrich filed suit to protect its mark, the court ruled that Zipper had become a common noun and was therefore generic.

Flip phone, which was once a trademark of Motorola, has similarly become a generic term through popular usage. Other marks that have become generic include App Store, granola, yo-yo, aspirin, cellophane, heroin, thermos and trampoline. "Today, the fear of genericide haunts the proprietors of Kleenex, Baggies, Xerox, Walkman, Plexiglas, and Rollerblade, who worry about competitors being able to steal the names (and the reputation they have earned) for their own products. Writers who use the names as verbs, common nouns, or in lowercase type may find themselves at the receiving end of a stern cease-and-desist letter."[41] The chief test for determining genericide is the primary-significance test, which provides that a mark is not generic when "the primary significance of the term in the minds of the consuming public is not the product but the producer."[42]

The Ninth Circuit upheld a lower court ruling denying a petition to cancel Google's trademark. Two business persons were forced to relinquish hundreds of domain names containing the term google, despite their contention that "the GOOGLE mark has become generic because the vast majority of the public understands the word google, when used as a verb, to mean the indiscriminate act of searching on the internet without regard to the search engine used." To defend its mark, Google conducted a survey, finding that the public overwhelmingly identified the term "Google" with the company when the term is used as a noun.

§ 8.2: FEDERAL TRADEMARK REGISTRATION

[A] The Mechanics of Registering Trademarks

Under the Lanham Act of 1946, the user of a mark can register it with the United States Patent and Trademark Office. The two principal rights in a trademark are: (1) federal trademark registration, and (2) the right to use the mark. In general, the first party who either uses a mark in commerce or files an application in the trademark office has the ultimate right to register that mark. Then, if the registrant satisfies further conditions, including continuous use for five consecutive years, the right to use the registered mark in commerce to designate the origin of the goods specified in the registration becomes "incontestable,"[43] apart from certain enumerated exceptions.[44] Trademark applicants need to consider:

(1) The mark they want to register;

(2) The goods and/or services in connection with which you wish to register the mark; and

(3) Whether they will be filing the application based on actual existing use of the mark or a bona fide intention to use the mark in the future.[45] A trademark application "must specify the proper "basis" for filing, whether current use of the mark in commerce or on an intent to use the mark in commerce in the future."[46]

The U.S. Trademark Office conducts a search for conflicting marks as part of the official examination of an application only after the filing of a trademark application. In evaluating an application, the examining attorney conducts a search of USPTO records to determine whether there is a conflict between the mark in the application and a mark that is either registered or pending in the USPTO.[47] "When a conflict exists between the applicant's mark and a registered mark, the examining attorney will refuse registration of the applicant's mark on the ground of likelihood of confusion."

The U.S. Trademark Office publishes approved trademarks on the Principal Register of the United States Patent and Trademark Office (USPTO). The term of a federal trademark registration is 10 years, renewable indefinitely with successive 10-year renewal terms. The terms "trademark" and "mark" are used interchangeably. A servicemark is "a word, phrase, symbol or design, or a combination thereof, that identifies and distinguishes the source of a service, rather than goods."

The U.S. Trademark Office allows a company to use the "TM" (trademark) or "SM" (service mark) designation, which signals rights even if the organization has not registered its marks. However, a company may not use the federal registration symbol "®" until the Trademark Office registers the mark and there is no longer a pending examination. Trademark registration is based on classes of goods or services and a company must pay a separate registration fee for each class. A trademark registration is restricted to those classes of goods or services that a company offers or plans to offer.

USPTO: Grounds for Refusal on the "Likelihood of Confusion"

The USPTO may be required to refuse registration of your mark on numerous grounds. The most common are:

Likelihood of Confusion: The USPTO conducts a search for conflicting marks as part of the official examination of an application only after a trademark application is filed. In evaluating an application, the examining attorney conducts a search of USPTO records to determine whether there is a conflict between the mark in the application and a mark that is either registered or pending in the USPTO. The principal factors considered in reaching this decision are the similarity of the marks and the commercial relationship between the goods and services identified by the marks.

To find a conflict, it is not required that the marks and the goods/services be exactly the same; instead, it is sufficient if the marks are similar and the goods and or services related such that consumers would mistakenly believe they come from the same source. Similarity in sound, appearance, or meaning may be sufficient to support a finding of likelihood of confusion. The following are some examples of marks that would be considered similar:

Sound

YOUR MARK	CONFLICTING MARK
T. MARKEY	TEE MARQEE

Although spelled differently, the marks sound alike; i.e., they are "phonetic equivalents."

Appearance

YOUR MARK	CONFLICTING MARK
T. MARKEY	

The marks look very similar, even though the one on the right uses a stylized font.

Meaning

YOUR MARK	CONFLICTING MARK
LUPO	WOLF

The marks are similar because, when the Italian word "LUPO" is translated into English, it means "WOLF."

Commercial Impression

YOUR MARK	CONFLICTING MARK

Because the marks include the same design element, they create a similar overall commercial impression, even though the one on the right also includes words plus the design.

YOUR MARK	CONFLICTING MARK
CITY WOMAN	CITY GIRL

The marks convey a similar general meaning and produce the same mental reaction. Even if two marks are found to be confusingly similar, a likelihood of confusion will exist only if the goods and/or services upon which or in connection with the marks are used are, in fact, related. To find relatedness between goods and/or services, the goods and/or services do not have to be identical. It is sufficient that they are related in such a manner that consumers are likely to assume (mistakenly) that they come from a common source.

Source: United States Patent and Trademark Office, *Protecting Your Trademark: Enhancing Your Rights Through Federal Registration* Retrieved at: https://www.uspto.gov/sites/default/files/documents/BasicFacts.pdf.

In addition to the Lanham Act, states also have enacted their own trademark acts, which give protection only within that state. To acquire trademark and/or service mark registration at the state level, applicants must file an application with the trademark office of the specific state where they seek protection. Courts subdivide state unfair competition claims arising out of the defendant's misuse of trademarks into two general types: (1) consumer confusion as to the source of products, and (2) unfair trade practices, a residual category of unfair competition laws.

Unfair competition occurs when the defendant makes representations to deceive the public such as palming off on the trademarks of others. "Palming off" occurs when a defendant uses symbols that are substantially similar to that of a trademark owner. "Reverse passing off" typically involves removing or obliterating an original trademark on the plaintiff's goods, without authorization, before reselling those goods. The defendant is masquerading in trademark or trade dress of the plaintiff who actually produced the goods or services.

Even if a registered trademark has not yet achieved incontestable status, a certificate of registration of the mark on the USPTO's principal register constitutes strong evidence of its validity.[48] Trademark owners must file an affidavit, or a declaration of continued use, with the USPTO to keep the registration alive between the fifth and sixth year after the date of initial registration. Failure of the registrant to provide this affidavit results in cancellation of the trademark registration. Trademarks may still be established by using a mark in commerce, without a federal registration. The USPTO, however, explains the advantages of owning a federal trademark registration on the Principal Register in Chart Two below:

CHART TWO: WHY REGISTER TRADEMARKS

• Public notice of your claim of ownership of the mark;
• A legal presumption of your ownership of the mark and your exclusive right to use the mark nationwide on, or in connection with, the goods or services listed in the registration;
• The ability to bring an action concerning the mark in federal court;
• The use of the U.S. registration as a basis to obtain registration in foreign countries;
• The ability to record the U.S. registration with the U.S. Customs and Border Protection (CBP) Service to prevent importation of infringing foreign goods;
• The right to use the federal registration symbol ®; and
• Listing proof of ownership in the United States Patent and Trademark Office's online databases.

[B] Trademark Causes of Action in Computer Cases

(1) Trademark Infringement

The Internet creates many legal dilemmas for courts in applying trademark law. For example, a trademark can have more than one owner if the companies are clearly distinguishable. Courts consider the following factors in determining whether there is a likelihood of confusion or unfair competition: (1) strength or weakness of plaintiff's mark, (2) the degree of similarity with defendant's mark, (3) class of goods, (4) marketing channels used, (5) evidence of actual confusion and (6) intent of the defendant. No one factor is determinative as the likelihood of confusion test considers the totality of facts under the circumstances.[49]

The Lanham Act permits concurrent uses of the same mark in different geographic areas, if there is no likelihood of consumer confusion, mistake or deception. However, consumer confusion becomes a more likely possibility when both have a presence in cyberspace. Two companies named California Pools, for example, operated in different parts of that state without confusion before the rise of the Internet. The date of first use anywhere, which is the date when the goods were first sold or transported to the public or when the services were first rendered under the mark in commerce, establishes priority. Such use must also be genuine and in the ordinary course of trade.

To prevail on a claim of trademark infringement under the Lanham Act, a plaintiff must show that: (1) it owns a valid, protectable and nonfunctional mark, (2) the mark is inherently distinctive or has acquired secondary meaning, (3) the defendant uses, produces, counterfeits, copies, or imitates the mark in commerce without the plaintiff's consent and (4) the consuming public is likely to be confused with the concurrent use of the defendant's goods or services.[50]

In *AMF Inc. v. Sleekcraft Boats,*[51] the Ninth Circuit set forth eight factors for courts to consider in determining the likelihood of confusion in trademark infringement cases:

(1) Similarity between the plaintiff's mark and the allegedly infringing mark;

(2) Relatedness or similarity of the parties' products or services;

(3) The strength of the plaintiff's mark;

(4) The marketing channels used by the parties;

(5) The degree of care exercised by the public in selecting the goods or services at issue;

(6) The defendant's intent;

(7) Evidence of actual confusion; and

(8) The likelihood of expansion of the parties' product lines.[52] Most courts will base a likelihood of confusion assessment on all of these factors.

(2) Federal Dilution

Dilution refers to "the lessening of the capacity of a famous mark to identify and distinguish goods or services, regardless of the presence or absence of (1) competition between the owner of the famous mark and other parties, or (2) likelihood of confusion, mistake or deception."[53] Trademark dilution occurs when the diluting action would lessen the strong positive association of a famous mark.

Under the Trademark Dilution Revision Act (TDRA), "a mark is famous if it is widely recognized by the general consuming public of the United States as a designation of source of goods or services of the mark's owner."[54] To determine the requisite degree of fame, the court may consider all relevant factors including:

(1) The duration, extent and geographic reach of advertising and publicity of the mark, whether advertised or publicized by the owner or third parties;

(2) The amount, volume and geographic extent of sales or goods;

(3) The extent of the mark's actual recognition; and

(4) Whether the mark is registered.

A key distinction is made between trademark dilution and trademark infringement. Trademark dilution occurs when use of a famous trademark by someone other than the owner, impairs the mark's distinctiveness.[55] Unlike trademark infringement, dilution may occur whether or not the mark is used on a competing product, used in a damaging way such as registration of a verbatim domain name, or in a way that is likely to cause customer confusion. To succeed in a federal trademark dilution claim, the trademark owner may prove either dilution by blurring or dilution by tarnishment.

The TDRA statute defines "dilution by blurring" as the "association arising from the similarity between a mark or trade name and a famous mark that impairs the distinctiveness of the famous mark."[56] Blurring is the "whittling away" of a trademark's distinctiveness, while tarnishment links trademarks to shoddy or unwholesome products. The TDRA statute defines dilution by tarnishment as the "association arising from the similarity between a mark or trade name and a famous mark that harms the reputation of the famous mark."[57] Similarly, a domain name can tarnish a trademark, as in *Mattel, Inc. v. Jcom, Inc.*,[58] where the Barbie trademark was used on an adult entertainment web site.[59] The court held that the use of the Barbie trademark combined with particular fonts and color schemes tarnished the mark.[60]

To state a federal dilution claim under the TDRA, a trademark owner must show the following:

(1) It owns a famous mark that is distinctive;

(2) Defendant has commenced using a mark in commerce that is diluting the famous mark;

(3) A similarity between the defendant's mark and the famous mark gives rise to an association between the marks; and

(4) The association is likely to impair the distinctiveness of the famous mark or harm the reputation of the famous mark.

In a social media case involving the website Pinterest, the site owned federal trademark registrations for word marks "Pinterest" and "pin." Pinterest filed a lawsuit against the operator of a website-based travel planning service that used "pintrips" and "pin" word marks. In *Pinterest v. Pintrips, Inc.*,[61] Pinterest asserted claims for both trademark infringement and trademark dilution, seeking a permanent injunction against Pintrips. The court found that Pinterest failed to prove a likelihood of confusion between Pinterest and the Pintrips marks.

The courts concluded that the trademarks Pin It and Pin were generic, ruling that Pintrips had a right to use the word pin through fair use. What was also damning for Pinterest's federal dilution claim was the fact that at the time of Pintrip's formation, Pinterest was not yet considered a famous mark. In addition, the companies were in two completely separate markets, so there was little likelihood of consumer confusion.

Ben and Jerry's Homemade Inc., a maker of ice cream, filed a trademark suit based upon tarnishment against Cabellero Video, "barring it from selling its "Ben & Cherry's" series of DVDs with sexually suggestive titles including "Peanut Butter D-Cups" and "Boston Cream Thigh."[62] The Ben and Jerry's tarnishment case arose out of the defendant's use of the mark in adult videos, potentially harming the reputation of the Ben and Jerry's mark by associating it with pornography. A judge issued a temporary injunction, ordering the pornographers to "stop offering the 10 titles in its Ben & Cherry's series in the interim and to remove all online mention of the X-rated products."

(3) False Designation of Origin

The Lanham Act provides remedies for false designation of original, false or misleading description of fact that are likely to cause confusion.[63] A plaintiff must allege that the defendant used the plaintiff's mark in a manner likely to confuse consumers about the source or sponsorship of the goods or services.[64] To prevail in a false designation of origin claim, or in an infringement case, the plaintiff must prove that a defendant's use of the trademark would likely cause an appreciable number of the purchasing public to be misled or confused as to the source, sponsorship or affiliation of the goods or services.

False endorsement occurs when a plaintiff's identity is associated with a product in a way that misleads the consumer about that person's sponsorship, as defined under Section 43(a) of the Lanham Act. To state a false endorsement claim, the plaintiff must allege facts that, if true, would establish that:

(1) His or her name was used in commerce,

(2) The name is sufficiently distinctive and

(3) A likelihood of confusion exists. Under the federal Lanham Act, the trademark owner can recover up to three time's actual damages and obtain injunctive relief.

In *Ron Paul 2012 Presidential Campaign Comm., Inc. v. Does*,[65] the defendants owned a YouTube and Twitter account named "NHLiberty4Paul." Under this pseudonymous website, the defendants uploaded a video on YouTube entitled "Jon Huntsman's Values" that attacked the former Republican primary nominee before concluding with the text: "American Values and Liberty—Vote Ron Paul." Shortly after the video's release, the Ron Paul Campaign filed a complaint asserting a claim for:

(1) False designation of origin in violation of the Lanham Act,

(2) False description and representation in violation of the Lanham Act and

(3) Common law libel and defamation.

The federal court denied the Ron Paul Campaign's request for expedited discovery, citing the court's grave doubts about whether the plaintiff had satisfied the commercial use requirement for false designation of origin. In a trade name false designation of origin case, the plaintiff must prove that the defendant made commercial use of the protected trade name. In the *Ron Paul* case, the pseudonymous website was not operating a business or misappropriating any commercial benefit from the infringement.

(4) False Advertising or Misrepresentation

The Lanham Act imposes liability on those who "in commercial advertising or promotion, misrepresent the nature, characteristics, qualities, or geographic origin of his or her or another person's goods, services, or commercial activities."[66] To prevail on a false advertising claim, the plaintiff must prove four elements:

(1) That defendant made material false or misleading representations of fact in connection with the commercial advertising or promotion of its product;

(2) In commerce;

(3) That are either likely to cause confusion or mistake as to (a) the origin, association or approval of the product with or by another, or (b) the characteristics of the goods or services; and

(4) Injure the plaintiff.

A court upheld a default judgment in *Yelp v. Catron*,[67] where a Yelp user offered to create paid reviews of businesses to post on the "Yelp" website, in violation of the site's terms of service. "Catron used the Yelp Marks, without alteration, in connection with his review-selling business without Yelp's consent in a manner that is likely to cause confusion, mistake, or to deceive."[68] Catron sold Yelp reviews and "displayed the Yelp Marks prominently on *adblaze.com* and *BuyYelpReview.com* in connection with his business."[69] Yelp alleged trademark infringement, unfair competition, dilution of a famous mark and cybersquatting, in violation of the Lanham Act.

The court found evidence supporting each of Yelp's federal claims as well as state false advertising claims, which also made the defendant liable under California's Unfair Competition Law.[70] Catron falsely represented that he offered real reviews but drafted Yelp reviews of businesses that he had never patronized. Catron's advertisements also offered assurances that its reviews "would not be filtered out," which is a practice Yelp implemented to regulate and prevent the exact type of false reviews that Catron was selling. Despite these promises, Yelp did indeed filter out the bogus endorsements.

[C] Defenses in Federal Trademark Cases

Trademarks may be used on the Internet without the owner's consent if the use is protected by fair use, nominative use, or is entitled to a First Amendment-related defense. Just as copyright law has built-in speech safeguards in the fair use doctrine and in the idea-expression dichotomy, trademark law also raises First Amendment concerns. This is, in part, due to the "Federal Dilution Act, which exempts from its coverage fair use in comparative advertising, noncommercial use and all forms of news reporting and news commentary."[71]

(1) Parody

Defenses in federal trademark cases primarily focus around the constitutional limitations involving First Amendment freedom of speech rights. A defendant may raise the fair use defense to prove their use of the mark was not a "trademark use," such as, for example, involving the mark in a parody or satire. A parody is a "simple form of entertainment created by juxtaposing the irreverent representation of the trademark with the idealized image created by the mark's owners."[72]

A parody must convey two simultaneous—and contradictory—messages: that it is the original, but also that it is not the original and is instead a protected parody. In the 1976 comedy, Silent Movie, produced by 20th Century Fox, the villainous corporation, "Engulf & Devour," parodies the real-world conglomerate Gulf+Western Industries, which had recently acquired Fox's rival, Paramount Pictures. The fictional company's motto was "our fingers are in everything."

Fair use is a court-created defense in trademark law, as opposed to the statutory law of fair use in copyright cases. In *Lyons Partnership v. Giannoulas*,[73] the Fifth Circuit ruled that the Ted Giannoulas's creation, a sports mascot called The Famous Chicken, which satirically assaulted a Barney & Friends-style purple dinosaur look-a-like in his performance, constituted a parody protectable by the First Amendment. The parody made a trademark the brunt of its joke and therefore did not infringe upon the Barney trademark owned by Lyons Partnership.

In *Hormel Foods Corp. v. Jim Henson Prods.*,[74] the Second Circuit observed that a successful parody "tends to increase public identification" of the famous mark with its source. In Henson's film, Spa'am is the high priest of a tribe of wild boars that worships Miss Piggy as its Queen Sha Ka La Ka La. The court observed that, "[a]lthough the name 'Spa'am' is mentioned only once in the entire movie, Henson hopes to poke a little fun at Hormel's famous luncheon meat by associating its processed, gelatinous block with a humorously wild beast."[75] Hormel contended, "Even comic association with an unclean grotesque boar will call into question the purity and high quality of its meat product." The Second Circuit noted that the district court:

> found no evidence that Spa'am was unhygienic. At worst, he might be described as "untidy." Moreover, by now Hormel should be inured to any such ridicule. Although SPAM is in fact made from pork shoulder and ham meat, and the name itself supposedly is a portmanteau word for spiced ham, countless jokes have played off the public's unfounded suspicion that SPAM is a product of less than savory ingredients.[76]

In *People for the Ethical Treatment of Animals v. Doughney*,[77] the animal rights advocacy organization People for the Ethical Treatment of Animals (PETA) brought action against Michael Doughney, citing trademark infringement, dilution and cybersquatting for Doughney's use of the domain name, *peta.org*. Doughney argued that his website, "People Eating Tasty Animals," was a parody of People for the Ethical Treatment of Animals and thus protected by the First Amendment. A Virginia district court granted summary judgment to PETA.

The court found that Doughney used PETA's trademark "in commerce" based on a two-part rationale; first, his website offered links to other websites offering "goods and services," thereby providing the needed "connection with goods and services" required by the Lanham Act, and second, Doughney recommended that PETA "settle" or "make him an offer" to purchase the domain name from him, thereby making Doughney a cybersquatter.

(2) Descriptive & Nominative Fair Use

Descriptive fair use is the use of a term to fairly describe a product or service. Nominative fair use is the use of a mark to refer to the actual product identified by a mark, such as a blog that reviews products or services. Nominative fair use is not infringement, so long as the use is:

(1) Not as a trademark, but

(2) Fairly and in good faith

(3) To describe the goods and services.[78]

Nominative fair use is when the defendant uses the trademarked term to describe the plaintiff's product, "even if the defendant's ultimate goal is to describe his own product."[79] A federal court ruled that use of a trademark in a site's metatags constitutes nominative fair use, because searchers would have a much more difficult time locating relevant websites if the law outlawed such truthful, non-misleading use of a mark. The same logic applies to nominative use of a mark in a domain name.[80]

In *Designer Skin LLC v. S & L Vitamins, Inc., et al.,*[81] the federal court dismissed a trademark dilution claim arising out of the defendant's use of plaintiff's marks in both metatags and search engine key words. The court reasoned that nominative fair use protected this practice unless there was a suggestion of sponsorship by the trademark owner. Notably, the court reached this result because the plaintiff failed to submit adequate evidence as to the impact this use of its marks had on search results for plaintiff's mark.

The nominative fair use analysis allows a defendant to use the plaintiff's mark to describe the plaintiff's product, so long as the goal is for the defendant to describe her own product.[82] The difference between nominative fair use and classic fair use is due to the modern recognition that a descriptive term that acquired distinctiveness was protectable.[83] A computer repair shop, for example, can advertise that it fixes Dell laptops even though "Dell" is a registered trademark. An over-the-counter medicine may advertise that it contains the same active ingredient as a famous, but more expensive, brand.

In *Playboy Enterprises, Inc. v. Welles,*[84] the Ninth Circuit reversed a federal district court's grant of a preliminary injunction that restrained the defendant, Welles, from using the registered trademarks "Playboy" and "Playmate" as metatags in her websites. Welles graced the cover of Playboy in 1981 as the Playboy Playmate of the Year for 1981. Playboy Enterprises International (PEI) contended that Welles infringed the following trademarked terms on her website:

(1) The terms "Playboy" and "Playmate" in the metatags of the website,

(2) The phrase "Playmate of the Year 1981" on the masthead of the website,

(3) The phrases "*Playboy* Playmate of the Year 1981" and "Playmate of the Year 1981" on various banner ads and

(4) Her repeated use of the abbreviation "PMOY '81" as the watermark on the pages of the website.

The *Playboy* court found that Welles's use of metatags was protected by the "nominative fair use" defense of another's trademark, particularly since she had been Playboy's Playmate of the Year for 1981.[85] The trial court refused to enter an injunction enjoining Welles's use of trademarked terms such as "Playmate" and *"Playboy"* on her website, as Playboy requested. The Ninth Circuit affirmed the lower court's ruling that the use of Playboy's trademarks in metatags in the wallpaper was not within the nominative fair use shield as it was not necessary to describe Welles. The court also rejected Playboy's dilution claim, since the defendant was only selling Terri Welles products. The court found that Welles was not trying to divert traffic from *Playboy* and recognized the nominative use defense of Ms. Welles's use of the "Playboy" and "Playmate" trademarks in her website advertisements.

[D] First Amendment & Gripe Sites

Companies often find it difficult to enjoin websites critical of their goods and services. The First Amendment generally protects fan sites, rogue sites, or grip sites that mention trademarks to criticize companies, unless a court finds that those sites are deceptive and create consumer confusion. "Gripe Sites," such as PissedConsumer.com, must make clear that they have no affiliation with trademarks that the domain name incorporates, to avoid the likelihood of confusion.[86]

In the early years of the Internet, trademark owners often won lawsuits against domain name registrants who incorporated their trade names or marks. An early example of such a complaint occurs in *Bally Total Fitness Holding Corp. v. Faber*,[87] where a critic of the chain of health clubs set up an anti-Bally website entitled "Bally's sucks." Bally Total Fitness (Bally's) filed suit for trademark dilution because the defendant was using its trademarks in an unauthorized manner.

The federal court in California granted summary judgment in favor of Faber, reasoning no reasonable person would think Bally's is affiliated with or endorses the anti-Bally website. The court also found "fair use" in the website's use of Bally's intellectual property.[88] In addition, courts have upheld the right to "Gripe Sites" where trade secrets where asserted by the trademark owner.[89] The gripe site cases demonstrate the First Amendment can trump trademark protection.

[E] The Uses & Abuses of Domain Names

The manifest function of a domain name—or Web address—is to identify and locate computers on the Internet. The Internet Corporation for Assigned Names and Numbers (ICANN) seeks ways to minimize the abuses and misuses of domain name registrations that include deceptive and fraudulent practices, such as: "cybersquatting, front-running, gripe sites, deceptive and/or offensive domain names, fake renewal notices, name spinning, pay-per-click, traffic diversion, false affiliation, cross-TLD registration scams, and domain kiting/tasting."[90] A Working Group for ICANN identified "cybersquatting" as an example of registration abuse. The ICANN study found certain other abuses, listed below, not classifiable as cybersquatting, but as separate forms of registration abuse:

> *Gripe/Complaint Sites a.k.a. "Sucks Sites"*: Websites that complain about a company's or entity's products or services and use a company's trademark in the domain name (e.g. companysucks.com).
>
> *Pornographic/Offensive Sites*: Websites that contain adult or pornographic content and use a brand holder's trademark in the domain name (e.g. brandporn.com).
>
> *Offensive strings*: Registration of stand-alone dirty words within a domain name (with or without brand names).
>
> *Registration of deceptive domain names*: Registration of domain names that direct unsuspecting consumers to obscenity or direct minors to harmful content—sometimes referred to as a form of "mousetrapping."[91]

[F] Remedies Against Cybersquatters

(1) Anticybersquatting Consumer Protection Act (ACPA)

During the mid-1990s, when the World Wide Web was in its infancy, "cybersquatters" created a land office business in registered domain names of famous companies or public figures, which were acquired in order to sell them to their natural owners for an extortionate price. Potentially valuable domain names such as sex.com were traded, hijacked or even converted, in a Wild West style virtual land boom. For example, Coca Cola and Nike were allegedly "victims of squatters of their Twitter identities."[92]

Congress enacted the ACPA on November 29, 1999, to protect consumers and American businesses, as well as to nurture electronic commerce, by prohibiting the bad faith and abusive registration of distinctive marks as Internet domain names. Congress passed the ACPA "in response to concerns over the proliferation of cybersquatting—the Internet version of a land grab."[93]

The ACPA amends the federal trademark statute (Lanham Act) by creating a cause of action for trademark owners against those who incorporate their mark, or one confusingly similar to it, into a domain name. To state a claim for cybersquatting under the ACPA, a trademark owner must show the defendant:

(1) Registered, trafficked in, or used a domain name,

(2) That it is confusingly similar to the plaintiff's trademark,

(3) Had a bad faith intent to profit from that domain name.[94]

Domain names represent valuable commercial commodities for companies, as they offer 24-hour-a-day exposure on the Internet. In 2009, talk show host Jay Leno won a cybersquatting case against a defendant who used the domain name, "thejaylenoshow.com to direct Internet users to a real estate website."[95] A more recently invented trademark-related abuse is username squatting where entrepreneurs register usernames containing another's mark with the intent to sell the username to the trademark owner at a profit:

> Thus, we have Taylor Swift buying domain names like TaylorSwift.porn and TaylorSwift.adult as well as TaylorSwift.sucks, and Kevin Spacey also appears to have bought his own .sucks domain, all the while paying these extortionist sunrise prices. ICANN's deal is, you can register your trademark with us, and that will gain you admission to the gauntlet first, during which you'll be despoiled. Otherwise, once it's open season, we'll sell your precious domain for a bargain price to the first buyer who comes along.[96]

Rev. Jerry Falwell's Lawsuit Against Cybersquatter

Rev. Jerry Falwell became a household name in 1979 when he founded the controversial "Moral Majority" political movement. This powerful voice of the Christian Right mobilized tens of millions of followers through vocal opposition to legalized abortion, gay rights and feminism. Christopher Lamparello registered the domain name, www.fallwell.com, and launched a website that was scathingly critical of Reverend Jerry Falwell and his views on homosexuality. The website displayed a notice that it was not associated with Rev. Falwell and a link to the minister's real site. Falwell submitted a complaint to the National Arbitration Forum (NAF), in accordance with the International Corporation for Assigned Names and Numbers (ICANN) Uniform Domain Name Dispute Resolution Policy (UDRP), asking that the domain name be reassigned to Falwell.

To prevail in such a claim, the complainant must show that the registered domain name is identical, or confusingly similar to, its trademark, that the domain name is being used in bad faith, and that the registrant has no legitimate interest in the domain name. Falwell prevailed in a UDRP proceeding by a vote of 2–1 and obtained a declaratory judgment to transfer the domain name to his organization, Liberty Alliance. The lower court had found a likelihood of confusion between Rev. Falwell's trademarks LISTEN AMERICA WITH JERRY FALWELL and common-law marks FALWELL and JERRY FALWELL, upholding the transfer of the domain name. In *Lamparello v. Falwell*,[97] the Fourth Circuit reversed on all counts, holding that the domain name did not infringe Reverend Falwell's trademark rights in his name, absent a showing of likelihood of public confusion, and notwithstanding any initial confusion. The court concluded that Lamparello was not using such confusion for financial gain and that users would not be misled into thinking that the Fallwell website was authorized or sponsored by Reverend Falwell.

(2) Uniform Domain Name Resolution Policy

Domain name registrants agree in advance to settle disputes with trademark owners through the Internet Corporation for Assigned Names and Numbers' (ICANN) Uniform Domain-Name Dispute-Resolution Policy (UDRP). Claims of abusive registrations "may be addressed by expedited administrative proceedings that the holder of trademark rights initiates by filing a complaint with an approved dispute-resolution service provider."[98]

Today, the UDRP has largely displaced court actions to resolve disputes between trademark owners and domain name registrants. UDRP panels decided more than 20,000 disputes between trademark owner and domain names during the period 2000–2011.[99] Many domain name disputes involve multiple causes of action. UDRP panels have the power to cancel or even transfer domain name registration. UDRP panels have no authority to award monetary damages, statutory damages, or any other remedies typically assessed for Lanham Act infringement or dilution claims.[100]

Five Types of Domain Name Disputes Decided by UDRP Panels

Five categories of cases are typically decided by UDRP panelists:

(1) Cases where the domain name and trademark are wholly identical, or, cases where the trademark owner has a registered domain name and the generic Top-Level Domain (gTLD) might be different;

(2) Cases where a registrant's domain name incorporates the surname of a celebrity;

(3) Cases where a generic or descriptive word has been added to the trademark (such as "my," "direct," "e-");

(4) Cases where anti-corporate websites append the word "sucks" at the end of trade names; and

(5) Typosquatting cases where the domain name registrant relies on Internet users mistyping famous trademark names.

Many celebrities and public figures have filed UDRP complaints to transfer or cancel domain names based upon common law rights, including "Madonna, Julia Roberts, Eminem, Pamela Anderson, JK Rowling, Michael Crichton and Ronaldo."[101] *Madonna Ciccone, p/k/a Madonna v. Dan Parisi and "Madonna.com"*[102] was a 2000 case decided by the WIPO Arbitration and Mediation Center. Madonna filed her complaint with the WIPO Arbitration and Mediation Center on July 21, 2000, via email, and on July 24, 2000, via hardcopy.

Madonna charged that Parisi's domain name was identical to her registered and common law trademark MADONNA, in which she owned rights. She further contended that Parisi had no legitimate interest or rights in the domain name. Finally, Madonna charged Parisi with obtaining and using the disputed domain name with the intent to attract Internet users to a pornographic website for commercial gain based on confusion with her name and mark. The UDRP panel found no other explanation for Parisi's choice of the Madonna mark. Parisi contended that he had rights in the domain name because he registered MADONNA as a trademark in Tunisia prior to notice of this dispute.

The panel stated that Parisi's registration of a trademark did not create a legitimate interest in Madonna's trademark. Parisi's registration of Madonna's mark in Tunisia, the panel concluded, was done pretextually to protect his interest in the domain name. In addition, the panel found evidence that Parisi adopted "madonna.com" for the specific purpose of trading off the name and reputation of Madonna.

The panel further found that Parisi offered no alternative explanation for his adoption of the name. Parisi did not sufficiently explain why "madonna.com" was worth $20,000 to him, or why that name was thought to be valuable as an attraction for a sexually explicit website. The WIPO panel had little difficulty in finding evidence of Parisi's bad faith registration and use of the disputed domain name, Madonna.com.

Actress Julia Roberts filed a similar suit against a cybersquatter. The defendant registered a domain name with Roberts' name and launched the website http://www.juliaroberts.com, which featured a photograph of a woman named "Sari Locker." The cybersquatter then placed the domain name up for auction on eBay. Asserting common law trademark rights, the famous actress contended the domain name "juliaroberts.com" is identical and confusingly similar to the name "Julia Roberts." The panel transferred the domain name to Roberts, finding bad faith registration on the part of the registrant because he had registered more than fifty other domain names, including movie stars' names such as "madeleinestowe.com" and "alpacino.com" and a famous Russian gymnast's name, "elenaprodunova.com."

U.S. trademark owners have a choice of either (a) filing a complaint in a U.S. federal court of proper jurisdiction against the domain-name holder under the ACPA, or (b) in cases of abusive registration, submit a complaint to an approved UDRP dispute-resolution service provider. Plaintiffs overwhelmingly choose to have their disputes handled by UDRP panelists. The advantage of the UDRP is speed and low expense. Trademark litigation in the U.S. federal and appellate courts may cost hundreds of thousands of dollars and take years to complete.

Another advantage of the UDRP is that every domain name registrant is subject to its jurisdiction, whereas a plaintiff will need to demonstrate minimum contacts with the state to establish jurisdiction and bring a defendant into U.S. federal court. In many instances, a trademark owner is only seeking transfer or termination of the domain name, which can be accomplished quickly and less expensively under the UDRP.

A domain name's registration agreement with all accredited registrars incorporates the UDRP provisions. One of the UDRP provisions states that the Internet domain name registrar will cancel, transfer, or otherwise make changes to domain name registrations in response to a court order. Chart Three summarizes the factors that plaintiffs consider in choosing which legal route to take, as shown below.

CHART THREE: ADVANTAGES AND DISADVANTAGES OF UDRP PANELISTS

Basis for Action: Right of Trademark Owner to initiate proceedings: The UDRP is a policy between a registrar and its customer and is included in registration agreements for all ICANN-accredited registrars. Each ICANN-approved registrar requires domain name registrants to agree to submit to the UDRP dispute resolution. The UDRP Policy is incorporated into all Registration Agreements and is followed by all registrars.	**Basis for Action:** Anticybersquatting Consumer Protection Act (ACPA), 15 U.S.C. § 1125(d), is a U.S. federal statute enacted in 1999 that established a cause of action for registering, trafficking in, or using a domain name confusingly similar to, or dilutive of, a trademark or personal name. Plaintiffs must establish jurisdiction over "cybersquatters" who register Internet domain names containing trademarks with no intention of creating legitimate web sites.
Advantages for Plaintiff: Inexpensive, quick, and easy process of gaining control of domain names that are confusingly similar or that dilute plaintiff's trademarks. Decisions are communicated to the parties from the UDRP Provider within three days. Plaintiffs prevail in eighty percent or more of the UDRP proceedings and the defendant has no right of appeal.	**Advantages for Plaintiff:** Trademark owners can seek remedies for infringement including (1) injunctive relief, (2) accounting for profits made while misusing the owner's trademarks, (3) damages (including treble damages for willful infringement), (4) attorney's fees in the "exceptional case," and (5) costs of filing the action. Courts can file an action against the domain name itself, if they cannot get jurisdiction over the defendant's persons. A court can also file an order to deactivate an infringing domain name.
Disadvantages for Plaintiffs: Arbitral panels do not permit discovery, are uneven in qualifications, and have no ability to issue injunctions or to order the cybersquatter to pay damages. The UDRP proceedings favor	**Disadvantages for Plaintiffs:** Federal courts can take years to decide an ACPA case and it can cost tens of thousands of dollars. An ACPA lawsuit typically is ineffective because the Internet is too fast moving. Defendants can tie trademark owners up in expensive discovery and other pre-trial maneuvers.

trademark owners over domain name registrants.	Defendants have a right to appeal adverse decisions by the trial court.

[G] Anti-Corporate Sites and the UDRP

Companies seeking to shut down gripe sites are far more likely to find success under the UDRP panels than in the U.S. federal courts, which often refuse to enjoin gripe sites because of the First Amendment right of free speech. In a UDRP proceeding, the domain name, AirFranceSucks.com, was transferred to the airline but "the airline's victory at arbitration was not without controversy."[103] UDRP panels have disagreed on whether the word "sucks" added to a trademark is confusingly similar.[104]

A UDRP panel found that the domain name Radioshacksucks.com was not actually a gripe website. It linked to various pay-per-click links mainly aimed at directing visitors to competing third party commercial websites. The panel ruled in favor of Radio Shack and transferred the name.[105]

In one case, the "sucks" site was found to be confusingly similar to the complainant's mark, because a search engine would bring up the "sucks" site when the mark itself was entered as a search term.[106] UDRP panels distinguish between complaint websites expressing feelings about products and services, and those constructed for the sole purpose of extorting money from the trademark owners.

§ 8.3: OVERVIEW OF TRADE SECRET LAW

A trade secret must be neither generally known, nor accessible. A trade secret is protectable even if it is minimally novel, but some element must be unknown to the public.[107] Three requirements are necessary for trade secret protection:

(1) The information must be kept secret;

(2) It has potential or realized commercial value because it is secret and

(3) The owner must implement reasonable efforts to keep the information secret.

In the 1970s, IBM was nicknamed Big Blue because of the generous benefits it provided for its workers and employment was long-term. Technology firms such as Hewlett Packard and Polaroid were famous for the loyalty shared between employer and employee. The contemporary highly competitive business environment, in contrast, has led technology companies to develop fluid workforce policies that create high levels of employee turnover, which place the employer's trade secrets at risk. A computer company will typically protect its trade secrets through internal security systems, encryptions of data and nondisclosure agreements with their employees, consultants and customers.

Palmer Luckey, who developed virtual reality headsets, founded Oculus VR (Oculus), a Menlo Park, California video game equipment creator. In March 2014, Facebook's CEO Mark Zuckerberg acquired Oculus for $2.3 billion. In February 2017, a jury awarded ZeniMax $500 million because Luckey and Chief Technology Officer John Carmack breached a nondisclosure agreement, "impermissibly treating ZeniMax's technology as their own and usurping ZeniMax's standing in the VR marketplace."[108] The jury determined that Oculus did not misappropriate ZeniMax's trade secrets, but rather fraudulently misrepresented the origin of the product and violated ZeniMax's copyright for VR software. The lesson from the Oculus case is the high risk of trade secret misappropriation lawsuits when two startups share data "to get off the ground, but only one company made it big."[109]

[A] Trade Secrets as Economic Assets

Prior to the 1980s, trade secrets were the chief means that technology companies used to protect their computer code.[110] Today, all technology companies use trade secrets to protect information that has economic value if kept secret. Computer software is the "single most important 'product' eligible for trade secret protection." Algorithms, formulas, flow charts, software design documents, technical data about digital product performance, software development agreements and pending patent applications are all protectable as trade secrets. Information technology companies are vulnerable to trade secret theft because of the widespread use of consultants, contractors, and increased outsourcing.

[B] Requirements of Trade Secret Protection

A trade secret may include a combination of elements, some of which are generally known to the public. "[A] trade secret can include a system where the elements are in the public domain, but there an effective, successful and valuable integration of the public domain elements has been accomplished, and the trade secret gave the claimant a competitive advantage which is protected from misappropriation."[111] Unlike patents, copyrights or trademarks, state tort law is the only form of protection for trade secrets. But increasingly, federal statutes such as the Economic Espionage Act supplement state law remedies for trade secret owners.

[C] Trade Secret Misappropriation

The tort of misappropriation of trade secrets requires the plaintiff to prove:

(1) The existence of a trade secret,

(2) The acquisition of the secret because of a confidential relationship and

(3) The defendant's unauthorized use of the secret.

Companies must implement reasonable security measures in order for information to be protectable as trade secrets. At a minimum, an Internet company must label source code, plans and other documents with a statement that these materials are confidential and proprietary.

"Reasonable efforts" can include advising employees of the existence of a trade secret, limiting access to the information on a "need to know basis," and requiring employees to sign confidentiality agreements. Disclosure is the death knell for a trade secret, destroying its emblematic feature of secrecy. For example, having been disclosed in public court files or transmitted on the Internet destroys the information's trade secret status.

For a plaintiff to recover for misappropriation of a trade secret, it must prove that the defendant used the proprietary information in question for some commercial use. The owner must also demonstrate that the defendant wrongfully acquired the information or data. Wrongful acquisition occurs when there is a breach of duty of trust implied or imposed by law against employees, corporate attorneys, or fiduciaries, such as outside counsel. Economic espionage, interception of electronic communications, or computer hacking are often key in demonstrating wrongful acquisition of trade secrets.

An Internet company's hardware design, future designs, specifications for software projects, customer lists and other information of actual or commercial value are protectable by trade secrets if the company makes "reasonable efforts" to conceal the valuable information. Chart Four provides practice pointers for information technology companies to protect their trade secrets.

CHART FOUR: PREVENTIVE ACTIONS TO PROTECT TRADE SECRETS

Reasonable Means	Company Culture
Access Controls on Confidential Information	Limit access to trade secrets on a need to know basis; prevent inadvertent disclosure
Identify and Audit Trade Secrets	Label and mark information or data as trade secrets; use popups to label digital information as confidential.
Socialization of Employees	Teach employees to identify and protect trade secrets; make trade secret protection part of orientation; require new employees to enter into nondisclosure agreements
Implement Reasonable Computer Security	Implement password and access controls; provide secure online transactions, firewalls, anti-virus software, and encryption; monitor e-communications; physically isolate computer tapes and storage devices
Departing Employees	Exit interviews: reminder of duties of confidentiality and nondisclosure; limit access to company's computer system and letter to ex-employee summarizing duties of nondisclosure
Third Party Consultants, Temporary Workers, Contractors, Joint Venturers, Computer Programmers, Website Designers	NDAs; access controls on a need to know basis; workplace training on how to protect trade secrets; policy outlined in employment handbook

[D] The Law Governing Trade Secrets

The Uniform Trade Secrets Act (UTSA) is a Model Statute drafted by the National Conference of Commissioners on Uniform State Law (NCCUSL) to update and harmonize the law concerning the misappropriation of trade secrets. Misappropriation under UTSA means "the disclosure or use of a trade secret of another without express or implied consent by a person who, at the time of disclosure, knew or should have known that knowledge of the trade secret was acquired under circumstances giving rise to a duty to maintain its secrecy."[112] The trade secret owner must prove that the defendant "under circumstances giving rise to a duty" to maintain confidentiality.[113] UTSA defines trade secrets broadly as information that has either potential or actual economic value.[114]

UTSA is the chief law for misappropriation claims in every state except Massachusetts and New York. The model statute defines trade secrets to include: "a formula, pattern, compilation, program, device, method, technique, or process, that:

(1) Derives independent economic value, actual or potential, from not being generally known to the public or to other persons who can obtain economic value from its disclosure or use and

(2) Is the subject of efforts that are reasonable under the circumstances to maintain its secrecy."

In contrast, The Restatement (Third) of Competition requires that information derive value from not being generally known and it focuses on whether a wrongdoer acquires the information during a confidential relationship.

In *Cellular Accessories for Less v. Trinitat LLC*,[115] Cellular Accessories fired its sales account manager who worked for them from 2004–2010. The ex-employee started his own mobile phone accessory firm, Trinitat. Cellular Accessories alleged that its former employee violated UTSA when he emailed himself a digital file that contained information on over 900 business and personal contacts and a separate file with client billing preferences and past pricing requests. Cellular Accessories also alleged that its ex-employee violated UTSA by maintaining his LinkedIn account that contained contact information. The court refused to enter summary judgment on behalf of the defendant and let the trade secret case proceed.

Information technology trade secrets can include source code, software specifications, the design of application program interfaces and almost any aspect of an online business. Courts consider six factors in determining whether confidential information constitutes a trade secret:

(1) The extent to which the information is known outside the business,

(2) The extent to which it is known to those inside the business, i.e., by the employees,

(3) The precautions taken by the holder of the trade secret to guard the secrecy of the information,

(4) The savings affected, and the value to the holder, in having the information as against competitors,

(5) The amount of effort or money expended in obtaining and developing the information and

(6) The amount of time and expense it would take for others to acquire and duplicate the information.[116]

[E] Nondisclosure Agreements to Protect Trade Secrets

Nondisclosure agreements (NDAs) bind an estimated thirty million Americans. If a software maker is developing customized software or building a specialized company website, counsel will typically draft NDAs that bind its employees, consultants, customers and other third parties. Typically, the NDA will stipulate that those subject to the agreement cannot disclose trade secrets unless they have the owner's written consent.

NDAs require customization to cover contractors, trade partners, licensees, bidders, the government or anyone else who accesses confidential information. NDAs must specify the subject matter that is covered. If a recipient of confidential information violates an NDA, the trade secret owner will not only have a breach of contract action, but often a misappropriation of trade secret cause of action. In April of 2009, a Rhode Island jury ruled that Microsoft should pay Uniloc USA and Singapore $388 million in damages for patent infringement arising out of a breach of an NDA. Microsoft had been granted access to Uniloc's system as part of a study to combat online piracy. The court ruled that Microsoft breached the NDA by using information gained during this investigation.

Silicon Valley companies must draft their NDAs narrowly because California courts will not enforce overly broad agreements. Courts will typically determine the enforceability of NDAs by asking two basic questions:

(1) Is the restraint, from the standpoint of the employer, reasonable in the sense that it is no greater than that necessary to protect some legitimate business interest of the employer? and,

(2) Is the restraint reasonable from the standpoint of the employee?

Some courts have adopted the Inevitable Disclosure Doctrine (IDD), through which an employer can use trade secret law to enjoin a former employee from working for a competitor, when such employment would inevitably result in the use and disclosure of trade secrets. A covenant restraining an employee from competing with a former employer upon termination of employment is considered reasonable if the restraint is no greater than what is necessary to protect the company and its intangible assets.

Information-based businesses will often adopt idea submission policies to avoid conflicts concerning ownership or interests in intellectual property rights. Idea submission policies are terms of service when customers, employees, or third parties submit ideas to the company. One of the chief purposes of an idea submission policy is to avoid disputes over whether the company misappropriated or disclosed an idea that was submitted to it. Some companies add a non-compete clause to employment contracts to prevent employees from entering into a similar profession or trade once their employment is terminated in a further effort to prevent disclosure of trade secrets. Many find this practice unethical, because it greatly interferes with an employee's right to seek future employment.

[F] Protecting Internet-Related Trade Secrets

Non-compete agreements have a variety of different provisions depending on where they are signed. How broad non-compete restrictions can be in terms of time, scope, or geographic location is the subject of much debate and litigation. Massachusetts courts tend to enforce more expansive agreements as compared to California courts.

In *Warehouse Solutions, Inc. v. Integrated Logistics, LLC*,[117] Warehouse Solutions, Inc. (WSI) developed software called Intelligent Audit, which is a web-based program that interfaces with UPS and FedEx to allow companies to track their packages and collect funds for late or missing packages. Intelligent Audit generates customer reports, performs e-bill audits and allows customers to view real-time data regarding their packages. ILL hired Langley to create its own version of the software.

Langley provided a demonstration of the program to Integrated who hired him. They then used the software under the name ShipLink. Lebovich, the developer of Intelligent Audit, verbally instructed ILL to keep Intelligent Audit confidential. There is some evidence that ILL required its own customers to sign confidentiality agreements. WSI did not require ILL to sign any written agreement before granting ILL "high-level administrative access" to Intelligent Audit.

ILL then hired Platinum Circles Technologies to develop its own program. Platinum received access to the interface of the Intelligent Audit program. It did not have access to the source code, only to the visual output of the program. The court concluded that the plaintiff's verbal instructions to keep the Intelligent Audit software confidential were not enough for the features and functions to be considered trade secrets or for the viewing of the visual output to establish misappropriation.

In *PhoneDog v. Kravitz*,[118] the court refused to dismiss a claim that an ex-employee misappropriated the password/login information and the list of followers for a Twitter account that were protectable as trade secrets. Kravitz, PhoneDog's ex-employee, continued to use a Twitter account to publicize PhoneDog's website after his employment ended. Kravitz argued that passwords to Twitter accounts do not derive any actual or potential independent economic value under the UTSA because they do not provide any substantial business advantage. Kravitz also contended that PhoneDog did not make any reasonable efforts to maintain the secrecy of its Twitter password.

The extent of Internet security measures taken by the owner of the trade secret need not be absolute but must be reasonable under the circumstances. In *PhoneDog*, the company password protected its Twitter account. The company requested that its ex-employee relinquish use of the account but he merely changed the Twitter handle on the account, while continuing to misappropriate confidential information. The court ruled that PhoneDog's efforts were sufficient to plead a misappropriation claim.

§ 8.4: GLOBAL TRADEMARK LAW

Globalized information technology companies face the problem that "uses by others that arise in foreign jurisdictions prevent efforts to establish a brand's reputation internationally."[119] Registration with the USPTO gives the trademark owner exclusive rights in the United States only. Trademark owners may obtain protection in the Eurozone through a single trademark filing in the Trademarks and Designs Registration Office of the European Union.

Alibaba, a Chinese e-commerce company operating in more than two hundred countries, is now the world's largest retailer, having overtaken Walmart. Gucci and Saint Laurent filed suit against Alibaba because it took too little effort to deter advertisements for cheap knockoffs that appeared on its website. In August 2017, the French luxury companies dropped the lawsuit because of Alibaba's new measures to stop counterfeits on its e-commerce portals.[120]

Global e-businesses face difficult barriers to establishing their trademarks worldwide. Amazon.com, for example, must ensure that no other company is using its mark in a foreign jurisdiction. Trademark law has been harmonized but there are still significant differences in how a company obtains trademark rights "for the same subject matter from one jurisdiction to another."[121]

Trademarks, by their very nature, are symbols and often language-based signifiers. Lawyers seeking trademark protection in foreign countries must consider translation challenges "particularly where multiple language may be spoken within a particular nation."[122] An Oracle Executive states that his company translates its products into "twenty-three different languages, including Spanish and Latin American Spanish, Portugal Portuguese and Brazilian Portuguese."[123]

The integrated petroleum company Exxon chose its name after determining that no language uses "xx," which lessened the problem of defending its marks globally. Social media companies face the most complex international issues. Facebook boasts that "to reach a global audience, Facebook supports 70-plus languages with a framework that enables you to translate text on Facebook."

[A] Non-Traditional Trademarks

The U.S. has the most expansive view of nontraditional trademarks. In the U.S., nonconventional trademarks have expanded to include single color trademarks, sound trademarks, three-dimensional trademarks, shape trademarks and even scent trademarks over the past two decades, as illustrated in Chart Five below.

CHART FIVE: EXAMPLES OF NONCONVENTIONAL TRADEMARKS

Type	Company	Trademark
Color Marks	Owens-Corning	Pink Color for Insulation
Trade Dress	Coca Cola	Shape of the Coke Bottle
Sound Marks	MGM	MGM's lion's roar
Motion Marks	Sony Ericsson	Flipbook of twenty images
Lacquered Sole on Shoes	Christian Louboutin	Lacquered red sole on footwear
Fragrance Marks	Kalin Manchev	Rose oil scent

[B] Immoral or Scandalous Marks & Policy Prohibitions

In 1994, the EU's Trademark Directive established the Community Trademark Regulation (CTMR), which prohibits trademarks from being registered if they are "contrary to public policy and the accepted principles of morality." However, "the concept of what is considered contrary to morality and public policy varies from country to country and evolves over time."[124] The European Union's Office of Harmonization for the Internal Market (OHIM) noted that it would not register a mark mocking a major religion or exploiting the founder of a religion such as a trademark for Jesus Juice Wine. It also noted that it could reject a profane trademark that might upset citizens, especially young children and the elderly.

In the United States, an examiner's determination of whether a mark is scandalous must be made in the context of the relevant marketplace for the goods or services identified in the application, and are determined by a "substantial composite of the general public." In contrast, OHIM applies a standard of a reasonable person, in a given context and will not refuse to register a mark because it offends a "small minority."

The OHIM permitted registration of SCREW YOU as a trademark for the goods applied for, such as artificial breasts and breast pumps sold exclusively in sex shops, because a trademark containing sexually charged language would not offend this type of clientele. The OHIM also ruled that the profane trademark could be registered to market condoms even if sold outside of sex shops, since consumers will be unlikely to be offended by the ScrewYou moniker. The OHIM, however, reversed registration for alcohol, a class that had been previously approved in the United Kingdom.

In the United States, the phrase, "Screw You, We're from Texas" was registered in 2001 for use on bumper stickers, baseball caps, t-shirts and beverage cans. In 2012, the U.S. Trademark Office approved the Screw You trademark for a broad range of classes including clothing, footwear and headgear. In 2013, the Trademark Office registered the word mark, "Screw You Cancer." It is likely that the U.S. Supreme Court will invalidate the scandalous clause just as it did for the disparagement clause in *The Slants* case.

§ 8.5: GLOBAL TRADE SECRET ISSUES

European users have a right to reverse engineer software to extract its non-copyrightable elements under the 1991 Software Directive.[125] Software makers cannot require consumers to waive this mandatory rule. The European Software Directive also permits "the making of a back-up copy by a person having a right to use the computer program [that] may not be prevented by contract insofar as it is necessary for that use."[126]

The misappropriation of trade secrets may be difficult to prove in some foreign countries that do not recognize this branch of IP law.[127] Japan had no formal legal protection for trade secrets until 1990. Most countries, however, will enforce license agreements and other contracts that impose an obligation to keep trade secrets confidential.

Cyberspace makes it possible for malicious actors, whether they are corrupted insiders or working for foreign intelligence services, to steal massive quantities of data at the click of a mouse. In May 2015, a Tianjin University Professor was arrested for economic espionage. "The 32-count indictment, which had previously been sealed, charged a total of six individuals with economic espionage and theft of trade secrets for their roles in a long-running effort to obtain U.S. trade secrets for the benefit of universities and companies controlled by the PRC government."[128] "Security company Mandiant published a report finding that the government of the People's Republic of China (PRC) is sponsoring cyber-espionage to attack top U.S. companies."[129]

§ 8.6: ETHICAL PERSPECTIVES: TRADEMARKS & TRADE SECRETS

[A] A Consequentialist View of Trade Secrets

The law of trade secrets gives intellectual property owners the means to protect information that has either potential or actual economic value, thus contributing to economic growth and healthy market competition. As Judge Richard Posner stated: "Trade secrets are of growing importance to the competitiveness of American industry. . . and the efficiency of industry depends . . . on the protection of intellectual property."[130]

In 2016, Congress enacted the Defend Trade Secrets Act (DTSA), giving trade secret owners a private cause of action under the Economic Espionage Act (EEA). Bloomberg BNA found that thirty-five companies working in robotics, semiconductors, online games and other emerging technologies filed thirty-five DTSA Act civil actions in California during the first months of 2017.[131] The DTSA gives businesses civil remedies for misappropriation:

> Although the Defend Trade Secrets Act of 2016 federalizes trade secret protection, it preserves state law trade secret protections. The act provides a uniform definition of trade secrets, a uniform standard for misappropriation, nationwide service of process, and nationwide execution of judgments.[132]

In June of 2016, Space Data, a U.S. company that developed balloon-based telecommunications services, filed suit against Google for misappropriating trade secrets in their "Project Loon." Space Data alleges that Google misappropriated trade secrets, causing it irreparable and substantial injury warranted injunctive relief. A federal court dismissed the DTSA trade secret claim because Loon did not provide an overview of what trade secrets were misappropriated.[133]

Consequentialists are supportive of trade secret law unless the doctrine expands to such an extent as to create excessive litigation. Trademark trolls, like patent trolls, register trademarks for the sole purpose of extorting settlements from companies who have a legitimate interest in a mark. The International Trademark Association charges that Chinese courts extract settlements from internationally known trademark owners, such as the French winemaker, Castel Frères SAS.[134] This unnecessary litigation is a tax on society that should be countered through revised international agreements.

[B] Virtue & Duty Theory

(1) Trademark Law and the Problem of Counterfeits

Trade secret law is full of ethical rhetoric. Its core prohibition is on the use of 'improper means to discover secret information."[135] A virtue theorist would argue that it is always wrong to sell counterfeits on the Internet because palming off other trademarks is a form of theft. Selling fake goods, such as "knock-off" Coach purses, is absolutely prohibited, even if the counterfeit products are sold at a lower price and may be better than the real thing. Manufacturers who create, as well as consumers who knowingly purchase, counterfeits are cheating trademark owners and are therefore behaving unethically.

Selling fakes undermines the moral basis of the good society. A Kantian would impose an absolute duty on eBay and Alibaba to aggressively cull counterfeit goods from their services. The categorical imperative that applies to counterfeits is that it is morally wrong to lie. Under Kantian theory, there is no exception for consumers who might benefit from the opportunity to purchase fake items.

(2) Trade Secrets & Virtue Theory

Trade secrets is the branch of IP law that best embodies the virtue theory and Kant's notion of duty, since an action arises only when defendants steal, bribe or induce others to breach their nondisclosure obligations. A misappropriation of a trade secret claim is always based upon bad faith and using "improper means" to gain control of information belonging to another.[136] Stealing another company's software specifications or violating a duty of confidentiality are morally reprehensible.

Virtue theorists would approve of NDAs to protect patented software and other property rights. Ex-employees or consultants who develop a software program for one company but and leave that company to begin marketing and selling a substantially similar program for another company, are a common form of bad faith in the software industry. For example, in the late 1980s, Par Microsystems, Inc. developed a computer software accounting program with the help of Robert S. Johnson, a computer design employee.

Johnson accepted employment with Pinnacle Development Corporation and shortly after, Pinnacle began the marketing and sale of a similar computer software accounting program. Upon Par's discovery of this program, it took legal action against Johnson and Pinnacle for copyright infringement. The jury awarded it $100,000.[137] Virtue theory would find it a moral wrong to breach a nondisclosure agreement and approve of the awarding of damages for breach of contract. However, excessively restrictive nondisclosure agreements may also be immoral.

[C] Trademark Bullying & Conflict Theory

A conflict ethicist would point to trademark bullying as an example of the corporate abuse of power in stretching trademark rights beyond the intent of the law. Trademark bullying occurs when a "trademark owner that uses its trademark rights to harass and intimidate another business beyond what the law might be reasonably interpreted to allow."[138] In 2010, President Obama signed S. 2968, Trademark Technical and Conforming Amendment Act, which requires the U.S. Department of Commerce to study the extent to which abusive trademark enforcement tactics harm small businesses.

Suffolk University Law School's Intellectual Property & Entrepreneurship Clinic represented a small business client, Li-Wei Chih, whose attempt to register the trade name "MonsterFishKeepers" was opposed by Monster Beverage Corporation. "The holding company for the Monster energy drink empire maintained that it owns the word 'Monster,' but the U.S. Trademark Trial and Appeal Board disagreed, dismissing the company's opposition to the name that Chih uses for his MonsterFishKeepers.com tropical aquarium website."

Chih had sought to register the brand name for use on apparel. "Monster Energy was deemed to be famous only for energy drinks, which will again negatively impact their ability to prevent others from using the word in other categories."[139] Without the good fortune of obtaining free representation from a university group, Li-Wei Chih is unlikely to have prevailed. Corporate trademark bullies often sue smaller companies, who lack legal resources to defend their interests.

A Vermont folk artist used social media aggressively to gain popular support after Chik-fil-A sued him, claiming his "T-shirt business built around the phrase 'Eat more kale' allegedly infringed on the restaurant chain's 'Eat mor chikin' slogan." Another Vermont trademark-bullying dispute culminated in a settlement when Hansen, a major beverage corporation, sued tiny RockArt Brewery, charging that Rock Art's "VERMONSTER" beer allegedly infringed on Hansen's "MONSTER ENERGY" trademarks. Rock Art Brewery retaliated with a YouTube video and Facebook group, "Vermonters and Craft Beer Drinkers Against Monster," which drew widespread popular support.

It is often difficult for courts to draw the line between trademark bullying and the legitimate protection of a mark. Conflict theorists tend to view the trademark bullies as a classic instance of larger companies abusing their power at the expense of small or medium sized companies, asserting that "large corporations have embarked on 'cease and desist' campaigns that are intended to 'bully' these small businesses and individuals into compliance."[140] Virtue theorists might also find this abuse of power to be morally objectionable.

Consequentialists might respond that while these large companies may appear to be bullies, they have legitimate reasons to police their marks. Trademark owners that do not aggressively defend their marks create a likelihood that a mark will become generic and, consequently, cease to be protectable.

[D] Updating the IP Social Contract

Social Contract theorists would agree with the consequentialists that the Lockean notion of property rights needs updating for the information age. The labor of trademark and trade secret owners gives them moral rights in cyberspace, just as their ancestors in Locke's time gained title to their property through industriousness. Defending their distinctive marks against tarnishment, parallels defending property from trespassers in the brick and mortar world. Social Contract theorists also stress the need to balance IP with free expression rights such as the exceptions for parody and gripe sites. The continuing expansion of trademark and trade secret law raises fears that an overly bloated IP regime might come to have a chilling effect on fundamental human freedoms.

[E] Preventing Government Oppression in Cyberspace

Libertarians would be concerned about the undue expansion of trademark rights as there is no clear limit to what can be trademarked. When trademark bullies engage in overreach to stifle competitors, it undermines the benefits of the free market. Libertarians would not be in favor of trademark examiners striking down marks on disparagement grounds because of the chilling effect on free expression.

Libertarians applaud THE SLANTS case because it invalidated the disparagement clause of the Lanham Act, thus strengthening the First Amendment's Free Speech guarantee. This U.S. Supreme Court decision will decrease the power of trademark examiners in deciding which marks are offensive and what is good for the rest of us. A Constitutional Fellow of the libertarian Cato Institute contended:

> Trying to stamp out "disparaging" speech is both misguided and unconstitutional. No public official can be trusted to neutrally identify speech that "disparages." Moreover, disparaging speech has been central to political debate, cultural discourse, and personal identity for as long as this country has existed. For example, we recently concluded a presidential campaign in large part defined by pronouncements that large groups of people found to be personally disparaging.[141]

The Cato Institute commentator also views the disparagement clause of the Lanham Act to be unconstitutionally vague:

> Its application will always be unpredictable, because nearly any brand or term could be taken as disparaging by some portion of some group. Take the low-hanging fruit of Aunt Jemima, Uncle Ben, the Cleveland Indians' Chief Wahoo, the women in La Tortilla Factory, or even the Keebler Elves. Determining whether a term should be seen as disparaging is an incredibly complex endeavor that the government can't possibly be equipped to handle.[142]

Libertarians would criticize the decisions of many of the UDRP panels and overly intrusive courts that resolve conflicts over domain names and trademarks as undermining free market property rights. Libertarians protest that officials subordinate basic rights to property through permitting "cancellation proceedings challenging a mark many years after its issuance and after the mark holder has invested millions of dollars protecting its brand identity and consumers have come to rely on the mark as a brand identifier."[143]

CONCLUSION

The Internet's disregard of geographic borders creates conflicts between concurrent users that would never have arisen between distant companies in the purely brick and mortar world. Owners of famous trademarks must register their marks in every country and be vigilant to avoid "territorially based claims of abandonment and to dilution arising from uses of confusingly similar marks."[144] To protect their intellectual property, information companies must master each country's different trademark laws.

Companies are turning away from patent protection and moving toward trade secrets to protect software assets. Trade secret protection is particularly vital in a networked world where intangible assets are easy to misappropriate misappropriation. The power of computer technology has increased exponentially, resulting in more powerful means for the theft and transfer of proprietary information. Calling something a trade secret is not enough in a world of mobile technology, smart devices and instant messaging. "Social media poses new risks for trade secrets that may be revealed to the public through inadvertent status updates."[145] Increasingly sophisticated and globalized laws must develop to more effectively protect proprietary information through the evolution of all branches of IP law.

CHAPTER EIGHT: REVIEW EXERCISES

8.1: Should the First Amendment protect rogue sites or gripe sites that mention trademarks when criticizing companies? Do gripe sites, such as PissedConsumer.com, play a significant role in American society? Should companies be able to sue when they believe that the false criticisms were posted to maliciously harm them? What rules are necessary to prevent critics from being intimidated by the threat of costly lawsuits?

8.2: In *Hormel Foods Corp. v. Jim Henson Prods.*,[146] the Second Circuit observed that a successful parody "tends to increase public identification" of the famous mark with its source. Henson's film pokes fun at Hormel's famous luncheon meat, spam, by associating its processed, gelatinous block with a wild beast. Hormel contended, "That even comic association with an unclean 'grotesque' boar will call into question the purity and high quality of its meat product." Does their argument have validity? Do companies or industries have a right to defend themselves from harmful portrayals?

8.3: Imagine that consumers are buying counterfeit goods from a company known as Huey Nuitton that sells its goods over the website Alibaba. Customers know that the products are of the same quality as the far more expensive trademarked version. What are the ethics of consumers purchasing counterfeit goods directly from Huey Nuitton if they are aware that the items are knock-offs? Should Alibaba be pressured to stop carrying such items? If so, what leverage might be used against this Chinese company?

8.4: Online shoe company Zappos has been actively using the hashtag #SHOEBACCA online, which has helped increase its sales. Zappos now wants to trademark this hashtag. How successful will Zappos be in obtaining this trademark? What companies would oppose the issuing of this trademark and what arguments can it make?

8.5: Lady Gidget, a prominent entertainer, is the owner of U.S. Trademark Registrations for the mark LADY GIDGET for entertainment services and related goods. Lady Gidget has used her name and mark professionally for entertainment services since 1999. Her music and other entertainment endeavors have often been controversial for featuring explicit erotic content. In addition, nude photographs of Lady Gidget have appeared in Penthouse magazine and she has published a coffee-table book entitled Lady Gidget's Sexting Book featuring sexually explicit photographs and text.

Parisia Enterprises is in the business of developing websites. On or about May 29, 2010, Parisia purchased the registration for the disputed domain name LadyGidget.com from Pro Domains for $20,000. On June 4, 2010, Parisia registered LadyGidget as a trademark in Tunisia. On or about June 8, 2010, Parisia began operating an "adult entertainment portal website." The website notice stated: "LadyGidget.com is not affiliated or endorsed by the Catholic Church or Lady Gidget or her various enterprises." What would be the advantages and disadvantages of Lady Gidget filing an UDRP proceeding, as opposed to filing a federal anticybersquatting case? To prevail in a UDRP proceeding, what would Lady Gidget need to prove?

8.6: What are some examples of trade secrets that a software company might want to protect? Unlike patent, copyright and trademark law, federal law does not protect trade secrets. What are some ways that companies protect their trade secrets?

8.7: What remedies may a trade secret owner pursue if a former employee misappropriates confidential information? What preventative steps can it take to prevent disgruntled ex-employees from revealing or selling trade secrets? What must the employer show to prove that it has a trade secret? Are hackers ever ethically justified in revealing trade secrets?

8.8: Why do some courts refuse to enforce some NDAs? Do you think that courts should broadly enforce NDAs or police them to prevent overly expansive terms? Is it unethical, for example, for a company employing student interns or co-op employees to require NDAs?

8.9: To what extent do you believe than non-compete agreements are justifiable to prevent former employees from revealing confidential information to competitors? Should courts prevent companies from requiring employees to sign very broad non-compete agreements or is this just an aspect of the free market? Under what conditions would you be willing to sign an NCA?

8.10: "Countries have laws to protect intellectual property for two main reasons. One is to give statutory expression to the moral and economic rights of creators in their creations and to the rights of the public in access to those creations. The second is to promote, as a deliberate act of Government policy, creativity and the dissemination and application of its results, and to encourage fair trade, which would contribute to economic and social development."[147] Which theory best explains U.S. approaches to intellectual property? Which approach best explains European approaches to intellectual property? Is there any evidence that countries are beginning to converge in their reasons for protecting intellectual property?

REFERENCES FOR CHAPTER EIGHT

1 LEAH C. THOMPSON & BRENT A. OLSON, 9A ARIZONA PRACTICE, BUSINESS LAW DESKBOOK § 35:3, Ch. 35: Internet Law (2014–2015 ed.).

2 *Trademark Law Developments*, 25 BERKELEY TECHNOLOGY LAW JOURNAL 4 (2010) (Complaint, No. 02487393 (Cal. Super. Ct. May 6, 2009).

3 World Intellectual Property Organization, *How Are Trade Secrets Protected?* (2017).

4 *See Kewanee Oil Co. v. Bicron Corp.*, 416 U.S. 470, 475 (1974).

5 World Intellectual Property Organization, *How Are Trade Secrets Protected?* (2017).

6 Dana Hull & Mark Bergen, Tesla *Sues Ex-Autopilot Director, Alleging Stolen Secrets*, ELECTRONIC COMMERCE & LAW REPORT (April 26, 2017).

7 Alexandria Sage, *Tesla Settles Lawsuits With Former Head of Its Autopilot System*, REUTERS (April 19, 2017).

8 Nicole Perroth, *Traveling Light in Time of Digital Thievery*, The N.Y. TIMES (Feb. 10, 2012), *available at* http://www.nytimes.com/2012/02/11/technology/electronic-security-a-worry-in-an-age-of-digital-espionage.html.

9 PAUL GOLDSTEIN, COPYRIGHT'S HIGHWAY: THE LAW AND LORE OF COPYRIGHT FROM GUTENBERG TO THE CELESTIAL JUKEBOX 10 (Stanford, California: Stanford University Press, 1994).

10 *The Coca Cola "Contour" Bottle Design Patent*, DESIGN PATENT: EVERYTHING YOU NEED TO KNOW, http://www.patentadesign.com/gallery/coca-cola-bottle-design-patent.html (last visited May 26, 2017).

11 Steve Brachmann, *Coca Cola's Patents: From Juice Dispensers to Artificially Sweetened Cereals*, IP WATCHDOG (Mar. 25, 2015), http://www.ipwatchdog.com/2015/03/25/coca-cola-patents-juice-dispensers-artificially-sweetened-cereals/id=55730/.

12 *Id.*

13 *Coca-Cola Bottling Co. v. Coca-Cola Co.,* 269 F. 796, 799 (3d Cir. 1920).

[14] Gene Quinn, *IBM's Formula for Success: Patents, Patents, and More Patents*, IPWATCHDOG (Jan. 11, 2012), http://www.ipwatchdog.com/2012/01/11/ibms-formula-for-success-patents-patents-and-more-patents/id=21722/.

[15] Julie Bort, *How This Regular Programmer Became a 'Master Inventor' at IBM*, BUSINESS INSIDER (Mar. 15, 2015), http://www.businessinsider.com/inside-ibms-patent-creation-machine-2015-3.

[16] Sam Chambers, *Amazon Sets Sights on U.K. Grocery with Checkout-Free TM*, ELECTRONIC COMMERCE & LAW REPORT (May 24, 2017).

[17] *Conditions of Use*, AMAZON.COM, INC., https://www.amazon.com/gp/help/customer/display.html?nodeId=508088.

[18] *Glaxo Wellcome UK Ltd. v. Sandoz Ltd.*, [2017] EWCA Civ 335, EWCA (Civ) (U.K.), No. A3/2016/2941, 5/10/17).

[19] *Id.* at § 11.83.

[20] *Northern Light Technology, Inc. v. Northern Lights Club*, 97 F. Supp.2d 96 (D. Mass. 2000).

[21] *Kremen v. Cohen*, No. C 98–20718 JW, 2000 WL 1811403, at *5 (N.D. Cal. Nov. 27, 2000).

[22] *Advertise.com, Inc. v. AOL Adver., Inc.*, 616 F.3d 974, 977 (9th Cir. 2010).

[23] *Park 'N Fly, Inc. v. Dollar Park and Fly, Inc.*, 469 U.S. 189, 193 (1985).

[24] 15 U.S.C. § 1052(a).

[25] *Pro-Football, Inc. v. Harjo*, 284 F. Supp. 2d 96, 124 (D.D.C. 2003) (denying cancellation of Washington Redskins trademark).

[26] Jux Law Firm, *Scandalous or Immoral, Disparaging, or Deceptive Marks: Can They Be Registered?* (2014).

[27] *In re Geller*, 751 F.3d 1355, 1358 (Fed. Cir. 2014).

[28] *Matal v. Tam*, 137 S.Ct. 1744 (2017).

[29] *Id.* at *15–*16.

[30] Ilya Shapiro, *Niggling Bureaucrats Shouldn't Be Telling Us What's "Disparaging"* (December 19, 2006). http://www.scotusblog.com/2016/12/symposium-niggling-bureaucrats-shouldnt-be-telling-us-whats-disparaging/.

[31] *In re Tam*, 785 F.3d 567, 568–569 (Fed. Cir. Apr. 20, 2015).

[32] *Id.*

[33] *In re Tam*, 808 F.3d 1321 (Fed. Cir. Dec. 22, 2015).

[34] *In re Tam*, 808 F.3d, at 1334–1339.

[35] *Id.* at 1339–1355.

[36] *Matal v. Tam*, 137 S.Ct. 1744 (2017).

[37] Brief of Law Professors as Amici Curiae in Support of the Petitioner, 016 WL 6833413 (U.S.) (Appellate Brief) in *Matal v. Tam*.

[38] *Id.*

[39] *Id.*

[40] *Id.*

[41] STEVEN PINKER, THE STUFF OF THOUGHT: LANGUAGE AS A WINDOW INTO HUMAN NATURE (New York, New York: Penguin Books 2007) at 165.

[42] *Kellogg Co. v. National Biscuit Co.*, 305 U.S. 111, 118 (1938).

[43] "A registered mark is presumed to be valid, 15 U.S.C. § 1057(b), and the mark becomes incontestable (with certain exceptions) after five years of consecutive post-registration use.

[44] *See* 15 U.S.C. § 1065.

[45] USPTO.gov, Trademark Basics (2012).

[46] *Id.*

[47] USPTO, *Possible Grounds for Refusing a Mark*, https://www.uspto.gov/trademark/additional-guidance-and-resources/possible-grounds-refusal-mark.

[48] *See* 15 U.S.C. § 1057(b).

[49] *See e.g., E. & J. Gallo Winery v. Gallo Cattle Co.*, 967 F.2d 1280, 1290 (9th Cir. 1992).

50 15 U.S.C. § 1114(a).

51 599 F.2d 341, 341 (9th Cir. 1979).

52 *Id.* at 348–349.

53 15 U.S.C. § 1127.

54 15 U.S.C. § 1125(c)(2)(A).

55 *Rosetta Stone Ltd. v. Google, Inc.*, 676 F.3d 144, 167 (4th Cir. 2012).

56 15 U.S.C. § 1125(c)(2)(B).

57 15 U.S.C. § 1125(c)(2)(C).

58 48 U.S.P.Q.2d (BNA) 1467 (S.D.N.Y. 1996).

59 *Id.* at 1470.

60 See also, *Hasbro, Inc. v. Internet Entm't Group, Ltd.*, No. C96–130WD, 1996 U.S. Dist. LEXIS 11626, at *2–3 (W.D. Wash. Feb. 9, 1996) (finding adult entertainment website tarnished distinctive mark of famous board game).

61 140 F.Supp.3d 997, 997 (N.D. Cal. 2015).

62 Bob Van Voris, BLOOMBERG LAW (Sept. 12, 2012), (https://www.bloomberg.com/news/articles/2013-07-31/apple-ben-jerry-s-georgia-code-intellectual-property).

63 15 U.S.C. § 1125(a).

64 Lanham Act, § 43(a), 15 U.S.C. § 1125(a).

65 No. C 12–0240 MEJ, 2012 U.S. Dist. LEXIS 30911, at *1 (N.D. Cal. Mar. 8, 2012).

66 15 U.S.C. § 1125(a)(1)(B).

67 70 F. Supp.3d 1082, 1082 (N.D. Cal. 2014).

68 *Id.* at 1095.

69 *Id.*

70 *Id.* at 1098.

71 BEVERLY W. PATTISHALL, DAVID CRAIG HILLIARD, JOSEPH NYE WELCH, TRADEMARKS AND UNFAIR COMPETITION 160 (New York, New York: Matthew Bender, 5th ed. 2002). Rebecca Tushnet, *Trademark Law as Commercial Speech Regulation*, 58 SOUTH CAROLINA LAW REVIEW 737, 748 (2007) (contending clash between commercial speech under the First Amendment and federal trademark statute).

72 *L. L. Bean, Inc. v. Drake Publisher, Inc.,* 811 F.2d 26, 34 (1st Cir. 1987).

73 179 F.3d 384, 384 (5th Cir. 1999).

74 73 F.3d 497, 503 (2d Cir. 1996).

75 *Id.* at 501.

76 *Id.*

77 263 F.3d 359, 359 (4th Cir. 2001).

78 *Cairns v. Franklin Mint Co.*, 292 F.3d 1139, 1151 (9th Cir. 2002).

79 *Mattel Inc. v. Walking Mountain Prods.*, 353 F.3d 792, 809 (9th Cir. 2003).

80 *Toyota Motor Sales, U.S.A., Inc. v. Tabari*, 610 F.3d 1171, 1171, 1179 (9th Cir. 2010).

81 *Designer Skin, LLC v. S & L Vitamins, Inc.*, 560 F. Supp.2d 811, 811 (D. Az. 2008).

82 *See* 15 U.S.C. § 1125(c)(3)(A).

83 Stephen W. Feingold & Howard S. Hogan, *Unique Online Trademark Issues* in G. PETER ALBERT JR. AND AMERICAN INTELLECTUAL PROPERTY LAW ASSOCIATION, INTELLECTUAL PROPERTY IN CYBERSPACE (Chicago, Illinois: American Bar Association, 2d ed. 2012) at 397.

84 279 F.3d 796, 796 (9th Cir. 2002).

85 *Playboy Enterprises, Inc. v. Welles*, 7 F. Supp.2d 1098, 1104 (S.D. Cal. 2001), aff'd by *Playboy Enterprises v. Welles*, 297 F.3d at 796.

86 *Ascentive, LLC v. Opinion Corp.*, 842 F.Supp.2d 450, 462 (E.D.N.Y. 2011).

87 29 F. Supp. 2d 1161, 1161 (C.D. Cal. 1998).

88 *Id.* at 1163.

[89] *Ford Motor Co. v. 2600 Enters.*, 177 F. Supp.2d 661, 662, 666 (E.D. Mich. 2001) (denying injunctive relief to Ford Motor Co., which sought to enjoin defendants from maintaining domain name, "FuckGeneralMotors.com," that takes user directly to Ford Motor Co.'s official website at "ford.com").

[90] Amy E. Bivins, ICANN Staff Seeks Comments on Uniformity of Contracts to Address Registration Abuse, ELECTRONIC COMMERCE & LAW REPORT (July 28, 2012).

[91] INTERNET CORPORATION FOR ASSIGNED NAMES & NUMBERS (ICANN) REGISTRATION ABUSE POLICIES WORKING GROUP FINAL REPORT (Submitted 29 May 2010), at 37.

[92] Lisa P. Ramsey, *Brandjacking on Social Networks:* Trademark *Infringement by Impersonation of Markholders*, 58 BUFFALO LAW REVIEW 851, 852 (2010) (describing misuses of brand names on the Internet).

[93] *Virtual Works, Inc. v. Volkswagen of Am., Inc.*, 238 F.3d 264, 267 (4th Cir. 2001).

[94] 15 U.S.C. § 1125(d)(1)(A).

[95] Stephanie Nebehay, *Jay Leno Wins Cybersquatting Case*, REUTERS (July 2, 2009) (reporting WIPO UDRP decision that real estate agent registered the domain name in bad faith and that Jay Leno had common law rights in his name).

[96] Roger Kay, *Saga of .Sucks Generates Laughter, Agony*, Forbes (June 29, 2015).

[97] 420 F.3d 309, 309 (4th Cir. 2005).

[98] *Domain Name Dispute Resolution Policy*, ICANN, https://www.icann.org/resources/pages/dndr-2012-02-25-en.

[99] Christopher Gibson, *The UDRP and Compagnie Gervais Danone v. Sequential Inc. Podcast*, http://www.law.suffolk.edu/about/news/pods.cfm.

[100] *The Uniform Domain Name Dispute Resolution Policy (UDRP), The Rules for Uniform Domain Name Dispute Resolution Policy*, ICANN, https://www.icann.org/resources/pages/rules-be-2012-02-25-en.

[101] *WIPO Continues Efforts to Curb Cybersquatting*, IPFRONTLINE (2005).

[102] *In re Madonna Ciccone, p/k/a Madonna v. Dan Parisi,* Case No. D2000–0847 (WIPO Oct. 12, 2000).

[103] *Air France Wins 'Sucks' Domain Name*, OUT-LAW.COM (May 31, 2005), https://www.out-law.com/en/articles/2005/june/air-france-wins-sucks-domain-name/.

[104] "The Panel is fully aware that there is a split among the UDRP decisions regarding whether a "-sucks" domain name is confusingly similar to the trademark to which it is appended. The majority of the decisions have found confusing similarity. In a minority of decisions, and in some dissenting opinions, Panelists have deemed a "-sucks" addition to a well-known trademark to be an obvious indication that the domain name is not affiliated with that trademark owner." *Id.*

[105] *TRS Quality, Inc. v. Gu Bei*, Case No. D2009–1077 (WIPO Sept. 25, 2009).

[106] *Cabela's Inc. v. Cupcake Patrol*, Case No. FA0006000095080 (NAF Aug. 29, 2000).

[107] *Kewanee Oil Co. v. Bicron Corp.*, 416 U.S. at 476.

[108] Alexis Kramer, *Game Maker to Facebook's Oculus: Stop Using Virtual Reality Code,* INTELLECTUAL PROPERTY LAW RESOURCE CENTER (Feb. 23, 2017).

[109] Alexis Kramer, *Trade Secret Cases Surge as Race for New Tech, Top Talent Heats Up*, ELECTRONIC COMMERCE & LAW REPORT (May 17, 2017).

[110] Mark Halligan, *Protection of U.S. Trade Secret Assets: Amendments to the Economic Espionage Act of 1996*, 7 JOHN MARSHALL REVIEW OF INTELLECTUAL PROPERTY 656, 657 (2008).

[111] *Rivendell Forest Products v. Georgia Pacific Corp.*, 28 F.3d 1042, 1046 (10th Cir. 1994).

[112] Cal. Civ. Code § 3426.1(b).

[113] *Avtec Systems, Inc. v. Peiffer,* 21 F.3d 568, 575 (4th Cir. 1994).

[114] UTSA defines a trade secret to mean means information, including a formula, pattern, compilation, program, device, method, technique, or process, that:

> (i) derives independent economic value, actual or potential, from not being generally known to, and not being readily ascertainable by proper means by, other persons who can obtain economic value from its disclosure or use, and
>
> (ii) is the subject of efforts that are reasonable under the circumstances to maintain its secrecy.

UTSA § 1(4).

115 2014 WL 4627090 (C. D. Cal. Sept. 16, 2014).

116 *State ex rel. The Plain Dealer v. Ohio Dept. of Ins.*, 687 N.E.2d 661, 672 (Ohio 1997).

117 610 Fed. Appx. 881, 881 (11th Cir. 2015).

118 2011 WL 5415612 (N. D. Cal., Nov. 8, 2011).

119 JOHN CROSS, AMY LANDERS, MICHAEL MIRELES & PETER YU, GLOBAL ISSUES IN INTELLECTUAL PROPERTY LAW (New York, New York: West, Thomson-Reuters, American Case Book Series, 2010) at 162.

120 Robert Williams and Marie Mawad, *Alibaba Fights Online Fakes in Deal With Gucci Owner Kering*, ELECTRONIC COMMERCE & LAW REPORT (August 9, 2017).

121 *Id.*

122 JOHN CROSS, AMY LANDERS, MICHAEL MIRELES & PETER YU, GLOBAL ISSUES IN INTELLECTUAL PROPERTY LAW (New York: LEXIS/NEXIS, 2010) at 162.

123 *Oracle Corp. Secs. Litig.*, 2009 U.S. Dist. LEXIS 50995 *14 (N.D. Ca., June 16, 2009).

124 Cross et. al., *Global Issues in Intellectual Property*, *Id.* at 370.

125 Council Directive of March 14, 1991, on Legal Protection of Computer Programs, 91/250/EEC, OJ No. L 122/42 (1991).

126 *Id.* at art. 5(2).

127 ALLAN S. GUTTERMAN, TECHNOLOGY-DRIVEN CORPORATE ALLIANCES: A LEGAL GUIDE FOR EXECUTIVES (New York, New York: Praeger Publishers, 1994) at 39.

128 *Chinese Professors Among Six Defendants Charged with Economic Espionage and Theft of Trade Secrets for Benefit of People's Republic of China*, UNITED STATES DEPARTMENT OF JUSTICE (May 19, 2015), https://www.justice.gov/opa/pr/chinese-professors-among-six-defendants-charged-economic-espionage-and-theft-trade-secrets.

129 Robert B. Milligan & Daniel P. Hart, *Top 10 Developments/Headlines in Trade Secret*, COMPUTER FRAUD, AND NON-COMPETE LAW IN 2014 (Jan. 6, 2014).

130 *Rockwell Graphics Systems, Inc. v. DEV. Industries, Inc.*, 925 F.2d 174, 180 (7th Cir. 1991).

131 Alexis Kramer, *Trade Secret Cases Surge as Race for New Tech, Top Talent Heats Up*, ELECTRONIC COMMERCE & LAW REPORT (May 17, 2017).

132 Patrick J. Coyne, *Expert Analysis: What You Should Know About The Defend Trade Secrets Act*, LAW360 (June 27, 2016).

133 *Judge Partially Dismisses Claims Against Google in Trade Secrets*, MEALEY'S (July 19, 2017).

134 *Id.*

135 James Grimmelmann, *The Ethical Visions of Copyright Law*, 77 FORDHAM LAW REVIEW 2005, 2008 (2009).

136 *Id.* at 2009.

137 P*AR Microsystems, Inc. v. Pinnacle Development Corp*, 995 F. Supp. 658, 659 (N.D. Tex., 1998).

138 Roxana Sullivan and Luke Curran, Trademark Bullying: Defending Your Brand or Vexatious Business Tactics? IP WATCHDOG (July 16, 2015), http://www.ipwatchdog.com/2015/07/16/trademark-bullying-defending-your-brand-or-vexatious-business-tactics/id=59155/.

139 *Suffolk Law Students Prevail in "Monster Case*, SUFFOLK UNIVERSITY LAW SCHOOL (Feb. 8, 2016), http://www.suffolk.edu/64761.php#.WS7vrTOZOV4.

140 Leah Chan Grinvald, *Shaming Trademark Bullies*, 2011 WISCONSIN LAW REVIEW 625, 628 (2011).

141 Ilya Shapiro, *Niggling Bureaucrats Shouldn't Be Telling Us What's 'Disparaging'* (December 19, 2006). http://www.scotusblog.com/2016/12/symposium-niggling-bureaucrats-shouldnt-be-telling-us-whats-disparaging/.

142 *Id.*

143 *In re Tam*, 808 F.3d 1321, 1339 (Fed. Cir. Dec. 22, 2015)

144 David R. Johnson & David Post, *Law and Borders—The Rise of Law in Cyberspace*, 48 STANFORD LAW REVIEW 1367, 1369 (May 1996).

145 *Id.*

146 73 F.3d 497 (2d Cir. 1996).

[147] *The Concept of Intellectual Property*, THE WORLD INTELLECTUAL PROPERTY ORGANIZATION (WIPO) (2016) at 3.

Conclusion: The Future of Global Computing

Protecting your company's rights and avoiding infringing the rights of others requires computer professionals and their attorneys to understand legal concepts in a globalized world. Creative solutions will need to be crafted for artificial intelligence, drones, robotics, the Internet of Things, 3-D printing, and other amazing innovations. Intertwined ethical and legal issues are not just academic exercises but critical tools for professional integrity. Computer professionals cannot simply assume that the general counsel's office will foresee and resolve all legal dilemmas. To be effective as an information-age professional, a basic understanding of preventive law is necessary to avoid becoming enmeshed in costly and time-consuming legal and ethical quagmires.

Ethical debates of the future will continue to draw upon consequentialism, virtue theory, conflict theory, social contract perspectives and libertarianism, as no single ethical perspective has a monopoly on good decision-making. The law as code approach, discussed in Chapter 2, illustrates how legal principles and technological knowledge interrelate. For example, in March 2017, a Twitter transparency report revealed that between July and December 2016, 376,890 accounts had been suspended for promoting terrorism. Twitter's proprietary spam-fighting tools identified seventy-four per cent of these accounts. Government takedown requests constituted less than two per cent of all Twitter suspended account for that six-month period. Twitter's computer professionals were more effective than government regulators at policing abuses on their social network.

A continuing battle between Twitter and organized hate groups are gaming Twitter's crowd sourcing efforts to make its service more welcoming. To control hate speech and harassment, Twitter's algorithms have been reconfigured to remove postings when users—or bots masquerading as users—record sufficient negative evaluations:

> Any organized group can now make Twitter work for them censoring the people they target, to make it label their tweets as "sensitive" or "potentially offensive", to delete all of them, to hide, suspend, and close the accounts as they may see fit. It's enough to launch an organized attack to denounce the targeted account as "sensitive", "offensive", "harming", "spam", and Twitter will obligingly censor it.[1]

Countering this new tactic will require coordinated actions by computer professionals and their attorneys. Twitter, as a U.S.-based global corporation whose platform hosts users from around the world, is working closely with a variety of governmental organizations to address these and many other difficult issues.

In the summer of 2017, Michael Rustad taught a course entitled "Emerging Issues in EU Business Law and Policy" in at the National University of Ireland–Galway's program with Suffolk University Law School. The theme of Rustad's Emerging Issues class paralleled each chapter of this book: the idea that U.S. companies doing business in Europe, or anywhere outside the United States, must familiarize themselves with diverse ethical and legal perspectives.

Dublin's Silicon Docks is the headquarters for the European branches of Facebook, LinkedIn and other top-ranked information technology companies including Google Dublin, Apple Operations Dublin, Cisco Galway, LinkedIn, EMEA, Dropbox, Citrix and EMC2. U.S. computer companies like Twitter Ireland, must continuously evaluate their practices to ensure that their contracts conform to EU mandatory consumer and privacy law. Michael Rustad took his National University of Ireland–Galway and Suffolk University law students to Twitter's Dublin headquarters, which is its largest office outside California.

Thomas Koenig, who was a guest speaker in Rustad's class, participated in the meeting with Twitter's Direct Legal Counsel for European Operations. The lessons we learned from speaking with the head of Twitter's public policy section and the chief legal officer confirmed the major themes of this book. Twitter's legal counsel stated that the lawyer of the future would need to be supremely flexible since his or her work is multi-faceted and "different every day."

Phillip Merrills-Dearn, who heads the Legal Department at Twitter International, explained the role he plays as Twitter's European corporate counsel. Merrills-Dearn is not a narrow specialist to be consulted only when Twitter must respond to lawsuits. He displayed a graphic that depicted the diverse legal issues he and his staff encounter daily, with ethics portrayed as the centerpiece. The company's legal department is tasked with ensuring that all Twitter personnel, and the platform itself, conform fully and continuously with the company's ethical code, which states:

> Everything we do in connection with our work is and should be measured against the highest possible standards of ethical business conduct. Our Code of Conduct is designed to deter wrongdoing and promote doing our jobs and operating our business with integrity.

While the Twitter ethical code does not explicitly refer to any of the five theories of computer ethics used in each chapter of this book. However, it draws heavily from each perspective. This book has provided a roadmap on how to identify and minimize risk factors in a globalized digital environment. Each chapter illustrates the importance of applying ethical benchmarks and legal expertise while operating in the midst of the Fourth Industrial Revolution. Computer professionals, and the lawyers who represent them, can no longer afford to be U.S. centric in their approach.

(1) The Consequentialist Perspective on Censorship

United Kingdom Prime Minister Theresa May has called for internationally coordinated censorship by Twitter and other social media to cripple violent extremism. Like most consequentialists, she would subordinate free expression in favor of promoting public safety. Prime Minister May contends, "We cannot allow this [violent] ideology the safe space it needs to breed."[2] She calls for an alliance of democratic governments to obliterate cyberspace-enabled terrorism:

> We need to work with allied democratic governments to reach international agreements that regulate cyberspace to prevent the spread of extremism and terrorism planning. . . We need to do everything we can at home to reduce the risks of extremism online.[3]

The United Kingdom's Investigatory Powers Act of 2016, derided by libertarians as the Snooper's Charter Act, has already given the government increased powers to conduct mass surveillance.[4] As U.S. Supreme Court Justice Robert Jackson famously stated in a dissenting opinion supporting a ban on incendiary speech, "the U.S. Constitution is not a suicide pact."[5]

(2) Virtue & Duty Theory Applied to Twitter

Twitter's mission statement incorporates an "ethical rudder" that guides the company's daily activities and long-term plans. Twitter expects its computer professionals and all staff members to understand and carry out the core mission to:

> Grow our business in a way that makes us proud. Integrity, honesty and trust are core to our business and the foundation upon which we are building Twitter. Our Core Values (go/core values) help us understand what it means to be a part of Twitter and help us retain a strong cultural identity. We also have a broad responsibility to our users, stockholders, each other and the world. This Code of Business Conduct & Ethics is one of the ways we put our Core Values into practice. We've developed these guidelines around the recognition that everything we do in connection with our work should be measured against the highest possible standards of ethical business conduct.[6]

Twitter's aspirational principles explicitly incorporate a Kantian emphasis on treating people as ends rather than means. The social media giant pledges to do well by doing good:

> We value our differences and treat each other with dignity and respect. At Twitter, we believe our differences make us stronger. We work to advance a culture of inclusion and diversity—something fundamental to our collective voice and core values. We believe that no one should be discriminated against because of factors such as gender, race, national origin, sexual orientation, gender identity or expression, religion, age, disability, and the like. While the laws protecting these values may vary in the countries in which we operate, we remain committed to fostering an inclusive and diverse workplace—where people can feel comfortable, be themselves, and do their best work.[7]

This Kantian influence does not mean that Twitter is not pragmatic, which is a central value in the social contract approach. Twitter incorporates pragmatism in its decision to comply with the laws of every country where it does business:

> Twitter takes its responsibility to comply with applicable law very seriously & you are also expected to comply with applicable legal requirements and prohibitions. While it's impossible for anyone to know all aspects of every applicable law, you should understand the major laws and regulations that apply to your work. You should consult the Legal team with any questions or concerns.[8]

(3) How Twitter Recognizes Conflict Theory

Twitter acknowledges the importance of understanding and dealing effectively with people of different cultures, races and gender differences. Awareness of these societal divisions is critically important to Twitter's continuing vitality in a multi-cultural business environment:

Be careful in the words that you choose: we are a community of professionals, and we conduct ourselves professionally. Be kind to others. Do not insult or put down other participants. Harassment and other exclusionary behaviors aren't acceptable. This includes, but is not limited to:

(1) Violent threats or language directed against another person.

(2) Discriminatory jokes and language.

(3) Posting sexually explicit or violent material.

(4) Posting (or threatening to post) other people's personally identifying information ("doxing").

(5) Personal insults, especially those using racist or sexist terms.

(6) Unwelcome sexual attention.

(7) Advocating for, or encouraging, any of the above behavior.

(8) Repeated harassment of others. In general, if someone asks you to stop, then stop.[9]

Twitter is continually working to mediate and moderate hate speech and harassment on its service. Dick Costolo, former Twitter CEO, acknowledges the difficulty in enjoining hostile postings. In 2015, Twitter developed new tools to improve "its notoriously arduous process for reporting abuse."[10] "Every day, Twitter users still face threats of physical violence, sexual abuse, and stalking—all forms of harassment that disproportionately affect women online."[11]

Twitter is constantly striving to bridge the gap between its aspiration of creating a safe space for "understanding and coping with different cultures, races and gender differences" and the reality of endemic conflicts around the world that surface in postings on its system.[12] Twitter is a company that knows it cannot succeed unless it embodies a corporate culture that is welcoming to diverse cultures and manages a platform that is a safe space for its users.

(4) Is Twitter Undermining the Social Contract?

A social contract theorist focuses on how to achieve the intricate balance necessary to protect fundamental human rights, while enabling the efficient coordination necessary for a democratic society. Twitter stands accused of threatening democracy by employing a format that rewards sloganeering over thoughtful discourse. Farhad Manjoo, a prominent technology journalist charges:

> Though the 140-character network favored by President Trump is far smaller than Facebook, it is used heavily by people in media and thus

> exerts perhaps an even greater sway on the news business... It exacerbates groupthink. It prizes pundit-ready quips over substantive debate, and it tends to elevate the silly over the serious—for several sleepless hours this week it was captivated by "covfefe," which was essentially brouhaha over a typo.[13]

This cultural critic also charges that bots designed to manipulate public perceptions have overrun Twitter:

> Research suggests that bots are ubiquitous on Twitter. Emilio Ferrara and Alessandro Bessi, researchers at the University of Southern California, found that bot generated about a fifth of the election-related conversation on Twitter in 2016. Most users were blind to them; they treated the bots the same way they treated other users... A trending hashtag creates a trap for journalists who cover the Internet: Even if they cover a conspiracy theory only to debunk it, they're most likely playing into what the propagandists want.[14]

Twitter would counter this claim by contending that its platform enables democratic participation and has been the catalyst for the Arab Spring and other movements against authoritarianism. Twitter must always be vigilant to keep pace with creative software bots and other malware that undermine its free expression ideals. The contradiction between Twitter's profit motive and its social mission to encourage constructive and respectful discussion is evident in its willingness to tolerate racist, sexist, or bullying tweets by celebrities. Twitter's 2013 IPO states that one of its primary goals is to:

> ... to foster a broad and engaged user community, and we encourage world leaders, government officials, celebrities, athletes, journalists, sports teams, media outlets and brands to use our products and services to express their views to broad audiences. We also encourage media outlets to use our products and services to distribute their content. If users, including influential users, do not continue to contribute content to Twitter, and we are unable to provide users with valuable and timely content, our user base and user engagement may decline. Additionally, if we are not able to address user concerns regarding the safety and security of our products and services or if we are unable to successfully prevent abusive or other hostile behavior on our platform, the size of our user base and user engagement may decline.[15]

Numerous commentators have called for Twitter to ban the divisive postings by President Donald Trump and numerous other prominent public figures.

When Rob Kardashian posted sexually explicit pictures of his ex-fiancé, Blac Chyna, on Twitter, the social media platform failed to remove her pictures as expeditiously as it does for non-celebrities.[16] In the first quarter of 2017, Twitter's monthly user base grew by nine percent in large part to President Trump's high-profile use of this social media.[17] Twitter must continually revisit its core ethical principles in making policy decisions about removing offensive tweets.

(5) Twitter from a Libertarian Perspective

Global information technology companies like Twitter must localize their policies while simultaneously functioning in multiple jurisdictions. This problem becomes particularly complex when Twitter operates in nations, such as some of those in Asia, where ethical, historical, philosophical, political and legal factors diverge more sharply than among the First World nations. Libertarians favor giving Twitter wide discretion to work out these issues without interference from government regulators.

Cyberlibertarians have proposed restructuring Twitter from a for-profit corporation to a user-controlled public service.[18] Twitter's value, they contend, lies in its user-generated content, not in its ability to commodify data for the capitalist system. To achieve this co-operative model, blocs of users would need to wrest control from traditional investors, who are concerned primarily with profitability.[19] Under user ownership, Twitter would serve users rather those seeking to monetize the website's popularity.

Traditional libertarians, in contrast, see nothing wrong with Twitter's pursuit of profits for its stockholders. Twitter once described its guiding principle as being "the free speech wing of the free speech party." But now it is involved, as are the other social media leaders, in balancing its own ethical code against the demands of a wide variety of stakeholders. Our purpose in writing this book is to help future leaders to navigate the increasingly complex ethical quandaries created by the contemporary technological revolution.

The emergence of a global marketplace provides exciting opportunities, yet it is associated with significant risks. Just as we were finishing this book, Facebook, Google, and Twitter were all sent a demand letter from the European Commission that gave these companies one month to revise their terms of service or face significant legal sanctions. The three agreed to comply with the Commission's demand that they conform to European consumer law. The giant cyberspace platforms are negotiating with nations around the world to avoid additional threatened enforcement actions.

The European Commission is close to reaching an agreement with Facebook, YouTube and Twitter regarding the removal of hate speech videos from their services.[20] Some U.S. companies doing business in Europe are particularly likely to be subject to regulatory actions and lawsuits because they mechanically deploy their U.S. centric terms of use that violate EU mandatory consumer laws.

(6) How Twitter Incorporates Ethical Theory in its Daily Operations

Twitter's corporate philosophy is to advance respectful communication around the globe. Attorney Merrills-Dearn stated, "It is true that third parties do the posting, but we are the conduit and we take that role very seriously." He also expects his lawyers to be fluent in at least two languages, to be familiar with multiple cultures, and to have at least a basic knowledge of computing technology. His key staff members share a global perspective, which includes a general familiarity with the laws, cultures, languages and economic realities of many nations. The legal personnel are paid for their moral judgment, mediating skills and understanding of diverse perspectives as much as for their legal expertise.

Twitter's legal director addressed the public policy role that the company must inevitably play in every country where it operates. Twitter frequently takes public policy stances on issues that affect its company's business objectives and corporate ethos. For example, Twitter filed a legal brief against President Trump's travel bans, and will oppose any Trump decisions that impose greater surveillance on citizens.

In another example, Twitter puts individual privacy at the heart of its operations. The company opposes repressive or overly intrusive political interference, but, at the same time, it is aggressive in taking down postings that encourage or enable violence. Twitter's counsel perceives the EU's data protection regulations as intended to be more extra-territorial than domestic, placing Twitter at the heart of the battle against terrorism since its platform is both global and instantaneous.

The corporate counsel closed our conversation by stating that the legal and political world is multifaceted and it will only become more so. The lawyer of the future must be comfortable operating in a rapidly changing environment that is full of uncertainty. As this book stresses, each technological advance creates additional legal dilemmas that must be navigated with a strong ethical rudder. As we learned at Twitter, there is little future for narrow practitioners, but bright and exciting careers for those with the imagination necessary to fill the gaps created by legal and ethical lag.

1 Alfons López Tena, *Twitter Has Gone from a Bastion of Free Speech to a Censor*, Business Insider (June 27, 2017).

2 Charles Riley, *Prime Minister Theresa May Has Called For Closer Regulation of the Internet Following a Deadly Terror Attack in London*, CNN TECH (June 4, 2017).

3 *Id.* (quoting United Kingdom Prime Minister May).

4 "Bill to make provision about the interception of communications, equipment interference and the acquisition and retention of communications data, bulk personal datasets and other information; to make provision about the treatment of material held as a result of such interception, equipment interference or acquisition or retention; to establish the Investigatory Powers Commissioner and other Judicial Commissioners and make provision about them and other oversight arrangements; to make further provision about investigatory powers and national security; to amend sections 3 and 5 of the Intelligence Services Act 1994; and for connected purposes." Act of Parliament, *Summary of the Investigatory Powers Act 2016* (2016).

5 *Terminiello v. City of Chicago*, 337 U.S. 1 (1949) (dissenting the Court's overturning of a Chicago breach of the peace ordinance).

6 Twitter Code of Conduct V2.0 (2017).

7 *Id.*

8 *Id.*

9 *Id.*

10 Nitasha Tiku and Casey Newman, *Twitter CEO: 'We Suck at Dealing with Abuse,'* The Verge (February 4, 2015).

11 *Id.*

12 *Id.*

13 Farhad Manjoo, *How Twitter is Being Gamed to Feed Misinformation*, THE NEW YORK TIMES (May 31, 2017).

14 Manjoo, *How Twitter is Being Gamed, Id.*

15 Alexei Oreskovic, *It's Looking More and More Like Twitter Actually Condones Some Abuse to Retain Its Celebrity Users*, BUSINESS INSIDER (July 9, 2017).

16 *Id.*

17 Seth Archer, *Twitter is Tumbling After Reporting Zero User Growth* (TWTR), BUSINESS INSIDER (July 27, 2017).

18 Angelo Young, *Meet the Tech Activists Who Want to Turn Twitter Into a User-Owned Co-op*, SALON (June 4, 2017).

19 *Id.*

20 Amare Toor, *EU Close to Making Facebook, YouTube, and Twitter Block Hate Speech Videos*, VERGE.COM (May 25, 2017).

Index